GALULA

GALULA

THE LIFE AND WRITINGS OF THE FRENCH OFFICER WHO DEFINED THE ART OF COUNTERINSURGENCY

A. A. Cohen

Foreword by John A. Nagl

 PRAEGER

An Imprint of ABC-CLIO, LLC
Santa Barbara, California • Denver, Colorado • Oxford, England

Library of Congress Cataloging-in-Publication Data

Cohen, A. A.
  Galula : the life and writings of the French officer who defined the art of counterinsurgency /
A. A. Cohen ; foreword by John A. Nagl.
     p. cm.
  Includes bibliographical references and index.
  ISBN 978-1-4408-0049-8 (cloth : alk. paper) — ISBN 978-1-4408-0050-4 (ebook)
1. Counterinsurgency—History—20th century.   2. Galula, David, 1919-1967.   3. France. Armée—
Officers—Biography.   4. Mao, Zedong, 1893–1976—Influence.   5. Counterinsurgency—United
States—History—20th century.   6. Guerrilla warfare—History—20th century—Biography.
7. Military doctrine—History—20th century.   8. China—History—20th century—Biography.
9. Algeria—History—Revolution, 1954–1962—Biography.   10. Jews—North Africa—Biography.
I. Title.   II. Title: Life and writings of the French officer who defined the art of counterinsurgency.
  U241.C62   2012
  355.0092—dc23
  [B]   2012020316

ISBN: 978-1-4408-0049-8
EISBN: 978-1-4408-0050-4

16 15 14 13 12   1 2 3 4 5

This book is also available on the World Wide Web as an eBook.
Visit www.abc-clio.com for details.

Praeger
An Imprint of ABC-CLIO, LLC

ABC-CLIO, LLC
130 Cremona Drive, P.O. Box 1911
Santa Barbara, California 93116-1911

This book is printed on acid-free paper ∞
Manufactured in the United States of America

Acknowledgments

Photographs, unless otherwise indicated, courtesy of Daniel F. Galula.

Extracts from *Counterinsurgency Warfare: Theory and Practice* (authored by David Galula) used by permission of ABC-CLIO, LLC.

Extracts from *Pacification in Algeria: 1956–1958* (authored by David Galula, 2006 edition) and *Counterinsurgency: A Symposium* (edited by Stephen Hosmer and Sibylle Crane, 2006 edition). Copyright RAND Corporation. Used by permission.

To those who saw through the masquerades
of tyranny and fought.

And to my father, who instilled in me
le devoir de mémoire.

Contents

FOREWORD

In the book of Mark, we learn that "A prophet is honored everywhere except in his own hometown and among his relatives and his own family." Jesus of Nazareth could have added "and in his own time" to make the verse even more applicable, not just to himself, but also to Lieutenant Colonel David Galula. Galula was a French officer who did his most important fighting in Algeria, his most significant writing in the United States, and had the most influence he would ever enjoy forty years after his untimely demise in 1967. He was so without honor at home that his most important book, *Counterinsurgency Warfare: Theory and Practice*, was not translated into his native French language until 2008. His ideas took more than forty years to make the voyage home, but when they did, they had been endorsed by American General David Petraeus and heavily influenced U.S. Army and Marine Corps counterinsurgency doctrine as well as the conduct of the two biggest wars of the early twenty-first century.

How this unlikely series of events came to pass is the story of this overdue biography, penned by Canadian Army Major A. A. Cohen. Like the subject of his work, Cohen is a young, bilingual army officer who benefits from both practical experience in the field and a passion for a series of ideas that can, and now have, changed the course of wars and of history. Cohen's work benefits from the compassion of one soldier for another and from its author having lived, as his subject did, through a revolution in warfare.

David Galula cut his teeth on revolutionary war. Graduating from Saint Cyr just in time for the fall of France, he fought for the liberation of his country and then was posted to Beijing in time to observe Mao's war of the people firsthand. Revolutions were sweeping the globe, populations empowered by new ideas were struggling to overthrow colonial overlords, and Galula saw governments both succeed and fail in attempts to suppress revolutions. He lived through popular uprisings and government attempts to subdue them in Greece, the Philippines, and French Indochina before being given the opportunity to put his learning to the test in Algeria in 1956. Assigned as a company commander with responsibility to pacify a sector, he developed, through trial and error, a system that worked.

Returning to Paris, Galula began lecturing and writing about his experiences in Algeria through the lens of nearly two decades of intensive study of revolutionary war. His ideas found purchase across the Atlantic Ocean, where the United States was struggling to understand the revolutions that were then reshaping Europe and Asia. Galula was encouraged by RAND's Steven Hosmer to write a major analysis of his combat experience, which was titled *Pacification in Algeria, 1956–1958* when published (unfortunately in classified format) in 1963. It was not released to the general public until 2006, when a failing counterinsurgency campaign in Iraq made its lessons painfully relevant and a worthy introduction by Bruce Hoffman put them in context.

Pacification in Algeria is largely a substantial, historical text. It provided the grist from which an elegant and ultimately influential theoretical work was distilled. *Counterinsurgency Warfare: Theory and Practice* was published in English in 1964, just as the United States was beginning to immerse itself into counterinsurgency warfare in Vietnam. Carl von Clausewitz observed that theory is most useful when it does not stray too far from the hard soil of practice. Galula's lessons—that the object of counterinsurgency warfare is the population, that intelligence derived from that population is key to success in this most frustrating kind of war, that areas must be progressively cleared of enemy forces and then held in order to build a secure area that will remain loyal to the government—were intensely practical ones. They were also, sadly, not followed during the early years of America's war in Vietnam. General William Westmoreland took a different path, one focused on searching for and destroying the enemy rather than on protecting the Vietnamese population. This ineffective and ultimately counterproductive strategy might have been avoided had Galula been more widely read, but it was not to be. He died in 1967, before the failings of American strategy in Vietnam became evident, and his ideas vanished beneath the wake of strategically failed counterinsurgency campaigns conducted by France and the United States. Both countries swore that they would never again engage in counterinsurgency, and Galula's ideas moldered on unvisited Staff College library shelves.

They remained submerged until America again found herself embroiled in another failing counterinsurgency campaign. In Iraq, attempts to sweep and clear insurgents became exercises in mowing the lawn, repeated weekly or monthly without changing the allegiance of the population. General David

Petraeus commanded the 101st Airborne Division in the initial invasion and then worked to rebuild Iraqi security forces as the commander of the Multi-National Security Transition Command—Iraq. Assigned to lead the army's Combined Arms Center at Fort Leavenworth in late 2005, he decided to renew the U.S. military's appreciation for lessons of previous counterinsurgency campaigns. Petraeus led a team of writers who, like David Galula, had experienced counterinsurgency warfare in both theory and practice. Over the course of 2006, as the war in Iraq spiraled downward, they produced the *U.S. Army/Marine Corps Counterinsurgency Field Manual*.

The manual's reliance on the thinking of David Galula is clear—in its focus on protecting the population as the key objective of any counterinsurgency campaign, its insistence on holding terrain that has been cleared of enemy forces, and its exhortations that counterinsurgents must continually learn and adapt to defeat their enemies by building secure areas in which secure governance can flourish. *Counterinsurgency Warfare: Theory and Practice* is one of just three sources acknowledged in the front of the manual. Galula would be justified in being proud of his influence.

Having rediscovered the work of Galula after so many years, we must not allow his ideas to again go fallow. Although counterinsurgency campaigns are messy and slow, they will remain an important part of what armies do as long as there are populations with unmet needs and revolutionaries with a burning desire for change. As Cohen writes, "Questioning whether an army should maintain a capacity for counterinsurgency is tantamount to questioning whether an army should maintain a capacity to operate abroad. The risk of having to face an insurgency has always, and will always accompany an army in its foreign expeditions." Whatever efforts we invest in avoiding large-scale ground interventions in the future, it would be irresponsible to ignore the odds of fighting counterinsurgency campaigns again. The cost in blood and treasure is far too high.

It is our moral obligation to ensure that the lessons learned over the past bitter decade of fighting and pacifying not be forgotten. Through this biography of David Galula, Major Cohen has taken an important step toward institutionalizing this great thinker's legacy and has given a prophet the honor he is due, in his own country and throughout the world.

John A. Nagl
November 2011

John A. Nagl is a retired U.S. Army officer who fought in both wars in Iraq and now teaches at the U.S. Naval Academy. He wrote the Foreword to a 2006 Praeger edition of *Counterinsurgency Warfare: Theory and Practice* and, with General David Petraeus, to the first ever French translation of the same work in 2009.

PROLOGUE

January 2008
Forward Patrol Base Sperwan Ghar, Kandahar
20 km SW of Kandahar City

We descended from our fortified knoll past the 155mm artillery pieces, past the 70-tonne main battle tanks, past the command post, past the barracks, past the mess hall, past the machine gun nest. Raise the gate. We snaked through the dogleg, finally emerging from the HESCO barrier. Stop. We checked the first culvert, the second, and the third, walking astride the oddly straight road we had built with a calibre of gravel that slipped and crunched under our weight. Turn Left. We stepped off onto a timeless path stitching along the southern belt of dust-colored hamlets. Hold. Half of ten of us looked through our rifle scopes at two impassive, darkly clad men, spotted by the drone circling up ahead. Report. They were crouching on a mud wall close enough to see us, but too far to understand our interpreter's yell. Go on. We walked in single file further down the now-silent path, flanked closely on either side by the thick walls of abodes. Fan out. We exited into the open, peering through rows of washboard-like grape fields, scrutinizing from afar the slits of the medieval-looking *kishmishkhana* huts. Slow down. We were encircled by loud and playful kids with extended hands chanting *pehn(!) pehn(!) pehn(!)* wishing for pens, pencils, or crayons—the currency, it seemed, of Kandahari children. Smile. So what's new? *Pehn! Pehn! Pehn!* Where are your parents? *Pehn! Pehn! Pehn!* Continue. We entered their tiny hamlet, climbing up and down makeshift stairs, past more mud-caked walls and shut little doors until we reached the small sunny square that hosted the white-bearded elders. Smile again. *Tsenga Yeh? Zhoray! Pe khayr!* All was fine, they said. The security was ok. The harvest had been ok. Their health was still ok. In summation, like the sporadic 25mm thumping in the distance, nothing had changed. Standby to move. A corporal noticed a seal and signature-bearing sheet of paper nailed to the old mosque door facing the square. *Da tso day?* Nobody had taken notice. Nobody knew. Really? Yes, we swear! Thanks. Loop back. We circled back towards the orderly grape field, carrying the night letter and the same entourage of children. *Pehn! Pehn! Pehn!* Show a pen. Do any of you know when this was placed on the door? Last night!, chanted the youngest with an outstretched hand, causing the two eldest, ten years his senior, to push away and hush the others with a practised authority. *Ho, yawa pehn zma andiwal.* Now, who put this there? Smack. The two youths grabbed the five-year-old's stained *shalwar* by the collar, and smacked him again across the back of his shaved little head, while the others ran home. Turn back. "Collaborators will be hanged," summarized the interpreter holding the cheaply photocopied letter, as we walked up the fortified knoll, past the sophisticated tanks that offered mobility across grape fields, and guns that offered firepower to penetrate thick *kishmishkhana* huts (which combined with other means, some had confidently said, would come to break the enemy's will of fighting).

> The minority hostile to the insurgent will not and cannot emerge as long as the threat has not been lifted to a reasonable extent. Furthermore, even after the threat has been lifted, the emerging counterinsurgent supporters will not be able to rally the bulk of the population so long as the population is not convinced that the counterinsurgent has the will, the means, and the ability to win.
>
> —*David Galula*[1]

INTRODUCTION

This discussion has been less an objective analysis than a groping for the truth. The reason is that this sort of warfare [the People's War] is not as yet very common; those who have been able to observe it for any length of time have not reported enough about it.

—Carl Von Clausewitz (1830)[1]

Believe me, those who will analyse the substance of my book and come out not only with criticism of what I suggest but also with alternatives will be very few. Never mind, there will be plenty of insurgency coming and we shall see who is right.

—David Galula (1964)[2]

DAVID GALULA, whose name has become synonymous with counter-insurgency in the international military and diplomatic communities in recent years, lived a brief but extraordinary life. A soldier-intellectual through and through, he devoted his life to France, her army, and to "Western Democracy's" struggle against totalitarian communist subversion. Graduating from Saint-Cyr military academy in 1940 at the age of twenty, he was rapidly immersed in France's uninterrupted stream of conflicts until his retirement from active duty some twenty-three years later. In the five years that remained of his life, he would publish what has been hailed as one of the most significant doctrinal masterpieces of the twentieth century: *Counterinsurgency: Theory and Practice.** He would also draft, during the same period, an

---

*For the sake of brevity, we henceforth refer to this work as *Counterinsurgency*.

illuminating report entitled *Pacification in Algeria: 1956–1958*[†] for the RAND Corporation. Though unavailable to the public until its declassification some four decades later, the report would come to perfectly complement his famous doctrinal work.

And that is certainly not all.

Galula's life and career were, against all odds and despite humble official advancements, as rich as they were fascinating. His fate led him to become intimately associated with the significant events and personalities of his time. He exerted a level of influence through the roles he occupied—and especially through the friendships he established—that was well out of proportion to his modest rank. He owed his influence instead to an uncommon intelligence, a flair for human behavior and relations, and a profound sense of humanity. Combined, these traits would propel him to enter the top military, diplomatic, and academic spheres, even though in truth, he was never a perfect fit within any of these. His strength resided in his capacity to adapt, though often with blinding loyalty and zeal.

Galula took on the unabashed character of France's famed Colonial Army turned Marine Corps, while remaining on its fringes throughout most of his career. He was a fantastic *raconteur*, as well as an able writer and orator. His wit, owed as much to genetics as to cultural background, endeared him to all who knew him on the four continents he came to call home. A quick read of the fictional publication he penned, *The Tiger's Whiskers*, provides a first and undeniable element of proof. Despite the clinical detachment that one may glean from reading *Counterinsurgency*, the man, as shall be seen, was anything but emotionally detached from his work.

Finally, Galula exuded self-confidence. He did so to such an extent that detractors claimed immodesty or over-assurance in his writings. Yet in *Counterinsurgency*, he had cautioned his audience:

> The enterprise is risky. First of all, whereas conventional wars of any size and shape can be counted in the hundreds, no more than a score of revolutionary wars have occurred, most of them since 1945. Is it enough to detect laws? Generalization and extrapolation from such a limited basis must rely to some extent on intuition, which may or may not be correct. Then there is the pitfall of dogmatism inherent in any effort at abstraction, for we are not studying a specific counterrevolutionary war, but the problem in general.[3]

Still, despite the "pitfall of dogmatism," Galula *knew*. He had not written in an intellectual vacuum, but at a time when Frederick Praeger and other publishers were churning out multiple titles a year on all things related to

---

[†]Henceforth referred to as *Pacification*.

revolutionary warfare. Galula was confident that his work would surpass them all. When a small minority of critics became vociferous, dismissing his theories as "typically French," or "overly colonial," and therefore irrelevant to American troops who would not be contested by populations over which they had no colonial designs, Galula contented himself by writing the stunningly prophetic words to his editor, "Never mind, there will be plenty of insurgency and we shall see who is right."[4]

David Galula owes his fame to his brilliantly lucid contribution to the art of irregular warfare. His ability to synthesize complex factors and dialectics across military, political, and even behavioral sciences remains, in my view, unmatched. Naturally, his coming into fame is also owed to fate and to the recent need for Western armies to relearn what they had quickly forgotten, or perhaps more candidly, to learn what they always disdained to institutionally learn. In the aftermath of their swift victories in Afghanistan and Iraq at the dawn of the twenty-first century, these armies were confronted with a chaos, which soon became more threatening than what they had faced during the invasions themselves. The costly oversights, as they were in the end, of having neither proper plans nor doctrine to counter what were soon, albeit reluctantly, acknowledged as insurgencies, prompted a survey of existing literature on the matter. The phenomenon, after all, was not new. The survey extended beyond the U.S. doctrinal arsenal, for despite Vietnam, little existed there that dug past the old adages of "human intelligence is the key," and "the population must be won over," as Galula had once lamented.[5] Fate therefore, and to a certain extent luck, would see his work rediscovered in 2004.

It was left to American generals David H. Petraeus and James N. Mattis to oversee a handpicked team of experts in the design and implementation of a much-needed counterinsurgency doctrine. The fruit of their labors was the dissemination of a combined U.S. Army-U.S. Marine Corps publication in late 2006. The new doctrine was deemed to have become ". . . the most important driver of intellectual change for the Army and Marine Corps."[6] It received unprecedented academic and media attention. NATO itself, and Allied military nations, such as Canada (for whom I proudly served), would come to inspire their own doctrines on the new U.S. "Field Manual 3-24."[7]

In a graceful gesture, the scholarly American generals and their dedicated advisors openly cited the work, which had influenced them the most in their drafting. Seldom had the U.S. Army and Marine Corps co-published a doctrine, and never before had such a doctrine included a bibliography.[8] At a time when U.S.-French relations were at their poorest since the 1960s, commonsense and courtesy prevailed to give credit where credit was due. Galula's 1964 seminal work was listed in both FM 3-24's short Acknowledgements section and Bibliography. His name was cited no less than nine times throughout the manual. More importantly, the essence of his works was undeniably reflected therein. Remarkably, forty years after they had been penned, Galula's writings were influencing wartime policy and strategy dictating the employment of hundreds of thousands of troops, and arguably, the lives of millions of people.

In a further demonstration of indebtedness and goodwill, General Petraeus and Lieutenant-Colonel John Nagl famously referred to Galula as the "Clausewitz of counterinsurgency"[9] in their laudatory foreword to the French edition of *Counterinsurgency*, which I have included with their permission as an appendix. To this, they added that Galula had been, from an American standpoint, "the most illustrious French strategist of the 20th century."[10] Given the enduring pre-eminence of Clausewitz in Western military thought, and the twentieth century's parade of Gal, Gallienis, Lyauteys, Fochs, de Gaulles, Falls, Challes, Bigeards, Trinquiers, Lacheroys, Aussaresses, Hogards, and others, the assertions had not been lightly made.

Irony surrounds Galula's legacy.

Galula remained unknown to the contemporary French military establishment until the resurrection of his writings by the American one. The first French exchange officer to attend the U.S. Army Command and General Staff College under General Petraeus's tutelage gallantly reintroduced Galula in France by translating *Counterinsurgency* on his own initiative from 2007 to 2008.[11] But Galula's official recognition by the conservative French establishment remained hesitant, if not guarded. Attitudes are slowly changing, however. Hopefully, the present work will complement the efforts of a few well-meaning others by putting to rest certain assumptions and misconceptions that I believe have stood as obstacles to a befitting recognition of Galula in France.

Some have gone as far as to imply that racial discrimination had thwarted Galula's career, and potentially his recognition. My research leads me to believe that this certainly did prejudice him at times, but that the effects were seldom lasting. Although the incidence of anti-Semitism is of little consequence to his writings, to which the lion's share of this work is devoted, it remains nonetheless important to the study of his legacy. Such allegations require an investigation that goes beyond simplistic assumptions. I have tried to avoid these at all costs, on this particular issue and all others—historic, biographic and analytical—leaving it up to the reader to decide when factual evidence comes up short of allowing for safe conclusions to be drawn. This said, I assume full responsibility for all errors of interpretation I may have made, as they are all my own.

What differentiates David Galula from his predecessors, peers, and contemporaries? Though fundamental questions such as this one are later addressed, we may set the scene now by considering his doctrine in light of three parameters: intent, basis, and approach. The first two parameters point to more similarities than differences between Galula's doctrine and that of his peers, the French *théoriciens de la Guerre Révolutionnaire* (revolutionary warfare theorists). The intent of these junior- and middle-ranked officers had been to countermand communist subversion in the aftermath of World War II. The *théoriciens* saw links between regional insurgencies, which led them to label the phenomenon as a global one. (Not unlike what some contemporaries have claimed about jihadist insurgency.) In their minds, proletariat-anchored Soviet doctrine threatened revolution in metropolitan France, and in its peasantry-anchored Chinese version, the revolutionary doctrine threatened uprisings in France's "colonial" and "semi-colonial" possessions. Mao's potent adaptation of the works of Lenin had already caused the downfall of French Indochina in the early 1950s, and if left unchecked, would also cause the fall of French Algeria. The *théoriciens* saw in revolutionary warfare a new method of political usurpation sponsored by an interested Sino-Soviet alliance over and above any nationalist underpinnings to the insurrections they fought and studied. The feared suffocation of the West by the totalitarian Communist Bloc was what had motivated Galula to write on the topic of counterinsurgency. Nothing else. He had written with defense in mind. The intent of Galula's doctrine, therefore, is important to bear in mind when interpreting his writings today.

In light of all of this, there is *some* credence to Galula's opinion that revolutionary wars were a phenomenon of the twentieth century,[12] if one considered the doctrines that spurred them, in lieu of the guerrilla warfare that exemplified them. As instruments of violent insurrection, terrorism and guerrilla warfare were not new. Clausewitz, whom Galula had unexceptionally studied in his time, had already written on "The People in Arms";[13] a phenomenon he attributed to the new totality of war brought on by Napoleon. In truth, the existence of guerrilla warfare long predated that too. But to Galula and his fellow *théoriciens*, the asymmetric warfare that the Spaniards and Russians had waged against the emperor's armies was but a single tool in an otherwise complex array of new political instruments held by the communist revolutionaries. Of guerrilla warfare, Galula would limit himself to writing, "The military tactics of revolutionary warfare are too well known to be elaborated in this summary."[14] And so, where others gleaned from Mao only a revolution in fighting tactics, and would become obsessed with formulating organizations, machines and techniques to counter these, Galula and the *théoriciens* perceived a revolution in grand strategy.

The second parameter of Galula's doctrine, the basis, is not only shared with the *théoriciens* of his own era, but also with those who preceded him. Galula believed that the population was the objective of the insurgent and counterinsurgent alike. "Population-centricity" was therefore the basis of his doctrine. The two most illustrious figures of France's Colonial Army at the turn of the century, Gallieni and Lyautey, also shared this view, as had Faidherbe, Bugeaud, and Pennequin decades before them. In their numerous

pacification campaigns, they had invariably chosen the population over
the enemy as their objective. To them, the defeat of the latter went through the
pacification of the former and not the other way around. They viewed the
population as the metaphorical ground over which contenders fought for
power. Through *tâche d'huile* and other complementing principles of pacification, they toiled to render this ground uninhabitable to the enemy. In so
doing, they rejected the Clausewitzian object of war of defeating the enemy's
will to keep fighting, in favor of defeating the enemy's *ability* to keep fighting.
Herein lay (and still lies), in my view, the crux of counterinsurgency warfare,
and the focal point of disagreement between population-centric and enemy-
centric doctrines.

It is with regard to approach, the third doctrinal parameter I have chosen,
that Galula would truly distinguish himself from all the others. First, we note
that in terms of form, Galula would devise the most structured counterinsurgency doctrine. Whereas a majority of his predecessors, peers and contemporaries would limit themselves to committing principles, guidelines, and case
studies to paper, Galula went further and drew from these a bold, step-by-step
approach. This led his acquaintance, the renowned military analyst Bernard
Fall, to write that *Counterinsurgency* was the best "how-to" book in the business.[15] Aided by the level-blurring nature of insurrectionary warfare, Galula
devised a countering approach that lent itself simultaneously to strategy and
tactics. There would be an unimpeachable clarity to his writings. These transitioned smoothly from no-nonsense philosophical discussion of his subject,
to practical application of his approach in the field. Galula refrained from
over-systemizing a phenomenon that had human beings at its core. His intelligence released him from an over-complication of things, rendering his writings accessible to all.

Galula's approach differed even more significantly in terms of content.
Of the four laws of counterinsurgency he proposed, the essence of his doctrine, I believe, was seeded in the third: "Support of the population is conditional."[16] He deduced a series of important principles from this law. From
these principles, he derived a method through which the favorable minority
in a population could be leveraged to sway the neutral majority, and suppress
the opposing minority. (Galula referred to this Maoist-steeped reasoning as
the "basic tenet of the exercise of political power."[17])

Still on account of his third law, Galula argued that the population's support could only be obtained if it could be effectively protected. Otherwise,
fear of the insurgent would preclude a population from collaborating with the
counterinsurgent, regardless of how meritorious his cause. Protection, therefore, addressed man's primal need for security, and freed him to rationally
choose the side that offered freedom and prosperity. Galula further argued
that effectively protecting a population could only be achieved by tightly
controlling it. Only through such a temporary exercise on the fringes of

liberal-democratic acceptability, but in respect of people's dignity—another important characteristic and sometimes differentiator of his doctrine—could one hope to truly "divorce" a population from an insurgency that resided within it. To this he added a second condition. The population had to be convinced that the counterinsurgent's capacity and determination to emerge as the victor in the long run surpassed the insurgent's. This condition, the fulfillment of which lay in the hands of politicians and their electorates, was absolutely critical in his view.

Favoring "minds" over "hearts," but without neglecting the latter—Galula was a proponent of dispensing education, medical care, and piloting local development projects—he thus recognized a hierarchy of human needs, which had to be addressed in sequential order. Indeed, this order would be reflected in the stepwise doctrine he proposed. Galula's genius, in my view, lay first and foremost in his embrace of this logic.

In 1960, Galula had written in a forgotten Staff College thesis, "If the word 'conventional' means what is usual, one may wonder which kind of war is now the conventional war."[18] He had been right in his prediction of the nature of wars to come in the nuclear era. What he had not foreseen perhaps was how quickly the global dialectic, which had motivated his writings, would come to be replaced by different ones, but that tellingly, his writings would maintain their relevance despite the change in contending actors and ideologies.

Henry Kissinger had written to Galula in 1964, ". . . could we adopt the tactics you recommend in Vietnam?"[19] The essence of the question remains true in the broadest sense today, and will remain so tomorrow. The human race's propensity to leverage *any* ideology to create rifts, amplify discontentment, mislead the less fortunate, justify or sponsor terrorism, destabilize established orders, etc., in the interest of gaining political power at home, or geopolitical advantages abroad, will remain immutable. And regardless of how dark and irrational the chosen ideology may be, Fear—the cheap and potent motivator of mankind—will forever be its catalyst. It therefore appears that the answer to Kissinger's question will remain "yes" for the foreseeable future.

This book is meant to be accessible and informative to those who, at all levels, military or civilian, have an interest in matters related to irregular warfare, Galula's writings, or Galula himself. Whereas certain sections lean more toward the biographic, defining the subject's character, intellect, and colorful path that fatefully led him to write about counterinsurgency, other sections lean more toward the analytical, delving into the very heart of his writings, and how they were shaped by his environment and the different schools of thought to which he was exposed.

I make, however, no pretention of being an academic. This book, though thoroughly documented and based on an extensive amount of research, is neither the derivation nor the evolution of a university thesis. I am a soldier who believes in the overall validity and brilliance of Galula's works, not merely from a theoretical standpoint, but from a very practical one. As such, I have tried to present the facts and my interpretations of these in the way that is most natural to me. I would ask the reader to pardon what may seem at times to be biographical empathy and attribute this instead to soldierly empathy.

No serious biographical investigation had yet been made about Galula prior to this writing. My research of the man and his life was facilitated by my knowledge of French (the translation of texts and interviews are my own) and by my closeness to the Jewish communities of North Africa from which he originated. This last attribute afforded me, I would like to believe, a socio-cultural understanding of the man that would have been difficult to come by otherwise. But fascinating as David's life may have been, it is for his shining intellectual legacy to Western military thought that he will be remembered. And though my own military background certainly proved to be an asset in interpreting his writings and career, I have deliberately refrained from drawing examples from my own experiences, with the exception of the prologue, where my sole intention was to reveal to the reader my motivations for this work. I have also attempted to shine a contemporary light on his writings, particularly in the epilogue and conclusion.

"Everything happens for a reason" is the old adage. "Maktoub" is the simple Arabic equivalent, meaning that "it is written." Galula became Galula because of a series of remarkable historical and personal circumstances. The demonstration of this is something toward which I will endeavor, for otherwise, the text would be nothing but a bland and monotonous chronology of milestones in his life. I have taken the liberty of surrounding biographical sections with historical context, particularly France's, which remains very much unknown to recent generations of North Americans, and I even dare say, to young Europeans and French persons. I think that a close attention to some of France's important wartime episodes during Galula's lifetime is critical to truly understanding him, and to no small extent understanding the context for his writings. Hopefully, as a fellow officer told me, a component of Galula's legacy will have been to act as a bridge between two long-lost and mutually indebted friends that are the French and U.S. militaries.

The story of David Galula could not have been written without the full participation of his endearing widow, Mrs. Ruth Morgan Galula. Ruth's courage and determination to see this endeavor through to a point where her husband's legacy would be firmly established cannot be overstated. Despite her advanced age and health woes, she braved long interviews at her home in California as well as countless others over the phone. She granted me unbounded access to her husband's extensive personal archives, a privilege that, at the time of this writing, she had refused to grant anyone else. I fondly recall the days when together, we patiently but excitedly peered over documents and photographs that had not been looked at in decades. For Ruth, the daily exercise of reliving her and her husband's past brought on a roller coaster of emotions. I was infinitely rewarded when she confided that the project afforded her closure, a closure that she had yearned for ever since her husband's passing away half a century ago. I have grown close to the small Galula family over the last three years of working on this book during every spare moment that I could find between my personal and professional obligations.

The boxes of documents, correspondence, and manuscripts Ruth preserved represented a tremendous source of information for the writing of this book. The vast majority of the contents of these archives were not known to the public prior to this publication. Ruth and I are both indebted to Professor Peggy Barlett for her help in organizing these. Alas, still more documents would have been available had the floods resulting from a hurricane not claimed them in Pensacola, Florida, where Ruth was living with her son up until 2007. It is my hope that this work will spur a reputable institution to offer to curate a collection of Galula's archives in France, as Galula would have probably wished, or in the United States, for which he had always demonstrated the utmost affection.

I will forever be indebted to professors Marie-Catherine and Paul Villatoux, whom I consider to be France's foremost academic authorities on the history of revolutionary and psychological warfare, for their selfless help, guidance, and patience. Humble as they may be, they have authored some of the most authoritative works on France's *guerre révolutionnaire* era. These are replete with valuable lessons that can be drawn and adapted for today. I hope that their works will be translated to English someday, so that they may be of benefit to a wider audience.

I am very grateful to all of those people who agreed to be interviewed, and who are cited throughout the texts. Their names also appear in the reference section at the end. These kinspersons, former classmates, colleagues, superiors, subordinates, and friends of Galula made the greatest efforts, often despite their advanced ages, to contribute to the story of the man whose early death they still recalled with great sorrow some forty years later. Their eagerness and ability to testify to Galula's character, intelligence, and achievements is telling of how profoundly they had been marked by him.

I am also grateful to those who did not know Galula but who were generous in their interpretations of his works, and in sharing instances where these had come to influence contemporary counterinsurgency doctrine and execution. They too are named throughout the texts, particularly in the epilogue, where Galula's modern legacy is discussed. I owe many thanks to facilitators of this work such as my father and his learned friends R. V., J. O., and A. M., who helped me to obtain rare, sometimes almost impossible-to-find reference material on France's colonial wars, and the institutions with which Galula was associated with his early life. I owe similar thanks to my sister-in-law,

T. H., for her help in proofreading parts of this work with a young but expert eye; as well as to Mr. Jacques Cataldo, for his enthusiasm and effectiveness in helping me as a "point-man" on the ground in France. Jacques acted voluntarily, driven only by his interest in seeing a biography of Galula published.

I also wish to thank the *Service Historique de la Défence* in Vincennes for granting me special access to Galula's personal military file, years ahead of the expiry of the prescribed confidentiality period. Naturally, I am thankful to the editors and staff at the Praeger Security Institute, Steve Catalano and David Millman in particular, for their involvement in rendering this project a reality. They indulged me in my desire to see this work on Galula published by the same reputable house that had believed in him forty-five years earlier.

Finally, none of this could have been possible without the support of my family and friends, but especially that of my wife. As I submit this manuscript, I am very aware that I will never be able to fully pay her back for her enduring patience, help and encouragements during this project in the aftermath of my return from overseas.

If this work succeeds in furthering the reading and understanding of Galula toward the same noble intentions he had written with in mind, the efforts that have been invested here by all will have been well rewarded.

Ruth Morgan-Galula passed away peacefully as I submitted this manuscript for publishing review, on April 24, 2011, in Pittsburgh, California.

SUMMARY EXCERPTS FROM COUNTERINSURGENCY: THEORY AND PRACTICE

Prerequisites for Successful Insurgency

1. A cause.
2. Weakness of the counterinsurgent.
3. Geographic conditions.
4. Outside support.

Insurgency Framework

The Orthodox Pattern
1. Creation of a [political] party.
2. United front.
3. Guerrilla warfare.
4. Movement warfare.
5. Annihilation campaign.

The Shortcut Pattern
1. Blind terrorism.
2. Selective terrorism.
3. Guerrilla warfare (if required).
4. Movement warfare (if required).
5. Annihilation campaign (if required).

Laws of Counterinsurgency

1. The support of the population is as necessary for the counterinsurgent as for the insurgent.
2. Support is gained through an active minority.
3. Support of the population is conditional.
4. Intensity of efforts and vastness of means are essential.

Counterinsurgency Framework

1. Destruction or expulsion of the insurgent forces.
2. Deployment of the static unit.
3. Contact with and control of the population.
4. Destruction of the insurgent political organization.
5. Local elections.
6. Testing the local leaders.
7. Organizing a [political] party.
8. Winning over or suppressing the last guerrillas.

Principles of Counterinsurgency

1. Economy of forces.
2. Irreversibility.
3. Initiative.
4. Full utilization of the counterinsurgent's assets.
5. Simplicity.
6. To command is to control.

1

The Galulas of Sfax

Pseudo-revolutionary mystification has acquired a new formula: all freedom must be crushed in order to conquer the empire, and one day the empire will be the equivalent of freedom. And so the way to unity passes through totality.

—*Albert Camus*[1]

Nothing in the technique offered here is incompatible with the democratic standards expected to be found in a democracy in wartime, whether in a civil war or in an international war. If the technique may seem slow and complicated, one must remember that the only way to bring a quick end to a rebellion is the Soviet way used in Hungary. But it is not our way.

—*David Galula*[2]

"THE GALULAS OF SFAX" sounds foreign enough to think that both the names of the family and the location were drawn from science fiction. Adding to the oddity is that the patronymic "Galula" would sound no more familiar in France today, than it would elsewhere, had it not been for the recent resurrection of its bearer's writings. Galula is not a French name. The common inference that David Galula was born into a family of *pieds noirs*[3]—French settlers living in North Africa—is rather far from the truth. He was, in fact, a first-generation Frenchman. Born in Sfax, Tunisia, on January 10, 1919, he and his family remained Tunisian subjects without French citizenship until 1924.[4]

David Galula, as his name somewhat betrays, and as his expulsion from the Vichy Army would coldly confirm, was Jewish. Culturally, he was Sephardic.[5] Both his parents were born and raised within Tunisia's considerable Jewish community. Like its Maghreb neighbors Morocco and Algeria, Tunisia was a Muslim state that maintained a relatively friendly and accepting attitude toward its Hebrew subjects. Naturally, this relation had had its ups and downs over the centuries, but such coexistence, particularly from a present—day perspective, was nonetheless remarkable. Galula was born when Arab nationalism was only nascent, and well before Islamic radicalism would succeed it as a galvanizing, albeit much more marginalized, ideology.

The Maghreb during the first half of the twentieth century was an enriching environment in which to grow up. Pluralism endows people with an openness of mind—sometimes—and more assuredly, with an ability to adapt to other cultures. Galula developed both. Jews and European Christians lived as minorities among Muslims. The cultural exchange between these minorities and the Muslim "masses"—the decidedly colonial term used then—was immense. It was not uncommon to find Jews and Muslims sharing identical superstitious beliefs and practices.

Cultural commonalities aside, lines were drawn socioeconomically between the French, the Jews, and their hosts. The French came first as the ruling elite. Jews came second, generally speaking, on equal footing with the disproportionately small Muslim middle class and aristocracy of the era. Combined, this second group—to which the Galula family belonged until its naturalization—fared very well under French rule. In third socio-economic standing were the Arab and Berber working and peasant classes. (That is not to say that there weren't any French working-class migrants. The stereotypical view that all *colons* were wealthy landowners is false.)

If Jews came proportionally ahead of their Muslim counterparts, it was due to their better access to education. Even the poorest of Jews were sponsored by well-organized charities. Basic schooling was guaranteed by *L'Alliance Israélite Universelle*. Headquartered in France, *L'Alliance* dispensed French and Hebrew education for children of Jewish extraction throughout the French dominion.[6] My grandmother, who attended both *L'Alliance* and secular French schools, recalled that there had been a few non-Jewish students in class with her at *L'Alliance*. The education it offered was on par with what was offered by the *lycées* (French schools) to properly French children. *L'Alliance* thus enabled its graduates to attend French universities, creating along the way a blossoming middle class and secular intelligentsia in North Africa. It is almost certain that Galula (along with his parents and siblings) owed his first years of elementary education to *L'Alliance*.

The Galulas endeavored to ascend socially to a point where they were considered first and foremost as Frenchmen. It is to this end that David's father, Albert Galula, applied for French citizenship for his family. It would be granted to him when his son was five years old.[7] Albert would retain his religion, but not its practice. His son, for instance, would not undergo ritual confirmation, bar mitzvah, at the age of thirteen. David's youth would be spent in cultural ambiguity, contributing perhaps to the conflicted sense of identity that persisted throughout his life.

Historical and environmental factors also played their natural part on Galula's developing perception of the world. First in Tunisia and then in Morocco, he was raised in a functional model of colonialism. He became its epitomic product. Born with a heritage that spoke of a completely different religion, ethnicity, language, and history, he grew up to fully embrace that which was offered by the colonial power.

Stigmatized as the act may be today, colonialism was still regarded as an acceptable form of geopolitical patronage during his youth. France, much like Britain, had long ago given itself a *mission civilizatrice* in which it genuinely believed. National prestige, geopolitical jockeying, and economic development through trade were also at stake, as was the access to human and natural resources that would prove useful in times of war. In a different category than Algeria (a true colony), Tunisia and Morocco came to be labeled as "protectorates," substituting the notion of political and socioeconomic patronage and assimilation with that of protection from banditry, anarchy, and the designs of other, allegedly less-scrupulous foreign powers.

Colonialism shared some common ground with the counterrevolutionary work that Galula's future promised, and the counterinsurgency work with which the West has been faced ever since the postcolonial era began. Denying this on moral or political pretenses may well be necessary, but refusing to draw lessons from history on account of these would be wasteful. There is little coincidence in the fact that Galula's four laws of counterinsurgency[8] would have found as much applicability to nineteenth century colonial warfare as they did to twentieth century counterrevolutionary warfare, and as they do now to twenty-first century counterinsurgency warfare given the elemental commonalities among these conflicts where people, more than material means, are at the center. It can be argued that the latest form of intervention, as practiced by the West, is not fueled by the same motives as its predecessors, nor is it free to apply the same degrees of force. It can be agreed, however, that all of these forms of intervention have historically been bound by a rather common end-state. They have ultimately sought to install or maintain a political order aligned with the intervener's interests. For this to be achieved, the concerned population's embrace of the proposed political order, or its submissiveness to it, has invariably been required, and set as the objective.

Pursuant to all of this, it is clear from his father's actions, and later his own, that Galula wholeheartedly embraced the French colonial cause. He embraced it in North Africa, and wherever else in the world the tricolored flag flew. "He loved France," his widow had unequivocally told me when I had first broached the issue of identity. It was her husband's ardent patriotism, and yet simpler motivations—not his religion, as has been mistakenly interpreted in recent times—that would motivate him to join the French military at the eve of World War II. Later, this same adoration for France would compel him to reintegrate the army despite having been expelled from it on unfathomable grounds.

Galula profoundly believed in the ability of France to better the lives of colonized and "semi-colonized"[9] peoples. From what his father had told him—Albert was born when the French had just arrived in Tunisia—and from what he had witnessed growing up in North Africa, Galula was convinced that French patronage resulted in higher standards of living. Sanitation, education, and commerce, to name a few areas, were all affected positively. As such, Galula believed that the French system was to the benefit of both the colonizer and the colonized.

It would be no wonder why, years later, Galula would so ardently defend the French model in Algeria. The tone, which he employed in *Pacification*, and in much of his correspondence, does not leave much room for interpretation; his was the belief that France had been both capable and justified in maintaining *L'Algérie Française*. Such a stand, though far from unique or even marginal, may have earned his legacy much controversy in France today. But unfounded extrapolation is chiefly to blame for that. As shall be seen, Galula had made his peace with de Gaulle's decision to grant Algeria its independence, understanding why it was politically imperative for him to do so well before the *Organisation Armée Secrète* (OAS)—the French splinter movement that violently opposed de Gaulle's decision—became active. Nonetheless, Galula foresaw the alternative in Algeria as a cruelly totalitarian one in the servitude of communist powers; far more oppressive, therefore, than what the prospect of continued French presence offered. This is the context within which Galula's initial inclinations towards French Algeria should be viewed. More broadly, I would submit that this is the humanistic context within which Galula's anti-communist and anti-revolutionary views should be judged.

The Galulas were exceptionally Europeanized for their time. From their clothing, as one can glean from family pictures, to their acceptance of interfaith marriage; they readily assimilated to the French. "They were still very proud of their Jewish heritage," David's widow had told me. Ironically, their nearly abandoned faith was what had allowed them to become French. Albert Galula had to appeal to the Crémieux[10] Decree of 1870, which granted the right of French citizenship to all Algerian-born Jews. Muslims, on the other hand, had been excluded from the offer.[11]

Galula wrote in *Pacification*: "When the French arrived in Algeria in 1830, they found a local Jewish minority in the same state of underdevelopment as the large Moslem majority. Both groups were given the same opportunities, yet only the Jews took advantage of it, and to such an extent that in two generations they became completely assimilated in terms of education and consequently in terms of social and economic advancement."[12] Galula had been unfair in omitting the instrumental role played by the well-established Jewish community in France in facilitating this assimilation leading up to the Crémieux Decree. As for his own citizenship, it had been acquired precariously. Albert Galula had appealed to the Crémieux Decree on account that his father had been born in Algeria. And though it is true that Albert's grandfather had been born there, it appears that the latter had already moved his family to Tunisia, where his son was born, well before the decree's enactment.[13] It is very possible, then, that Albert had stretched the truth regarding his father's nationality in order to qualify his family for citizenship.

Religion had indirectly afforded David Galula French citizenship, but paradoxically, it is the absence of religion in the family household that allowed him to contemplate a military career. Young men of Galula's background, as a general rule, did not seek to undertake careers in the French Army, let alone attend Saint-Cyr. The existence of Jewish communities in the Maghreb predated the French colonization by centuries; and so the allegiance of these young men was first and foremost to their own communities. The lands that they inhabited had changed hands too many times, and too often with dreadful consequences for them to owe their allegiance to any other cause but their own. Algerian Jews, given their stronger bonds to France, were the natural exception to this rule. But Galula was not Algerian.

David's character too, was naturally affected by his cultural heritage. His sense of humor, for instance, was typically Sephardic: gently sarcastic, self-mocking, and often cynical, but shy of sardonic. It lent itself well to satire of the kind found in his lesser-known fictional writings. Parts of *Pacification*, as well as much of his correspondence, are also infused with it. Those who knew him spoke of an "endearing" kind of humor. "My English," Galula would write in his final years to the famed strategist Alistair Buchan, "is not quite the King's, due to my strong French accent, but I have never had any difficulty in getting my ideas across."[14] And when, in a conference he had organized, Buchan referred to Galula as a lieutenant-colonel to bolster his credibility as a speaker, the latter replied, "I would be grateful if you could correct a mistake in my title as it appears in your program: my Army [rank] is Major, not Colonel, although I feel of course that I should have been made a General long ago[!]"[15]

Non-practicing as his father may have been, the values associated with his religion were never brushed away. Despite the clinical detachment found in some of his works, evidence abounds that Galula was a Humanist. His thoughts and positions on counterinsurgency were anything but aseptic. Quite on the contrary, his career and his actions were those of a man who fought passionately against veiled tyranny. His writings make clear that he could not palate the relativism by which the communists stood by to criticize Western colonialism and patronage, while justifying their own methods of expansion through exported ideology and subversion. This deeply rooted dislike of communism was more likely to be born out of Humanism, than out of zeal to prove his French republican patriotism.

Far from resembling his famous peer, Colonel Roger Trinquier (to whom a section in a later chapter is reserved), Galula was a theorist and practitioner of war who sincerely believed in the imperativeness of acting morally, regardless of the circumstances imposed by the struggle. (That is not to say that Trinquier is amoral or immoral. Quite to the contrary, he goes to great lengths to illustrate the necessity of leveling modus operandi with terrorist-insurgent organizations in *Modern Warfare*. He argues in favor of limitless coercive interrogation by noting that as a soldier accepts the dangers inherent in war, a terrorist, who has refused to accept these same dangers by operating incognito and against civilians, must accept the dangers that await him in capture. In essence, one cannot ask for the same protection that is afforded to a prisoner of war, if one has not acted as a soldier.) During an important RAND symposium on counterinsurgency he later attended, Galula admitted to his peers, for instance, that he had been "temperamentally unsuited to organizing and exploiting children for the purpose of gathering intelligence through them,"[16] despite having learned from communist guerrillas what value they could bring.

And yet, Galula was far from *soft*. In *Pacification,* for instance, the officer coolly relates how he had had a rebel executed on-the-spot for assassinating one of his militiamen. His doctrine was not *soft* either. The imperative of exercising a firm control over a population in the midst of a counterinsurgency effort is a central theme. Some of his proposals, such as the forced enlistment of local labor (paid at a nominal rate) to build roads and defensive works, would raise more than a few eyebrows today.

David Galula's birth brought disproportionate joy to his parents in that he was the first son, and that five daughters had preceded him. His father, a Sephardic man despite himself, had always wished for a son. At the age of 42, Albert's wish had finally come true. For his 33-year-old wife, Julie Cohen, her son's birth was a harbinger of salvation—or so she thought. Albert, the avid gambler that he was, insisted on trying for a second son. But the odds seldom favored the poor man. A sixth daughter was born two years later.

David was born into a relatively prominent family of Sfax's Jewish community. Albert was not to credit for this; his father was. David's grandfather, David Dekyar Ghalula, born in Tunis in 1844, was the son of Jacob ben (son of) Jacob born in Bône, Algeria, 34 years earlier. I discovered that David Dekyar had held municipal office in Sfax as one of the two representatives of the Jewish community in 1888.[17] This exemplified one of the ways by which the French unburdened themselves from the costly administration of their colonies and protectorates, while allowing for some degree of representative governance. Financially successful, David Dekyar had carved himself a fair share of the city's important olive business. He came to own oil presses, bottling facilities, and by some accounts, even a small fleet of boats dedicated to carrying his products across the Mediterranean.[18] It was after this grandfather that David Galula had been named in accordance with Sephardic tradition. In all likelihood, it is also from him that David inherited some of his intellectual prowess and charisma.

The patronymic Galula was, as above, spelled Ghalula at the time of David Dekyar. The "h" represented a more accurate reflection of the name's Arabic or Berber pronunciations. But the letter was eventually dropped to Europeanize the name. A number of sources corroborate that the Ghalula family originated from an ancient village of the same name in Tripolitania (a region in present day Libya, bordering Tunisia). The village had been set at the foot of Djebel (Mount) Nefoussa, and founded by Troglodyte Berbers.[19] Historical records further indicate that "Ghalula" hosted Jewish enclaves until the late fifteenth century.[20] If this is so, then it follows that Galula's ancestry in North Africa predated the Spanish Inquisition of 1492. The alternative explanation to the origin of the family name is that it may have been borrowed from the Arabic word for "to cheat," or "to deceive," pronounced *Ghalul*.[21] This proposition however, as amusing as it may have been to a family where the men of Albert Galula's generation were avid card players, is downplayed by most authorities.

Galula remains, to be sure, an uncommon last name for North African Jewry. There are two branches to the family. It seems that the split occurred towards the end of the nineteenth century when David's grandfather David Dekyar moved his family from Tunis, the capital, to Sfax, some 300 kilometers to the south.

David was raised until the age of seven in coastal Sfax, Tunisia's second largest city. Although Sfax had prospered briefly under Ottoman rule, it was under the French, a century and a half later, that it would truly flower. Demographic censuses of that era quantified the French Administration's successes in improving local living conditions.[22] A modern port was built and electricity was brought to industrial areas and well-to-do residential neighborhoods. An import-hungry Metropole meant that vast olive groves and grain fields would soon saturate the countryside. David Dekyar's olive business thrived under these conditions, enticing or at least enabling the family to Europeanize itself as it did.

I had the pleasure of interviewing sisters Yolande Bismuth and Magda Ericson over the phone in late 2009. The daughters of Victor Galula, Albert's brother, Yolande and Magda fondly remembered their cousin David, though their brief encounters had occurred long ago. Yolande recalled the story of how David Dekyar's fortunes had changed for the worse when the uninsured family estate went up in flames.

"The house had burnt down *to the ground*," she stressed over the phone, speaking to me in French from her Paris flat. "According to family lore, the fire was started accidentally by one of my aunts who had gone to her room to change. She had opened the closet with one hand, while holding a lit candle with the other. A dress caught on fire. The house had burnt down so quickly . . . and this too is part of family lore . . . that my uncle Élie, though paralyzed by a childhood illness, stood up from his wheelchair and sprinted out of the house. Thankfully, nobody had been hurt."

"After the house fire," Yolande continued, "the family business plummeted. David Dekyar's three eldest sons were more interested in gambling than in working. There was a lot of card playing in Sfax's upper social circles at that time. It was a ruinous vice! The sons got themselves and their father into debt like this. And who knows . . . maybe that's what forced them to sell or abandon the olive business."

The financial misfortunes that originated there had perhaps been fateful in the upbringing of David Galula. Albert's lack of financial stability had led to the precipitated betrothals of his daughters. Had these same woes encouraged David to seek a career where financial compensation was meek, but at least stable?

Albert was born in the middle of six siblings. Joseph, named after his paternal grandfather, had been the eldest. Next came Victor, born in 1880, followed by Albert, two sisters, and a brother. Joseph had been the brightest and most successful of the boys. He had been the first to leave Sfax, and the first to settle in Casablanca, the El-Dorado of the era.

"Joseph did very well in the grain business," Yolande told me. "He held an executive job with the old and powerful *La Maison Louis Dreyfus* company. But Joseph had a very strong character, too."

"Too?" I repeated.

"Yes," she answered, "all the brothers had strong, obstinate characters, and were outspoken like their own father. . . . In any event, his character was perhaps too strong, given the reaction he had to his supervisor's criticism one day."

"And what reaction was that?" I asked, grinning in anticipation.

"Joseph wrote a scathing letter stating that everybody in the company, from top to bottom, from the highest director to the lowliest steno writer, was incompetent. Completely incompetent!"

"Ah, well done," I commented, laughing.

This was perhaps another sign of genetic character influence, so to speak. Whether coincidental or actually hereditary, Galula would come to have a very outspoken manner about him. And though his unguarded intellectual

Galula family portrait taken in 1912. From left to right, Joseph and his wife Senegalia, David Dekyar and his wife Deya (Chemla), Julie (Cohen) and Albert, Jenny (Albert's younger sister) and her husband Darius Cattan. (Courtesy of Magda Galula Ericson)

expression promoted the circulation of his ideas, it was sometimes detrimental to the advancement of his career according to his widow. A superior of his had once pleaded with Ruth, "Can't you convince your husband to avoid always speaking his mind in front of senior officers at work? I have tried my best, but he doesn't listen!" Galula was not outspoken, however, to the point of recklessness. He enjoyed having the ear of senior commanders and officials. The intelligence of his arguments, his self-confidence, and his wit afforded him that.

David's second eldest uncle, Victor, had been a gifted student in school. His father had agreed to send him to Liège, Belgium, to earn a degree in electrical engineering. He had been the first and only one of the brothers to seek and attain a university degree. Higher education was evidently a value that Victor would instil in his daughters. Yolande, for instance, earned degrees in philosophy and art. Her younger sister Magda, born in 1929, earned a PhD in physics from the renowned Sorbonne University in Paris, at a time when women in that field, and at that level, were nearly unheard of. During David's lifetime, she and her husband Dr. Torleif Ericson were already well on their way to becoming titans in the field of nuclear and condensed matter physics.

Did Victor's attainment of a higher education entice his nephew to do the same? Or what of the fact that Victor served as an infantryman throughout the First World War? Tempting as it may be to draw conclusions, it is unlikely that these were decisive factors. Victor had established his family in Algeria soon after Albert moved his to Morocco, precluding significant interaction between David and his uncle.

At the risk of shocking some readers, I will note that marriage between cousins was still acceptable in North Africa in the early twentieth century—the legacy of secluded village life in earlier times. David's parents had not taken exception to this, as they were in fact first cousins. Still, this revelation surprised me because both Albert and Julie had sprung from liberal and modern families. "The offspring, from what I gathered, turned out to be either brilliant, or a bit cuckoo," Ruth Galula had told me in an innocent way, causing us both to laugh.

Ruth believed that her mother-in-law would have liked to be more traditionalist, but was held back by Albert. Julie nonetheless remained superstitious, like many Tunisian Jews. Ruth recalled an instance when her mother-in-law had spilled water down the stairs outside of her apartment following her son's visit: "She said it was to make sure that we would return. She stood there spilling the glass as if it were the most normal thing in the world to do!"

"Julie was very proud of her family name," Ruth added. "She wanted me to know that Cohen was a noble and priestly name, and that I should consider it quite the privilege to have married the descendent of one!" Of priestly descent or not, Julie's family too was relatively assimilated, as intermarriage was well accepted. Julie's older sister, for instance, married a Catholic Spanish diplomat serving in Morocco. Another sister, Mathilde, married a gentile French Army officer stationed in Morocco. Interestingly, Yolande Bismuth did not believe that this army officer could have had much of an influence over David, given that he soon returned to France with his bride. Ruth thought otherwise. She shared that David spent a year living with them in France during his "preparatory" year for Saint-Cyr. The story of Colonel Pasthier will be saved for the next chapter.

I honed in on David's father. I only knew from David's birth certificate that his father had declared himself to be a *négociant*, or a businessman. I asked Yolande to describe what memories she had kept of her uncle. She had never met him by her own admittance, but had been told about him by her own father.

"Albert was a 'Jean-de-la-Lune' [space cadet] character," she said. "He was the kind of man who seldom worked. His being a poor provider compelled his daughters to become seamstresses in Casablanca at young ages. David too, I suppose, must have had to fend for himself."

Ruth's depiction of Albert matched Yolande's. "I was given the impression that Albert had held a high opinion of his social status. He had many friends, which meant that they must have accepted him at his own valuation! Granted, he was said to be a marvellous storyteller, possessing a terrific sense of humor. He spent his days in the cafés of Casablanca telling stories to those who, like him, had not much else to do. David, however, never held his father in poor esteem."

Idleness, evidently, had not been passed on to his son. In addition to his busy military and later civilian career, Galula had written more prolifically than what was publicly known up to now. I recalled how his brother-in-law, Jere Rowland, who was one my first interviewees for this work, had told me that "there was never a day in David's life when his mind was idle." Albert's redeeming qualities were to be found in his son, however. A resilient sense of humor and the ability to be sociable and entertaining were part of these. Galula would acquire the reputation of being able to captivate the attention of any individual, regardless of rank or social status. He also enjoyed, somewhat like his father, having an audience. He had written only half-jokingly to his editor, who had wished that he write more on the subject of counterinsurgency, "The trouble with me is, I am a man very sparse of words, at least in writing because when I talk, it's another affair."[23]

The inherited-humor and storytelling skills were also perhaps to credit for the style of his writings. (With the exception of certain parts of *Counterinsurgency*, where he mimicked, knowingly or not, Mao's scholastic-administrative language.) His published fictional piece, *The Tiger's Whiskers,* for instance, is the transcription of one of many humoristic tales he used to tell at dinner parties in Hong Kong. Reading *Pacification* too, one is never bored despite the length of the work. Galula's sense of humor transpires through what could otherwise have been a rather macabre tale.

The many testimonials I gathered about Galula pointed in the same direction: he was a man in whose company one was never bored. Such talents served him well in his *attaché* postings in Hong Kong, for instance, where he successfully entertained princes, generals, senior officials, academics, journalists, and others who were always of much higher rank or standing than he. His pleasant manner was complemented by a still more impressive intelligence, which could stimulate debate on any issue. All of this was often enough to pardon his unguarded outspokenness.

A man who shall be introduced later, but whose influence over Galula can be stated here as having been immense, spoke the following in 1967:

... Galula struck everyone, not only because of his intelligence, but because of his type of intelligence: quick, dynamic, and penetrating. It allowed him to delve with equal zeal and passion into the most varied of subjects: politics, war, science, technology and arts; as long as these were situated in living actuality, in his current of thoughts, and in reality. It is this that allowed him to write simultaneously the most serious publications on the gravest of topics, and books of humor containing a surprisingly vivacious style.[24]

2

CASABLANCA

Every new construction yard is worth a battalion.

—Marshal Lyautey[1]

The population represents this new ground. If the insurgent wishes to disassociate the population from the counterinsurgent, to control it physically, to get its active support, he will win the war because in the final analysis, the exercise of political power depends on the tacit agreement of the population, or at worst, on its submissiveness.

—David Galula[2]

DAVID GALULA spent eleven of the most formative years of his youth in North Africa's grandest metropolis, Casablanca. He was seven years old when his father decided to follow his older brother, Joseph, to Morocco. Casablanca's economic boom during the interwar period was said to be unparalleled in the region, but the move did little to reverse Albert's financial woes.

David grew up in a relatively spacious downtown apartment on Général Poeymirau Boulevard. A central and pretty street, it had been named after the French officer who had been instrumental only a few years earlier in the pacification of Morocco. The general had served under none other than Marshal Lyautey, France's *pacificateur par excellence*. As of 1907, Lyautey led the conquest and pacification of Morocco, inspired by his previous campaigns under Marshal Joseph Gallieni's tutelage in Tonkin and Madagascar.[3] In 1913, Lyautey became Morocco's first *Résident Général*. His name was later lent to a number of streets and institutions in Morocco, including the prestigious high school Galula attended.

Both Morocco and Tunisia had fostered insurgencies at the outset of their respective occupations, and both had been placated successfully and relatively swiftly. Morocco had been a credible sultanate—a traditional kingdom—whereas Tunisia had not. The latter had been left with a struggling dynasty of Turkish begs from whom the French had easily usurped any remaining power thirty years prior to their foray into Morocco. As such, Morocco was destined to retain more autonomy. The cultured Lyautey did not wish to see a true colonization of Morocco, and had said to this effect: "*ici, nous avons réellement trouvé un État et un peuple*"[4] (Here, we have truly found a state and a nation). To his dismay however, an impatient Paris pressured him to draw more economic returns from the protectorate, leading him to resign in 1925.

Morocco was not very different from Tunisia as far as Galula's upbringing was concerned. Colonial history aside, resemblances between the two protectorates abounded: from climate to culture, to the languages spoken on the street, and onto the social dynamics between the French, the Muslims, and the Jews. Needless to say, Galula's first cultural shock did not occur during his transit from Tunisia to Morocco, but rather later, during his transit from the Maghreb to metropolitan France.

The city of my grandparents' and parents' youths was rapidly modernizing in the 1930s. Casablanca quickly outpaced Sfax's own considerable development. It became the Maghreb's largest city. Casablanca had been home to 25,000 people at the onset of French involvement in 1907. By 1931, this number had grown to 90,000, and nearly tripled again to 257,000 by 1936.[5] By then, it had the air of an up-and-coming European city, drawing crowds of tourists for world-class events such as the prestigious *Grand Prix* races. It is generally recognized that the city owed much of its heyday glory to Lyautey, whose sepulchre at the Pantheon in Paris bears the inscription "*Bâtisseur de Villes*" (Builder of Cities).

Such exposure to a modernizing world was conducive to expanding one's horizons and ambitions. Galula benefited from an excellent education in Casablanca. Elementary school in Sfax with *L'Alliance* had been on par with French education anywhere else, but the Lycée de Casablanca, later renamed Lycée Lyautey, was Morocco's elite institution.[6] It prepared Galula for the rigorous Saint-Cyr admittance exam, while completing his cultural assimilation. Galula's teenage years in the Hollywood-storied urbanity seem to have been happy ones. Surrounded by the affection and adulation of his sisters, he grew up with privileges that were unaffected by his father's financial woes.

Julie Cohen Galula continued to live on Poeymirau Street long after her children had moved out, and long after her husband Albert had passed away from natural causes during the War. A recently engaged Ruth Morgan visited her in 1949. Gifted with an awe-inspiring memory, Ruth recalled, 60 years later, a large and bright third-floor flat with high ceilings. "It must have felt much smaller when David had lived there with all of his siblings. There was a wide hall in the middle where the family ate their meals together. They had a *Fatima*[7] to help with the cooking and cleaning. She stayed mostly in the kitchen, which still had its original coal stoves when I visited."

"Had David been spoiled?" I asked, somehow certain that he had been.

"Oh yes!" Ruth exclaimed. "With his mother around, six sisters, and a *Fatima* . . . he couldn't boil water when I met him!" Catering to his every need, Ruth recalled how his mother and the maid had ensured that he was always happy as a child.

"He hated bland foods, and only cared for red meat," Ruth illustrated her point. "If he didn't touch his plate, his mother would say: '*Mon chéri . . .* we'll just have to make you something else!' And the maid would be sent out to purchase whatever he fancied."

"He was really handicapped by this," Ruth added on a different tone. "At formal dinners, I had to make the most elaborate excuses to hostesses to explain why he alone wasn't eating. I am sure that the wives of senior officers and diplomats often took offence to this." Thankfully for Galula, his wife adored cooking. She is, as far as I know, Julia Child's most loyal fan. She reveled at how much she had in common with America's original television celebrity chef. Both had worked for the State Department, lived in China in pre-revolutionary times, and then followed their husbands to France before finally returning to the United States.

Galula's sense of humor and personable style made him fond of practical jokes. "David had thought it a good idea to place a piece of camembert cheese under one of his sister's bed one day," Ruth recounted. "The girls were driven crazy for days trying to figure out where the smell was coming from. They turned the room upside down before they could finally find the hidden piece of cheese. In the heat of Casablanca, it must have been unbearable!"

Another testimonial regarding Galula's propensity toward practical jokes came from Anne-Louise Rosensohn, Ruth's niece. A person who exudes positivism and kindness, she was particularly excited at the prospect of a book being published about her uncle. "My parents and the Galulas brought us, the children, on a weekend trip to Cape Cod," she told me over the phone. "David used to always play tricks on us. One morning, he sprinkled our eggs with Tabasco sauce without telling us. We laughed so hard with our mouths burning! He had an unforgettable French accent which made everything funnier."

Galula was affectionate, much more so perhaps than the typical career officer of his era. He was, moreover, completely uninhibited, sometimes to the point of mild eccentricity. His cousin, Yolande Bismuth, told me that he assumed a martial, rigid allure only later (and temporarily), while attending Saint-Cyr, where one can assume he was trying to fit in.

"David was incredibly loving with his sisters," Ruth told me. "He was particularly fond of the youngest one, Esther." Nicknamed Tételle, she had suffered from polio. "They all doted on her," Ruth continued. "She had a wonderful personality . . . always full of joy. Much to David's delight, she would happily marry and have children, gaily overcoming her handicap."

Although David reserved his warmest affections for Tételle, he saw a kindred spirit in Henriette. "She was his favorite," Ruth felt. Henriette had been the second eldest, born eleven years before him. Wise and mature, she had served as a good counsel to her brother throughout his youth, and probably a good intermediary between him and her father. Henriette had been preceded by Deya-Laure (named after her paternal grandmother), and followed by Marie-Helène, Madeleine, and Sarah-Claire Cécile.

"David's older sisters were ecstatic to have had a brother," Ruth remarked, "but when their father tried for a second son and Tételle was born, they told him 'ça suffit' (that's enough)! There were limits to how much of a financial burden they would carry for his sake."

The next topic of interest regarding Galula's youth was his schooling. I knew from his widow and his personal papers that he had attended Casablanca's Lycée Lyautey from 1930 until his preparatory year for Saint-Cyr in 1938.[8] Lyautey had personally ordered the construction of the *lycée* on Casablanca's Mers-Sultan hill.[9] The campus came to include ten pavilions, its own dormatory, a gymnasium, and a stadium. The student population quadrupled in the ten years that spanned the campus's inauguration and the beginning of Galula's attendance. The sons and daughters of French civil administrators, officers, soldiers, expatriated professionals, businessmen, teachers, and others surrounded Galula. France's social and political spectrum was well represented in his classes. Jews and Muslims from well-to-do Moroccan families were also accepted at the *lycée* in small numbers.

It was naturally left for French schools to promote French values among the sons and daughters of Muslim elites. If a "leverageable" segment of the population could be molded in the administration's image, the latter would be able to rule with a minimalist footprint. Nonetheless, secondary education, even that which was dispensed by auxiliary *écoles musulmanes*,[10] was not available to all in Morocco. (Retrospective opinions on the causes for this shortcoming range from the desire to maintain ignorance, to a willful restraint in the imposition of French culture, and on to a simple lack of resources). Much to my surprise, Arabic was not taught at the French *Lycée* until the end of the Second World War. And so save for a few words and expressions, Galula could not speak the language.

The French education system of Galula's era was recognized as one of the best, if not *the* best in the world. It famously endowed its graduates with a

A teenaged Galula stands next to his older sister "Lolette" (Deya-Laure).

rich general culture and a wide knowledge base. Tellingly, there was a great amount of pride in being admitted to the teaching profession, which was viewed as an elite corps. "My husband could not believe," Ruth would tell me, "that I had gone through high school and four years of college without having studied any serious chemistry or physics in the American system of education." (In fairness to the latter, however, I hasten to add that her husband had held a particularly strong affection for natural sciences.)

Ever since Napoleonic times, one had to pass a lengthy *Baccalauréat* exam at the completion of high school in order to accede to France's dual university system.[11] Although the *"Bac"* guarantees access to public universities, it does not do so for the elitist *Grandes Écoles*, a banner that includes Saint-Cyr and world-famous institutions such as École Normale Supérieure and Polytechnique. Admission requires one to complete an additional year or two of intensive preparatory studies in order to compete in a gruelling national exam known as the *Concours*. Admitted candidates owe the State a number of years of public service after graduation, but are practically assured prestigious careers.

"Salomon Pimienta was David's closest childhood friend," Ruth told me with a tone that announced remorse. "When David passed away, I had not had the presence of mind to inform Pimienta in time for him to make it to the funeral in Paris. He was still living in Morocco, and . . . I had not seen him in years! He never forgave me . . . and we never spoke again."

Pimienta and Galula had started classes together at the age of eleven at the *Lycée*. Galula's friend was not a French citizen, but came from a similar background. He remained in Morocco during the War and afterwards, doing well for himself in mineral mining ventures and mechanical automation. His friendship with Galula never diminished despite the distances that came to separate them.

Marcel Kadosch was another classmate and friend of Galula's in his senior year at the *lycée*. He and I corresponded frequently during my research. I recall being humbled time and again by his long and informative letters. Kadosch had chosen to study engineering after graduation from the *lycée* with Galula. Like Pimienta, Kadosch was also without French citizenship. But like so many of the Lycée Lyautey alumni, he was destined for a life of accomplishments. In 1952, he collaborated with Jean Bertin, the chief scientist behind the *aérotrain* (hover train) project, to invent the world's first jet engine reverse thruster. The three boys—Galula, Pimienta, and Kadosch—had shared a common cultural heritage, as well as a passion for sciences and mathematics.

"David and I played chess frequently at the *lycée*," Kadosch reminisced in an early letter. "One day, we signed up together for a tournament to play against Morocco's champion: Mr. Kulczar. The man played simultaneously against twenty of us. He defeated all but one." In 1967, Pimienta reunited Kadosch and Galula in Paris over dinner at the Place d'Alma. The two had not seen each other in nearly thirty years. Kadosch recalled that Galula's first words to him were: "Do you remember the face Kulczar made when you took away his queen!?" Kadosch had won the game.

Galula and Kadosch were enrolled in the same advanced mathematics program in their graduating year. "There were 35 of us in 'Math Elem'," Galula's classmate wrote me. "Twenty-five boys, six of which were Jewish, and 10 girls. There was a single Muslim boy amongst us: Bou Yacoub. Not admitting more Muslim students was one of the great failures of the Protectorate's policies at that time. Thankfully, Muslim students were more present in philosophy classes that year, and I know that they were better represented at other *lycées* in Morocco."

"Many of us," Kadosch continued, "were later accepted in the *Grandes Écoles*. Galula and Jacques Gros went to Saint-Cyr. Jean Hentschel, who later headed the national electrical company, and Henri Le Masne de Chermont, who was killed at Monte Cassino in 1943, went to Polytechnique. Three of the girls also attended a *Grande École*, and all returned to the *lycée* to teach."

Nothing in Galula's early academic performance had foretold admittance to a *Grande École*. "He had not been a top student during his *premières années* [first years]," Ruth informed me, finishing her sentence with remarkably well-maintained French, as she often did in my company. "He played hooky all the time. He loved to swim, play tennis and ride horses. Albert pulled him out of the *lycée* at 14, figuring that he would be motivated to go back after being put to work."

Albert Galula had been understandably displeased about his son's lack of interest in school. David had been given an opportunity that his sisters had not.

"The outcome?" I asked Ruth.

"Completely contrary to his father's intention! David enjoyed work too much . . . so Albert put him back in school."

Character and temperament had likely been at play. Galula had never been the scholastic type, and felt ill at ease in academic circles later in life. (A regrettable fact, as he would surely have written more otherwise.) His decision to apply himself in school likely coincided with his decision to attend Saint-Cyr.

"David must have *become* an excellent student," Kadsoch replied in a later letter, conveying his surprise that this had not always been so. He sent me a copy of the *lycée*'s honor roll, which he had preciously kept. In the year that preceded graduation, Galula had finished among the top five students in half of his courses. He had topped his class in physical education (Galula was athletically inclined throughout his life), finished second in physics and chemistry, third in mathematics and bible studies, and fourth in French composition.[12] The final year was not as fruitful in prizes, despite his good grades. He only finished first in physical education. "The reason for this," Kadosch explained, "was because the *Math Elem* class was generally composed of the *lycée*'s brightest students. This raised the average considerably." Kadosch had ranked first overall that year, winning the *lycée*'s *Prix d'excellence*. All of this was more than impressive. For the two boys to perform as they did was a testament not only to their intellectual capacities, but also to their determination to succeed. One must be reminded that Kadosch was not even French, and that Galula had been naturalized! Moreover, Galula could not have counted on much help from his parents or siblings, who were unlikely to have completed higher studies.

I questioned Kadosch on classroom life. He admirably recalled how the students debated political and social matters, reflecting the opinions their parents expressed at home. In 1938, the left-leaning Front Populaire was governing France at a time when Western Europe was well on its way to fascist hegemony. The presidency of Léon Blum, a Parisian Jew with Sorbonne University diplomas in literature and law, would do little to curb the anti-Semitic scapegoating in the aftermath of France's defeat. Vichy France's minister of the interior, Marcel Peyrouton, candidly expressed that it was Blum and his Jewish acolytes who had "done all this harm to France."[13] Kadosch's sense of conflicted identity comes through in his letters, as the notions of religion, race, and nationality had so often been forcibly tied in his youth. Undoubtedly, this had been the case for Galula too.

"My father was a teacher at *L'Alliance*," Kadosch volunteered. "He was also a Free Mason, believing in God and secularity. I am none of these. He believed in the God of Victor Hugo, Voltaire, and Rousseau. I do not believe in any God, not even Spinoza's. I strongly suspect that this was the same for David, though we never spoke of religion together. In any event, I cannot allow myself to speak for the departed . . . " Galula had been agnostic, according to his widow, but this will be left for later.

"I never heard Galula express any political preferences," Kadosch continued, "but his friend Pimienta manifested a decidedly hostile attitude towards the *Front Populaire*, or at least, towards the Communists, and I always thought that the same went for Galula. I suspect that I was not mistaken given what one can glean from his writings."

"Did the students believe that Germany would dare invade again the mightier France?" I asked him.

"All of us certainly had the impression that war was imminent," Kadosch replied. "Curiously, it was the *professeurs de gauche* [Left-leaning progressive professors] who were most preoccupied by Hitler's aggressiveness. They thought that he would go to war as soon as possible because Germany had secured a lead in the arms race. One of these professors had even dared to ask in class: 'What shall we do if tomorrow France was to become a German colony?'"

Already intent on applying for Saint-Cyr by then, Galula would have tightened his fists at such a question. France's progressive system of education was also singled out as a cause for defeat. Marshal Philippe Pétain, the head of the provisional Armistice government based in Vichy, told the American ambassador to France that ". . . if France has lost the war, it is because its Reserve officers have been educated by socialist professors."[14] Notwithstanding the issue's complexity, which renders such a statement ridiculous, one cannot refrain from noting that it was France's Socialist and Communist citizens who initially played the greater role of resistance to the Fascist occupation.

"The *professeurs de droite* [Right-leaning, or conservative professors]," Kadosch continued, "on the contrary, like our history professor Mr. Proutier, were confident that the superiority of the French infantryman would be decisive. They saw other factors such as aviation as the lofty domain of Guynemer and Mermoz.[15] Proutier went as far as implying—as if he was privy to some state secret—that France possessed special weapons capable of ensuring an easy victory against the Germans."

"The Third Republic was also on the agenda, and we were given a class on the Dreyfus Affair,"[16] Kadosch concluded on the subject. "To my surprise, Mr.

Proutier declared that it was just about certain that Dreyfus had been guilty of nothing, and that the military tribunal had erred. This raised the immediate ire of those sons and daughters of military families in the classroom. They, and I suppose their parents, were absolutely convinced that the captain had been a traitor, thirty years after his rehabilitation process! A few Jewish students attempted to defend the captain. Galula said nothing, at least, not in my presence."

I was naturally inclined to discover what had motivated David Galula to pursue a military career upon graduating from the *lycée*. Military tradition, for one, simply did not exist in his immediate family. Nor did martial spirit run deep in the Sephardic community of that era. (This would change with the growing influence of Zionism during and after the Second World War.) And finally, France had dubbed the Great War "*la der des der*," or the Last of the Last, after winning a Pyrrhic victory in 1918. Officering was consequently seen as a derelict profession in the interwar period, and applications for Saint-Cyr plummeted.[17]

As mentioned previously, the inference that Galula would join the French Army to fight Nazi Germany on account of his being Jewish cannot be given much credit. Had it been true, many others like him would have done the same. A quick inspection of Saint-Cyr's cadet roster for his year disproves that. It must be reminded that: (1) popular opinion in France (and particularly in her protectorates and colonies) was that France could not be defeated; and (2) the anti-Semitism of the Nazis had yet to come close to its wartime climax. In the antebellum years, Germany's anti-Semitism appeared as a mere intensification of what had been regularly manifested in Europe, and even in French Algeria at times.

What influence had the French officer who had married Galula's aunt exerted on him? Colonel Albert Pasthier had been a Saint-Cyr alumnus according to Ruth. He and his wife Mathilde agreed to host David during his preparatory year (known as *Cornishe*). Pasthier would have been an able mentor to Galula who still, according to Ruth, had had to compress two years of preparatory studies into one because of the year of schooling he had missed. (The compression may also have been due to the mobilization effort in France.) Ruth was told that Pasthier became a hero of the Resistance in the area of Limoges during the war. Eventually betrayed by one of his own, he was sent to Dachau and never returned.[18]

Marcel Kadosch met Galula on two or three occasions shortly after the *baccalauréat*. He informed me that Galula had spent some time as a school monitor in Oujda, near the Algerian border. This had been a way for Galula to earn some money in anticipation of his stay with his aunt and the Colonel in France. I asked Kadosch if his classmate's decision to join the army had been expected.

"There were a few signs, but not many," he answered. "Galula enjoyed physical activity and training. At the *lycée*, one could already guess that he had the profile and the intellectual capacity for Saint-Cyr. It was, however, atypical for a Jewish boy in North Africa to do so. Although France was still a democracy in 1939, and although Captain Dreyfus had been rehabilitated and his honor restored in civil society, Galula must have known that he ran the risk of being rejected by the military establishment, especially in North Africa. For as far as I know, it was only much later that the military establishment admitted *du bout des lèvres* (reluctantly) that Dreyfus had not betrayed his country. Galula did well, I think, to leave for China, Greece, and the United States at different times in his career. I suspect he had always asked to be sent away." Even in his decision to join the army, Galula had shown the daring and non-conformism that would later define him and his doctrine.

It is of course unlikely that Colonel Pasthier had exerted the sole influence over Galula's career choice. Such decisions are rarely ever driven by a single factor. Galula was probably born with a more martial spirit than others, and may have developed, in his youth, a fascination for history and adventure. He may have been attracted by the prospect of a steady income given his father's financial woes. And finally, he may have been lured by the promise of acceptance, which remained precarious throughout his life, despite his unfailing loyalty and abnegation for his adoptive nation.

3

SAINT-CYR

We have entered the habit of selecting personnel based on the complexity of the equipment they must use. The most intelligent are assigned to operate radars, and the dumbest are made to become riflemen. Let our engineers design idiot-proof radars then! The rifleman must be the smartest soldier in Revolutionary Warfare . . .

—Charles Lacheroy[1]

The student learns in military schools what he has to do in each phase [of conventional warfare], according to the latest doctrine. Field games are staged to give him the practical training in the maneuvers he may have to conduct. When he is in the field under actual war conditions, his intellectual problem amounts to determining which phase of the battle he finds himself in, then he applies to this particular situation the general rules governing the phase.

—David Galula[2]

HIGHLY INTELLIGENT, athletic, and looking the part at just under six feet tall, the twenty-year-old David Galula was not out of place at France's foremost military academy.

But a perfect fit, he was not.

Saint-Cyr embodied France's rich military heritage and high tradition. In a broader sense, the academy embodied republican elitism. Galula was surrounded by cadets of nobler birth or higher bourgeois standing than he. Both still mattered to a degree in post-revolutionary times. For those of humbler origins, and in fairness, they were not few at Saint-Cyr; the academy offered a step up the Republican ladder.[3] But for many of those in this category, officering, at least, was part of family tradition. That a French colonel had married one of Galula's aunts, and that another uncle had served in the Great War as a foot soldier, did very little to place him in that category. And although it is true that one's admittance at *L'École Spéciale Militaire* depended on the *Concours*, other, more subjective considerations could sometimes be at play. Galula, who was not born French, let alone with any real social standing or militaristic family background, could not have benefited from such considerations.

There was also the bothersome question of race.

The French military establishment was not, as the Dreyfus affair had previously demonstrated, and as its behavior under the Vichy Regime would soon reiterate, very favorably inclined toward Jews. Of course, there had been laudable exceptions at the institutional and individual levels. Historical context must also be kept in mind. The French military, at the eve of the Second World War, was in all likelihood not much better or worse than any other in this regard—save for the obvious exception of the Wehrmacht.

The imminent threat posed by Germany had played in favor of Galula's application to Saint-Cyr in 1939. This was one of the many fateful ironies of his career. Although the Nazi threat had done little on its own to motivate Galula to pursue a military career, it became a *sin qua non* circumstance for his admittance. The academy's quota had been exceptionally doubled in 1939 in view of the mobilization.[4] Galula, it turned out, had ranked a paltry 643rd out of 762 admitted candidates from the *Concours*.[5] (His widow attributed this to his shortened preparation time.) It follows, therefore, that Galula would not have been admitted under normal circumstances when typically, the academy accepted approximately 400 candidates per year.

France and Great Britain were already at war with Germany when Galula began classes in October 1939.[6] His class was christened *La Promotion de l'Amitié Franco-Britannique* to highlight the alliance. Rarely had the academy diverged from naming a class after a great battle (though not always a victorious one), a campaign, or an illustrious figure. The "A.F.B.," as it was known, was a tribute to the solidarity that had won the Great War, and that assuredly, would win the present one. The A.F.B. was the 126th class to attend the academy since Bonaparte's founding of the school in 1802. It would be the last to be hosted near the town of Saint-Cyr, on the outskirts of Paris,[7] and the last to include air cadets in its ranks.[8] Historic significance pervaded the cadets of the A.F.B. as they walked through the halls of their country's most illustrious military academy at the onset of total war. The prospect of leading men into battle was a terrifying one, as the memories of the Great War and of colonial expeditions were kept alive by the academy's senior cadres. For those who had enrolled out of patriotic fervor and yet simpler aspirations of adventure and glory, this proud fate would have meant everything in the world and more.

Discipline was notoriously strict at Saint-Cyr, but Galula's record of punishments and reprimands remained blank.[9] Outspoken though he may have been, a rebel he was not. The *Saint-Cyriens* were organized along the lines of two battalions—one regular and one reserve—each of which contained five companies. Galula, a regular cadet, belonged to the 3rd company headed like the others by a captain. Subordinated to the company commander were four lieutenants, each of whom was in charge of a platoon of twenty cadets or so. The school commandant, a colonel, oversaw all aspects of the academy. His was a prestigious appointment, entrusted with shaping an entire future generation of officers.

The cadets were made to sign six-year engagement contracts.[10] The vast majority, including Galula, were assigned to the infantry branch. Wartime circumstances dictated that the curriculum for infantry officers would have to be compressed from the traditional two years down to a mere six months. General studies were sacrificed to allow for essential tactical field training. The pressing expectation was that cadets would lead platoons into battle immediately upon graduation. The A.F.B. would not have the leisure of studying colonial history, let alone pacification and counterinsurgency warfare at Saint-Cyr, as shall next be seen.

In 2010, I had the honor of corresponding with Colonel René Lantelme, a distinguished officer and alumni of the A.F.B. As luck would have it, Lantelme had been assigned to the same cadet company as Galula. His recollection of Galula was faint, however. "Those were a very rushed six months," he pointed out to me in a first letter, "an insufficient amount of time for any particular cadet to stand out, or to leave a mark on one's memory that could last this long." At ninety years old, he corresponded with remarkable patience and clarity. I gleaned from our exchanges that his belonging to the fateful class had been a mark of pride throughout his life. The feeling had been undoubtedly shared by all of the A.F.B. alumni. Colonel Lantelme volunteered, as his class's surviving alumnus secretary, to depict the atmosphere that prevailed at the academy in 1939.

"As war with Germany had already been declared," he wrote to me, "we knew full well that we were preparing for combat. We were constantly reminded of that." A sense of urgency permeated the cadets' routine. "We woke up at five every day to eat a hurried breakfast followed by physical training. We practiced tactical manoeuvres in the vicinity of the school, but on grounds that had always proven to be too small for that purpose. Next, we attended classroom lectures throughout the late morning until noon, when all we could do was fight to stay awake."

Page taken from the yearbook
of Saint-Cyr's 126th Class,
"A.F.B."

The rest of the day was equally saturated. Afternoons were dedicated to further training in the field, while evenings were dedicated to the theoretical study of tactics and doctrine.

"Our lieutenants and captains were only a few years older than us. All had graduated from Saint-Cyr themselves. Their influence and their authority depended, of course, on their characters; but, the majority left us with excellent impressions of their qualities and exemplary style of leadership."

"What of the school commandant?" I had asked, after seeing a picture of the powerful and intelligent looking man in a yearbook Galula had preserved.

"Colonel Groussard," Lantelme replied, "was a great figure of *l'Infanterie de Marine*. Of average height, Groussard cultivated an air of originality with his shaved head and monocle. We, the cadets, occasionally imitated him . . . only because he looked like a popular actor of that era. During the German occupation, Groussard established an intelligence-gathering service to feed information to the American OSS and to the British." This revelation, corroborated by other sources, had probable implications for Galula's wartime service to which the next two chapters are devoted.

Galula's cultural shock at Saint-Cyr was undoubtedly compounded by austere living conditions. Accommodations and communal life at the academy were a far cry from the plush treatment he had been accustomed to at home. The picky eater would be confronted with cafeterias that were notorious for serving bad food, almost to a purposeful extent.[11] Acclimatizing to the cold posed another challenge, exacerbated by wartime fuel rationing. "We had an exceptionally difficult stay at Saint-Cyr through the winter of 1939 to 1940," Lantelme reminisced. "Colds, bronchitis, frost-bitten ears, etc., were the norm. The infirmary was so full that the fencing hall had to be annexed to allow more room for sickbeds."

I asked the Colonel about the curriculum.

"All training," he replied, "was focussed on producing platoon leaders who would be capable of fighting a conventional war on our borders. All of the other traditionally-taught general studies, including military history and the colonial campaigns of Lyautey and Gallieni, were excluded." Lantelme informed me that anything related to pacification had only been studied superficially and individually by the cadets of the A.F.B. prior to the *Concours*, as the latter had always included a section on France's imperial history. Given Galula's performance there, and the A.F.B.'s truncated curriculum, it is doubtful that the influence of pre-WWII counterinsurgency thinking on his writings had been very strong. Without being *ignorant* of France's rich pacification history, as shall be discussed in this work's second interlude, I believe that Galula was much more of an *auto-didacte* than what some today give him credit for. It is equally important to note that the influence of French pacification tradition on his writings would pale in comparison with that of Chinese Revolutionary doctrine.

March 20, 1940, marked the hasty graduation and commissioning of the A.F.B. cadets. A majority of these, like Galula, were sent to instruct at training depots overflowing with mobilized reserves. The rest were integrated into line battalions mustering at the borders. Galula was sent to a Colonial Army depot in Morocco. Fate would postpone his participation in combat operations for another four years.[12] "If only a few of us saw action on French soil," Colonel René Lantelme had volunteered on this point, "it is because of how rapidly and catastrophically the war devolved into the Armistice of 1940."

The A.F.B. suffered *relatively* light casualties in May to June of 1940 as a result. Fourteen graduates were killed in action, and forty-two were captured.[13] Sinister as these figures were, the ratio was modest for *Saint-Cyrians* in arms. Later in the war, twelve would die fighting in the Resistance, while sixty-two more would perish in the liberation of France. Still a handful of others would die fighting each other on either side of the Vichy-Gaullist divide.[14] Of the 756 graduates of the A.F.B., a staggering 163 were killed in action in

Galula, left, honing his equestrian skills at Saint-Cyr.

the final tally of World War II, Indochina, and Algeria.[15] One out of five had died in battle—a ratio consistent with Saint-Cyr's history. Such figures indoctrinated those who attended the famed academy to contemplate the issue of death very casually. Indeed, these figures played on Galula's conscience, and would come to influence career choices that became fateful to his legacy.

The 585 remaining able graduates of the A.F.B. were reunited once more following the signing of the armistice for a four-month complementary course intended to narrow the training gap with previous classes. In April 1941, Galula was instructed to leave Morocco for the unoccupied southern region of Aix-en-Provence, where the military academy had been evacuated to prior to being overrun by German units.

The cadets were split into two successive classes of roughly equal size.[16] Galula attended the second class starting in May 1941, a full year after Germany's invasion of France. Cadets once more, their lieutenancies were revoked for the duration of the training. This was partly a ruse of the French high command to maximize the number of commissioned officers employed at any given time, without exceeding the quotas set by the German Armistice Commission.[17] France was allowed to maintain an army of 100,000 men with a prescribed amount of commissioned officers. Hitler had seen in this an economical alternative to policing French territory with German troops, while limiting the number of disbanded soldiers that could potentially turn into insurgents. (Needless to say that the logic has been too easily brushed away in recent times.)

Raising a new generation of officers was of paramount importance to the Vichy government, for it believed that the nation's rebirth and moral reinvigoration would be achieved through its most emblematic institution, the armed forces. An important shift in curriculum and pedagogy awaited the returning cadets, as described in a French Army journal of that period: "Military education [at Saint-Cyr] has now moved away from teaching vast quantities of general and professional knowledge, and is aimed more at forming cadets as soldiers and leaders, that is, to render them morally, physically, and intellectually apt to command. . . ."[18]

Such a shift may have affected the predisposition of incumbent generations of French officers toward counterinsurgency work. It was good to render officers "morally, physically, and intellectually apt to command"; but one infers from this that officers were henceforth indoctrinated for a more dynamic, aggressive, and technical style of warfare centered on mechanized maneuver. Officers were made to value shock-action, swiftness, and technical synchronicity that forced Jominian "decisions" on the battlefield. The merits of such indoctrination—championed by the Germans and Guderian's armored school in particular—had been made perfectly clear in the summer of 1940 through Germany's stunning victory.

Stripped of its colonies after the Treaty of Versailles, the bulk of German military activity in the interwar period had *not* been geared towards pacifying possessions overseas, as had been the case for the French. Germany, therefore, had been released from the obligation to endow its officers with "general knowledge" and aptitudes that lent themselves well to the exercise of pacification as Lyautey had emphasized in his *Du rôle colonial de l'Armée* manifesto. (The German record of pacification in occupied territories during the war was condemned in advance perhaps as much by Nazi ideology, as it was by a complete lack of understanding of how to obtain a population's support.)

It follows that the French Army had been either unlucky or unresponsive in its assessment of changing circumstances. Prior to the blitzkrieg of 1940, it had provided its officers with a broadly scoped education, best suited for colonial pacification. Afterwards, it had provided its officers with a technocratic training best suited to face a Soviet invasion.[19] Regrettably then, it had consistently groomed its officers for conflicts in which they would not participate, at the detriment of grooming them for conflicts in which they would. And yet, one style of training and education need not be exclusive of the other.

Galula recuperated his commission upon graduating from the complementary course at Aix on August 31, 1941. Three days later, as he returned to North Africa, his commission was revoked once more; but this time in the spirit of German policy, and not against it.

4

UNDER VICHY

A government after having lost a major battle, is only interested in let-
ting its people go back to peace as soon as possible, and, overwhelmed
by feelings of failure and disappointment, lacks the courage and desire
to put forth a final effort, is, because of its weakness, involved in a major
inconsistency in any case. It shows that it did not deserve to win, and,
possibly for that very reason was unable to.

—Carl Von Clausewitz[1]

The population's attitude is dictated not by the intrinsic merits of the
contending causes, but by the answer to these two simple questions:
Which side is going to win? Which side threatens the most, and which
offers the most protection? This is why a counterinsurgency is never lost
a priori because of a supposedly unpopular regime.

—David Galula[2]

THE FRENCH DECLARATION OF WAR on Germany on September 3,
1939, was followed by *sitzkrieg*, not blitzkrieg. France anticipated that her
enemy would attempt yet another Schleiffen*esque* offensive through open
country. She prepared to absorb the blow through another rigid defense. For
three entire seasons, France and her British ally waited on the Maginot Line.
The monotony proved disastrous for morale and strategically deceiving, as a
German offensive was thought to be less and less likely as the months went by.
The events surrounding Guderian's *percée* in May through the town of Sedan,

nestled in the Ardennes on the Meuse River, and General Gamelin's ineptitude at coordinating a timely response, need not be reminded here. France's
defensive posture—in both physical and doctrinal terms—utterly failed.

David Galula remained garrisoned in Morocco throughout the Battle of
France. His was a simple case of good or bad luck, depending on one's point
of view.

In June of 1940, the French government sued for peace.[3] An armistice was
signed with Germany and a second one with Italy. (The latter had sought to
profit from her ally's successes, but her foray into French territory amounted
to an embarrassing military failure.) A military government headed by Marshal Philippe Pétain, the elderly hero of Verdun, replaced the parliamentary
democracy that had been the Third Republic. The ambitious commander of
the navy, Admiral Darlan, took charge of the important ministries, and seconded Pétain.

The Armistice left French North Africa under French sovereignty. Hitler believed that allowing Pétain's Vichy-based government to rule over the
unoccupied south of France and her colonies would result in a significant
economy of German forces. Hitler also believed that such a show of leniency would render industrialized France more susceptible to supplying his
war effort. Finally, Hitler gambled that "sweetening the deal" for the French,
as he did, would reignite the age-old animosity between the French and the
British. The key was to entice the French to defend their colonies against the
British (and later the Americans), who would sooner or later seek to acquire
additional bases from which to wage war, in addition to depriving Germany
of French resources.

Hitler's gamble succeeded.

Vichy French and British forces had squared off on more than one bloody
occasion by the following year. After an episode of bitter fighting for the
control of Syria, a French protectorate, Vichy's defending General Dentz
addressed his troops with the following telling words:

> . . . As for the British, you have rediscovered in them our secular ene-
> mies, who wish only to find in Peace, a France without a navy, without
> colonies, and without any military traditions. . . . This Peace, to which
> they may aspire, is nothing but one of compromise and lassitude, which
> will bring us back to those very things, which caused our downfall:
> Freemason-styled democracy and Jewish-Saxon financing. These rep-
> resent the past, [and] nothing constructive.[4]

The rhetoric outlined sombre traits of the French military regime, one
of which was the anti-Semitism that would have unarguable repercussions on Galula's wartime service. Secondary as the issue may appear to

his contribution to counterinsurgency thought, its effect on him may have steered his career toward our subject of interest afterwards.

Xavier Vallat, Vichy's first commissioner-general of Jewish affairs, called for the enactment of "State Anti-Semitism."[5] American historians Robert Paxton and Michael Marrus wrote, with abounding evidence, "Without direct German prompting, a local and Indigenous French anti-Semitism was at work in Vichy—a homegrown program that rivaled what the Germans were doing in the occupied north and even, in some respects, went beyond it."[6] In a pathetic twist of history, Vichy would hold Jewish *emprise* responsible for losing to Germany, while the latter had held the same minority responsible for its defeat by France in the last war.

The physical eradication of Jews was *not* on the Vichy agenda; although that regime's participation in deportations would result in the killing of over 70,000 of them.[7] Paxton and Marrus wrote: ". . . Vichy France became in August 1942, the only European country except Bulgaria to hand Jews over to the Nazis from areas not directly subject to military occupation."[8] Vichy also instituted labor camps in North Africa, where non-citizen, conscription-aged Jewish males, including demobilized colonial soldiers, and a host of other minorities and *indésirables* lived and worked in harsh conditions.[9] Vichy's aim vis-à-vis the Jews, in the words of its Minister of Justice, was to perform "the surgery necessary to cure the French patient."[10] The "surgery" would thus rid French society from a Jewish presence in government, education, science, media, finance, etc. It wished to emulate Germany, whose addressing of the Jewish issue had demonstrably served her well. Unlike Germany's Final Solution (which came about afterwards), however, the "surgery" was to be more of a societal one than a physical one. To this end, Vallat promised no less than a "return to national health," adding the caveat, "We have tried to be brain surgeons and not butchers and certainly not torturers. . . ."[11] The Vichy regime would be discriminate in its discrimination. It would seek to distinguish between Jewish veterans and non-veterans, long-standing citizens and recent immigrants, etc.

Vichy enacted a multitude of anti-Semitic laws and measures to attain its goals. The racial law that saw Galula expelled from the officer corps was inspired by "the studies of measures taken abroad."[12] General Paul de la Porte du Theuil, the overseer of a German-inspired paramilitary youth program in France, banned Jews from participation on account that they were a harmful "source of disunity" and that, moreover, they were "inaccessible to the work of moral education."[13] The French military went even beyond those anti-Semitic measures sanctioned by Pétain. In October 1940, for example, the army, air force and navy agreed to extend the application of the law that banned Jews from serving as officers and non-commissioned officers to include enlisted men, vaunting the additional restriction as an incentive for the recruitment of non-Jews![14]

Tainted were Vichy's institutions, at the center of which stood the army. Tainted was the latter's representation of the nation that stood for liberty, equality, and fraternity; that had seen the Dreyfusards prevail; and that had been the first in Europe to grant its Jews full civil rights, as far back as 1791.

David Galula's wartime service was directly affected by two principal Vichy laws: the first and second *Statuts des Juifs*. The first statute was spelled out in the Law of October 3, 1940. Drafted by Justice Minister Raphaël Alibert, it ordered the banning of Jewish officers and cadres from the military, the public service, and certain industries. The first article of the statute stipulated that one was considered Jewish if one had a minimum of three Jewish grand-parents, but that two sufficed, if the person happened to be married to a Jew. Galula, whose four grandparents had been Jewish, qualified perfectly. The ninth article stipulated that the statute's application extended beyond metro-politan France to "Algeria, the colonies, and the protectorates."[15] Serving as a commissioned officer in Morocco, Galula should not have been spared by this law. And yet he was.

Why or how Galula was able to remain in the military following the enact-ment of the first statute is a mystery toward which I can only offer a hypoth-esis, despite having researched the matter extensively. Paxton and Marrus wrote that the first statute was only "spottily applied in practice."[16] It is con-ceivable that nobody had paid much attention to a young lieutenant serving in the colonial garrison of a small Moroccan town. Moreover, I discovered that Galula had been placed on a 60-day Armistice leave period starting in November 1940, while the measures outlined by the first statute only came into effect the following month, meaning that Galula would have been tem-porarily out of sight.[17] Nevertheless, the hypothesis presupposes benevolence in his immediate hierarchy. His military file supports this. His battalion commander wrote the following performance evaluation of him in February 1941: "The young Saint-Cyrian promises to become a very able officer—pos-sessing a sharp mind, and very ardent in his work, he serves without com-plaining, always seeking to do more and better despite the difficult situation in which his *origins* [my italics] place him, thus demonstrating a most admir-able abnegation."[18]

Galula would not escape the following year's second statute regarding France's Jews, however. The Law of June 2, 1941, was in essence a stricter version "designed to fill lacunae in the earlier law."[19] It also outlaid harsher sanctions for transgressors. Any Jew caught exercising a forbidden profes-sion was subject to a prison term ranging from one to five years, and a fine ranging from one to twenty thousand francs.[20] The first article of the law was also revised to eliminate a semantic loophole that some had found. The distinction between one's belonging to the Jewish faith versus one's belonging to the Jewish race would henceforth be inconsequential, as both were rendered equally incriminating. France's assimilated Jews could no longer claim to *not* be Jewish on account that neither they, nor their grandparents, had ever practiced that religion. (It is possible that Galula may have resorted to this argument too, initially.) Incredibly, and I believe this to be worth noting here, the second statute offered a two-month "leniency" delay for its application to French Jewish soldiers still held in German P.O.W. camps, starting on the day of their return. (And to think that Pétain had claimed that de Gaulle had been a "*tâche d'honneur*" [honor stain] on the French officer corps![21])

The second statute came into effect midway through Galula's complementary training course at Aix. In all likelihood, he was allowed to complete his training because the cadets' commissions had been temporarily revoked. The cadets were given back their commissions at graduation on August 31, 1941, and Galula was unceremoniously expelled from the military two days later.

Equally as significant for Galula and his family was Vichy's abolishment of the Crémieux Decree in October 1940.[22] In a single stroke, citizenship was annulled for all Jews of Algerian decent.[23] It is unclear whether Galula's citizenship was actually rescinded, despite the mention in his military file of his naturalization by virtue of the decree. It is unlikely that it was. He could not have returned to Saint-Cyr as a non-citizen, nor could he have later been reintegrated into the military with his commission without holding citizenship. Had this been another case of his chain of command benevolently turning a blind eye, or rather one of spotty administrative application?

Operation TORCH saw the landing of Allied troops in French North Africa in November 1942. Hitler reacted by dissolving the Vichy government for its unconvincing defense of the North African coastline, and by ordering German forces garrisoned in occupied France to push south across the Armistice line to hold the Riviera against an eventual Mediterranean landing.

This watershed in the war convinced a majority in the French North African command to rally to the Allies in the weeks that followed the landings. Regrettably, Vichy's anti-Semitic legacy in North Africa survived past this point. Galula's reinstatement into the military, for instance, was delayed until May 1943. The Allies did not wish to pressure French authorities to abolish anti-Semitic laws for fear of antagonizing their hosts.[24] General Nogues, the French governor-general of Morocco, told President Roosevelt in January 1943 that "it would be a sad thing for the French to win the war merely to open the way for Jews to control the professions and the business world of North Africa."[25] Roosevelt agreed that quotas, at least, should be maintained.

Marcel Kadosch, David's *lycée* classmate whose promising scientific career was delayed on racial grounds, harbored strong feelings on this issue.

"Admiral Darlan,"[26] he wrote me, "did not reverse Vichy's edicts concerning the Jews. When he was assassinated, his successor, General Giraud,[27] expressed the mindset of the military establishment rather well when he said, *'Nous allons reprendre le combat, mais je veux que l'arabe reste dans son champ et le juif dans son échoppe; le decrét Cremieux reste abrogé'* [we will resume fighting, but I want the Arab to remain in his field, and the Jew to remain in his shop; the Crémieux Decree remains abrogated]."

Giraud had resisted the reintegration of Jews "for fear that they would spoil the future of [their units]."[28] He signed the order for the reintegration of Jewish servicemen reluctantly, only after being coerced by his more enlightened rival, Charles de Gaulle.

Galula had thus remained stripped of a commission for nearly two years, and theoretically stripped of citizenship for nearly three. Both injustices had outlived Vichy.[29]

In the days that preceded the signing of the 1940 armistice, a relatively unknown general Charles de Gaulle delivered his first of many famous radio addresses from London, calling on all of France to resist the Axis occupation. De Gaulle undertook a campaign of subversion with Allied help. Through charisma and perseverance, he soon became France's most iconic wartime figure, slowly rallying a fighting force under his "free French" banner. His position on the legitimacy of insurrection as a strategic defense was in tune with Clausewitz, who had written, "A government must never assume that its country's fate, its whole existence, hangs on the outcome of a single battle, no matter how decisive. Even after defeat, there is always the possibility that a turn of fortune can be brought about by developing new forms of internal strength. . . ."[30]

De Gaulle was swimming against the tide, however. In the eyes of many, particularly in those of France's career soldiers—and this is important to note—de Gaulle was considered a dissident, a rogue, and a traitor for his efforts to undermine the legitimacy of the military government based in Vichy, headed no less by a French Marshal.[31] This point of view was particularly shared by officers serving in French North Africa who were not confronted with the occupation, and whose chains of command had been left nearly untouched by the armistice. These officers reasoned that collaboration with the Allies would only lead to a more complete and brutal German occupation of French territories. De Gaulle's rhetoric, they felt, was upsetting the precarious state of affairs between Vichy and the Nazis.

Adding to the initial non-popularity of de Gaulle within conservative, French military circles was a host of other circumstances. The first of these was that the armed forces now effectively governed the country, which would allow for the military to reform the nation in its own image. The army's defeat, ironically, had returned it its clout in society. It was not inclined to let it go. Another circumstance lay with the communist threat. The considerable anti-communist faction within the French military believed that fighting Nazi Germany, in the aftermath of Operation BARBAROSSA, would only contribute to the spread of communism in Europe.[32] Colonial Army officers in general, Galula included, were vehement anticommunists. Communist subversion posed the greatest threat to the colonies their corps had bled to acquire, and would soon again bleed to preserve. And as a final circumstance disfavoring de Gaulle, there was the British attack on the French Navy fleet stationed in Algeria. British guns, bombs, and torpedoes killed over 1,200 French sailors in a single action at Mers el-Kebir in the summer of 1940.[33] Yesterday's ally had turned out a traitor. De Gaulle was considered as such too for siding with the English. It was felt by some—especially in the Colonial Army—that the latter would have traded anything with the British, including French blood and colonial possessions, in return for political recognition by the Allies.

On the other side of the divide, Marshal Pétain naturally attracted many. The stately white-haired figure symbolized the French triumph over Germany in the Great War. His cabinet propagandized his intent of *preserving* the French nation. Many refused to attribute collaborationism to him, believing instead that he was playing both sides, in the interest of France.[34] The common perception was that anything "bad" emanating from Vichy was simply a German diktat.[35]

The result of all of this was that de Gaulle's rallying of the French population was far from spontaneous. The fundamental principles of insurrectionary warfare were at work. The tide of the war would first have to change, and outline an incontestable Allied victory on the horizon, to sway the majority of the French population to side with de Gaulle. This, in itself, lends credit to Galula's later theories on the secondary importance of a cause or ideology after the initiation of hostilities. De Gaulle adopted a cause—France's liberation from Nazi occupation—that should not have failed to rally the entire French population to his side from the outset. And yet it did. A minority of the population actively supported him, and came to be known as the Gaullists. A minority of the population actively opposed him, and came to be known as the Vichyists. As for the majority of the population, despite the obvious merit of the patriotic cause—and the French are very patriotic—it remained neutrally submissive to its fate until a tipping point in the war was reached.

I found no record or indication of Galula having officially fought with de Gaulle's "Free French." It is my own impression that Galula would not have left the ranks of the Colonial Army under Vichy had he not been forcibly expelled from them on September 2, 1941.[36] I base this impression on the circumstances mentioned above, but also on a particularly strong character trait I discovered in him: blind loyalty. His lifelong mentor and friend, who shall

be introduced later, stated that Galula had been an exceptionally loyal officer, even in the most trying of circumstances. His loyalty was proven under
Vichy, until he was shown the door, while others had already defected, and
later again during the Algerian War, where as shall be revealed, his heart had
been with *L'Algérie Française* (maintaining French Algeria), and yet his duties
in the final years of the war contributed to granting Algeria its independence.

If Galula's loyalty to Vichy is morally questionable, it is only so in hindsight,
as one cannot but acknowledge the sum of the extenuating circumstances
already mentioned. It must also be reminded that Galula was barely over
twenty then, and freshly conditioned for obedience by Saint-Cyr. Explainable as it may be, however, this loyalty revealed something else profoundly
rooted in him. It became apparent to me through my research that Galula
had harbored the deepest desire for acceptance by French secular society,
and by the army in particular, and that this desire was deepened every time
his belonging was challenged. His father's dream had been one of complete
assimilation into French society. How proud Albert Galula must have been to
see his son accepted at Saint-Cyr a decade after his precarious naturalization?
When David, at 17 years old, had kept mute in class through a heated debate
about the Dreyfus Affair, it had probably been because of the importance
he attached to *belonging*. Renouncing Vichy in 1940 would have been tantamount to renouncing acceptance by the majority of his peers and superiors
in the Colonial Army.

It is likely that Galula refused to acknowledge to himself, and more certainly to others, that there was a latent anti-Semitism that would stand as an
obstacle to his acceptance. Pretending it didn't even exist, he wrote in *Pacification*, "There had been no racism in the French Army." More than repression
of feelings, this was repression of reality. I asked Colonel Lantelme whether
he felt that anti-Semitism had affected his fellow cadets at Saint-Cyr or afterwards. His response was stern. "There was, in France, no anti-Semitism
whatsoever amongst the population, with only a few exceptions. In any event,
there was none within the army, and especially not at Saint-Cyr. Galula was
removed from the officer corps through the application of a law that was
aimed at all Jewish public servants. Things were quickly re-established following the liberation of Algeria in 1942."

I agreed, not on the basis of a single testimony, but on the basis of two years
of research, that after Vichy, the army had not held Galula's "race" overtly
against him. But the choices he made to remain on the army's fringes, driven
perhaps by a subconscious fear of rejection, may have indeed limited his official progression. It was there, on the fringes, where his powerful intellect,
about which he was prouder than any rank he could have ever held, would
become his defining characteristic, not his race or religion. It was also there,
on the fringes, where Galula would soon be exposed to the greatest insurgencies of all—in China.

"My husband, you must know, had a tremendous amount of self-confidence," Ruth had told me. "This showed immediately. And socially, he wasn't hampered . . . as he might have been in those years . . . by his belonging to the Jewish faith. He did not look Jewish, and his last name did not give it off either. David never reacted when he heard disparaging comments being made about Jews by fellow officers. There were lots of these comments thrown about. I knew though, that he was proud inside of who he was."

Nonetheless, Ruth insisted, very strongly I should add, that her husband had never been a direct victim of anti-Semitism within the French Army. I noted the extent of this belief when she felt that it was impossible that her husband could have ever been expelled from the officer corps on racial grounds. But facts are facts. His military file proves that his expulsion had been very real. So repressed were Galula's feelings on the matter that he had omitted to tell his own wife about what had happened to him under Vichy. His abnegation was such that he would soon reembrace the same institution that had rejected him, proof again that his love for his adoptive nation knew no bounds.

5

FIGHTING WITH *LA COLONIALE*

Et au nom de Dieu, Vive La Coloniale!
—French Colonial Army Motto

In a conventional war, the same rules, the same principles of warfare hold
true for both sides; what varies is the relative strength. In a revolutionary war ... there is no such symmetry; the revolutionary camp and the
opposite camp are bound to fight according to two different sets of rules.
—David Galula[1]

"ONE'S CHOICE OF REGIMENT had to do with one's ranking upon graduation from Saint-Cyr," David Galula's widow told me when I broached the
issue of her late husband's wartime service. "David did not have much choice
in the matter. His academic performance at Saint-Cyr had not been stellar
because he had had a shorter preparation period than most of his peers. He
was assigned to an Indigenous regiment in North Africa, and had little to say
about it."

Galula's military file reveals that he had ranked 212th out of 580 upon
graduation. He elected to serve in Morocco, near his family, with the Colonial
Army, for which he was a natural match.

The French Colonial Army, known as *Les troupes coloniales*, or simply
la Coloniale, had historically held a similar mandate to its British counterpart, the Royal Marines. *Les troupes coloniales* had been named *les troupes de
marine* until the turn of the nineteenth century, and then again following the

pullout from Algeria in 1962, by which time anything "colonial" had become unfashionable.[2] The *troupes de marines* traced their roots back to the seventeenth century, when the Cardinal de Richelieu, the First Minister of France, had decreed that one hundred infantry companies would be raised to "garrison the King's ships." The corps was formalized in 1831, as France's second colonial era got underway with the conquest of Algeria.[3]

Galula wore the corps' insignia on his wedge cap: a simple golden anchor intertwined with rope that identified him as a *marsouin*. The latter nickname, meaning porpoise in French, was analogous to "Jarhead" for U.S. Marines and "Bootneck" for their royal counterparts. The onus of the French nickname belonged to the French Navy, which mocked the infantrymen onboard its ships for following along for the ride.

The European race to acquire colonial possessions in the nineteenth century, combined with the evolution of naval warfare led to a reorientation of the corps' mandate. Fighting at sea was replaced by colonial conquest, pacification, and administration. An acumen for civil affairs and counterinsurgency work among the corps' officers and NCOs was institutionalized. Galula wrote of his NCOs in *Pacification*, "We were much luckier that the Metropolitan Army in regard to our NCOs. The Colonial Army, a prestige outfit offering assignments in exotic places from Timbuktu to Tahiti, attracts easily the best professional NCOs. Selection is stiff, and a sergeant has to be very good. . . . Three sergeants in my company had fought in Indochina, where two of them had been in command of one hundred natives in isolated posts with no other Europeans around."[4]

A senior officer of the Colonial Army wrote in a brief history of his corps: "Experience has shown, much more so in developing countries than in ours, that relations between humans are what matter most."[5] Cognizant of this fact, this officer reasoned, had always been critical to his corps' success abroad. He concluded with what one may recognize as the making of successful small war practitioners:

> . . . the adaptability of [the Corps'] officers and NCOs is owed to their long tradition of exercising diverse functions, facing changing situations, transitioning between different environments and breaking free from conventional thinking—the bane of those who have served for too long in headquarters or in line battalions.
>
> And so, *les troupes de marine*, armed with the experience of their leaders . . . and able to adapt themselves to any function—administrative, political or military—will remain, for very long still, one of France's best foreign policy tools. . . .[6]

The description suited Galula perfectly. His career choices precluded his fertile mind from conventionalism. A résumé he had drafted summarized what his career in the Colonial Army had required from him, and what it had given him in return:

> I am accustomed to living abroad and can establish friendly relations with people of all races and nationalities. Through my years abroad, I have acquired many friends in the military, diplomatic, newspaper, business, and academic professions.
>
> France has been at war, and the French Army has been fighting, continuously for the last twenty years. Like all my fellow officers, I have lived a hectic life. I have had to adapt myself rapidly to new situations, and to face extraordinarily varied problems at many levels, more often than not with limited material means. Making prompt decisions and dealing with all kinds of people have become second nature.
>
> Unlike most French officers, however, I have spent ten years of my career abroad, most of the time being on my own with tasks and responsibilities far above the norm for my rank and age. I have had to show initiative, to use my imagination in order to detect important problems, to study them in detail, and to find practical and reasonable solutions.[7]

Indeed, the pedigree of a successful counterinsurgent.

Galula was assigned to the Colonial Army's 4th *régiment de tirailleurs marocains* following his initial phase of training at Saint-Cyr. One month later, in May 1940, he was reassigned to the 1st *régiment de zouaves* garrisoned in Settat, a town located forty miles south of Casablanca. I discovered this to be an odd assignment for a Colonial Army officer, since the Zouaves belonged to *l'Armée d'Afrique*, which was distinct from the Colonial Army. "North African Jews were very numerous in the *zouaves*," a well-meaning retired French colonel who sat on the editing board of the corps' magazine suggested over the phone, puzzled just as I was.[8] Officered by whites, the Zouaves were easily identifiable by their customary baggy trousers and colorful attires. Their name was owed to the Zwawa tribe of Berber Kabyles, highland warriors that had once served as mercenaries for Algeria's Turkish begs.[9]

The bulk of the 1st Zouaves had already been sent to Europe by the time of Galula's transfer in 1940, leaving behind a small garrison to train draftees and to fulfill its colonial security mandate.[10] Galula only served for six months with the *zouaves*, but his exposure to the remaining Kabyles among them, if there were any, earned him cultural insight that proveed useful in the Kabyle area he pacified some fifteen years later in Algeria. In *Pacification*, he demonstrated a stereotyping preference for these Berbers over their Arab neighbors.

Someone in Galula's hierarchy felt that his expulsion from the military on racial grounds had been wasteful. That same someone saw in the twenty-two year old a strong intellectual capacity and a burning desire to contribute to the war effort. Hearsay in the Galula family is that David had been involved in espionage. Yolande Bismuth was the first to tell me this. Ruth was next. A curriculum vita written by Galula stated that he had been sent on a "special mission" to Tangiers in 1942. I found a second piece of modest evidence in his military file at Vincennes. His cadet booklet from Saint-Cyr bore the following hand-written note: "[The officer cadet] recognizes to have received counter-espionage training, and commits to prescribing to military secrecy in his writings and his conversations."[11]

Whether as an agent-handler, or at the very least, as an eyes-and-ears informant, Galula had been singled out to gather intelligence covertly in Tangiers. But on whose account? The Vichystes? The Gaullists? The Giraudistes? The Allies? Although my impression is that Galula would not have left the ranks of Vichy had he not been expelled, it does not preclude Galula's having held strong sympathies for the Allied cause. Historian Robert Paxton demonstrated that French officers in North Africa could be incredibly loyal to Pétain, while wishing for an American victory. By process of elimination, it is most likely that Galula had served the Allied cause. Had he served de Gaulle's Free French, his record of service would have shown it. Furthermore, Galula's attitude towards Gaullists, in his correspondence of later years, seemed too lukewarm for him to have adhered to that movement from early on. As for Vichy, it is simply unreasonable to consider that he would have been employed by the same regime that held disdain for him and his kind, or that he would have wished to risk his life for it, once his rejection became a *fait-accompli*.

Who had guided Galula toward espionage or counter-espionage? I could not find the answer from his files, nor from those whom I had interviewed. My hypothesis lies with Colonel Groussard. Galula's commandant at Saint-Cyr was responsible for setting up information gathering networks to feed into the British *Intelligence-Service* and the American OSS from the onset of the Armistice.[12] It is a known fact that he had put some of his graduates in contact with Allied agents.[13] Groussard had initially remained loyal to Vichy, believing like so many others that Pétain was planning *la revanche*. And though Groussard's loyalty changed once he became disillusioned, he did not rally to de Gaulle's Free French. (He went so far as to refuse de Gaulle's offer to promote him to the rank of general.)

Adding credence to the above hypothesis is the fact that Groussard[14] was a fervently anti-communist Colonial Army officer who had served in Morocco just before the War. He was reputed to have had an influence over his cadets and their opinions that went well beyond that of the average military academy commander. Groussard would have known that Galula was to be expelled from the army on the morrow of his graduation. Would he not have found the cadet predisposed for intelligence work in Morocco? Galula's upbringing

The fateful and enigmatic Colonel Groussard commanded Saint-Cyr. He would orchestrate a vast intelligence network in collaboration with the Allies during the War.

there and his belonging to the ubiquitous Jewish community—very present in Tangiers—would allow him to blend in without raising suspicions.

"David's cousin owned a busy store in Tangiers," Ruth told me the little she knew about his mission. "David used that as his cover. He worked there, exchanging information with people who came by the store." Like any story her late husband had shared with her, there was also a component of humor. "The spies all new each other," she continued, "and they would get together every night to drink themselves under the table! David blamed this episode of his life for not being able to stomach alcohol. My husband, you see, was a mess after two drinks."

William Breuer wrote in his entertaining *Undercover Tales of World War II*, "Tangiers was a hotbed of espionage and intrigue, the most critical cockpit of intelligence in North West Africa."[15] Tangiers was precisely that because of the liberties that its "International Zone" designation allowed for, and because of its pivotal location on the Strait of Gibraltar at the juncture of Spanish, British, and French territories. Adding to the "intrigue" was the Monte Carlo–like setting created by the war (which undoubtedly appealed to the Galula one discovers from reading *The Tiger's Whiskers*).

Spies and counter-spies of every allegiance buzzed about Tangiers. The OSS ran its most important station in North Africa there, paving the way for U.S. involvement in the Mediterranean.[16] The British, for their part, unraveled Germany's Operation BERNHARD in Tangiers, putting an end to the mass forgery of Sterling currency. The German *Abwher* was active in monitoring Allied shipping through the Strait, while trying to get wind of when and where the Allied landing would materialize.[17] As for the French, their agents sought to discover what plans the Germans, the Spanish, and even the Americans and the British had for Morocco and French North Africa. Secret liaisons were undoubtedly maintained with all of these, that is, when Vichyists, Gaullists, and French Communists were not too busy spying on each other.

Galula's reintegration into the officer corps in the middle of May 1943, six months after the Allied landing in North Africa, came with a lieutenant's promotion and the promise of fighting for the liberation of France. His first orders were to report to the Colonial Army Training and Organization Center in Mostagenem, Algeria. Vichy soon became a thing of the past. Although metropolitan France was now ruled entirely by the German occupier, North Africa, at least, was governed by generals de Gaulle and Giraud through the French Committee of National Liberation—a power-sharing instrument the two rivals had created. As the committee busied itself to organize and equip a French expeditionary corps in North Africa and Britain, it broadcast the following orders to the Metropolitan population in Maoist terms:

1. Every French citizen must henceforth consider himself to be engaged in a Total War against the invader for the liberation of the Homeland;
2. The citizen can no longer choose between fighting or abstaining from fighting, nor when he must fight; Every single one is now a soldier under orders;
3. Every French citizen that is not a combatant, or that is not yet, must consider himself as an auxiliary. Whatever his role and responsibilities may be, the citizen must support the Interior French Forces (FFI), aid them materially, supply them, guide them, inform them on the enemy's moves. . . . Assisting the FFI is an immutable obligation, anybody that chooses to not do so will be guilty of treason, and will be answerable to this government.[18]

Galula was assigned to a storied formation of the Colonial Army: *les tirailleurs sénégalais.* This corps was comprised of Indigenous troops from Senegal and other West African protectorates.[19] *Tirailleur* was the Napoleonic designation for sharpshooting skirmishers; but the *sénégalais* had always been employed as line infantry (and occasionally scouts in their very beginnings).[20] The tall and lanky troops represented a substantial portion of the standing

Colonial Army. The *sénégalais* had earned a reputation of fearlessness. German and Italian troops feared the mythical "savagery" of these African warriors the most in both World Wars.[21]

The *tirailleurs* had played important roles in France's colonial pacification campaigns. Lyautey, for one, had employed them skillfully in a *quadrillage* (grid-like occupation) of the Moroccan Rif during the revolts that erupted there.[22] So had Gallieni before him, in Madagascar, writing of them to the Minister of Colonies: "The *tirailleurs sénégalais* have always proven themselves through their endurance, their professional demeanor, and their bravery, which has now become legendary. . . ."[23]

Galula was given command of a platoon in the 3rd company of the newly reconstituted 1st Battalion of the 4th *régiment de tirailleurs sénégalais* (4th RTS) under Colonel Borgnis-Desbordes (undoubtedly a descendent of the famed *pacificateur* who had led the conquest of French Nigeria).[24] In April 1943, the entire regimental headquarters staff along with the 1st Battalion had been wiped out at sea. The liner ferrying them from Morocco to Algeria had been torpedoed by a German U-boat, killing 763 *tirailleurs*, including the regimental commander.[25]

Two months following Galula's reintegration, the 9th Colonial Infantry Division (9th CID) was created under General de Larminat's 2nd Army Corps. The division was assigned the 4th and 13th RTS, as well as the 6th RTS commanded by the fateful Colonel Raoul Salan. Structured and equipped in the image of a U.S. "partially-motorized" infantry division, the 9th CID trained hard throughout the summer and fall of 1943 on amphibious landing tactics at the U.S. Fifth Army Invasion Training Center on the Algerian coastline.[26] Galula's commanding officer wrote of him, "A valuable officer with a strong sense of duty. Very complete general and military knowledge. He is a solid platoon commander with a strong morale."[27]

Changes to the leadership of the 9th CID occured in 1944, and with these came a growing anticipation of operations to come. General Magnan, a de Gaulle supporter, was appointed to replace the previous divisional commander. (Magnan had worked towards facilitating the Allied landing in Morocco, and had been jailed for it by Vichy French authorities.) Galula's regimental commander was replaced with Colonel Cariou. In March, the division was reassigned to the French 1st Army Corps. By April, the latter was assigned in turn to the legendary General Jean de Lattre de Tassigny, and his massive expeditionary task force, Army Group B.[28]

The long awaited order to participate in operations in Europe arrived on March 27, 1944. The 9th CID was embarked at the port of Oran, Algeria, and landed in Corsica, from where it staged its first offensive. Although eager to land in France, the men were told that they would first be launched against the German-held island of Elba, off the coast of Italy, where Napoleon had once been imprisoned. The Germans had reinforced the Italian garrison

holding the tiny island with two infantry battalions and several coastal batteries covering the naval passage. The 9th CID had been selected to spearhead
the operation. June 17, 1944, would mark Galula's "D Day."

Under the cover of darkness, Magnan sent his *Commandos d'Afrique* to
neutralize the enemy batteries perched on the hilly flanks of the island's
southern beaches where he intended to land the bulk of his division. Salan's
13th RTS was the first in the order of landing at dawn, and consequently suffered the heaviest casualties. Stiff German resistance forced the landing sites
to be shifted to the east, from Marina di Campo, to the beaches of Nercio
where Galula's 4th RTS landed. The *tirailleurs* were able to reach the north
side of the tiny island on D+1, but an additional four days were required to
secure the entire island. The French had suffered 252 killed and 635 wounded.
Their enemies had lost 500 men, with nearly four times that number captured. American onlookers dubbed the landing as "the hardest conducted in
the Mediterranean campaign."[29]

Galula saw action four years after France had signed the Armistice; but the
fierceness of the fighting at Elba had made up for the wait. De Lattre wrote
in his *History of the First French Army* that the *sénégalais* had resorted to
using flamethrowers to dislodge the Germans from their positions dug into
the rocky hills.[30] It was said that Galula's battalion commander, *Commandant* Gufflet, had commanded brilliantly. An officer of his battalion wrote,
"He was, without a doubt, the most complete officer I had ever met, through
his intelligence, character and courage."[31] The young lieutenant Galula had
shown his valor under fire under this inspirational leader. He was awarded
the Croix de Guerre with a Vermeil Star after receiving an Army Corps citation. "A masterful and decisive platoon commander," the citation read, "He
relentlessly led his platoon forward on the Island of Elba in spite of heavy
enemy artillery barrages. He demonstrated initiative and leadership in all
circumstances, and succeeded in capturing, through rapid manoeuvres, 50
withdrawing enemy soldiers, including 2 officers."[32]

Galula was wounded in July of 1944. His military file states that the wound
was inflicted by grenade shrapnel in his right buttock in Corsica. Ruth completed the story.

"It was a silly training accident," she said, chuckling. "He and his sergeant
were giving a demonstration on the use of grenades to new recruits when it
happened. One of those two had made the mistake, but only David was hurt,
and thankfully not seriously. He kept a deep scar in his upper thigh from that
episode."

"Later on," Ruth continued, "David and his sergeant were involved in a
road accident. David was unscathed, but the sergeant and the jeep's two other
passengers suffered some fractures. David followed his sergeant to the field
hospital. He teased him that it was perfectly normal that he should take his
turn at being wounded!"

On August 17, Galula and the rest of his division stood in line once more on the docks of Ajaccio, Corsica. This time, they embarked to participate in the liberation of France.[33] The plan was for de Lattre's Army Group B, to which the 9th CID still belonged, to land on the Riviera, two days after General Truscott's U.S. 6th Army Corps had established a bridgehead.[34] De Lattre was given three objectives: (1) To roll up German positions from east to west along the Riviera, seizing the city-ports of Toulon and Marseille; (2) To thrust northwards along the Rhone Valley to link up with Eisenhower's Normandy-landed force in an attempt to trap withdrawing German forces in the southwest of France; and (3) To establish a new line of Allied supply extending from the Mediterranean to the western edge of the Reich.[35] A flotilla of 2,000 ships was mustered for Operation DRAGOON. On the French side alone, 260,000 men would participate. Of these, nearly 90 percent originated from France's colonies and protectorates. Africa had supplied the lion's share.[36]

Toulon, located to the east of Marseille, was the first major objective assigned to the landed French forces. A reinforced garrison of 25,000 Germans under Admiral Rhufus defended what was the strongest point in the Axis defense of the French Riviera.[37] Hitler's orders to Rhufus were clear and characteristic. The admiral was to make a fortress out of Toulon, and "defend it to the last man."[38] By August 20, three days after his first units had landed, de Lattre could only muster a vanguard of 16,000 men against this force. Still, as his scouts reached the outskirts of Toulon, he decided to capitalize on his momentum to establish a foothold within the city. By doing so, he discarded the plan to lay siege to Toulon for fifteen days, which would have allowed him to fully deploy his corps.[39] The barely disembarked 9th CID was ordered to penetrate the inner core of the city, and seize the important Arsenal.

August 20, 1944, marked Galula's second D-Day. This time, however, the landing itself would be unopposed. The 4th RTS disembarked on the beaches of La Nartelle, across the bay from Saint-Tropez. Now under the orders of Lieutenant-Colonel Bourgund,[40] the regiment moved by night and day across crammed and narrow roads towards La Môle, located some fifteen miles inland. The laborious deployment required three days, following which Galula's battalion, the I/4th RTS, was ordered to lead the way towards Solliès-Pont, a northeastern suburb of Toulon. From Solliès-Pont, the I/4th RTS swung north, and thrust into Toulon from the northwest, through the villages of Signes, Saint-Anne-d'Evenos, and finally Ollioules.[41] At Signes, the battalion was met by de Lattre himself. The soon-to-become Marshal of France ordered the officers of the battalion to step down from their GMC troop lifts so that he could address them before they went into battle.[42]

In the evening of August 23, *Commandant* Gufflet ordered his sleepless battalion to leave its motorcade behind, and march south towards Revest, on the periphery of Toulon, at best speed. Walking in single file in the darkness, the men covered some fifteen miles of hilly mule trails in under four hours.

They were met by guides from another Colonial Army regiment to conduct a relief-in-place. By 0200 hours, on the 24th, the tricky operation was completed. The prospect of fighting for the liberation of Toulon suddenly became very real. Toulon was the home of the Colonial Army. The 4th RTS itself had been garrisoned there from 1922 until the war began. With dawn breaking, Gufflet led his battalion across the Line of Departure towards the Arsenal.[43]

By the early afternoon of the 24th, the battalion had gained a foothold in the neighborhood of Sainte-Anne, just north of the Arsenal, at a cost of twenty-five casualties. In doing so, they had captured 150 of the enemy, and left an unknown number lying dead on the streets. At 1500 hours, Gufflet maneuvered his rifle companies into a south-facing axis of advance centered on Toulon's Faron Boulevard. Galula's company, the 3rd, led by Captain Nogret, assumed the forward-left position, clearing down Boulevard Saint-Anne. The company came under heavy fire from the defenders' 20mm guns hidden within the Fort of Malbousquet. The bleeding and pummeled company fought its way to the Arsenal wall in the vicinity of the Castigneau door and breached it. With the prize in sight, Gufflet was given an unbelievable order: he was to stop his progression into the fort, withdraw, and consolidate. Higher headquarters had decided that the Arsenal would be assaulted later that evening by another unit, to which a share of the glory had been promised. The withdrawal alone cost the battalion eleven dead and thirty-five wounded.[44]

The assault by another unit never materialized. Galula's battalion was ordered to reenter the Fort of Malbousquet the next day. Again, the 20mm guns exacted a heavy toll on Gufflet's exhausted men. Breached once more, a definitive foothold was established in the fort by the afternoon. The final assault was ordered for 2000 hours.[45] The *sénégalais* fought in close quarters with fixed bayonets to reach their designated assault positions. The fort was an intricate maze, but many of the colonial officers knew it well from having been garrisoned there in the past. Faced with a growing carnage on both sides, Gufflet suggested that an ultimatum be sent to the enemy prior to the assault. Bourgund, his superior, agreed. A staff officer volunteered to deliver the ultimatum. He was met by desperate and haggard German soldiers who took him to parley with their commander. Captain zur See Hellhoff of the *Kriegsmarine* surrendered the Fort with full battle honors at 0730 hours the next day to Bourgund and his regiment's assembled officers.[46] On the 28th, Admiral Ruhfus ordered the surrender of the entire Toulon garrison. French losses amounted to 2,700 men. The deepwater port had been secured an entire month ahead of schedule.[47]

The 9th DIC was regrouped on September 5, and bid farewell to its commander, General Magnan, appointed by de Gaulle as the military governor of Toulon. The following week, Army Group B's northbound vanguard linked up with Leclerc's Normandy-landed 2nd Armored Division. The much celebrated event led to the creation of the 1st French Army under de Lattre, henceforth directly subordinated to Eisenhower.[48] Aided by American logistics and air power, de Lattre had advanced 400 miles in forty days.[49]

"Our division barely had time to regroup after the fall of Toulon before we were ordered to make best speed towards Voiron," Colonel Pierre Boré wrote in recollection of his service with the 4th RTS. This officer had passed away at the age of eighty-five, in 2008, shortly before I could reach him. His wife Viviane agreed to share the memories her late husband had preserved in writing. "The lack of fuel was our biggest impediment. We snaked up towards Pontarlier and Lomont (in the Rhone Alps). . . . Finally, on the 25th and 26th of September, the main body of the division caught up with its vanguard on the Doubs River Loop [An area located 100 kilometres to the southwest of Mulhouse.] By then, we were not only lacking in fuel, but also in ammunition, which stopped us from pushing any further."

"On September 27th," Boré's testimonial continued, "the division maneuvered into a defensive position. Orders were given to hold the line. . . . But the cold and rainy weather started to become an issue for our Senegalese troops." Fifty-six percent of Galula's division was comprised of Indigenous Africans.[50] In October, it was decided that these would be replaced by white French Forces from the Interior (FFI). (As absurd as such a measure may seem today, the racial swap on the front lines at the onset of winter had its precedent in the First World War.[51] Winter clothing being what it was then, the *sénégalais* were said to be at greater risk of frostbite and hypothermia. But as these troops were replaced with Metropolitan Frenchmen, many wondered whether the real motivation had been instead of putting a white "face" on the Liberation of France. Had the British themselves not insisted that Leclerc's 2nd Armoured Division be "whitened" prior to arriving in Britain to participate in Operation OVERLORD?) In the absence of Senegalese troops in a regiment of Senegalese *tirailleurs*, the 4th RTS was renamed the 21st *régiment d'infanterie coloniale* (21st RIC).

The 9th CID remained dug-in some fifty miles away from the German border that lay to the east, as it contemplated Wehrmacht-occupied Mulhouse and Strasbourg to the north. "By early November," Boré wrote, "we were told that we were once again headed for action. . . . On November 13th, both Churchill and de Gaulle came to witness the launch of our offensive. But it snowed heavily that day, and everything had to be postponed. . . ."

On the morrow, the 9th CID pierced the German lines at Belfort. The Rhine had finally been reached.[52] By the end of the month, Galula's regiment arrived in Mulhouse. The New Year of 1945 was followed by bitter cold and a German counterattack, which was soon repelled. The 9th DIC pushed further north on January 20, capturing Mulhouse's outlying areas. The Division was allowed some rest, finally, in Strasbourg. On March 28, two months later, Galula crossed the Rhine with a reconnaissance party two days ahead of

Military identity card.

his battalion.[53] Combat operations awaited them in the Karlsruhe, and then across the Siegfried line.[54]

Galula had served as a platoon commander throughout the Battle of Toulon. Noticed for his analytical skills, however, he was soon appointed to become the battalion's intelligence and signals officer. Colonel Bourgund, his regimental commander, had written the following evaluation of him on his twenty-fifth birthday: "A young officer who has demonstrated a high degree of intelligence and energy. He possesses a very sharp and active mind that remains, however, too mobile. He pursues too many ideas at once, which sometimes results in unbalancing his work." Seven months later, it was up to Colonel Delteil, Bourgund's replacement, to evaluate Galula just as tellingly: "Intelligent, dynamic, expending himself in his work, he has rendered excellent services. Armed with tremendous self-confidence, he sometimes lacks a sense of reality. Imbued with leadership, he attaches himself to his men; he will be more likely to succeed as a staff officer, than in troop duty. Very good general culture, excellent military spirit, good presentation."[55]

The spring of 1945 brought an end to the fighting for Galula. The 9th CID, and the 21st RIC under it, had seen action at Elba, on the Riviera, in Alsace, and finally across the Rhine. Given the eagerness of the High Command to re-establish French honor, the G.I.-dubbed "Champagne Campaign" had never really been that for Galula and his fellow *marsouins*. Naturally, between the battles, not everything had been horror. Excitement, fascination and even pleasure could find their way into daily life.

I found a series of surviving agendas that had belonged to Galula in his wife's dearly preserved memorabilia. The first of these covered the year 1945. Tiny in size, the agenda carried pencil-scribbled inscriptions. Though scarce and barely legible, the inscriptions offered something of a diary of his adventures. The first ten entries read as follows:

January 1st, 1945   Camping at the airfield. Cold and calm day. Fritz aircraft in the evening. Nice view of the Vosges.

January 2nd, 1945   Same place. Conducted liaison with artillery. Gun duel in the evening.

January 3rd, 1945   Same place. Calm day. Visited by General. Heavy guns fired at night.

January 4th, 1945   Multiple reassignments. Paudlet goes to the 6th, Guardin to the 2nd. Calm day. The rich are playing La Marseillaise. We were invited for wine and food by Miss de Juge.

January 5th, 1945   Calm day. Heavy artillery barrage overnight on Napoléon Island. De Sartège transferred to 2nd Battalion. It's snowing. Glorious morning.

January 6th, 1945   Another calm day. Read, play cards, shower.

January 7th, 1945   Busy night.

January 8th, 1945   Cantonment picked-up and moved to Rischerm. Intestinal gripes.

January 9th, 1945   Rinherm. Minister's visit. Sled race.

January 10th, 1945   Forgotten birthday . . .

As the weeks went by, and as his Regiment was pushed further north and then east across the Rhine, Galula's entries dwindled to one or two words a day, and sometimes none. He resumed his entries in the spring, by which time he was allowed some leave in liberated territory. His entries reflected those of a young man determined to live every day to its fullest; a desire heightened by the euphoria of a soon-to-be-over war. The names of girls appeared increasingly frequently in his agenda. In Strasbourg for instance, he had met a girl named Nini. Next to her name, he had added two "X's." Her name appeared again three times in the spring. Charlotte, to whom he attributed not two, but three "X's," appeared on May 10, in Mulhouse. The previous day, he had scribbled the name of Marguerite, but she had only received a single "X." There were also Suzies, Angelas, Helgas, and Colettes! And, of course, there were other ways in which to entertain oneself. The May

26 entry read, "Swim in the Danube, fish with grenades," followed by "Harmonica" the next day.

"David loved and admired women," Ruth told me with a smile as we browsed through his miniature agenda. "Some men are more lustful than others," she shrugged her shoulders casually, and laughed. "Before we got married, he told me jokingly: 'dear, you know that I will not be able to be faithful to you forever. I have been accustomed to too much variety in women!' A young and attractive bachelor crisscrossing Europe at the end of the war could not have turned out any differently."

"Had David had a serious girlfriend before marrying?" I asked her, without much purpose. "Jeanette had been a serious girlfriend during the war," Ruth allowed, keeping her smile. "David had decided to let her go though. She was too religious for him."

"And that bothered him?"

"Well yes," she hesitated, suddenly blushing. "She would go to confession in the morning . . . after getting out of bed with him. . . ."

"Ah."

"David thought it was senseless," she continued, "not the fact that she was praying . . . but *why* she was praying. David was agnostic, you see. But he certainly was not an atheist. I remember him looking at our baby, after his return from Algeria, and saying: 'How can anyone not believe that there is a God out there?'"

6

JOURNEY TO THE FAR EAST

The war that we are fighting today for the emancipation of the Chinese people is a part of the war for the freedom of all human beings, and the independent, happy, and liberal China that we are fighting to establish will be a part of that new world order. A concept like this is difficult for the simple-minded militarist to grasp and it must therefore be carefully explained to him.

—Mao Tse-Tung[1]

I have been convinced for a long time that the only possible way to cope with the Chinese Communist tactics, not only in China, but also in the rest of Asia, and especially in Indochina, is to "take a leaf from their own book," and mobilize the masses against them. I use "mobilize" in the fullest Communist sense of the word, i.e., politically, economically, ideologically, and last, militarily. Achieving this is only a matter of technique. I have seen the communists operating in China in 1945–1948, and I am sure that they did not have the support of the majority of the population as they claimed; they only used, efficiently, the minority in their favour to activate and control the rest of the population.

—David Galula[2]

I ASKED RUTH GALULA what she thought had attracted her husband to spend three years in China immediately after the War. Had it been the remoteness? The promise of adventure? Some childhood novel he had read?

"No," she had replied smiling. "It was a simple matter of chance."

Jacques Guillermaz embodied that chance. A Colonial Army officer himself, he had served as a company commander in the same battalion as Galula at Elba and Toulon. Later, he assumed command of the entire battalion as it reached the Doubs to repel a German counteroffensive.[3] The battalion's intelligence officer had made a strong impression on him, strong enough that Guillermaz invited Galula to follow him back to China as his assistant-attaché as soon as the fighting ended.

"Guillermaz was, without a doubt, the most influential person in David's life," Ruth told me over a French breakfast at her son's home. My research had led me to fully agree. Galula and Guillermaz became professionally and personally inseparable. Luck, and to a certain extent design, intertwined their military careers. I believe that in many ways, Guillermaz provided Galula with the intellectual mentorship that the his father was not able to offer. He helped shape Galula's gifted mind. Most of all, Guillermaz strove to impart on his protégé a methodology to military and geopolitical analysis, without trying to impose his own opinions. This distinction was especially true on the subject of counterrevolutionary warfare. There, master and disciple not only cordially disagreed, but also did not share the same passion for the subject. Nonetheless, as Guillermaz can be credited for having traced Galula's career path, he can also be credited for setting the conditions that led to the latter's legacy.

Guillermaz was eight years older than his protégé. Regardless of how close they grew to one another, one senses that there was a willful deference in Galula toward his mentor throughout his life. Seen in this light, Guillermaz became to Galula, in many ways, what Scharnhorst had been to Clausewitz. Just like Scharnhorst and Clausewitz, mutual esteem did not translate into perfect agreement or into character synonymy. Jacques Guillermaz was a brilliant and cultured man. His were the traits of academia: intellectually cautious, diligent, patient, and prude. Galula, equally brilliant if not analytically sharper, was nothing of the above. (His passage at Harvard did little to change that.) Cerebral though he was, the conclusions Galula drew were bold, daring, and sometimes impetuous.

"Guillermaz was every bit the intellectual," Ruth told me of a man she had held in the highest esteem. "He was much more reserved than David as you can imagine. He was the product of a traditional military family. David was a *bon vivant* in comparison. On certain occasions, for instance, when I inadvertently let a vulgar word out in French like '*merde!*,' Guillermaz would look at me sternly and chide me with: 'that language is not appropriate for a lady!'"

Galula's unfailing good humor and personable style made him the more capable socialite of the two. Guillermaz detested that unavoidable aspect of an attaché's life, preferring to devote his time to his scholarly passions. Galula, by contrast, was a crowd pleaser and a fine networker, eager to stimulate conversation with senior figures. In mainland China, and later in Hong Kong, such skills would prove invaluable to the intelligence work that was integral to his attaché responsibilities. In contrast to this, Guillermaz lamented in his memoires with irreproachable integrity, "I should have gotten closer to the population, and sought to increase my personal interaction with it, if I was to better understand the events that were transpiring, and the effects that these were having on the people."[4] Was this not precisely Galula's forte? In China, Galula convinced Guillermaz to travel to the hinterlands with him not just to see the beauty of the land, but also to mingle with the population and witness the bizarre war unfolding on the ground. Later in Algeria, Galula succeeded on account of the level of interaction with the population he required of himself and of his troops. It became clear to me that where Galula was strongest, Guillermaz was weakest, and vice versa. They complemented each other like yin and yang.

In China, Guillermaz characteristically maintained an impartial attaché's view of the raging civil war and of the rising communist tide. "I expressed what I felt to be the truth, regardless of the consequence this held for my name," he wrote in his memoires, bitterly reflecting on the communist sympathies some had accused of him of harboring. "This frankness, which seemed to me desirable, sometimes led others to label me as something that I was not . . . I favoured reason and conscience while others lost themselves in ideology or sentiment."[5] Certainly, Galula had never been one of Guillermaz's accusers. Moreover, one finds abundant proof in their extensive personal correspondence that Guillermaz had never harbored such sympathies; but only that his *anti*-communism was not nearly as visceral as that of other Colonial Army officers, including Galula.

As characteristic as Guillermaz's academic objectivity had been in carrying out his attaché duties, Galula would carry out his own in a much more analytically daring manner. He studied the communist underdog's spectacular rise to power with the intent of deciphering its method, so that it could be turned against similarly fueled revolutions brewing in other parts of the world. Motivation was not lacking, as Galula quickly came to see the Chinese Civil War as the spark to the "brush fires" that threatened to ravage France's overseas possessions.

"The young officer has demonstrated a superior intelligence and work ethic," read the first evaluation of Galula written by Guillermaz in 1946. "Very active, he remains somewhat impatient and too quick-to-conclude."[6] The statement summarized well Guillermaz's overarching impression of his protégé that would persist throughout their lifetimes. The following year's evaluation by Guillermaz conveyed a similar impression: ". . . possessing a brilliant intelligent and sharp mind, he is conscientious and hard-working, capable, and desirous to observe. He will have to rectify, nonetheless, his overly-impulsive and subjective judgement."

But Galula was not to be tempered.

"David thought that quite on the contrary," Ruth told me, "it was Guillermaz who was often much too prudent and resigned in his reports, and not sufficiently alarming at times when he should have been."

The correspondence I peered over, spanning twenty years, corroborated her claim. I discovered there a particularly telling letter written by Guillermaz to Galula in 1954:

> I think that it is somewhat imprudent to conclude as you did, based on a single phrase, that there will be some serious quarrels between Moscow and Peking. I believe, as you do, that the Chinese will increasingly try to assert themselves, and try to draw advantages from their alliance. But presenting it as you have, the prospect of tensions will inevitably lead "wishful thinkers" to jump on your conclusions, extrapolating these further than you had ever intended.[7]

This was one of many instances where Galula's analysis had been too bold for Guillermaz to endorse. Yet in this instance and others, the boldness did not preclude the analysis from being very good. Guillermaz, who was well on his way to becoming one of France's top political sinologists, failed to recognize here that his protégé had been right. Mao would publicly declare two years later, "The Chinese Revolution was victorious in spite of the will and wishes of Stalin."[8] What ensued in Sino-Soviet relations need not be reminded here.

In another telling instance, Dr. Doak Barnett, a Hong Kong friend of Galula's, reminisced about the Great Leap Forward and the Cultural Revolution it gave rise to. Addressing Galula, he wrote, "I remember, too, though, that you were one of the few people who were convinced that there were significant tensions and problems under the surface, in [China's] military establishment as well as in other sectors of the political system. Subsequent developments have certainly supported your judgements of that time, as I recall them."[9] Barnett was no featherweight. He would become a key advisor to President Nixon on U.S.-China relations, coining the phrase "containment without isolation."[10]

Differences of character and opinion thankfully remained inconsequential for the esteem in which Guillermaz and Galula held one another's judgment. Even when their paths temporarily split in the early 1950s, Guillermaz wrote regularly to his junior, separated by two ranks, to seek his opinion on evolving geopolitical matters in Asia. In their correspondence, they included integral copies of the reports they cabled to Paris, willingly submitting their analysis to each other's criticism, knowing that they would always benefit from it. The difference in rank and seniority highlighted Guillermaz's professionalism, and the absence of vanity in him. In 1955, he graciously wrote to his protégé who had reached the end of a six-year assignment to Hong Kong: "I wish to seize this opportunity to tell you how much I appreciated this period of renewed collaboration, and how much esteem I have for the vivacity and value of your judgement."[11]

In light of the above, it is unlikely that Guillermaz approved wholeheartedly of Galula's *Counterinsurgency*, and even less so of *Pacification* (for reasons detailed later). He would have likely found Galula's interpretations to be intelligent, but imprudent in their occasional lack of nuance, and too shallowly sourced in the academic sense. Guillermaz may have also found the laws, principles, and procedures his protégé derived to be too readymade, or incompatible with changing times and growing political constraints. Galula would have known this. Nevertheless, of all of the people he knew, he sought Guillermaz's recognition first. As Galula waited for a first published copy of *Counterinsurgency* to arrive to him by mail in France, he wrote to his editor at Praeger: "I know exactly how I will open the air parcel, glance at my name on the jacket, show the book to my wife and boy, then rush to bring it to my best friend, Colonel Guillermaz." Impatient, he continued his letter to his friendly American editor with self-mocking humor: "I am calm, I am very calm, I have tried to be very calm every morning for the last few days [when] the mail is carried upstairs by the concierge . . . well, no air parcel yet, which is curious since I heard of no plane crash over the Atlantic. Never mind. I am still calm. . . . [But] let us not forget that I am on my way to becoming a rich capitalist!"[12]

Urged by General Edward Lansdale and his editor Frederick Praeger to write a second book after *Counterinsurgency* that would delve deeper into "Chinese communist insurgency and its exportabilities,"[13] Galula replied tellingly: "While at Harvard, I debated with myself what book I ought to write: the one on counterinsurgency which was on my chest for a long time, or another on how the Chinese communists . . . rose to power. I drafted the plan for that second book, but I dropped the idea because it entailed too much research. I don't like working from research material. . . ." Instead, Guillermaz would write that book. In 1968, he published the highly authoritative *Histoire du Parti communiste chinois: 1921–1949*, and its sequel covering the period of 1949 to 1972, four years later. Galula concluded his letter to his editor with: "Ed Lansdale's suggestion is very flattering, but what can I do? . . . I feel I said already in my book everything I knew, everything that mattered on China's insurgency technique and threat. Writing another one on the subject would just add more details, certainly interesting but not absolutely necessary."[14]

The post-military careers of the two friends reflected the differences between them. "Guillermaz was a real *Sinologue*," Ruth told me, according a lot of weight to the title, as she too had spent ten years in China, fascinated by its civilization. Guillermaz went on to lead a successful academic career in his cherished field after retiring from the military as a general, with a bearing on France's diplomatic relations in the Far East.[15] By contrast, Galula joined the business development branch of a large defense firm after writing *Counterinsurgency* at Harvard.

Guillermaz's wartime years were marked by personal and family turmoil. Serving as the deputy attaché to China at the outbreak of the War, he confided in his memoirs that he had wished to rally himself to de Gaulle from the outset. A man of untainted integrity, honor, and modesty, his claim was undoubtedly true. But he too had been put off by the British attack on the French fleet at Mers El Kebir, and his wife had been vehemently opposed to him defecting.[16] When Pearl Harbor finally convinced him to leave Asia to join the Free French, his wife refused to follow him. She left with their children for French Indochina instead. Guillermaz wrote, with the sorrow of having postponed his decision in vain, "I realized then that I had lost everything in my attempt to reconcile my loyalty to my country and family, and my loyalty to my conscience which, to speak like Chateaubriand, is of all the witnesses, the one whose judgement I fear the most."[17]

"His wife forsook him and started a new life in Hanoi," Ruth shared. "He found her involved with a French doctor when he returned to Indochina after the war. She told him that she had been entitled to start anew, as he had abandoned her. She asked him to move past the whole affair. Jacques couldn't. It was too much for his honor to forgive."

In 1944, Guillermaz personally briefed generals Giraud and de Gaulle on the evolving Sino-Japanese war, and how it related to French Indochina. He warned the two generals of the Japanese threat posed to the French colony, and of the Maoist-inspired insurrectionary threat brewing within. The impression Guillermaz made on the generals was enough for them to designate him as the next attaché to China.[18]

"For weeks on end," Guillermaz recalled, "I tried to obtain from *les troupes coloniales* qualified officers for our intelligence services in China...."[19]

France was desperate to reassert herself in that part of the world after the War. She needed good representation and good intelligence. True to his professional ethic, Guillermaz sought men who would complement him, and not merely mirror him. Galula was one of these. Bright and already experienced in both covert and conventional military intelligence, he was a natural match. Louis Léouzon,[20] who had been a classmate of Galula's at Saint-Cyr, was another. Pierre Bourgeois was third, and Maurice Raymond was fourth. All belonged to *les troupes coloniales*. Each of them had been handpicked by Guillermaz, and forewarned that diplomatic staff postings were not conducive to rapid career progression in the French Army. Each of them agreed for his own reasons, which included, no doubt, the desire to follow the officer that was Guillermaz. The five of them became lifelong friends.

Guillermaz had already accumulated six years of experience in China before returning with his new team in 1945. He had lived through the Japanese occupation of both Peking and Nanking, and had met the likes of U.S. general (then lieutenant-colonel) "Vinegar" Joe Stillwell serving as Chiang Kai-shek's chief-of-staff.[21] Guillermaz had arrived in China at the same age as Galula had, twenty-six, and equally as ignorant about the country.[22] Guill-ermaz recalled, however, that as an officer of the Colonial Army, it had been *expected* that he adapt quickly to his new role in a foreign country. This, he admitted, had "hurried [his] professional and intellectual maturity."[23] The same was true for Galula who would have to report on a different form of conflict from the one he had just experienced in Europe, and studied at Saint-Cyr. In a people's war, politics, Guillermaz would underscore, played the most important part. Guillermaz had introduced Galula to the problem; and the latter took it upon himself to devise a solution.

As Guillermaz had previously done himself, Galula began his assignment with intensive Chinese language training.[24] It fell upon him to self-teach about Chinese history and culture during his spare time, and to inform him-self about the civil war he would soon be expected to report on. In his mem-oires, Guillermaz recalled reading Edgar Snow's iconic *Red Star over China*, and later U.S. Marine Corps General Evans Carlson's *Twin Star of China* at the onset of his assignment. It is very likely that Galula, an avid reader by all accounts, had done the same. Galula would later get access to a host of com-munist doctrines such as Mao Tse-Tung's *On Guerilla Warfare* translated by another U.S. marine, General Samuel Griffith, who became a good friend of Galula's in later years. Mao's other works such as *Strategy of Revolutionary War for China*, *On Protracted War*, etc., as well as the works of Lin Biao, Liu Shaoqi, Zhou Enlai, and others also captured Galula's interest as they became available to him. (How and when Galula came across some of these is dis-cussed in the next chapter.)

Galula's tiny 1945 agenda introduced in the previous chapter, and from which the following is extracted, sells the young officer's adventure rather short.

August 24th	Depart for Malta
August 25th	Depart for Cairo
August 26th	Depart at night for Schiba
August 27th	Arrive at Schiba. Arrive at Karachi.
August 28th	Depart for New Delhi. Arrive at Calcutta. Saw severe burn victims.
September 27th	Parachute course
September 28th	First jump
September 29th	Second and third jumps
October 10th	Saw Capt Guillermaz and Raymond
October 24th	Travel preparations
November 3rd	Depart for Chungking. Mithyina, Kunsuing, Arrive Chungking. Saw Léouzon, Bourgeois.
November 4th	Visit city
November 5th	Go out with Léouzon

November 7th   Reception at the Russian Embassy
November 11th   Reception at the French Embassy
November 13th   Start Chinese language studies with Mr Ku Wang Sian
November 14th   Second teacher, Misses Tung Po Soo
November 15th   XX

The trip from Europe to Asia, through the Middle East, south-central Asia, over the Himalayas, and into China was one that could not have failed to fascinate him. Flying in Gooney birds and Skymasters across civilizations, daunting mountain ranges, vast deserts, and buzzing jungles, he disembarked every time in a land more unfamiliar than the previous.

In Calcutta, Galula and his fellow assistant-attachés waited nearly two months for the weather to clear over the "Hump" for flights to China to resume. "Guillermaz allowed them to kill time by jumping out of airplanes," Ruth recalled shaking her head. "It was too risky to fly over the Himalayas, but they felt it was okay to practice parachuting!" I gleaned from his agenda that parachuting was not the only distraction the charismatic Galula had found.

Guillermaz, in the meantime, promoted *à titre fictif* to the rank of lieutenant-colonel, left for China in October 1945, ahead of his assistants, with the exception of Maurice "Coco" Raymond. The latter was an intelligence officer belonging to the Colonial Artillery (known as "*bigors*"). In China, he worked undercover as an agent handler, according to Ruth. Otherwise, as the most senior of the subordinates, he served as Guillermaz's deputy, responsible for overseeing the intelligence-gathering efforts of the three other assistant-attachés; all of whom were officially attached to the *Deuxième Bureau* (G2—Intelligence staff), leaving little doubt as to what their primary functions would be.[25]

Guillermaz established his attaché post with the French delegation stationed in Chungking, Chiang Kai-shek's wartime capital, which lay outside of Japanese-controlled areas.[26] Coco Raymond and Pierre Bourgeois remained with Guillermaz in Chungking, until the embassy was moved to Nanking, the southern capital, following the Japanese withdrawal. Léo Léouzon was detached to Shanghai, the coastal hub where French commercial interests were significant.[27] As for Galula, he was assigned to Peking by Guillermaz,[28] the latter's former posting. The ancient city was a sinophile's dream, Guillermaz's favorite in all of China. Galula had been favored. Peking had been left relatively unscathed by the War. Ancient monuments, temples, and palaces were scattered throughout the city. Walls and ancient gates outlined Peking's quarters: The Imperial, the Forbidden, the Tartar, the Chinese, and the Diplomatic. The elegantly appointed French embassy, established in the latter, now served the French consulate, where Galula established his office.[29]

"My husband made many friends in Peking, including a young French sinologist by the name of Robert Ruhlman. He was slightly eccentric, and

Galula at consular office in Peking.

very nice, save for the occasional outburst of 'Alsatian' temper." A graduate of
the most prestigious *Grande École*, Ruhlman became close friends with Alain
Peyreffitte, who certainly came to know Galula too during that period. Peyreffitte became one of de Gaulle's closest collaborators in the 1960s, and rose
to become one of France's most iconic scholarly statesmen, a French Henry
Kissinger of sorts.[30]

"The fictional character of Lieutenant Jean Leone is based on David Galula,"
the author of the novel entitled *The Peking Letter* wrote me. "It will give you
the flavour of his personality and of how we lived in Peking."

   I reached Seymour Topping in the fall of 2009. A distinguished American
journalist, writer and professor, he was then in the final stages of editing his
memoirs, *On the Front Lines of the Cold War*, which I would come to read the
following year. My first contact with him was over the phone, in the presence of Ruth Galula, whose friendship with Topping's wife, a photojournalist
herself, was entering its seventh decade. Topping's intrepid coverage of the
Chinese Civil War had launched his career. He continued to cover communist and Asian affairs in following decades, rising to the position of managing
editor of the *New York Times*.[31]

   When Topping had first befriended Galula, the two had had much in
common: age, religion, wartime service as junior officers, and even a shared
passion for horseback riding.[32] Both were keen observers and analysts, which
made them very good at their essentially similar occupations. Once demobilized, Topping opted to enroll at the American missionary-supported

College of Chinese Studies in Peking. His intent had been to study Chinese while freelancing as a war correspondent. He arrived in the city in September 1946, equally as disoriented as Galula had been the year before. "It was beyond my imagination," he wrote in his memoirs, "that in a matter of weeks I would be flying from Peking to report from Mao Zedong's headquarters in Yunnan, and that I would be covering the Chinese Civil War for the next three years."[33]

"Peking was the center of war activity in North China and Manchuria," Topping wrote me. "When not out reporting," he continued, "I took language lessons [at the College] from a bespectacled Mandarin-like professor who insisted that I apply myself rigorously, and had me practicing Chinese tones endlessly."[34] He would meet Galula there. The language school was located in Peking's Inner City, adjacent to the Forbidden City and the Legation Quarter. Galula had also studied at the College, but had soon discovered complementary ways of learning Chinese. His agenda entries above for November 14 and 15 of 1945 reveal just that. Miss Tung Po Soo's teaching pedagogy came highly recommended no doubt!

"On some evenings Galula and I would go by rickshaw down the narrow, cobbled toutiao hutung (alleyways) along Hatamen Street," Topping recounted in his memoirs, "past the crimson walls of the Forbidden City, pausing at times to gaze at the purple and golden tile roofs of its palaces and temples before being wheeled through the Front Gate of the Outer City into the old Chinese Quarter. There we would loll in the boisterous wine shops exchanging gossip and quips with Chinese acquaintances, at times visiting the company houses where slim joy girls with tinkling voices in silken cheongsams slit to the thigh offered tea and other delights."[35]

Ruth Galula had not been unaware of her husband's rambunctious bachelor's past, quite normal for a single man his age after all. But she recalled how Guillermaz had turned red with embarrassment when she had asked him, after her husband had passed away, to translate a writing exercise the latter's tutor-mistress had given him to complete. "It was much too risqué for poor Guillermaz to read out to me!" she told me laughing. "Then again, it was very common for foreign officers to have that kind of relationship with their tutors in China."

"After several months," Topping continued, "I left the school dormitory to share a house with Captain David Galula, a brilliant young French assistant attaché, who confided in me details of the briefings he was getting from his excellent Chinese and diplomatic sources."[36]

Topping shared Galula's house for six months, developing a lasting friendship. "He traveled occasionally into the various war zones . . . sharing with me his impressions and details of briefings he received from Nationalist army officers," Topping completed the portrayal in an email.

But Galula had kept mute on other things.

"Zero on captivity," Topping replied to my question about Galula's detention by Communist forces during a fact-finding trip to the western provinces. Nor had Galula ever shared any details about his time under Vichy.

"He was highly thought of by his peers and Guillermaz placed great trust in him," Topping added in his correspondence with me. "He got on very well with the military and diplomatic community." Galula often loitered at the Peking Club, lunching or drinking with foreign correspondents and diplomats, many of whom were much older than him no doubt, with the purpose of gathering and trading information. Galula fostered very strong relations with the press corps throughout his diplomatic postings, first in mainland China, and then in Hong Kong. He understood the power of the media. Galula's journalist friends were almost invariably American. Beyond his innate affinity for America, it seemed that he trusted these journalists more than their French counterparts who were susceptible to harboring socialist or even communist sympathies. Galula saw value in exposing the truth about the rise of the communists to American journalists, who according to Guillermaz, "could not find in their embassies any impartial information, nor with their military attaché missions, which were too committed to the Nationalist cause, and were therefore bound to be [overly] optimistic."[37] Later in Hong Kong and in Algeria, Galula sought to leverage his relationships with the press to favorably influence American readership about France's counterinsurgency campaigns.

Chinese identity card.

Sent by an exasperated President Harry Truman, General George C. Marshall succeeded in imposing a ceasefire between the Kuomintang (KMT) and the Chinese Communist Party (CCP) in January 1946. Marshall had weighed in heavily with his prestige, dictating what concessions each side would have to make in order to coexist.[38] But by March of the following year, the reforms he had called for had failed. The French attaché team would not be afforded a quiet posting after all. The resumption of hostilities announced the final episode of the Chinese Civil War, which had begun in earnest in 1926, when the KMT and CCP had joined forces against the Feudal Lords. The rupture of that alliance had led to the Long March, until the Japanese invasion provided a notional hiatus to intensive fighting.

Galula left China a year prior to Mao's victory speech in Peking,[39] by which time the final outcome of the Civil War had undoubtedly been known to him. His witnessing of an overwhelming communist victory over a massively favored Nationalist Army marked him profoundly. U.S. Lend-Lease and other military assistance programs had afforded the Nationalists an uncontested air force and a vast superiority on the ground in terms of mechanization and firepower. But the communists had been armed with an ideology, and more importantly perhaps, with an incredibly effective "technique of mobilizing the masses,"[40] as Galula came to write. Mao had famously told American journalist Anna-Louise Strong that even in the nuclear era, "The outcome of a war is decided by the people, not by one or two new types of weapons."[41] The primacy of political strength over military strength in revolutionary warfare—active popular support in other words—was the first lesson that Galula would glean from Mao. It was reinforced by Guillermaz who seldom, if ever, mentioned conventional military activity in his correspondence with his protégé; knowing full well that it would never decide the overall outcome of such a struggle.

The French had retaken possession of their colony in Indochina after the Potsdam Conference, holding much less credibility in the eyes of the Vietnamese. (The British return to Malaya would suffer from the same psychological handicap.) The Viet Minh and other revolutionary groups had benefited from the ousting of the French by the Japanese during the Second World War. In addition to following the Chinese Civil War, Guillermaz and his team concerned themselves with what repercussions a communist victory in China would have on an adjacent French Indochina. (Those same repercussions would create a need for U.S. involvement in Vietnam the following decade.) Guillermaz directed the efforts of his subordinates towards answering the following critical question: On the morrow of their victory, would the Chinese Communists intervene on the side of the Viet Minh against the French?

"I held full responsibility for the unveiled views I expressed to higher headquarters in Paris and Saigon," Guillermaz wrote in his memoires, "but I must acknowledge that these views relied on the products of a worthy team. Captain Bourgeois brought to the table detailed information concerning the [Chinese] belligerents' orders of battle, and thorough descriptions of their respective operations. Captain Galula displayed, throughout our discussions and interpretations of events, a spirit that was particularly fertile and prompt."[42]

The intelligence delivered by Guillermaz's team had strategic implications for Paris in its relations with China. The intelligence also had a bearing on the conduct of France's counterinsurgency campaign next door. Both Guillermaz and Galula would come to write that the intelligence they had produced had served the French expeditionary command in Indochina to formulate its strategic deployment. With resources being limited as they were, the theater commander was faced with the recurring dilemma of whether to invest his forces in the pacification of the interior, or to divest these to strengthen the northern border to stave off the risk of a Chinese invasion. (A dilemma compounded by the fact that the United States was initially very cool at the prospect of France maintaining herself in Indochina in the first place.)

When, by late 1947, the tide of the Chinese Civil War was deemed by those who understood it to be turning decisively in favor of the Communists, Guillermaz felt that France should enter into negotiations with the Viet Minh. Procrastination or obstinacy, he felt, would only lead to a weakening of the French position. "For reasons of national self-interest, history and ideology," Guillermaz wrote, "[a Chinese communist government] would support, via one way or another, the military effort of the Viet Minh, and sustain it for as long as necessary to avoid its collapse, and then, weigh in heavily on our own dialogue with Ho Chi Minh."[43]

This call to negotiate did not earn Guillermaz many sympathies within the military establishment. In 1948, he put the idea to General Salan, the commander of ground forces in Asia, who had commanded the 13th RTS at Elba. Salan was receptive, but did not commit to the idea.[44] "Not only did my warnings go unheeded," Guillermaz reflected bitterly, "but five years would go by until the Geneva conference of 1954 would put an end to a war which … could not have had any favorable outcome for France."[45] Bernard Fall wrote with the benefit of hindsight in 1961, "The arrival of the Chinese Communists on the borders of North Viet-Nam in November 1949 closed the first chapter of the Indochina war and doomed all French chances of full victory. From then on, the Viet-Minh possessed, like the Reds in Korea, a 'sanctuary.' …"[46]

If gathering intelligence in the dens of Peking was not risqué enough to satiate Galula's appetite for adventure, a few journeys into the Chinese hinterland, in the midst of a Civil War, would do the trick. When KMT-CCP hostilities resumed in the early spring of 1947, the young officer drove an American Jeep into no-man's-land and beyond in order to see the civil war's progression for himself, and to gain a better understanding of how the communists were swaying the population to their side. For this, he would risk life, limb, and diplomatic incident.

In an early book describing Mao's revolution, French Air Force General Lionel Chassin referred to a report Galula had submitted to Guillermaz upon his return from his first trip to the Interior as follows:

In April 1947, a French observer commenting on Communist operations in southern Shanxi wrote: "... The relative ease with which Communist forces have won [their battles against Nationalists] can only be explained by the superiority of their moral force. A disgruntled and passive Nationalist soldier who is turned to the Communist side becomes, once he is indoctrinated and politically educated, a willing and aggressive fighter."

And this perceptive observer concluded: "When the population is not outright hostile, it is completely unsympathetic to the Nationalists. Their own generals do not agree, nor do they cooperate. Their troops loathe fighting. They have no suitable weapon to bear against their elusive and resolute enemies. The American military aid they receive ends up in the hands of the Communists, often during the first clashes. If only military considerations had been stake, the outcome would not have been this doubtful."[47]

Galula had traveled alone on his first long-range expedition. French-flag hoisted on his Jeep, and with nothing but a fuel drum strapped to the back seats to keep him company, he did not care to take a guide, figuring that it would be cumbersome and perhaps detrimental to the "neutral observer" image he wished to maintain.

Galula drove his Jeep west out of Peking and then south across the Northern Province of Chahar (present day Beijing Province) into Shanxi. He was detained by communist guerrillas he encountered in Tatung, and shortly thereafter released. Unbothered, he pushed further to Taiyuan, where he was met by an important provincial governor and warlord, Marshal Yen Hsi-shan, who treated him as a guest of honor.[48] Ruth cherished this particular episode of her husband's travels. "The soldier-poet took an immediate liking to David," she told me, as she reached for a shoebox where she kept her most treasured mementos. She pulled out a parchment. "He dedicated this idiom to my husband." Guillermaz had translated the Chinese calligraphy after David had passed away. The verses echoed the essence of Galula's interpretation of the use of force, and its relation to cause and ideology in revolutionary warfare.

> Reason strengthens Strength;
> Reason, because of Strength, can spread.
> Strength without Reason, shall wither;
> Reason, without Strength, shall fail to spread.
> (*Addressed to 'Chalula', on the 29th of March 1947*)

From left to right, Galula, Robert Ruhlman, and Coco Raymond. Photo was taken prior to Galula taking off on a solo expedition into China's hinterlands to report on the progress of Communist rebel forces.

Galula developed a fascination for Chinese idioms, reflecting his admiration of the Chinese mindset. Twenty years after his first assignment to China began, he told a friend who had asked him what living in Asia had been like, "I have never met a Chinese person who wasn't intelligent."[49] Ruth added that her husband considered all Chinese, "from the warlord to the coolie," to be endowed with superior wisdom and admirable cunning.

Following his encounter with Hsi-shan, Galula continued south, following a railway, as Nationalist forces were generally only capable of securing these main lines of communications. He stopped at the next gated village as night fell. "During the night," Guillermaz recounted his subordinate's exploits in his memoires, "communist guerrillas scaled the walls of the little village, in the purest style of ancient warfare. Galula was captured a second time, and remained in the custody of General Ch'en Keng, the regional military commander, for nearly two weeks."[50]

Captivity was welcomed by the inquisitive captive. Again, Galula was treated with deference.

"Captain Galula was thus able to visit communist-controlled areas," Guillermaz continued, "converse with communist officers including Ch'en Keng, visit and question Nationalist soldiers, inquire about the organization and status of forces in the Northwest, and even on the progression of the battles."[51]

In *Counterinsurgency*, Galula wrote, recalling this period of captivity, "Various military and political cadres undertook to explain to me their policy, strategy, and tactics."[52] Of all the things he observed, he seemed most impressed by the indoctrination and release of prisoners by communist forces. Galula promoted this approach in Algeria, preaching the merits of turning arrested insurgents. The insight Galula gained into other methods of communist indoctrination was similarly invaluable to his later writings. Communist indoctrination took every audience involved in a revolutionary war into account. Not only was the peasant population continuously indoctrinated by communist soldiers, but so too were their enemies, prisoners, and they themselves. Galula was highly impressed by the insurgency's emphasis on governance, recalling from his captivity: "In 1947, when the author was captured by the Chinese Communists in Hsinkiang . . . he noticed that a team of Communist civil servants immediately took over the administration of the town. . . . These officials, he was told, had long before been designated for the task and had been functioning as a shadow government with the guerrilla units in the area."[53] Galula thus witnessed the Communists out-governing the Nationalists. He would report back on these and other seemingly intangible factors that went beyond orders-of-battle and troop deployments, feeding into Guillermaz's view that victory, both in China and Indochina, would likely go to the revolutionaries.

After his release, Galula headed for Xi'an, and left his Jeep there to board a plane for Nanking, where he briefed Guillermaz on what he had seen. The lieutenant had driven some 800 miles, amazingly, without any mechanical breakdowns. Amazingly too, he had not been forced to surrender his camera or his film despite being captured twice. Galula convinced his superior to extend the adventure together. Despite his fascination with China, Guillermaz had yet to undertake such a voyage. At Galula's request, they returned to pick up the Jeep in Xi'an by train. Travel by rail took two days, but Galula disliked flying in China. According to his apologetic widow, "He felt that Chinese passengers were sick at the drop of a hat, which turned him off flying." Recuperating the miraculous Jeep, the officers headed toward Tibet, through China's northwestern provinces. They reached Lanchow, the capital of Gansu Province, first, and then Qinghai.

"We crossed the Wei [River] at Hsienyang (Xianyang), the storied city of Chinese Antiquity," Guillermaz wrote. "We then drove across a series of hills, and onwards through poor villages announcing the dryness of Central Asia. These were followed by the valley of the Chin River: almond, jujube, and pear trees flowering, crisp fresh air, and clear blue skies. How often did we stop, amazed and enthralled, after reaching a bend of a winding road, or a vantage point on a slope!?"[54] At Pingliang, still in the Province of Gansu, they discovered a medieval-like city steeped in Muslim culture. They remained there overnight, hosted by Spanish monks. The next day, they reached Lanzhou, on the Yellow River, to the south of the Great Wall. Having crossed the famed river, they drove on to Xining, where they met Ma Pu-fang, the Muslim general and provincial governor who would win a major battle against communist forces later in 1949, skillfully employing horse cavalry as he did so.[55]

At 6000 feet above sea level, the French officers deviated south toward the Tibetan Buddhist temple of Kumbum, the Place of One Hundred Thousand Holy Images, bringing along a German priest-scholar they had met as their interpreter of local dialects. They were received at the temple by the fateful Panchen-Lama, second in holiness only to the Dalai Lama. The youth grew up to play a pivotal role in Chinese-Tibetan affairs, opposing his counterpart, the Dalai Lama, in a complex geopolitical struggle that involved much more than freedom of religion.[56]

Passing through a caravan of yaks, still gaining altitude with their Jeep that now carried a French diplomat they had met, they continued through to Tangar (Huangyuan). They were flanked by snowy peaks on their way to the mystical Koko Nor Lake set at 10,000 feet. Getting lost, and then back on track, they drove the trusted Jeep through a mountain pass set at over 12,000 feet, brushing with Mongolian men-at-arms, wild horses, and antelopes, finally emerging to the beautiful blue image that was Koko Nor.

"Captain Galula," Guillermaz concluded jovially, "whose sense of humor was impervious to disappointments, begged me to find some reason to charge him with four days of disciplinary detention, and for it to be recorded with the date and place; so that, he laughed, his personal file would contain the irrefutable proof that he had ventured all the way to Lake Koko Nor, a feat, which would otherwise be unbelievable to his peers."[57]

7

INTERLUDE: MAO'S DISCIPLE

To learn is no easy matter and to apply what one has learned is even harder.... The important thing is to be good at learning.

—*Mao Tse-Tung*[1]

... Just like my master, quite in spite of him, that dear Mao Tse-Tung, I have faith in Theory only when it is combined to Practice, and founded on Experience....

—*David Galula*[2]

OF ALL THE INFLUENCES over Galula's writings, some of which have already been alluded to, and others, such as the French Psychological Action program that shall be discussed later, the Chinese Revolution was the most significant. Galula was one of a handful of French observers witnessing the struggle on the ground as it entered its final phase. The impressions he gathered between 1945 and 1948 came to permeate his writings. Later, during his six-year assignment to Hong Kong, he would undertake a post-mortem reflection of what had happened in mainland China. The hypotheses he drew then about revolutionary warfare were strengthened by a seemingly identical scenario being repeated in nearby Indochina.

Influenced by their own trials and errors, and in turn by earlier Soviet doctrinaires, the Chinese Revolution's leaders became prolific commentators on the art of revolutionary warfare. Their manifesto-styled writings were seldom limited to military content. Beyond trying to achieve some form of standardization in tactics and organization, communist fighting doctrines were written with the intent of *indoctrinating* in every sense of the word. Soldiers and auxiliaries were politically educated. They were imbued with the ideology of the Party, and provided with the tools of propaganda applicable to themselves, the populations they lived off of, and their enemies, which they invariably sought to rally.

Dozens of doctrinal texts were drafted both prior to and after Japan's expanded occupation of Chinese territory. The doctrinal amalgam, which had first been intended to defeat the Kuomintang, would prove equally handy against the modern Japanese Army. The latter's counter-doctrine on the matter—contained in the hastily written *The Essentials of Pacification*—adopted a brutally ineffective enemy-centric approach. "Pacification must utilise surprise attacks and raids as their main tactic," a captured manual read, "The aim of pacification is extermination."[3]

"Galula was a superb observer of the Chinese revolutionaries," Seymour Topping wrote to me. "Counterinsurgency was not defined as such at the time, but he was a student of Maoist guerrilla tactics." Topping adopted the Maoist definition of guerrilla warfare, which encompasses military tactics as well as political and psychological warfare.

Galula became passionate about Mao from early on. Motivated by his increasing obsession to deal communist subversion a blow, the avid chess player found a worthy opponent in the iconic leader of the Chinese Communist Party. By 1945, when Galula first arrived in China, Mao had already penned, or lectured, *Problems of Strategy in China's Revolutionary War* in 1936, *On Guerrilla Warfare* in 1937, *Problems of Strategy in Guerrilla Warfare against Japan*, and *On Protracted War* in 1938. These works were in addition to a vast number of others on a great variety of topics. One of his most significant philosophical writings, *On Contradiction*, was not specifically tied to revolutionary warfare, but spoke to the importance of a cause and ideology in a revolution's viability. And though Galula's opinion on the importance of causes and ideologies in insurgencies became mitigated over time, he remained undeniably sold to Mao's interpretation of dialectics, and how these created exploitable rifts within populations.

Galula came to refer to Mao as his master "quite despite himself."[4] It should come as little surprise that Galula would later introduce *Counterinsurgency* with a quote drawn from the first work of Mao to which he had had access to.[5] Of all of the revolutions Galula encountered and studied, he cites none as often as the Chinese. And yet, his exposure to that particular revolution had not been the lengthiest or the most intimate, although it had been his first. The Algerian War, by virtue of his origins, felt closer to home. His involvement there was also more direct, serving two years on the ground, and another three years in a headquarters position at the national-strategic level in Paris.

Galula studying in Peking.

In Galula's eyes, the Chinese Communists epitomized the art of revolutionary warfare. He was more impressed by them than by their Soviet predecessors about whom he seemed to know or care about much less. He was most impressed, perhaps, by the intellectuality of the Chinese model that was founded on patience manifested by the notion of protracted warfare. It is likely that Galula saw in that model the same refinement and wisdom that he saw in the Chinese people as a whole. His admiration was uninhibited by his visceral dislike of the ideology the Revolution upheld. All of this was in stark contrast with the Algerian revolution for which he expressed only contempt and disdain. "Having refused the help of Communist technicians (thank God)," Galula would later write in *Pacification*, "the [Algerian] rebels are not shining with organizing talents."[6]

Mao's influence over Galula's writings is evident to the point of style. Galula's often conversational style of writing, so present in *Pacification* and across his correspondence, is absent from his capstone book. In the latter, his tone is replaced by a Maoist one at times, which his peers at Harvard cautioned him to dampen. It is left to the reader to decide whether Galula's nod to Mao was deliberate. Illustrating the resemblance, we consider how Galula concludes the first chapter of *Counterinsurgency*: "We have indicated above the general characteristics of revolutionary war. They are an ineluctable product of the nature of this war. An insurgent or a counterinsurgent who would conduct his war in opposition to any of these characteristics . . . would certainly not increase his chances of success."[7] Similar language can be found in the introduction to Mao's *Problems of Strategy in China's Revolutionary War*: "Revolutionary war . . . has its own specific circumstances and nature, in addition to the circumstances and nature of war in general. . . . Unless you understand its specific circumstances and nature, unless you understand its specific laws, you will not be able to direct revolutionary war and wage it successfully."[8]

The scholastic, administrative language used by Mao, so common to totalitarian regimes—as the French philosopher and playwright Albert Camus commented—lent itself well to Communist-styled dialectics.[9] Arguments are often expressed through "Unity of Opposites," or yin versus yang. Furthermore, as many of Mao's and his acolytes' writings were transcriptions of oral lectures and presentations, the style remains persuasive and accessible.

Galula's study of Mao most likely began in the field. Although Galula could cite the sayings of Chu Teh in 1947,[10] it is questionable whether his access to written communist doctrines had been substantial during his assignment to Peking. Galula's firsthand observations combined with his debriefing of sources had likely constituted the stuff of his first studies. His correspondence reveals that it is only afterwards, when he was assigned to Hong Kong as of 1950, that he would gain greater access to revolutionary literature.

Chinese revolutionary doctrines were not readily available to French officers to study in the early stages of the Indochina War (which spanned from 1946 to 1954). The first work to be translated into French was Mao's *Problems of Strategy in China's Revolutionary War* in 1950.[11] Only *On Guerrilla Warfare* had been translated into English by Samuel Griffith earlier, in 1940, with extracts of it published in the Marine Corps Gazette.[12] (Griffith's work was published commercially in 1961, by Praeger.) The next Western-language translation of Chinese revolutionary doctrine to appear was *Problems of Strategy in Guerrilla Warfare against Japan* in 1952,[13] followed shortly by a "source book" compiled and translated by Columbia University professor Gene Hanrahan.[14] Entitled *Chinese Communist Guerrilla Tactics*, Hanrahan's 134-page booklet became instrumental to Galula's study of Chinese revolutionary doctrines. It includes doctrinal essays written by Mao, Chu Te, Lin Piao, Hsiao k'e, Ming Fan, P'eng Te-huai, and other Red Army cadres.

Galula obtained a copy of the source book in the spring of 1953 through his friend and collaborator Howard Boorman, a young American sinologist

Galula interacting with
Chinese peasants.

in charge of translation and open-source intelligence at the U.S. consulate
in Hong Kong.[15] (I found this copy in Galula's archives some fifty-five years
later.) Impressed by the work that the source book represented, Galula wrote
to Hanrahan:

> [The texts] are indeed invaluable to anyone attempting to understand
> the *real* military strength of the Chinese Communists. . . . [They]
> provide my thesis with plenty of additional ammunition. I have tried
> for a long time to find the original documents here but without suc-
> cess. I found only "On Protracted War" by Mao Tse-Tung, which my
> office translated. I believe Mr. Boorman will send you a copy of it. . . .
> If by any chance you have not [also] read "[Problems of] Strategy in
> China's Revolutionary War" by Mao Tse-Tung, I would be glad to send
> it to you.[16]

Galula was ecstatic. His letter to the professor was biographically revealing in that he claimed to have a counterrevolutionary "thesis" by 1953. In the

same letter he wrote: "I intend to send an official request through appropriate channels to Army G-2 in the Pentagon for a number of copies of your book for the French Army." It was by luck and by virtue of his association with Boorman, therefore, that Galula was able to assist in disseminating part of the enemy's doctrines to the French High Command. The discovery would be of little avail, however, as the Viet Minh was already well into the maneuver warfare phase of its revolution by then, culminating in the Battle of Dien Bien Phu the following year.

The above discovery is also important because it discredits any contending theory that Galula had been significantly influenced by the works of Lionel Chassin,[17] whom the former never mentioned in his correspondence or in his writings, and who wrote about Mao *after* Galula had access to the latter's first works.

Mao was not an exception to the rule that every thinker, great or small, is influenced by others before him. He had been a disciple of Lenin on the subject of revolution. He had studied Sun Tzu (like Galula, I discovered) and Clausewitz. From the latter he had retained the idea that war was an extension of politics, and that insurrections were akin to "strategic defences" comprised of "tactical offences"—a recurring theme in Maoist texts. Mao had also studied Napoleon and his *Grande Armée*'s disintegration at the hands of harassing guerrillas. He had reflected on the Italian occupation of Abyssinia, and had read Lawrence's *Seven Pillars of Wisdom*, drawing from each of these examples of success and failure.

Mao cautioned his followers against transposing historical lessons too quickly, however. "The guerrilla warfare conducted by the Moroccans against the French and the Spanish," he cited as an example, "was not exactly similar to that which we conduct today in China. These differences express the characteristics of different peoples in different periods." Galula, in turn, would caution his readership along the same lines, while narrowly avoiding the trap of dogmatizing Mao.

Galula's enthrallment with Maoist doctrine led him to methodize two models of insurgency. He labeled the first the "Orthodox Pattern," and based it entirely on the Chinese Communist revolutionary model. He outlined five phases for it,[18] stating that the "blueprint" had belonged to Liu Shaoqi.[19] The seed of the dialectic model, however, had been sown earlier by Mao himself in *On Protracted War*, who wrote: "The first stage covers the period of the enemy's strategic offensive and our strategic defensive. The second stage will be the period of the enemy's strategic consolidation and our preparation for the strategic counteroffensive. The third stage will be the period of our strategic counteroffensive and the enemy's strategic retreat."[20] An even closer match could be found in Mao's stepwise revolutionary process outlined in *On Guerrilla Warfare*:[21]

1. Arousing and organizing the people;
2. Achieving internal unification politically;
3. Establishing bases;[22]
4. Equipping forces;
5. Recovering national strength;
6. Destroying the enemy's national strength;
7. Regaining lost territories.[23]

At the outset of the Algerian War, Galula had mistakenly gone as far as attributing the FLN's rebellion to Chinese Communist designs, before being brought back to reality by Guillermaz.[24] If nothing else, this demonstrated to what extent Galula perceived an exportable and timeless quality to the Chinese revolutionary pattern that had proved its effectiveness in places such as Indochina and Malaya. Only his direct participation in the Algerian War, two years after it began, would convince him that an offshoot pattern of insurgency had grown out of the "orthodox" pattern he attributed to Mao. Galula labeled the offshoot "the Bourgeois[25]-Nationalist Pattern" or the "Shortcut Pattern." This too he viewed through the prism of Maoist doctrine.

The difference between the Orthodox and Shortcut patterns of insurgency lay in the first two steps. Since the goal of nationalist revolutionaries was "generally limited to the seizure of power"[26] from their colonial overlords, the creation of a political base and of a united front—the first two steps of the Orthodox pattern—could be skipped and replaced by blind and directed terrorism to expedite the process. "Promoting disorder," Galula wrote in *Counterinsurgency*, "is a legitimate objective of the insurgent. It helps to disrupt the economy, hence to produce discontent; it serves to undermine the strength and the authority of the counterinsurgent. Moreover, disorder—the normal state of nature—is cheap to create and very costly to prevent."[27] Once terrorism achieved the desired outcome of polarizing a population, the "shortcut" patterned joined the "classic" one in its third step: guerrilla warfare.

Galula's obsession with the Chinese model nearly blinded him to fundamental differences between the revolution he had witnessed in China, and the one he would later come to witness in Algeria. An insurgency's reliance on terrorism, for example, made for a weak differentiator between his two patterns of insurgency. Terrorism was not exclusive to the FLN in Algeria. The Maoists had, after all, made full use of terrorism in China, and the Viet Minh had done the same in Indochina (two cases he described as "orthodox"). The absence of a political base or of a united front was a similarly weak differentiator between the two patterns. The rebel movement in Algeria had evolved from a political party whose roots extended back twenty years.

The "shortcut pattern" adopted by the nationalists in Algeria had been less of a reason for their relatively quick victory over the French, than an effect of the particular circumstances of that war. A truer differentiation between

Galula's two patterns of insurgency depends more on the character of the counterinsurgent, than that of the insurgent's. (The latter dialectically adapts to the former after all.) Whether the counterinsurgent is a domestic or foreign entity, for instance, is pivotal to an insurgency's adherence to a particular pattern. The stakes involved for the Kuomintang counterinsurgent in China were significantly higher than those involved for the French counterinsurgent in Algeria. For the ruling Kuomintang, survival depended on the outcome of their counterrevolutionary effort. Chang Kai-shek could not refuse battle, so to speak. For French President Charles de Gaulle, on the other hand, withdrawing from Algeria was not only feasible, but also politically preferable by the time he decided to do so. It was much easier to lose one's will for a war that was ultimately "optional." Not all revolutionary wars are protracted for this very reason, despite what Mao had written, and what Galula had restated in the introduction to his treatise, somewhat contradictorily to his own thoughts on the "shortcut pattern."

The *optionality* of a counterinsurgency campaign does little to favor the determination of a foreign counterinsurgent to see it through. This can lead to a self-fulfilling prophecy as the population and the insurgent will equate *optionality* with ephemeral determination on the counterinsurgent's part, thus simultaneously discouraging the population to side with the counterinsurgent and encouraging the insurgent to continue on fighting. For the foreign counterinsurgent, political support at home for the counterinsurgency campaign is commensurate with the said *optionality*. Thus, the determination of the counterinsurgent, dictated by the *optionality* of his involvement, is what often determines how protracted a struggle will be. The Chinese Civil War had not been "protracted" on account of Mao's desire for it to be so—for surely he too would have opted for a "shortcut," but on account of the tenacity of his opponent.

Infatuated as Galula was with Maoist doctrine, there is little doubt that Galula's most important doctrinal themes were rooted there. Nonetheless, a tall intellectual step remained to be taken between the correct interpretation of that doctrine, and the formulation of a response. "The one who directs a war against a revolutionary movement will not find in Mao and in other revolutionary theorists the answers to his problems," Galula reflected on account of the asymmetry inherent to revolutionary wars. "He will surely find useful information on how the revolutionary acts, he may perhaps infer the answers he is looking for, but nowhere will he find them explicitly stated."[28] Galula took that intellectual step unaided, but influenced to some extent, as shall be discussed in a later chapter, by French revolutionary warfare theory of his era, which was also influenced to some extent by Maoist doctrine. It is hoped then, that by drawing parallel lines of thought between Mao and Galula, the reader will not be misled to conclude that the latter's ideas lacked originality.

Galula's remedy to Mao's self-proclaimed "irreversible" method of revolution was his own.

"Mao Tse-Tung contends that the phenomena we have considered are subject to their own peculiar laws, and are predictable," Samuel Griffith wrote in the introduction to his pioneering translation of Mao's *On Guerrilla Warfare*. "If he is correct, and I believe he is, it is possible to prevent such phenomena from appearing, or, if they do, to control and eradicate them. And if historical experience teaches us anything about revolutionary guerrilla war, it is that military measures alone will not suffice."[29] Griffith stopped short of elucidating countermeasures, but marked an important point: if revolutionary warfare was indeed a methodological form of warfare, and not merely spontaneous violence and chaos, then it could be opposed methodologically too. Galula embraced this reasoning to the extent of producing a stepwise approach to his counterinsurgency theory. And as could be expected from such an attempt, which in essence mirrored Mao's pragmatic style, some criticized him for being dogmatic despite his own warnings on the matter.

Galula complements his Clausewitzian definition of an insurgency—"the pursuit of the policy of a party, within a country, by every means"—with a Maoist one: "An insurgency is a *protracted struggle*[30] conducted methodically, step by step, in order to attain specific intermediate objectives leading ultimately to the overthrow of the existing order."[31] The "slow and methodical" process, so central to Maoist doctrine, is equally central to Galula's doctrine. "There are no magic shortcuts,"[32] Mao wrote. Galula believes that the same held true for the counterinsurgent. Agreeing with Pen'g Te-huai[33] as to the cause of this, Galula writes, "The protracted nature of revolutionary war does not result from the design of either side, it is imposed on the insurgent by his initial weakness."[34]

The asymmetry between insurgent and counterinsurgent led to another underlying theme: the adaptation of yin and yang dialectics to revolutionary warfare. Samuel Griffith pointed this out in his introduction to Mao's *On Guerrilla's Warfare*: "Of opposite polarities, they represent female and male, dark and light, cold and heat, recession and aggression. Their reciprocal interaction is endless."[35] In *Problems of Strategy in China's Revolutionary War*, Mao called on his followers to oppose their superior adversary's strength not by matching it, but by applying a complementary opposite; as yin could not be met with yin, nor yang with yang. He provided examples:

Oppose protracted campaigns and a strategy of quick decision, and uphold the strategy of protracted war and campaigns of quick decision.
  Oppose fixed battle lines and positional warfare, and favour fluid battle lines and mobile warfare.
  [. . .][36]

Galula synthesizes Mao's dialectical analysis as follows:

An appraisal of the contending forces at the start of a revolutionary war
shows an overwhelming superiority in tangible assets in favour of the
counterinsurgent. . . . The situation is reversed in the field of intangibles.
The insurgent has a formidable asset—the ideological power of a cause
on which to base his action. The counterinsurgent has a heavy liability—he is responsible for maintaining order throughout the country.
The insurgent's strategy will naturally aim at converting his intangible
assets into concrete ones, the counterinsurgent's strategy at preventing
his intangible liability from dissipating his concrete assets.[37]

Galula adopted Mao's argumentation that the laws and principles applicable
to one side of a revolutionary war were not applicable to the other. Mao wrote:
". . . since revolutionary war and counterrevolutionary war both have their
special characteristics, the laws governing them also have their own special
characteristics, and those applying to one cannot be mechanically transferred
to the other."[38] By the same token, Galula felt that the counterinsurgent could
not "borrow characteristics" from the insurgent, in spite of how appealing that
could be. More than a question of ethics, which he only indirectly addresses
in *Counterinsurgency*, it was a question of practicality. He agrees with Mao
that two competing "shoals of fish" cannot survive in the "same medium."[39]
Galula's rationale for this is disarmingly clear: "Were [the counterinsurgent] to
operate as a guerrilla, he would have to have the effective support of the population guaranteed by his own political organization among the masses; if so,
then the insurgent would not have it and consequently could not exist. . . ."[40]
Such reasoning led Galula to oppose the French Psychological Action Bureau's
bid to create a rival clandestine organization in Algeria, for instance.

Galula's merit does not lie with the elaboration of these dialectic principles, but with his acceptance and integration of them into his counterinsurgency doctrine. Mao and T. E. Lawrence felt that guerrillas had to remain
"fluid" and "gas-like" to oppose the counterinsurgent's "linear" organization
and style of warfare. Galula does not challenge this. He writes, "The insurgent
is fluid because he has neither responsibility nor concrete assets; the counterinsurgent is rigid because he has both, and no amount of wailing can alter
this fact for either side. Each must accept the situation as it is and make the
best of it."[41] This is precisely what his counterinsurgency framework seeks to
do. He notes:

If the insurgent is fluid, the population is not. By concentrating his
efforts on the population, the counterinsurgent minimizes his rigidity
and makes full use of his assets. His administrative capabilities, his economic resources, his information and propaganda media, his military

superiority due to heavy weapons and large units, all of which are cumbersome and relatively useless against the elusive insurgent, recover their full value when applied to the task of obtaining the support of the static population. What does it matter if the counterinsurgent is unable on the whole to run as fast as the insurgent? What counts is the fact that the insurgent cannot dislodge a better-armed detachment of counterinsurgents from a village, or cannot harass it enough to make the counterinsurgent unable to devote most of his energy to the population.[42]

This adherence to the dialectical conception of revolutionary warfare distinguishes Galula from many other thinkers in his field and underpins his doctrine's success.

"What is a political problem?" Galula asks in his discussion of potential causes for revolution in *Counterinsurgency*. "It is 'an unsolved contradiction,' according to Mao Tse-tung. If one accepts this definition, then a political cause is the championing of one side of the contradiction."[43] The cause need neither be real, nor highly meritorious according to Galula. It is but a leveraging tool for a contending political party to rise to power. But in principle, the chosen cause should be sound, polarizing, and most importantly, resilient to the counterinsurgent's ability to address it, or to adopt it himself. Mao acknowledged that the Communist Party's early decision to abandon the path of the workers' revolution—more applicable to industrialized nations in Marxist thought—in favor of a peasant revolution, was what had saved the Communists in extremis. Galula saw political opportunism in such instances.[44] And so, when interpreting Galula's definition of insurgency as "the pursuit of the policy of a party, within a country, by every means," it follows that the only immutable "policy of a party" is perhaps that of seizing power. This has important implications when trying to eliminate "the root cause" of an insurgency, as any cause or subset of causes may change during a campaign. The Taliban's shifting stance on narcotics trafficking illustrates this point rather well. Prior to the U.S. invasion of Afghanistan, the Taliban had resolved to eradicate the opium trade. After their ouster, the Taliban resolved to condone it in order to generate income and to rally poppy farmers to their side. Another illustration resides in the fact that the Taliban and their affiliates have gradually shifted their principal cause from one of upholding a puritanic ideology, to a simpler and more appealing one of "ousting the foreign occupier."

"To deprive the insurgent of a good cause amounts to solving the counterinsurgent's basic problems," Galula writes. "If this is possible, well and good, but we know now that a good cause for the insurgent is one that his opponent cannot adopt without losing his power in the process. And there are problems that, although providing a good cause to an insurgent, are not susceptible

to solution." To this he adds, revealing his position on the relative importance of cause and ideology, and his predilection for "minds" over "hearts":
"Alleviating the weakness in the counterinsurgent's rule seems more promising. Adapting the judicial system to the threat, strengthening the bureaucracy, reinforcing the police and the armed forces may discourage insurgency
attempts, if the counterinsurgent leadership is resolute and vigilant."[45] Galula
considered to his regret that this had been why the Chinese Communists were
not at risk of being toppled by a counterrevolution, even during the tumultuous periods of the regime's early years.

Galula argues that the value drawn from a particular cause by an insurgency depends on how deeply it could polarize the population in its favor.
"The first task of the insurgent," he writes, "is to make [the cause] acute by
'raising the political consciousness of the people.'"[46] Mao referred to this
imperative as "creating a United Front." The minority actively supporting the
cause would be employed to sway the neutral or apathetic majority, and suppress the active minority in opposition. Galula saw in this "the basic tenet of
the exercise of political power," and would base his Second Law of counterinsurgency—"Support is gained through an active minority"[47]—on it. This
exercise of control-through-segmentation, fundamental to Galula's doctrine
(especially to the latter steps of his process), was evidently inspired by the
Chinese revolutionaries. Mao's deputy, Liu Shaoqi, gave the example of how
this concept translated into practice in a 1940 doctrinal-manifesto intended
for the Red Army: "You must carry out extensive front work so as to win
over the middle forces . . . differentiating them from the collaborators and
anti-communist diehards. You must . . . keep your attacks against the collaborators within bounds, as not to encroach on the interests of middle-of-the-
roaders and arouse their fear."[48]

To Mao and, subsequently to Galula, the population represented the
objective of revolutionary war. It also symbolized the ground insurgent
and counterinsurgent fought to seize. "Revolutionary war is political war,"[49]
Galula writes in the first pages of Counterinsurgency, revealing the elemental
Maoist influence. He derived from this his First Law of counterinsurgency:
"The support of the population is as necessary for the counterinsurgent as it is
for the insurgent."[50] Galula reasons that, "In conventional warfare, strength is
assessed according to military or other tangible criteria, such as the number
of divisions, the position they hold, the industrial resources, etc. In revolutionary warfare, strength must be assessed by the extent of support from the
population as measured in terms of political organization at the grass roots."[51]
Agreeing with Mao, he adds, "And so intricate is the interplay between the
political and military actions that they cannot be tidily separated. . . . "[52]

Galula had thus touched upon a thorn in the side of depoliticized Western armies in the postcolonial era. Griffith, another student of Mao, complemented this view with brilliant insight:

A revolutionary war is never confined within the bounds of military action. Because its purpose is to destroy an existing society and its institutions and replace them with a completely new state structure, any revolutionary war is a unity of which its constituent parts, in varying importance, are military, political, economic, social, and psychological. For this reason, it is endowed with a dynamic quality and a dimension in depth that orthodox wars, whatever their scales, lack.[53]

Mao wrote in *On Guerrilla Warfare*: "There are some militarists who say: 'We are not interested in politics but only in the profession of arms.' It is vital that these simple-minded militarists be made to realize the relationship that exists between politics and military affairs . . . it is impossible to isolate one from the other."[54] Consequently, Galula believed that officers in the counterinsurgent camp should be assigned roles according to their ability to grasp the politico-military, or civil-military, interplay. He chastised those who were solely interested by the mechanics of war, when involved in conflicts whose outcomes relied on anything but.

Galula remained pragmatic, however. Military force was indispensable to political work in the context of insurrectionary war. The most potent cause and ideology still required the application of force to rally the majority. He draws his Third Law of counterinsurgency from this—"Support from the population is conditional."[55] The latter is his most significant and original in my view. It is worth noting that Galula drew this law not from Maoist texts, but from the field. Galula had been able to reach this conclusion, while others had not, precisely because of his privileged witnessing of those elements that were not committed to paper by the revolutionaries. Communist ideology on its own had not rallied the masses. Fear and terror, as political instruments, had been required to rally them. (The Red Army itself was notorious for self-purging to instil fear, thus catalyzing the indoctrination of its own fighters.) Galula was confirmed in his impression in Algeria where he obtained the collaboration of the villagers only after the shadow rebel organization in the area had been successfully eliminated.

The Maoist prescription for insurgents to embed themselves within the population certainly influenced Galula to argue the merits of counterinsurgent troops doing the same. Protecting the population, the conditionality for support, could only be achieved through control; and control could only be achieved by living among the population. In this spirit, Hsiao K'e,[56] the author of *On Plain Guerrilla Warfare* Galula had read in Hanrahan's compilation, disavowed the supremacy of difficultly accessible terrain (mountains, jungles, etc.) as a medium of fighting for guerrillas: ". . . it is definitely untrue that guerrilla warfare cannot be carried on in the [inhabited] plains . . . Comrade Chou En-lai has compared guerrilla warfare in its relationship with the total-masses, as that between the fish and the water . . .

similarly, only in a place where there is a mass-people's movement can guer-rilla warfare be produced."[57]

Conditioning a population toward obedience, an admittedly somber pro-posal, was another notion Galula gleaned from the Chinese Revolutionaries. The notion would be recuperated by the Viet Minh, and even by the French Psychological Action Bureau later in Algeria. People could also be conditioned for obedience through the imposition of small and seemingly benign tasks and restrictions in their daily lives, as could be common in organized religion (which revolutionary communism unarguably took the form of in practice).[58]

Communist doctrine also heavily emphasized the need to conduct propa-ganda and "political work." In doing so, it promoted the creation of civic com-mittees to raise political awareness. In practice, these often served to instil fear and foster mutual suspicion to breed zeal, and weave a tight mesh around all aspects of people's lives. What mattered too, finally, was to try to "wet" the population by forcing its involvement in the struggle. Galula adhered to all of this, writing: "The guerrilla operations will be planned primarily not so much against the counterinsurgent as in order to organize the population. An ambush against a counterinsurgent patrol may be a military success, but if it does not bring the support of the village or implicate its population against the counterinsurgent, it is not a victory because it does not lead to expan-sion."[59] He applies the same reasoning to the counterinsurgent camp: "The strategic problem of the counterinsurgent may now be defined as follows: To find the favourable minority, to organize it in order to mobilize the popula-tion against the insurgent minority. Every operation, whether in the military field or in the political, social, economic, and psychological fields, must be geared to that end."[60]

On the broad issue of political work and propaganda, Chu Te writes in his 1938 essay *On Guerrilla Warfare*, "Guerrillas must never forget that primi-tive weapons alone, without political work, will never suffice to gain victory over a stronger enemy. Every guerrilla fighter must engage in political work, becoming an armed agitator and organizer in the war of resistance."[61] And for this, Mao outlined a trinity of propaganda: "There are three additional mat-ters that must be considered under the broad question of political activities. These are political activities, first, as applied to the troops; second, as applied to the people; and, third, as applied to the enemy. The fundamental problems are: first, spiritual unification of officers and men within the army; second, spiritual unification of the army and the people; and, last, destruction of the unity of the enemy."[62] Indeed, in his keystone chapter of *Counterinsurgency* dedicated to operations,[63] Galula applies this trinity to each of the eight steps of his framework. He also stresses the importance of devolving propaganda (what would be called information or psychological operations today) and intelligence collection to the lowest levels. A set of instructions Galula had written for his company in Algeria, in October 1957, would speak to this too (see Appendix A). He concluded those instructions with "two broad goals," and "nine rules" for soldiers to follow; undoubtedly inspired, in form, if not as much in content, by Mao's famous "Three Rules and Eight Remarks" that could be found in *On Guerrilla Warfare*.[64]

Finally, Galula's Fourth Law of counterinsurgency, "Intensity of efforts and vastness of means," also finds some parentage in Mao. Galula writes, "Operations needed to relieve the population from the insurgent's threat, and to convince it that the counterinsurgent will ultimately win are necessarily of an intensive nature and of long duration."[65] Mao had recognized that for guerrilla operations to be successful, they could not be sustained across an entire territory, without risking dilution. In turn, Galula preached for the application of effort in a successive fashion, area by area as well as for the fielding doctrine through the notion that "the first area is a test area,"[66] underscoring the importance of continuous learning and adaptation in irregular warfare.

8

THE BACHELOR'S CHAMPAGNE

Too often there are those who only see arms as the basic factor of warfare.

—Chu Teh[1]

The counterinsurgent reaches a position of strength when his power is embodied in a political organization issuing from, and firmly supported by, the population.

—David Galula[2]

IN SEPTEMBER OF 1948, Galula's first three-year assignment in China was coming to an end. He bid farewell to Peking, and left for Nanking to spend the final two months of his assignment with Guillermaz. In Peking, he also bid farewell to his friend Seymour Topping, to whom he owed a case of champagne for having "left the estate of bachelorhood."[3] Galula's turn to do the same would come very soon.

David met Ruth Morgan for the first time at the inaugural party of the Egyptian Mission to China.

"There were only three Egyptian diplomats at the embassy," Ruth introduced one of her favorite memories. "The rumour running in Nanking was that King Farouq had established the Mission only to get its incumbent ambassador, Fouad Sadek, as far away from Egypt as possible. Sadek had romanced a powerful man's wife at court . . . ," she paused and grinned, "he was admittedly a very good looking man. It wasn't long until another rumour spread, probably true mind you, that he was having an affair with the French Air Attaché's wife!"

Ruth had been invited to the party along with other unmarried staffers from the American embassy. "I was sitting at a table with friends when David arrived," she recalled. "I saw him walk in accompanied by the Egyptian diplomat Mr. Morghan." The latter had met the tall, twenty-six year-old brunette foreign service secretary before. "He was very fond of me. He was always happy to remind me that we shared the same last name . . . phonetically, at least." The short, dark-skinned Egyptian promptly introduced the French bachelor who had just befriended him. "David sat next to me, and we talked well into the evening."

Galula proposed the following month.

Engaged, the couple was forced to wait nearly a year before obtaining permission to marry. "The French Army," Ruth explained, "since Napoleonic times, had maintained stiff regulations with regards to its officers marrying foreign women. Official permission had to be granted. I was asked to supply character references. I gathered 15 of these in my favor! I included the U.S. ambassador, senior military officers, and even the FBI agents who were attached to us in Nanking."

"Guillermaz, whose opinion David valued so much, thought that the whole affair had been much too precipitated." Ruth had met Guillermaz before in Nanking's social gatherings. "He was not opposed to me, quite on the contrary. It's just that he felt that a month wasn't enough to really know for sure. He had, after all, been very hurt by his marriage to a woman who turned out to be so different than him."

"Did David heed his advice?"

"Oh no. . . . Not for this," she gently scoffed, smiling.

Ruth was already worldly despite her young age. She had been serving with the U.S. Department of State since her graduation from college in Minnesota, during the War. China was her second assignment after a three-year posting to Ecuador. Open-minded, socially graceful, and very cultured, her nationality was another facet that made her ever so appealing to David, who was infatuated with everything that was American.

"David and I loved music," Ruth offered. "Much to his regret, he did not play any instruments. Playing the piano, as his sisters did, had been considered unmanly. This was too bad, because he had such a good ear! He whistled Bach, his favourite composer, and Mozart, to perfection. I, on the other hand, loved the opera, more so than he did. He thought it was so sweet that I cried every time we went to the opera."

NANKIN—SHANGHAI—TOKYO—HONOLULU—SAN FRAN-CISCO—LOS ANGELES—SAINT LOUIS—CHICAGO—WASHING-TON—NEW YORK—CHERBOURG—PARIS.[4]

Ruth Morgan and Jacques Guillermaz in front of the latter's residence in Nanking. Guillermaz became Galula's lifelong mentor and friend.

Guillermaz signed a travel order with the itinerary on November 17, 1948, authorizing Galula to return to France by way of the United States, which he had never seen.

"I had to submit my resignation at the embassy in order to travel with my fiancé," Ruth remembered, pursing her lips with guilt after sixty years. "I disappointed a lot of people by doing that of course. I received numerous calls, some from the United States. Everybody tried to change my mind. But I wouldn't. I was engaged to Nanking's most eligible bachelor!"

The couple traveled by airplane, train, bus, and ocean liner. "We flew during Thanksgiving," Ruth began on an anecdote, "and with the time zone changes, this meant that we would sit down for not one, but two Thanksgiving dinners ... one in Guam, a refuelling stop, and another in Hawaii.... David of course, had never tasted American cooking yet. It was much too bland for him! He just sat through these dinners, feeling miserable from the flights and miserable because the food was so unpalatable to him."

In Tokyo, the couple spent a few days touring the resuscitated capital of a recent enemy. In Honolulu, they indulged in an out-of-order honeymoon at the beautiful Royal Hawaiian Hotel on Waikiki beach. In San Francisco, they strolled through the bustling wharfs before taking a train bound for Los Angeles. In Hollywood, they visited a movie set where Bob Hope happened to be filming that day, much to David's delight. Leaving Los Angeles, they would stop by the Grand Canyon on their way to Saint Louis, where a first family visit was scheduled. Laure, or "Lolette," David's eldest sister, married an American G.I. stationed in Casablanca during the War. They bought a small house together on the outskirts of Saint Louis. "Lolette became like a grandmother to our son in later years," Ruth said.

Saint Louis was followed by a trip to Chicago. Satisfied with their sightseeing, they headed east toward Washington, D.C. Ruth could barely contain her excitement as she led her fiancé to her parents' home in Falls Church where they would spend Christmas and New Year's.

"My mother, I guess, was disappointed by the prospect of me having to live abroad for the rest of my life," Ruth reflected, ". . . and that is what David represented for her. My father's reaction was completely different."

Ruth had been very close to her father. "I was his first child, and we were very much alike. We shared a profound passion for travel." Fred Jenison Morgan had served as a doughboy with the U.S. Army in Europe during the War. He relished every moment he had spent in France and Belgium after VE Day. "My father was overjoyed. He doted on David from the moment he met him, until the moment we left. He dreamt of returning to visit us in France one day. To my greatest regret, he passed away before he could do so."

"I remember, years later, crying for days when David delivered the news of my father's death. He was of no use in such circumstances. He told me to take a hot shower, and gave me a copy of Einstein's Theory of Relativity to read. He thought that that would calm me down," Ruth shook her head, still in disbelief at her late husband's Saint-Cyrian treatment of death and grievance.

Ruth's perception of her father's life would deeply influence her relationship with her husband. Her father studied civil engineering after the War. "His dream of a life of travel and adventure nearly came true when he was offered work on the Pan-American Highway project. He would have loved it . . . living in Central and South America for a few years." But Ruth's mother had refused. "My father submitted to that. I know that he was miserable every day of his life because of my mother's constant refusal to allow him to travel." Ruth felt that her father's life had been shortened by these sorrows. "I swore to myself that I would never interfere in my husband's career." She kept true to her promise.

David and Ruth set sail for France from Manhattan on board the *de Grace*. They disembarked at Cherbourg, and headed for Paris by train. Ruth discovered a metropolis where utilities were still rationed four years after the War had ended. Her husband inquired about the status of their request for permission to marry.

"There was nothing to be done," Ruth recalled. "We were met by a haughty administrator who asked my husband if there was any '*pressing* reason' why the process should be expedited. David turned to me and said in English 'now we'll know to stuff a pillow under your dress the next time we come here!'"

Galula decided that they would visit Morocco with what remained of his leave allowance. The couple traveled south, to Marseilles, and boarded a ship bound for a familiar Tangiers. "There was so much family to visit!" Ruth exclaimed.

She anticipated my next question.

"His family was split into two camps," she said, "one side accepted me and was very kind, and the other . . . well, not as much."

Hélène, David's sister, and Ruth's most fervent objector, thought that she had already found the perfect match for her brother: the pretty Jewish daughter of her well-to-do employer. "Miss Perez and I got along better than Hélène and I would!"

"What of his mother?" I asked.

"She was always very sweet to me and certainly very civil," Ruth answered, adding with an earnest smile: ". . . and I made sure to acknowledge the significance of her lineage. Our interaction was limited by language, of course, as I only learned French later."

"I don't think she liked the fact that I was American," Ruth added after a pause. This surprised me, because North African Jewry during and after the War were generally head-over-heels for Americans. "I *know* that she hated the fact that I smoked. It was considered vulgar for a woman to smoke. She also thought that American women led their husbands by the nose! And that simply would not have done for her dear boy!" We both laughed.

"How did this affect David's perception of women?" I prodded the issue.

"There were some women which he thought to be intellectually on par if not superior to men. Nevertheless, his attitude was that women should be sheltered and cared for, and not bothered with issues such as military affairs that they were unlikely to grasp, or simply had no need of knowing."

Galula seldom consulted his wife on important decisions. Years later, when he would volunteer for service to Algeria despite his promise to the contrary, his behavior had been consistent. "I begged him to renounce to the whole affair of going over there," his wife reminisced. "I told him that I just couldn't bear to see him leave. But he just said 'yes, yes dear', and then went and did it. That was his way."

Ruth felt that her husband's reluctance to speak about his work was as much due to his attitude toward women as it was to issues of confidentiality. "Thankfully, my time in the Foreign Service and State Department had conditioned me to such things. The principle of 'need-to-know' was engrained in me." I asked Ruth if this had bothered her. She answered with uttermost honesty: "My husband *had* to be intellectually superior to me. That's how I wanted it. He was, as I think you know by now, a very brilliant man."

Returning to work after nearly six months of leave, Galula reported for the first time in his career to National Defense Headquarters in Paris. He was assigned to the G2's *Service des missions à l'étranger.*[5] There, he did not last. He was eager to return abroad, away from the environment in which he was but a very small cog in an otherwise very large and at times perhaps unfriendly machine. He applied for a military observer position with the United Nations in Greece with Guillermaz's endorsement. His candidacy was accepted. He left for the Balkans in May 1949.

Ruth returned to stay with her parents in the United States. "As luck would have it, we were granted permission to get married the following month, I received a letter from David stating that the situation in Greece would soon be stable enough for me to join him. I left on a ship that July."

Ruth found a place to stay at the American Anatolia College in Thessaloniki. She found enough work to stave off boredom, while her husband partook in monitoring operations. "The director of the College, Mr. Sheppard was very kind to us." A Congregationalist like Ruth, and an ordained minister, Mr. Sheppard would soon volunteer to officiate their wedding that was set for the 21st of August, 1949. The date coincided with Ruth's birthday and with her parents' wedding anniversary. But the scheduling of a major military offensive against the communists that week forced Galula to change the date to the week before. The reception took place on the 14th, on the college's manicured grounds, attended by the college's staff and many of Galula's peers from the UN mission.

Galula left as planned to monitor the offensive against communist forces in the Mount Grammos sector of the Greco-Albanian border.[6] Upon his return, he borrowed a trusty American Jeep to drive Ruth on a honeymoon excursion from Salonika to Kavalla that took them from the shores of the Aegean Sea, up to and across snow-covered mountain passes. Nostalgia of past adventures was at play.

Ruth was in for a surprise when they came upon their first river. "My new husband was fascinated with big rivers ever since the War. He stopped the vehicle on the bank, and stepped out. He looked at me, and explained that he and Coco Raymond had started a tradition of marking every new river they came across." Smiling half apologetically, Galula walked down to the edge, and peed into the water. "He did so without a care in the world! There were some poor old women some distance down the stream washing clothing . . . my God was it ever embarrassing!"

I obtained a similar testimonial from Ruth's brother-in-law, Jere Rowland. A retired architect living in New England, he held Galula in the highest esteem. He imitated Galula's French accent as he told me about a time when his late wife had driven her brother-in-law to Manhattan. "David was in the passenger seat, and busy looking at the map as military men do. My wife and him were approaching the Manhattan Bridge when David exclaimed: '*Stop ze car!*'

'What? Why?!'

'*I need to pee!*'

'I can't stop here on the middle of a New York City bridge!'

'*Yes, yes, it is ze afternoon, zere is no traffic!*'

She stopped the car. David stepped out and quickly relieved himself over the side, into the river below. When he got back into the car, he smiled and said proudly: 'Zat is two rivers in one! Ze Hudson and ze East River!'"

Rowland informed me that Galula had exercised his rite of passage in the Nile River too, and even in the Yellow River while being held in captivity by the communists. "The house in which he was being detained was located on the river's shore. One evening, he walked to the edge of the water and started to relieve himself until a perplexed Chinese guard on the rooftop spotted him and asked him to go back inside." Whether some of Albert Galula's *raconteur* talents passed down to his son were at play here or not is the reader's guess.

9

U.N.S.C.O.B.

There is no unbreachable gap between a common man and a soldier as he can be a soldier in a minute if he wishes to do so. It does not matter whether or not you are a common man, as your ability to engage in a battle of words is even an asset. . . . Guerrilla warfare is a military college and a few trials on the battlefield would transform you into a capable general.

—*Mao Tse-Tung*[1]

I was sent to Greece, where I expected to see another communist insurgency snowballing. I saw instead its defeat, a revealing experience.

—*David Galula*[2]

DAVID GALULA ARRIVED in Greece in May 1949 with much simpler aspirations than to undertake a comparative study of insurgencies. His motivation to deploy under the United Nations banner to a civil war–torn country was candidly explained to me by his widow: "Counterinsurgency warfare as a subject on its own had yet to become an interest of his. He had devoted himself to studying Chinese political and military affairs under Guillermaz, but I don't think he foresaw, at that time, writing on the broader topic of counterinsurgency."

"Then why Greece?" I asked.

"Two things were going through his mind," she replied. "Firstly, we were engaged, and he wanted to be able to provide for me. He knew that his captain's pay in France would not suffice. The UN paid its observers handsomely." Service abroad entitled one to a foreign living allowance. In China, for instance, his salary had amounted to only half of what this indemnity provided him with.[3] "Secondly, David had become accustomed to a degree of adventure that only a foreign posting could provide." His correspondence confirms that he had little patience for headquarter work in Paris.

Nonetheless, the Greek Civil War presented Galula with a case study that starkly contrasted with what he had just witnessed in China. As such, the year and a half he spent in Greece contributed significantly to his understanding of insurrectionary warfare. The comparison highlighted certain fundamentals that would find their way into his writings, not the least of which was the need for an insurgency to adopt a cause that could be suitably leveraged to polarize a population in its favor. He wrote the following in *Counterinsurgency*:

> The 1945–1950 Communist insurgency in Greece, a textbook case of everything that can go wrong in an insurgency, is an example of failure due, among other less essential reasons, to the lack of a Cause. The [communist] party, the EAM, and its army, the ELAS, grew during World War II when the entire population was resisting the Germans. Once the country was liberated, the EAM could find no valid cause. Greece had little industry and consequently no proletariat except the dockers of Piraeus and tobacco factory workers: the merchant sailors, geographically unstable, could provide no constant support. There was no crying agrarian problem to exploit.[4]

Eight percent of the Greek population of seven million had perished during World War II, and another two percent would perish during the civil war that followed.[5] What had started as an ideological rivalry between two underground resistance movements during the Nazi occupation, would culminate in a vicious internal struggle for power. The communist EAM-ELAS pitted itself against the British-backed National Republican Greek League (EDES). The ELAS renamed itself the Greek Democratic Army (GDA), while Western-backed forces were reorganized into the Greek National Army (GNA). Following a half-heartedly applied peace treaty, the communist guerrillas retreated to Greece's mountainous borders where they benefited from the support of neighboring Communist regimes such as Albania, Bulgaria, and Yugoslavia.[6] (Under Tito, however, the latter would soon turn against the Stalin-aligned Greek Communists.)[7] The Greek Civil War, far from being inconspicuous on the international scene, became a catalyst for the elaboration of the Truman Doctrine.

The twenty-eight-year-old Galula's already mature appreciation for war and geopolitics was expanded in Greece. His revulsion to communist revolutions was deepened there, too. "He saw some very horrible things over there," his widow told me. "There was one particular instance when he came across two older men walking away from a village. One of them was wounded and hobbling on makeshift crutches. He told David that communist fighters infiltrated from Bulgaria had cut off his buttock and forced him to eat it as a punishment for something he had done, or refused to do." Galula came to understand that such brutality was calculated. It had an aim. He would see in it not a simple expression of hatred as some had come to label terrorism, but a method of achieving control over a population through fear. (I asked Ruth whether her husband had exhibited signs of post-traumatic stress disorder after Greece, or after Algeria later on. "No" had been her answer. "No, and if he had, he certainly hid it very well.")

As a result of U.S. and British pressures, the United Nations Special Committee on the Balkans (UNSCOB) was created on October 21, 1947. Headquartered in Salonika, UNSCOB was assigned "conciliatory and observational" functions.[8] As Professor Amikam Nachmani wrote in his authoritative *International Intervention in the Greek Civil War*, "the main aim of the observers was to ascertain the type and scope of aid extended by the Balkan states to the Greek guerrillas."[9]

UNSCOB's mission was a complicated one. It was criticized by some nations and praised by others, naturally, depending on where a nation stood ideologically, and where its interests lay in reference to the Iron Curtain. Volunteered officers from both democratic and communist nations were mixed into observer teams in order to give as much of an appearance of impartiality as possible. France strived to remain particularly impartial given the precariousness of her position vis-a-vis the Soviet Union in those years, and the considerable segment of her electorate that voted communist at home.

A solid understanding of political sensitivities was required of all observers. Reports that concluded too strongly against one side or the other were generally shunned for being inflammatory. Galula's very analytical style of reporting was more likely than not to raise a few eyebrows. Nevertheless, the head of the French delegation, Lieutenant-Colonel Vernier, commented that Galula "displayed initiative and judgement in many circumstances, notably during a particularly delicate contact with Bulgarian border authorities." And that moreover, during operations, Galula had demonstrated "initiative, objectivity, intelligence, and *sang froid*."[10]

In addition to the criticism UNSCOB attracted, there was also ridicule. The observers' need to display absolute impartiality led many of the locals to complain about their ineffectiveness. According to Nachmani, a funny story ran "about a mule that had strayed over the Albanian border. When the Albanian border guards asked for its return, the Greek guard firmly replied that this was impossible as the mule had violated the territorial integrity of Greece and was at present being interrogated by UNSCOB[!]"[11]

Compounding the political and diplomatic risks associated to the mission were physical hardships. "Beyond the issue of impartiality," Nachmani wrote, "the qualifications demanded of the observers were knowledge of Greek, physical fitness, and a tough character. They had to be willing to cover long distances in all weather by jeep, mule, or on foot. . . . Those subsequently chosen were all majors and lieutenant-colonels, veterans of World War II."[12] With the exception of speaking Greek, Galula was well suited for the job. His work in China had prepared him perfectly for it. Vernier noted how Galula was particularly appreciated by his Chinese, American, and British colleagues for his ability to interpret for them.[13] Galula's ability to be charming with his Chinese communist colleagues, for whom he held no personal ill feelings, very certainly played in his favor.

An official from the U.S. Department of State offered the following testimonial of the dangers faced by the observers:

> . . . Every time they leave Ioannina they immediately are in danger of mines planted in the roads by the guerrillas or of being shot at or captured by the guerrillas. . . . While the observers are in the field they have to carry their own food and all other equipment and usually sleep in some primitive stone hut in a little village with only such comforts as they can carry with them. I should add that the men I met seemed of the highest type and not only had no complaint to make but appeared to be enjoying their dangerous job.[14]

So grave was the danger posed by guerrilla-laid mines to the observers' safety that reconnaissance flights over border areas replaced travel by land. That danger was soon replaced by another. UNSCOB's "fleet" of two-seater airplanes (of which there were only three available, none equipped with radios) began to attract small-arms fire from the guerrillas. The cavalier observers claimed that this, if nothing else, helped them to identify the positions of belligerents on the ground. Nevertheless, an UNSCOB pilot was killed in February of 1949.[15] A few months later, on July 6, 1949, Galula came close to suffering the same fate. "When the plane landed," Ruth related, "they found a dozen bullet holes in one of the wings, and a bullet lodged right under David's seat!"

The Greek guerrillas' tactics were in some respects not dissimilar from those of contemporary insurgents. The use of mines and improvised explosive devices, for instance, was widespread.[16] Nachmani noted how, "Some villages were emptied of their inhabitants to prevent them from providing information about the guerrillas' strength and movements. In others, the villagers were paid to plant mines for the guerrillas (they then reported the discovery of the mines to the GNA and claimed a reward). All in all, the government's inability to protect the villagers was clearly demonstrated, thereby discrediting its authority."[17]

Henry Grady, the U.S. Ambassador to Greece, objected to blindly increasing the size and means of the GNA:

> The key to success according to [this] thinking is always more: more men, more money and more equipment. . . . This armed force . . . has been unable to make appreciable progress . . . against a bandit organization of some 25,000 men fed with what they could steal or buy locally, clothed in remnants, armed with old weapons . . . transported on their own, or their donkey's legs, and trained by their own leaders. . . . [The bandits] are not backed by a single airplane, heavy gun, or naval vessel. In view of fact we have [already] increased the size and equipment of Greek armed forces, during which time strength of bandit forces has remained proportionally constant to that of the Greek army, and as we do not achieve greater security by these actions, it seems to me that we are not justified now in [applying] the old method of increasing again the size and equipment of armed forces.[18]

Galula fielded similar objections to conventionally minded thinking. It was not only a question of numbers, and certainly not one of material means. More than anything, in Galula's opinion, the success of a counterinsurgency effort depended on the technique employed and on the top-level determination to succeed.

In Greece, Galula noted how the insurgency had self-defeated by foregoing key fundamentals of irregular warfare. The insurgency had failed to grow roots in the population. Worse yet, its guerrilla fighters had morphed prematurely into a regular army, allowing for their tidy destruction on the battlefield.[19] An insufficiently polarizing cause and the loss of external support had dealt the fatal blow. Galula concluded in *Counterinsurgency*: ". . . the Communist insurgents were able to wage commando-type operations but not true guerrilla warfare, in fact, their infiltrated units had to hide from the population when they could not cow it. . . ."[20]

The Greek insurgency's bid to follow the orthodox pattern of revolution had failed.

10

THE STRATEGIC CAPTAIN

And that is why it is so important to understand that guerrilla warfare is nothing but a tactical appendage of a far vaster political contest and that, no matter how expertly it is fought by competent and dedicated professionals, it cannot possibly make up for the absence of political rationale. A dead Special Forces sergeant is not spontaneously replaced by his own social environment. A dead revolutionary usually is.

—Bernard Fall[1]

Our plans essentially differ on the following: your methods rely on shock and speed, whereas I lean towards continuous action that is systematic, meticulous, and therefore yes, slower and less spectacular. You pick your activist candidates (from the local population) on criteria which I must admit, seem to me obscure, whereas I allow my candidates to emerge by themselves.

—David Galula[2]

MY RESEARCH OF DAVID GALULA'S Hong Kong assignment was marked by regret in April of 2010. Robert Morot, Galula's chief warrant officer and close friend throughout the six years they had spent together in the Crown Colony, had just passed away. I had called his home to ask his endearing wife whether her husband was predisposed to grant me the phone interview we had recently set ourselves on doing. "I am afraid that that will no longer be possible," she replied with a pained voice. "You are not aware then . . . my husband past away last week." I expressed my sincerest condolences. I hung up the phone and called Ruth Galula. She had been friends with the couple for over fifty years. "How could it be?" She asked. We had both heard Morot's voice, frail but confident, two months prior, eagerly agreeing to contribute to this work. I was sad for Morot's family and, naturally, sad for the memories that had been lost.

I intensified my search for other sources of information. After some success, it became clear to me that Hong Kong had been a highlight in Galula's life. He shined in military, diplomatic, and press circles. He seized every opportunity afforded by his attaché role to influence decision-makers in Paris and in Indochina. Jere Rowland, Ruth's brother-in-law, summed up the period over the phone: "Ruth and David lived at the peak in Hong Kong, enjoying the lives that diplomats had in the 1950s. David took on very large responsibilities, and was held in very high esteem." My research proved that to be entirely true.

Ruth had not been surprised when, in the summer of 1950, her husband had expressed his desire to terminate his UNSCOB assignment ahead of schedule. "He felt that there was little remaining for him to observe, let alone do, once the insurgency subsided," she told me. It was difficult to renounce to United Nations pay and the increasingly comfortable living in Salonika, but the boredom soon exceeded Galula's threshold. "David never had the patience to sit around and do nothing. When the fighting stopped, he just had to leave. His fellow observers remained there happily collecting large sums of money with no risk involved." The French Army had no trouble in finding a replacement for Galula under such circumstances.

The couple returned to Paris in September of 1950. They found temporary lodging with Coco Raymond, while they shopped for an apartment they could finally afford. Galula was granted a month of leave by the commander of the 1st Colonial Infantry Regiment, headquartered at Versailles, to which he had just been nominally assigned.[3] The following month, he was reassigned to the *Deuxième Bureau* (G2) of the *État-Major Particulier de l'Infanterie Coloniale* in Paris. He immersed himself once more in intelligence work, this time under the direction of Colonel Petit.[4] The latter was appreciative of Galula, recognizing "*une intelligence vive et originale*," but also that the young officer would have to acquire "*une certaine pondération*."[5] Galula lasted six months before caving to an offer he could not refuse: an invitation from Jacques Guillermaz to return to the Far East.

Guillermaz had been ordered to remain in China, nearly alone, after the triumph of Mao in 1949. France had made a show of severing diplomatic ties with the communist regime by recalling its ambassador, but had dampened the blow by maintaining its principal military attaché there.[6] Louis Léouzon, who had previously been based in Shanghai, was ordered to set up an attaché post in Hong Kong, where countless refugees fleeing the mainland and much of Nanking's displaced diplomatic and press corps had resettled.

Guillermaz had been one of the very few Western observers to remain on the mainland on the morrow of the communist victory. He would later write in his memoirs, "I witnessed firsthand a rare phenomenon: authorities progressively taking control of a large city's population, and the transition from an often sad but free world, to that of a universe dominated by a totally excluding ideology, and run by pitiless organizations."[7] Guillermaz escaped the mainland after two years of living in hellish surroundings. He left behind a population brutalized by draconian measures aimed at the "suppression of counterrevolutionaries." This dark and nearly forgotten episode of Chinese history added fuel to Galula's counterrevolutionary fervor; for what Guillermaz had witnessed then, he related to his protégé. This would be evidenced years later in Galula's satirical writings to which the next chapter is devoted.

Guillermaz arrived in Hong Kong in January of 1951 to take over from an Indochina-bound Léouzon. Guillermaz invited Galula to relieve him in June. The former wrote, "I had bartered my title of military attaché to China . . . for that of assistant military attaché to London, detached to Hong Kong." Although the transfer was a demotion in title for him, the opposite held true for Galula; for the attaché to Hong Kong essentially assumed the functions of attaché to China in absentia of diplomatic ties between France and Peking. With the remote help and council of his mentor, Galula became his government's primary source of information and analysis regarding an increasingly cloistered but dangerous Communist regime.

In Hong Kong, prior to Galula's arrival, Guillermaz had been warned to mind his steps. "Colonel Guillermaz," his British diplomatic contact had said to him, "you are no doubt aware of how delicate our relation is with the government in Peking. We expect that you will do nothing to complicate that situation any more than it already is."[8] In other words, he was to refrain from running a network of agents in Hong Kong with a view of gathering intelligence on the mainland. Such activity had put Léouzon in hot water in previous months. Ruth informed me, supported by correspondence, that Léouzon had become *persona non-grata* with the British.

However, none of the above sufficed to dissuade Galula from running agents and otherwise collecting intelligence in Hong Kong, as his personal papers testify. He coyly wrote retrospectively in *The Tiger's Whiskers*, with his distinctive brand of humor, "Some people went as far as to say that one out of two Chinese was an informer. Making due allowance for exaggeration, let us say the percentage was one out of three."[9]

Galula's ability to speak English combined with his friendly manner allowed him to develop a positive relationship with his British hosts. His sharing of the intelligence he gathered likely contributed to keeping him out of trouble. The senior British intelligence officer in Hong Kong would not only turn a blind eye to his activities throughout his posting, but would also

Shaking hands with Sir Alexander Grantham, Governor of Hong Kong. The wife of
the French consul stands in the background.

write Galula to thank him for his ". . . help during [his] term of office[!]"[10]
Galula made friends in American intelligence circles as well, such as Howard
Boorman, introduced earlier as an analyst working at the U.S. consulate.

The focus of Galula's intelligence-gathering efforts in Hong Kong was not
dissimilar to the one he had under Guillermaz, prior to Mao's victory. Galula
wrote to a friend in later years, ". . . my primary mission was to assess for our
command in Saigon and for the government in Paris the possibility and the
likelihood of a Chinese Communist intervention in Indochina. On my judgement depended in part the deployment of our forces in that theatre and their
freedom of action."[11]

The distance between London and the Crown Colony provided Galula with
nearly complete autonomy. His relation with the French Attaché-General to
the United Kingdom was only administrative, since Galula sent his reports
directly to the G2 in Indochina and Paris. He was otherwise loosely subordinated to the French consul, Mr. de la Gourrurec, and later to his replacement
Jacques Dubuzon, both of whom were seconded by Mr. Willocquet. An informal subordination link also persisted with Guillermaz, by then the attaché to
Siam, with the acknowledgment of Paris.

With the Korean War raging in the north, and the Philippine insurgency
festering in the south, Honk Kong stood at the center of a region embroiled in
conflicts spanning the full spectrum of warfare. The colony became a point
of liaison for senior Allied officers and diplomats, as well as a rest and transit
hub for Allied naval forces. "Every senior French officer serving in Indochina

came through Hong Kong," Ruth affirmed. "David and I were responsible for hosting and entertaining them. As the attaché, my husband came to know a lot of important people during those years." Indeed, Galula never missed an opportunity to share his analysis on Chinese and communist affairs. His correspondence attests to the number and seniority of officers he hosted and fostered relationships with. Ruth recalled, for instance, the fateful visit of the commander-in-chief of French forces in Indochina: "General Salan, exhausted by the war, fell asleep in our living room after a lengthy discussion he had had with David over lunch."

"There is no place like Hong Kong for sheer beauty," Galula wrote. "One can live there for years without tiring of the landscape."[12] Demographics were exploding in the early 1950s. Industrialists, merchants, bankers, the poor and the rich fled the mainland in droves to the Crown Colony, while the Kuomintang and its diehard supporters took refuge in Formosa (present-day Taiwan). Squatter towns appeared wherever there was room, ushering in the implementation of multi-story building standards by the British, and fathering today's remarkable skyline.

"The summer here is less hot than what it was in Nanking, you have the beaches, and the landlord will be able to install air-conditioning in one or two of your rooms ... ,"[13] an outbound Guillermaz wrote to Galula from Hong Kong. The Galula couple moved into Guillermaz's modern apartment afforded by an indispensable foreign living allowance. "We lived on one of the lower floors of the Djibato Building on Peak Road," Ruth told me. "The building was owned by a French bank whose executives lived on the upper floors." Ruth benefited from the help of three house servants: a cook, a "boy," and an "amah." These had all previously worked for Guillermaz, who advised Galula that they were ". . . from the North, and so do not have any bad accent." They remembered David from previous years, when he had visited their former French employers in Nanking. "The 'boy' Wang and the cook 'Huang' speak French and are conversant in English. They are stalwart people," Guillermaz added, "and as far as I know very honest."[14]

"Those three were so devoted to David that they refused to take any days off despite our strongest insistence," Ruth recalled, adding with a touch of laughter: "Even on the Chinese New Year, they would not go home until David, the '*Monsieur*,' had had his breakfast!"

In Hong Kong, one's social life was as demanding, if not as important, as one's professional life. The Western military and diplomatic communities threw countless receptions and dinner parties to compensate for what Galula considered to be an otherwise entertainment-less spot. In *The Tiger's Whiskers*, Galula colorfully described the mood as follows: "Hong Kong was as dead as a doornail. ... [It] had none of the attractions of Shanghai before Mao

Reading in the living room
of the Djibato apartment.
Galula remained an avid reader
throughout his life.

Tse-tung, of post-Tojo Tokyo or even of Murmansk after de-Stalinization.
There were a few night clubs, but they were models of dullness. At midnight
sharp the band struck up 'God Save the Queen' and 'Goodnight, Ladies'."
This, he added with humor, was owed to the "famous Anglo-Saxon puritan
spirit," and to the fact that "Her Majesty's government . . . did not relish being
accused by the . . . communists of favouring debauchery among the working
class in order to cater to vices of the bourgeois imperialists. . . ."[15]

The Galulas were socialites indeed. David was an outstanding networker,
completely uninhibited by his relatively low rank, and completely self-
assured in his intellectual prowess. Real intelligence, probably as much as
amusing gossip, was shared between Western attachés. "They met over dinner with their wives once a week," Ruth told me. "The gatherings were held
on a rotational basis, with each attaché couple hosting the others in turn.
After dinner, the men would retire to the living room and share information
and opinions on the latest issues." Galula, though outranked by his counterparts, was singled out as being particularly astute and well informed. A
1952 performance evaluation of him by the chief-of-staff of the intelligence
branch in Paris reads: "[He] is very hard working, active, and always seeking
to know more; he does not hesitate to step out of the closed circle of Western
observers in Hong Kong."[16] His ability to speak Mandarin and his previous
intelligence-gathering experiences in Peking afforded him a definitive edge
in recruiting sources, particularly among deserters and refugees who still
had ties to the mainland.

Major Fielding "Doc" Greaves and his wife, Jean, were friends of the Galulas
in Hong Kong. Greaves, a U.S. Army intelligence officer, was number two on
the American attaché team. "Doc is an unassuming gentleman from an old
Virginia family," Ruth had told me before we phoned him. "His ancestor had
married Betty Washington, and had built the Kenmore Plantation with her.
Doc was the workhorse at the U.S. embassy. He was their brightest one."

"I recognized in David an intellectually markedly superior individual," Greaves stated in our first email exchange. "He was exceptionally bright, highly intelligent, able to quickly grasp the essentials of any situation, as well as being naturally good humoured, socially charming, and a delightful friend. . . . We naturally often discussed what was going on in Hong Kong's northern neighbour, that 'elephant in the living room of the Far East,' and we were both active in interviewing foreign missionaries and Chinese and foreign businessmen being forced out of, or fleeing from China."

"David did not yield easily to obstacles," Greaves ensued with a personal anecdote, "as we learned one evening when Jean and I were giving a small cocktail party in our apartment on the south side of the island at Repulse Bay. Our timing was bad. A typhoon hit Hong Kong late that afternoon. It blew down a tree across the main road between Victoria and our apartment. Somehow, David forced his small *Morris Minor* over, through, or around, the tree and arrived—he and Ruth being the only guests who made it that night. We had a great time sitting on the rug while David taught us a mind-stretching five-letter word game by candle light."

Far from being restricted to military and diplomatic circles, social life in Hong Kong included the prominent business community, the *raison d'être*, after all, of the colony. Galula was friends with the likes of wealthy French businessman de Santerre, his wife, and their pretty daughter Danielle. Philippe Simon, with whom Galula played copious amounts of golf, also belonged to this category.

Galula entertaining Danielle de Sansterre and other guests with characteristic humor during New Year's Eve at the Correspondent's Club in Hong Kong.

"The Royal Hong Kong Golf Club, for some bizarre reason, did not allow women to join without their husbands," Ruth explained how her husband, an avid tennis player, swimmer, and equestrian picked up this game, too. "When I told him I wanted to start playing with the other wives, he said: 'Hell's Bells! I will play too if I have to pay for two memberships!'" Sundays were increasingly dedicated to golf. "Simon and David played eighteen holes in the morning and eighteen in the afternoon. I think that without that distraction, David would have otherwise burned himself out." Her husband was the only commissioned officer attached to the French consulate, whereas other nations maintained teams of two or more.[17] (Galula became so infatuated with the sport that he would tell Guillermaz, prior to leaving, that his golf bag would be the last thing that he would pack.[18]) Galula also belonged to the Hong Kong Yacht Club, having bought a tiny sailboat with a British intelligence officer he befriended. "After sailing," Ruth said, "they would scout the best floating kitchens at the harbour, mingling with the refugees who operated them . . . rather purposefully I gathered."

Finally, there was also the press with whom to make friends. Galula was, as mentioned previously, highly appreciated by journalists. He felt that it was good practice to reveal what was truly happening in China, as many in the West still felt that the communists had risen to power on account that they were a popular, egalitarian, and humanistic movement. Galula felt that the international press had a key role to play in what he perceived to be a globalized Communist insurgency, which warranted a comprehensive and global response. Joe Alsop, the well-known "Matter of Fact" columnist for the *Herald Tribune,* became such a friend. Some years later, he would write of Galula in his column, "[he was] one of the few who were really informed about Communist China, David made a lot of Newspaper friends in Hongkong."[19] "Alsop admired David's intellect," Ruth had told me.

Galula also grew close to Henry Lieberman, the bureau chief for the *New York Times* in China, whose wife had been a friend of Ruth's since college. Lieberman would prove instrumental in Galula's post-military career, as shall be seen, and fateful, therefore, in the writing of *Counterinsurgency.* There was also Tillman Durdin, the famed *New York Times* correspondent, and Fred Hampson, of the Associated Press, to befriend. All would maintain a correspondence with Galula until his death.

"My husband was happy," Ruth concluded simply. "The attaché position in Hong Kong was much more interesting than what he could have had in Paris given his junior field rank."

What was initially intended to be a two-year assignment, ended up lasting six years. Ruth explained: "When David's first two-year term was up, Pierre Bourgeois was earmarked to take over the position; but he was ordered to remain in Indochina. When David's second two-year term was up, it was up to Louis Léouzon to replace him, but the British refused. He was still *persona non grata.*" Galula did not object to having his mandate renewed twice, even though it meant that his career progression would stall. His position precluded him from exercising a command, however minor, which was necessary for him to advance past the rank of captain. Guillermaz offered characteristic encouragement: "I hope that you will be promoted this year. If not, know that you have still gained the better reward, because of the interest that your work has solicited, and the moral credit that it affords you."[20]

Ruth recalled how Guillermaz had never been one to push for his subordinates' promotions. "It was a question of honor and abnegation for Guillermaz," she said. "He felt that every officer had to do his duty, and give his all, without expecting anything in return. It was up to the army to promote based on what needs it had. My husband accepted that. He always preferred to be considered for his intelligence, and not for his rank." The inconsistency between Galula's rank and responsibilities became his mark of pride. According to his wife, he would go so far as refusing a temporary promotion when it was finally offered to him in Hong Kong to place him on equal footing with his U.S. and British counterparts.

China's predilection for subversion over direct aggression to establish a regional buffer zone is what led Galula, *en finale*, to study subversive warfare, and to devise a counterinsurgency doctrine. He attributed a tremendous amount of importance to the following statement he related in the conclusion to *Counterinsurgency*: "In June 1951, Liu Shao-Chi claimed that 'the prototype of the revolution in capitalist countries is the Soviet type, the prototype of revolution in colonial and semi-colonial countries is the Chinese type.'"[21] This created a paradox in Galula's doctrine. Although he perceived a timelessness and universality to his writings, he would anchor them on a snapshot of a geopolitical era that was bound to evolve.

Galula's forced resignation to the sidelines of the Indochina War grew his desire to contribute in some cognitive way to the counterinsurgency effort being waged there. Surviving copies of the reports he submitted to his chain of command attest to his strong desire to inform and influence decision-makers well above him. "This officer answers perfectly to the intelligence needs of the National Defense Headquarters, rendering his, one of the most profitable attaché stations in the Far East,"[22] reads a telling 1952 performance evaluation of him. There is little doubt that Galula played a strategic role in Hong Kong through the analysis he provided to the French Command. The weight of his judgement seemed to have been unabated by his rank.

"[David] became an authoritative figure amongst the numerous foreign experts there: officers, diplomats, and journalists. His analyses were unconventional and bold, and were always followed with great attention,"[23] Guillermaz observed. General Bourgund, Galula's regimental commander during the liberation of France, later entrusted with the command of all French

ground forces in central Vietnam, would begin a letter to an ill-forgotten Galula stationed in Hong Kong with: "My dear comrade, you have the reputation
of being the Providence of visitors to Hong Kong whom do not wish to leave
Asia without having been made aware of the latest developments in China.
Even your hospitality and kindness has become legendary in Indochina."[24]
France's chief of staff of the army, General Guillaume,[25] would also write personally to Galula to thank him after passing through Hong Kong: "I knew in
advance that you were one of the best specialists of Chinese affairs and I was
able to appreciate in Hong Kong your profound knowledge in this complex
domain."[26] Little more proof should be required of Galula's originality, influence, and early renown in Chinese affairs.

Such acclaim inevitably earned Galula the jealousy of others at times.
Some saw arrogance in the junior officer's outspokenness and self-confidence
in dealing with higher officials. An expatriated veteran of the Free French
living in Hong Kong wrote to Guillermaz to complain about his protégé, who
had omitted to invite him at a consular party, "I do not want to make a big
deal out of this, but Galula is really starting to think too highly of himself,
and forgets too often that he is dealing with people that are older than he . . .
I have always acted as a friend towards him, but he has never reciprocated,
which only half-surprises me, for a multitude of reasons. . . ."[27] The inference
was a shady one.

True to his ways, Galula's analysis and communications with superior
headquarters continued to be unorthodoxly conclusive, against the counsel-
ing he had always received. The method paid off because he was more often
right than wrong. In September of 1952, he wrote a secret briefing note on the
communist bloc's "Peace Congress," to be held in Peking later that year. He
focused on Chinese communist subversion, concluding that China preferred
to address itself "to the peoples of the world above the heads of their governments." He highlighted similarities between the Viet Minh's methods in
Indochina and earlier Red Army methods in China.[28] In the wake of a Korean
War armistice, he predicted that China would not agree to a compromise
in Vietnam, contrarily to mainstream opinion, and to Guillermaz's mitigated position. Galula was proven right. His analysis also extended beyond
the realm of politics and military affairs. In a 1953 report, for instance, he
predicted that China would face economic difficulties because of how expedi-
tiously their agrarian reforms were being undertaken.[29] Indeed, they would
prove to be economically disastrous, leading to widespread famine.

In addition to submitting intelligence reports, Galula also drafted a
series of memoranda proposing methods to counter Maoist subversion,
pushing the envelope of his attaché mandate as he did so. His correspondence with Gene Hanrahan and others indicates that he had developed a
"thesis" on counter-subversion.[30] I found multiple references to a report
he had drafted on this theme; a report that may well have constituted his

first attempt at doctrinal writing on counterinsurgency. Unfortunately, the report has not survived in Galula's papers. In a response he received from the chief intelligence officer in Indochina, I could glean that Galula had centered his thesis on the idea of promoting a "*démocratie intérnationale unificatrice*" (unifying international democracy).[31] He proposed this as a counter-cause to communist ideology, capable of taking the wind out of the sails of Sino-Soviet subversion in the developing world. This proposal was consequent to his impression that counterrevolution was handicapped from the outset by the "reactionary" negativity associated to it. He felt that the West would only be victorious in the longer term, if it could be perceived as fighting *for* an ideal, and not merely *against* one. This notion was strikingly similar to the one that would be put forward by America's Edward Lansdale, to whom we return in a later chapter. For the moment, in 1953, Guillermaz cautioned his protégé that his proposal to sponsor a competing counter-cause in the communist camp would "encounter stiff resistance by those who have an interest in doing so,[32] in addition to mental inertias."[33] A year later, in the aftermath of Dien Bien Phu, Galula would take up the issue again with his mentor:

> I am not discouraged. There are still too many resources in the Free World remaining for us not to be able to defeat the communists on their own ground, via their own means, once we become better organized. But we have no time to waste on exhortations. What is to be done? I have a little idea, which I had started to elaborate to you in Saigon: the creation of a political, economic, social, moral, *democratic and international* weapon. Without waiting for the communists to impose on us their system, there is a revolution to be made in the world, starting with France. This will remove the purely negative connotation from the fight against communism, which paralyses us from the outset.[34]

Galula shared these and other thoughts with officials transiting through Hong Kong, and in reports he submitted to the French Command.[35] I discovered the following letter written by Galula, still a captain, to General Clément Blanc, the Inspector-General of French ground forces, on January 20, 1954:

> During your stay in Hong Kong, I would have liked to show you what are the aims and goals of communist China, and what methods it has to achieve them. Moreover, I would have liked to convince you of China's determination, and of her resolute hostility towards us. Unfortunately, I barely had enough time to present you with a few elements of the problem. I am therefore sending you a few basic notes in a hurry. You will perhaps wish to read them prior to questioning Guillermaz whom you have summoned to Saigon.

The most important one, in my opinion, is the note on the basis of China's foreign policy. I drafted it in February of 1952, and though two years have elapsed since, I do not see a single modification that needs to be made. Not because I am a prophet, but simply because the Chinese Communists resolutely follow their own doctrine, and that they do not hesitate to spread their ideas. . . . This note, which is based on official texts and on a whole slew of other evidence, demolishes the [current] thesis that a [peaceful] coexistence with the communist world is possible.

The note *Nature of operations to consider against Communist China* will inform you directly of the military power of that country, and on its formidable defensive capacity.

The note *Consequences of the Korean War Armistice* will inform you on the repercussions for Indochina; no direct aggression, but an intensification of efforts to assist the Viet Minh.[36]

General Blanc, a veteran of Verdun, was on his way to visit French troops in Indochina when Galula handed him this letter in Hong Kong. (Guillermaz referred to General Blanc as Galula's "friend."[37]) Blanc visited Dien Bien Phu on January 26, 1954, with an entourage comprised of Generals Navarre[38] and Cogny,[39] Commissioner-General Maurice Dejean and Secretary of State for Associated States Marc Jacquet. Navarre explained the situation: "What we're trying to do is draw the rebel forces to Dien Bien Phu, to keep them from invading Laos. We've had American generals, veterans of Korea, tell us how satisfied they were with our deployment. They invested a lot of money here and they don't want to lose."[40]

Dien Bien Phu would fall five months later. At the ensuing Board of Inquiry, a regimental commander who had witnessed the VIP visit was asked to testify. "Did it seem to you that these high personages wanted to know if you could hold?" asked the general heading the inquiry. "They displayed optimism typical of official visitors," the commander answered. "The only one who had any doubts was General Blanc." The latter had been worried by the sustainability of the defense.[41]

In the aftermath of Dien Bien Phu, Galula was personally summoned by Raoul Salan who wished to be briefed on the likelihood of a Chinese aggression during the withdrawal of French forces from Indochina. Galula did so, but would narrowly miss a second equally, if not more significant opportunity to go to Washington to address Pentagon officials on the overall situation in Indochina.[42] His conventionally minded friend, Pierre Bourgeois, was chosen to go instead as a result of his more direct experience. Bourgeois had served as an intelligence officer at theater headquarters in Saigon. One can only assume how differently the two officers would have presented the problem to their American audience at the dawn of U.S. involvement in South Vietnam.

Galula's morale and enthusiasm plummeted as the situation in Indochina started to become hopeless for French forces prior to Dien Bien Phu. Despite the congratulations he received from top echelons for his work, he felt that the substance of his reports went unheeded. Guillermaz tried his best to motivate him. The scholarly colonel sympathized with uncharacteristic criticism of the military and political establishment that lay above them. "Our addressees in Paris are generally incapable of appreciating the opportunities found in our reports, or to detect themselves the meaning and gravity of unfolding events."[43]

Galula responded to Guillermaz's encouragements by attacking the ineptitude of the traditional intelligence function to address modern needs. He felt that if Indochina had been lost to a communist revolution, and other countries were on the brink of suffering the same fate, it was partly because higher echelons failed to understand the nature of these conflicts in their beginnings. He wrote to his mentor:

> We must reorganize our intelligence services in the Far East in line with what we want . . . why do we keep creating folders of targets which we will never bomb? Or establishing complex and detailed orders of battle for our opponents, when broad brush figures would often suffice instead? Sure, if we could afford these luxuries, then we could always entertain ourselves by gathering intelligence for the sake of gathering intelligence. . . .
>
> The communists are those who have the upper hand at the moment, while we content ourselves with accepting what comes from that, reacting here and there. However, communist activity is not exclusively military, especially now that they have taken a preference to subversion. It follows that it is *this* activity that must be followed attentively in all of its forms: legal, clandestine, political, economic, cultural, etc.
>
> There is no longer "military intelligence," there is instead "national security intelligence." The military attachés will thus find themselves entering the realm of diplomats—it is true—but it is a problem that will have to be solved.[44]

This reasoning had led Galula to blow off Pierre Bourgeois earlier in the campaign, when the latter had asked him to focus his intelligence-collection efforts on troop movements and the quality of road networks in southern China, with a view on updating French targeting folders. Bourgeois explained, to an incredulous Galula, who knew that France would never dare bomb Chinese territory, ". . . we see things through a different prism here. We, at the 2nd Bureau in Saigon, are not at the same level as National Defense Headquarters in Paris, we are often obliged to focus on very down-to-earth details that have nothing to do with grand politics."[45] Galula seethed at the realization that

Theater-level intelligence was concerning itself with the width and condition of roads behind enemy lines when the overall outcome of such a war would never depend on that.

And yet, the French were not stupid. Was it not thought and acted upon later, by another Power, that bombing jungle trails would decisively stifle the same enemy?

On May 28, 1954, as surviving French and Indigenous troops were being ruthlessly marched north away from the hell of Dien Bien Phu, towards the hell of the Viet Minh prisoner camps that awaited them, Galula wrote to a superior officer with palpable anguish:

> ... I find myself brooding from morning to evening and from evening to morning, unhealthily, on the tragedies of our Expeditionary Corps, of France, and of the Free World. Unhealthily that is, because I think of my impotence as an individual, and because I am relegated to reading arrogant Chinese propaganda every day, the imaginings of a neutralist British press, not to mention the foolishness of AFP [Agence France Presse] and of American news. We will pay dearly for that imbecile Eisenhower's popular grin.[46]

Two months later, Galula would mull angrily at the overall outcome of the war. Vietnam was set to be partitioned with the ephemeral promise that a referendum to consider reunification would be held within two years. Overcome with emotion, Galula allowed himself to get upset with Guillermaz who reflected that the fall of Indochina had been inevitable after all. (Galula would come to the same conclusion in later years, but for different reasons that would not include historical determinism.)

> What a catastrophe this armistice is for the Free World! It marks the failure of the so-called "containment policy," the failure of the present American administration, and the triumph of a little clique of determined communists.
>
> Because this communist victory is the outcome of a handful of leaders whom you know of,[47] and it is because of this that I do not follow you entirely when you raise the issue of historical determinism.
>
> There indeed exists historical currents against which we cannot swim; the entire communist strategy relies precisely on leveraging the present anti-colonial nationalist currents, with little means, just as a judo master throws down his opponent by using his opponents weight and strength. But there also exists counter-currents, presently, the latent hostility of the Chinese, Czech, Russian lao pai hsing[48] towards their leaders. What have we done to exploit this? Here we are still debating

on the theory of coexistence whilst the communists decided long ago to destroy us.[49]

Galula had been marked by the cataclysmic battle at Dien Bien Phu without having participated in it. The impotence he felt in Hong Kong pushed him to the brink of despair. Overworked, angry and frustrated, his hopes for a counter-cause to communism slowly disappeared from his correspondence. Galula's ill feelings worsened as another insurgency threatened France's control of Algeria, where a majority of Colonial Army officers, including himself, saw communist designs. Worse still, on the morrow of New Year's Day 1956, a national election in Metropolitan France resulted in the Communist Party under Maurice Thorez winning more seats than any other individual party. Galula wrote the following to Guillermaz later that week:

> On this stance of mine that is as radical as usual, I would like to touch on another subject, the recent elections. Their results do not surprise me nor affect me, they simply confirm my ideology. I think that the time has come to rely on our own salvation and not on some personality compromised by the very fact that he is tainted by the present regime. The time has come to look for, identify and regroup those who are willing to act. En route for the first [revolutionary] cell! I have not spent 10 years in the shadow of communism without having retained something.[50]

Galula was emotionally compromised. I never found any other trace or indication of political defiance on his part in the course of my research. Guillermaz's reaction to the letter may have been furious, but his unfailing politeness and reserve seemed to have withheld him from replying to Galula, whom he cared for as a disciple, but also as a young brother. Letters such as these proved, if nothing else, to what extent Guillermaz had been a trusted confidant.

Galula's feelings were exacerbated by personal guilt. "He realized that nearly a quarter of his classmates from Saint-Cyr had been killed or captured in Indochina," his widow told me. "This realization, more than anything, led him to volunteer for Algeria as soon as we returned to France. This was a shocking blow to me. He had sworn to me in Hong Kong that he wouldn't."

Galula's correspondence offers no hint as to whether he ever volunteered for service in Indochina. Such a request, I assume, would have likely been rejected in favor of maintaining him in Hong Kong. His insightfulness on Chinese affairs seemed to be too appreciated by senior circles to allow for his dismissal. His role in providing strategic intelligence had been undoubtedly more valuable than what his field contribution as a captain could have represented in such a vast war. And yet, none of this could have subdued his guilt for not participating in the fighting. Such feelings, irrational as they may

David and Ruth ferrying in
Hong Kong. Ruth is holding a
Graham Greene novel.

seem, can run very deep in a professional soldier. He wrote to Guillermaz, prior to leaving Hong Kong, "... it is time for you to pass to from the G2 to the G3 staff,[51] from intelligence to action."[52] The comment was subconsciously self-directed. Well aware of his protégé's worsening state-of-mind, Guillermaz wrote him back, "I feel that you are right to wish for a little distancing from Chinese affairs. It seems to me that once you will have completed some indispensable command time in Germany, your place will be assured with Paris's SEATO delegation. . . ."[53] Galula had no inclination, however, to further sideline with Paris's SEATO delegation, or to become an anonymous company commander in Germany for the sake of a promotion. He volunteered for Algeria instead.

Galula continued to be solicited by think tanks and universities for his insightfulness in Chinese affairs long after his departure from Hong Kong in 1956. Alastair Buchan, for instance, invited him a decade later to contribute to a compilation of texts by leading Cold War academics. His essay titled *Subversion and Insurgency in Asia* reads, "In the first ten years that followed the end of the Second World War six large revolutionary wars occured in Asia—China, Indo-China, Indonesia, Burma, Malaya, the Philippines—as against only one conventional war, in Korea. This six-to-one ratio was obviously no accident." With the benefit of hindsight, Galula reflected on Chinese intentions as having been on the fence between inward-looking and expansionist political agendas. He recognized that after Indochina, the Chinese had tapered off their efforts of exporting their revolution to surrounding Asian countries.[54]

In retrospect, Galula got carried away in his enthusiasm when depicting China's threat of revolutionary contagion to the world, beyond her regional sphere of influence. What seemed to be an unstoppable movement in the early

1950s, had already lost its steam half a decade later. China adopted a humbler foreign policy, no doubt fueled by its alienation from the Soviet Union, calling for isolationist prudence, and an unspoken temperance vis-a-vis the United States and her allies. Nevertheless, Galula's perception of that threat had led him to devote his mental energies on how to combat it. This was not in vain. Those deliberations contained the seeds of the counterinsurgency theory he would soon experiment with in Algeria.

11

Jean Caran

Ideology, whether communist or fascist, is nothing more than a pretext for dictatorial rule.

—*Harry Truman*[1]

The participation of the population in the conflict is obtained, above all, by a political organization (the party) living among the population, backed by force (the guerrilla gangs), which eliminates the open enemies, intimidates the potential ones, and relies on those among the population who actively support the insurgents. Persuasion brings a minority of supporters—they are indispensable—but force rallies the rest.

—*David Galula*[2]

GALULA'S DECADE-LONG EXPOSURE to revolutionary communism in Asia inspired him to write satirically about the subject, in addition to his more commonly known doctrinal works. This was a strange undertaking for an avid reader of anything but fiction. Guillermaz had said that books on warfare and warriors were all that had captivated his subordinate's interests.[3] Ruth agreed, adding that her husband's interests exceptionally extended to physics, chemistry, and mathematics, but indeed, never to fiction. Still, she felt her husband was a born storyteller armed with a great sense of humor.

"Any number of people had told him that this one particular story would make a great book," Ruth explained how her husband would come to write *The Tiger's Whiskers* ten years later in 1964. He had told the rambunctious tale of an unyielding entrepreneur, Mr. Pang, at more than one Honk Kong dinner party.

The Tiger's Whiskers spoke to the agility and cunning of the Chinese mind Galula admired, while satirically describing the prevailing mood in British-ruled Hong Kong at the height of the Korean War. "That novel," confided a friend of Galula's in an email, "though mostly unread, gives a pretty good indication of the character of the man that I knew and grew to like."[4] The storyline reflected the author's enthusiasm for the fairer sex as much as it did his typifying sarcasm. "On April 12, 1952," a random passage from his short novel reads, "the USS *Bull Run*, commonly known as 'Big Bully,' followed by the destroyer *MacBain*, sailed through the narrow strait of Lei Yue Mun and majestically entered Victoria Harbour. . . . The *Bull Run*'s arrival had been kept secret, and for this reason no more than five or six hundred Chinese guides were huddled outside the gate."[5]

"He was looking for work when he wrote *Les Moustaches du Tigre*," Ruth informed me, using the original French title of the novel her husband drafted in late 1963, in the middle of a three-year sabbatical leave from the army. He was hopeful that the royalties would complement those of a just-published *Counterinsurgency*.

Mindful to disassociate this light read from *Counterinsurgency*, Galula adopted a *nom de plume*. He chose "Jean Caran" which, as Ruth recalled, had something of a Russian meaning. In fact, "Caran d'Ache" (or *carandash*) phonetically sounds out "pencil" in Russian. Caran d'Ache was also the pen name of a French political satirist and cartoonist who had become famous for his coverage of the Dreyfus Affair (unfortunately, with unbridled anti-Semitic zeal).[6] As for the title of Galula's novel, it alluded to the Chinese idiom of "if one pulls a tiger's whiskers one may end up inside the animal's mouth." In other words, one took a great risk in offending an entity more powerful than oneself. The idiom applied perfectly to the tiny British colony nestled on China's coastline.

The novel succeeded well beyond Galula's and his publisher Flammarion's expectations. While the latter had been drawing up a publishing contract, Galula had sent a copy of his manuscript—still in French—to his editors at Praeger, and to his friend General Sam Griffith who had translated and pro-vided analysis on Mao's *On Guerrilla Warfare*. The retired Marine loved it. He would show the manuscript to the director of sales at the Walker Pub-lishing Company over lunch.[7] Within a week, Walker informed Galula that they were interested in publishing his novel for the American market. "I must congratulate you on your versatility," the director of sales wrote him, "to turn out first what is rapidly becoming the classic study of counter-insurgency, and then write a charming, witty book on a somewhat more pleasant aspect of Sino-American relations is indeed a feat."[8] Walker's only concerns lay with the shortness of the story, and its somewhat flat ending. Galula would ask for a week off from his new employer to address these. Still, those two issues remain the pleasant novel's only faults.

Walker grew frustrated with Flammarion's tough negotiating over distribution rights for the U.S. market. One senses from the tone of the letters that the dispute may have been fueled as much by strained Franco-American relations in the early 1960s, as it was by genuine commercial considerations! Walker complained to Galula that they would have offered him higher royalties, and more flexibility to publish the book abroad, had he chosen them as the primary publisher. Galula's response was telling of his patriotism:

> When I had finished the manuscripts of the "Tiger's Whisker's" last spring, I realized that it was meant more for the American and British markets than for the French. . . . However, in spite of the fact that I certainly do need money (if only to buy a house here as I am now doing) I decided to go the other way around. The reason is hard to explain fully because it is purely sentimental and consequently illogical. My first book, "Counterinsurgency: Theory and Practice," was written directly in English and published in New York by my friend Praeger. I wanted this second one to be published in France first, simply because I am French and French is after all my native language.[9]

Les Moustaches du Tigre was nevertheless translated into English, Italian, and German. Astonishingly, Galula's fate skirted Hollywood fame, when the Twentieth Century Fox Company nearly brought the story to the silver screen. Fox paid ten thousand dollars to Flammarion, a whopping sum for 1963, to secure an option on the movie;[10] out of which Galula received a much needed four thousand dollars.[11] An additional twenty thousand dollars would be paid if the movie made it to production.

"David came home and said that he had something 'important' to tell me," Ruth recalled. "I burst into tears! I assumed that something terrible had happened. He calmed me down, and told me about the movie offer. It was as if we had just won the lottery." Unfortunately, the movie was never produced.

Armed with the confidence drawn from having published *The Tiger's Whiskers* in 1964, Galula set out to write the manuscript for a second one in a similar genre the following year.

La Guerre bactériologique, or *Germ Warfare,* as Galula titled the manuscript, was written as a political satire describing the birth and infancy of Communist China. Material on which to base the story was not lacking for Galula. For six years in Hong Kong, he had peered over newspaper clippings and editorials from the mainland, such as the one from the Peking Journal that ". . . harped on the necessity to reinforce the people's vigilance against saboteurs . . . and on what terrible punishments were inflicted on counter-revolutionaries and other agents of the Enemy."[12] Galula made a poignant mockery of Mao's bloody *Three Antis* campaign aimed at eradicating corruption, waste, and bureaucracy, which he felt was only aimed at galvanizing the masses around the new regime through fear.

Galula wrote to his editor at Praeger, Phyllis Freeman, with unrelenting humor:

> Please give my regards to Sam Griffith. Tell him that I have finished the draft of my book about germ warfare in China and will spend my next vacation polishing it. It's a nasty one and my friend Mao Tse-tung won't like it at all. Maybe Khrushchev will give me the Lenin prize and make me a hero of the Soviet Union. In which case you will be all invited to a huge vodka and caviar party.[13]

Frederick Praeger insisted on publishing the manuscript, even though, as a work of fiction, it fell outside the scope of his publishing house.[14] However, it was not to be. Galula appears to have been responsible for holding back. Having found employment as a business developer in a French defense firm by then, he may have feared being portrayed as an overly politicized "reactionary" at a time when China's relations with the West, and with France in particular, were rapidly thawing. Phyllis Freeman wrote to a self-dismissive Galula: "Even though the book . . . is not serious, Mr. Praeger and I are most interested in seeing it. It will be quite a feat to pull off this approach, and it might make a very good musical comedy."[15]

Germ Warfare would have likely surpassed *Les Moustaches du Tigre* in sales and in legacy. Drawing on the quick-witted satirical style of *The Tiger's Whiskers*, Galula maintained the formula of a plot evolving through rapid iterations of increasingly sardonic and ridiculous situations made possible by human ingenuity on the one hand, and gullibility on the other. From a literary point of view, *Germ Warfare* was fleshier, its characters more defined. Of greater importance was the strength and intelligence of the message the author delivered. Galula sought to demystify through parody how ideology propagated through fear could be used to achieve total control over a population; a prevalent theme in Galula's non-fictional writings, and in the opening chapter to *The Tiger's Whiskers*.

Galula sets the story of *Germ Warfare* in a small agrarian village in the province of Szechuan following the rout of the Kuomintang. The hero, Misses Li, is portrayed as the young, beautiful, and ardent fiancée of the zealous political commissar Comrade Fu, a volunteer for the ongoing war against the "imperialist and bloodthirsty" Americans in Korea. "One evening, Misses Li, no longer capable of hiding her feelings, admitted to Comrade Fu her love for him. He buried his face in his hands and after a long silent pause, reached for Misses Li's hand and held it." Comrade Fu replies:

> Comrade Li, love can only be a decadent *bourgeois* feeling. This sort of love, I cannot share. At the opposite of this, love can be the cement that unites two comrades dedicated to the good of the People, to the Revolution, to the destruction of the old unjust society, and to the construction of a new and fair society led by comrade President Mao Tse Tung . . . if these are the feelings that you feel, Comrade Li, then I share them with you wholeheartedly.[16]

Li is soon elected mayor after making promises to uphold the communist cause like no other. Smart and ambitious, she sets out to distinguish her tiny village from the others in Szechuan. She creates a series of committees that slowly begin to permeate the lives of her villagers. The opportunity to demonstrate an unwavering adherence to Mao comes soon when the Central Party announces that General MacArthur, the "puppet of Wall Street," has launched a biological warfare campaign against Korea and North-Eastern China. A dispatch from Beijing reads: "The bandits of Wall Street, incapable of resisting our heroic volunteers' offensives, have demonstrated their infinite cowardice and criminal mindedness by mobilizing microbes. They have raised ticks and rats with the expressed purpose of dropping them on our territories from their airplanes in order to spread diseases and kill our pacific populations. . . ."[17]

The villagers are whipped into action by their young mayor, who falls prey to the fear-instilling, galvanizing propaganda concocted by the regime. Li commits her village to the defense of the mainland by ordering the extermination of vermin and all forms of insects; the would-be carriers of deadly biological agents. Minimum quotas are set for the number of rats and insects to be killed by villagers each day. Penalties are imposed for defaulters.

Galula's parody demonstrates to what extent an ideologically fueled system becomes humanly flawed like any other. The ideology that rests at the center of the effort quickly becomes a secondary preoccupation. Hypocrisy, double-standards, jealousy, greed, and most of all fear, factor in. No ruse or tactic is to be disdained if it increases the tally of vermin killed: ". . . Other comrades from the village suggested that the enemy should be forced to concentrate, which would make his destruction easier. . . . Carcasses of dogs were left to rot at strategic locations. With a single carcass, 647 green flies, 72 wasps, 1,112 regular flies, and 4 rats were eliminated on a single day. . . ."[18]

A black market crops up to satisfy the demand for contraband rat tails expressed by villagers who are incapable of meeting the imposed quotas. But the rat tails turn out to be hoaxes; lizard tails rolled in greyish clay! School children also participate in raising the enemy death count by breeding rats in their classrooms. Although encouraged and acclaimed by the provincial governor, Misses Li is understandably exhausted:

> When one is a member of the Party, mayor of an ideologically advanced village, delegate to the popular consultative political council of the sub-district, president of the woman's association and of seven other important committees (such as the Resistance to America committee, etc.), vice-president of five other just-as-important committees, active member of nineteen other committees and popular organizations, and in addition to all of this, one is engaged since twenty-two days in a shock-action campaign that is vital to the fate of the Nation, one then has good reason to feel tense and fatigued, irritable and exhausted.[19]

And the delectably entertaining parody continues. The nearly completed manuscript of *Germ Warfare* that sits in Galula's papers is a testament to its author's ability to dissect, analyze, and simplify human collective behaviors and motivations. He wished to reveal the naked truth behind communist expansion, which he saw fueled by a technique reliant on force and terror, more than on ideology alone. Just as *Counterinsurgency* had been addressed to the Western military, political, and civil servant communities, *Germ Warfare* would have been addressed to the Western public at large. Galula saw in it perhaps his own psychological warfare contribution to influencing the "home front," still split between apathy and empathy for the communist agenda, particularly in France. The question of whether *Germ Warfare* would have succeeded in meeting Galula's intentions is a valid one. So too is the question of whether a similar method of demystifying contemporary totalitarian ideologies anchored on religious or other beliefs would work today.

12

This Cannot Be another Indochina

With regards to Algeria, some have said: "the mission that is assigned to our army is the same mission that has always been assigned to it: the destruction of armed opposition." Gentlemen, I am sorry, but if this were so, we would be committing a fundamental error.

—*Charles Lacheroy*[1]

As for the Muslim masses, their main problem was one of security. And the FLN threats and assassinations had greater effect on them than had the better educational opportunities and land reforms.

—*David Galula*[2]

ALGERIA MAY FAIL TO APPEAR in Galula's correspondence predating his return from Hong Kong in 1956, but it is unlikely that the troubles that followed the *Front de Libération Nationale* (FLN) bombings on November 1, 1954, had escaped his notice. The French, not unlike the British, were suffering drearily from anti-colonial fever. French North Africa had reached its boiling point, fueled by Pan-Arab nationalism, vying Soviet interests, America's push for self-rule, and the alleged "Anglo-Saxon" desire to please oil-rich Gulf States. Violent independence movements were manifested in Tunisia, Morocco, and finally in Algeria. By March of 1955, France had granted Morocco and Tunisia their full independence. Only Algeria would not be given up so quickly or benevolently.

The loss of Indochina affected Galula because of Hong Kong's proximity to that theater, the involvement of a hated communist adversary, and the guilt and remorse resulting from the tragic fate of so many of his comrades. The loss of Tunisia and Morocco was yet more painful to endure. Galula was, after all, born in the former and raised in the latter. His family had wholeheartedly embraced French rule and culture within those protectorates. And though the troubles that led to the independences of Morocco and Tunisia could not be compared in scale, brutality, or significance to those of Indochina and, soon, to those of Algeria, they had also added to Galula's frustration. He felt that France had given up easily in those first two protectorates, plying to the brief terror campaigns he later deemed to fall under the "shortcut pattern" of insurgency.

Galula claimed the following in his introduction to *Pacification*: "I felt that I had learned enough about insurgencies, and I wanted to test certain theories that I had formed on counterinsurgency warfare. For all these reasons I volunteered for duty as soon as I reached France."[3] Was this motivation genuine? Probably. But his desire "to test certain theories" was likely subordinated to his desire for vindication his widow had spoken about, and his desire to keep Algeria French.

Galula and Guillermaz were at odds over France's commitment to preserve her colonies and protectorates. Although Guillermaz would also later serve in Algeria, motivated by feelings of guilt tied to Indochina, he was personally convinced that it was as unjust as it was unfeasible to halt a people's aspiration for independence. Moreover, as shall be touched upon in the next chapter, his soldier's honor interfered with the work that pacification required. Notwithstanding his more right-leaning stance, Galula was a product of North Africa, whose French population was naturally not all in favor of the metropolitan government giving anything up. It was, furthermore, Galula's luck that his great-grandfather had been born in Algeria, by virtue of which, he had been granted the French citizenship he so cherished. It was to Galula's credit, in the end, that he would remain as professionally detached as he later did while serving on the ground from 1956 to 1958, and then at the highest level of headquarters until 1961, in a conflict where civil, political, and military domains became so embroiled.

After ten years of intelligence and diplomatic work, Galula volunteered for field duty in a line battalion assigned to one of the worst areas of operation in Algeria. His plea to the *2ième Bureau* (G2) must have been a strong one. How else could a valued military attaché, fluent in Mandarin and possessing recognized analytical skills, be sent off to command a company of draftee infantrymen in the mountains of Kabila? Although the 1956 troop surge required the French Army to draw nearly indiscriminately on its resources, Galula's file clearly destined him for staff employment. His correspondence unraveled the mystery. He submitted his request for field command directly to General Ely, the Chairman of the French Chiefs of Staff, and to General Guillaume, the commander of the army, both of whom knew Galula personally as a result of their stays in Hong Kong. Guillermaz would also help by putting in a good word with the director of the Colonial Army.[4]

On Red All Saints Day, 1954, the FLN conducted upwards of thirty terrorist actions across Algeria's densely populated north. The majority of the victims were Muslims, targeted because of their publicly known allegiance to the French. This initiated what Galula and others would describe as *la bataille du silence* (battle for silence).

Galula attributed the rebellion in Algeria to Communist subversion (initially, at least) and to the rebels' willful polarization of the racial divide that persisted between the colony's Europeans, of which there were one million, and the Arab and Berber Muslims, of which there were nine million. He would later write to Colonel Goussault, the commander of the Psychological Action Bureau in Algeria, in Chinese proverb–inspired style: "There is a racial problem in Algeria that is doggedly exploited by our adversaries; it is their only argument, but one that is able to flare passions. And when passions flare, they smother reason and even one's best interests."[5]

Galula otherwise acknowledged the Algerian nationalist cause only fleetingly. In all likelihood, he viewed Algeria and the United States in the 1950s in a similar light, where civil rights contentions, not nationalist sentiment, underpinned racial unrest. (Algeria had been part of France for too long for the French to view themselves as foreign occupiers.) Galula singled out the inadequate administration of the colony as the primary enabling condition for the rebellion. A weak security apparatus had also played in the rebels' favor. In the *quartier* (district) of Aissa Mimoun, where he was stationed, he remarked how a single salaried policeman had been entrusted with protecting a population of fifteen thousand.[6] Galula never felt, therefore, that the FLN owed its existence to some implacable cause, ideology, or charismatic rebel leadership.

Galula partly attributed the insurgency to a matter of timing and context. Both of Algeria's neighbors had already entered the final phase of their struggles for independence—Tunisia under the banner of Bourguiba and his *Neo-Destour* party and Morocco under Sultan Mohammed V. The FLN felt that it could benefit from these neighboring precedents. (Momentum matters greatly in civil unrest, as contemporary events in the Middle East have proven.) A major difference lay, however, in the stronger bond that tied Algeria to France. The "optionality" of a French counterinsurgency effort in Algeria would be much less. Morocco and Tunisia were protectorates, with only small fractions of their populations consisting of European settlers. Algeria was much more than that. So strong was Algeria's integration with France that it was genuinely considered to be a domestic theater of operations, designated as the 10th Military Region (the Paris Region, for instance, was the 1st). Political and economic implications lessened the optionality of

the conflict for France. Settlers voted in metropolitan elections, and their economic clout was made significant by the commercial trade between Algeria
and the Metropol that depended on them.

By virtue of this stronger integration with metropolitan France, Algerian
Muslims should have benefited from greater social equities than did their
counterparts in neighboring protectorates. A rare proof of this—the one that
Galula highlighted in his writings—lay in the ease by which Arab and Berber Algerians traveled to France to study and work. Nevertheless, France had
refused to grant French citizenship to all Muslim Algerians for fear that millions of them would migrate permanently to metropolitan France, and for
fear that the latter would effectively lose political control over Algeria.[7]

Muslim Algerians had been elected to Algeria's legislative assembly since
1947, but their representation was not proportional to their numbers. Furthermore, the assembly's role was essentially confined to issues of budget,
taxation, and to the "local adaptation" of laws passed by its metropolitan
counterpart. The latter reserved the not-insignificant right to veto any motion
passed by the Algerian assembly.[8] Economically too, the European population swayed disproportionate power in Algeria. But Galula saw in this the
flipside of the contradiction, whereby this small segment carried half of Algeria's tax burden on its own.

Galula leaned decidedly to the right in proposing to manipulate the standard of living that France had afforded the Indigenous population as a means
of countering the insurgency. Without entering into specifics, he included the
following reflection in an early memorandum to his chain of command:

> There are two ways to show the carrot. We can make the Algeri-
> ans promises of magnificent progress, starting from what they have
> today. . . . But I know enough to fear that we will not be able, in gen-
> eral, to make good on our promises. . . . Is it not better then to deprive
> the inhabitants of part of the material and social benefits which we
> already have brought them, and to restore these progressively as they
> co-operate? Are not peace and the return to normal conditions the
> soundest of all promises?[9]

Although essentially population centric, nothing in this proposal rang of
mildness, let alone softness. Galula reasoned that it would be pointless and
even counterproductive to make promises of socioeconomic development
that could not be kept. He further believed, in contrast to the insurgent, the
counterinsurgent is judged for what he achieves, and not what he promises to
achieve.[10] From an ethical perspective, his argument in favor of withdrawing
benefits in view of progressively restoring them was one of an end justifying
the means. From a practical perspective, his argument sought to afford local

commanders the ability to impose rewards and consequences, in other words, to have recourse to both the carrot and the stick in their dealings with the population. He recuperated this theme in *Counterinsurgency* five years later, while adding a strong caveat that demonstrated maturation and rebalancing in his thinking:

> It would be a mistake to believe that a counterinsurgent cannot get the population's support unless he concedes political reforms. . . . He may very well withdraw whatever benefits the population receives from the mere existence of his regime—a measure of law and order, a more-or-less running economy, functioning public works and services, etc.—and restore them gradually as a premium for the population's cooperation. . . . But such a policy of pure force could bring at best a precarious return to the status quo ante, a state of perpetual tension,[11] not a lasting peace.[12]

Addressing an insurgency's root cause, therefore, remains a central tenet of the Galula Doctrine.

The inherent weakness of the French Fourth Republic for which Galula had revealed his revulsion in a letter to Guillermaz was aptly exploited by the FLN.

Born on the morrow of World War II, the politically chaotic French Republic saw its coalition governments dissolved at an average rate of once per year in the lead up to the Algerian War. Communist and socialist parties represented nearly half of the French National Assembly when combined. These were generally anti-colonial, spurred on to some extent by Soviet leanings on the matter. The FLN thus found sympathizers and willing propagandists, even in France, creating a political discord that did little to advance governmental policy in Algeria.

The FLN benefited from considerable external support too—a requirement for an insurgency to succeed according to Galula.[13] Morocco and Tunisia were natural allies of the FLN, although the courtship would not last long after the war; so was Egypt with a charismatic Nasser at the helm, who dreamt of pan-Arab nationalism. Encouraged by the Soviet Union, Nasser harbored the FLN's top leadership. Weakening the French would further his aims of nationalizing the Suez Canal; an endeavor that was ultimately aligned with Soviet strategic interests.

Publicly, the FLN claimed that it did not wish to be subjugated to Soviet ideology or embrace, as it was, a Muslim, rather than a communist, movement. But *realpolitik* dictated otherwise in some regards, and confirmed that Galula and others had been right to suspect Soviet involvement. (They had been wrong, however, as Guillermaz pointed out, to see *only* that in the insurgency's beginnings.) Khrushchev would come to write in his memoirs:

The liberation struggle of the Algerian people was something we [the politburo] regarded with great attention and sympathy. . . . We aided them by all means available to us . . . although this was difficult to accomplish. The French imperialists at that time were doing everything they could to prevent weapons from reaching the Algerians. It was necessary to send them by way of Morocco or other countries.[14]

The FLN also found tacit support from an unexpected source. The United States, under President Kennedy, stayed neutral throughout the conflict to be sure; but its young president made the following reproach in 1957, while still a senator, to the Eisenhower administration that had provided arms to the French: ". . . we cannot long ignore . . . a struggle for independence that has been and will be a major issue before the United Nations, that has denuded NATO and its armies,[15] drained the resources of our French allies, threatened the continuation of Western influence and bases in North Africa and bitterly split the Free World we claim to be leading."[16]

Like the majority of French Army officers at that time, Galula was critical of the American (and British) stance on Algeria. His widow related how he deplored that a few American NGOs had offered medical relief to the FLN in camps along the Algerian border. He was also made upset by the skewed media coverage. He would complain about this to Henry Kissinger, while at Harvard, as French forces were withdrawn from Algeria. Ruth recalled, "Kissinger looked at him and said very frankly: 'the media here does not need to concern itself with the truth David, there aren't enough people here who know the truth to cause a stir.'"

In a secret-labeled "Annual report on the state of morale" Galula submitted in late 1957, he described how the influx of Western-made weapons in the hands of insurgents had affected the morale of his company. His inference regarding their origin and the motive for supplying them was strong: "The delivery of Anglo-Saxon weapons to Tunisia has upset [my troops]. The [issue of] Saudi petrol is often discussed."[17] The broader predicament was depicted by Joe Alsop who had left Hong Kong to become *Time Life*'s chief correspondent in Lebanon. He wrote Galula the following after a layover in Paris:

. . . I was especially sorry to miss your views, David, on Algeria. Is this another Indo-China, where the outcome is already hopelessly inevitable? As you certainly know, the Arabs in this part of the world belabour the U.S. ceaselessly for what they call our "support" for the French in Algeria, yet I gather the French think we have failed to support them enough. . . . In fact I think a good part of the alleged interest of the Levantine Arabs in Algeria is phony; they're too much wrapped up in their own problems, like Israel, to give much of a damn. In a sense Algeria is a convenient device for the pro-Western Arabs . . . to stay right with Arab ikons (*sic*) by condemning Western policy in Algeria while knowing full well that they will never have to do anything about it. . . .'[18]

Nothing indicates that Galula ever believed in a "hopeless-inevitability" to the Algerian War. He had felt that even the loss of Indochina had not been wholly inevitable. (He colorfully considered, however, that Napoleon himself could not have won the war with so few troops![19])Of Algeria he would write rhetorically in a 1956 memorandum to his chain of command, "Is our cause necessarily lost then? Not at all, for in every situation, whatever the cause, there will always be a favorable minority, a neutral majority, and a hostile minority. . . ."[20] The rest was a matter of determination and technique.

In truth, Galula was contemptuous of the Algerian insurgency and its leadership. As stated in an earlier chapter, he did not share the same level of respect for the FLN as he had for the Chinese communist rebels. Although he disliked both and what they stood for, he deemed Mao's movement to be more refined, its approach to insurgency more scientific, methodical, patient, and clever. In truth, there was likely to be an element of cultural bias, too. He was the product of a colonial environment that often harbored stereotypical views. After the war, he would write in *Pacification*:

> One may wonder why it took so long, more than a year, for the insurgency to spread all over the territory. The fact may be attributed to the incompetence and inexperience of the leaders; to the Arab's notorious inability to organize (I sound no doubt terribly colonialist, but it's a fact, as witness the small Israeli Army and the huge Arab manpower all around it); to their tendency to bicker among themselves; to the FLN's ignorance of insurgent warfare except in its crudest form; to the rebel's vanity, which led them to refuse expert communist advice.[21]

Still, Galula respected the fighting prowess and courage of FLN fighters, just as he respected the fighting prowess of the Muslim troops enlisted on the French side. He had fought, after all, alongside such troops in the past. He balked, however, at the tactical acumen of the FLN's cadres. Here again, the Saint-Cyr graduate writing in the early 1960s could indeed sound very "colonialist," and forgetful of his own origins. "Yet even in Tunisia," he commented in *Pacification*, "where [the FLN] had every facility, the rebels very seldom attempted to create diversions along the border fences, thus occupying our reserves while crossing at a weak point. There is no question that Algerians are good individual fighters, but they do not make an army unless officered by European cadres."[22] He reserved his greatest disdain for the FLN's top leadership. He often recalled how these men had been political non-entities prior to the rebellion. Adding insult to injury was that key leaders such as Belkacem and Ben Bella had served as non-commissioned officers in the French Army, and that both had been decorated for their service during the Second World War. Ruth told me that her husband had gone as far as naming two stray cats he adopted in Algeria after these leaders, much to the delight of his troops!

Galula downplayed the "colonialist" attitude he expressed at times with humor, but in practice, his respect for the local Algerian population seemed beyond reproach. This was so not only for garnering that population's active support, but also because it was in him, I believe, to respect the dignity of others.

(Firmness and respectfulness in dealing with a population are not incompatible with each other in the midst of a counterinsurgency campaign. Behaviors become counterproductive [at either end of the scale] when officers and soldiers fail to understand this.)

France's teetering Fourth Republic issued promises of resolve as frequently as they were broken. This, the bane of any counterinsurgency effort, would lead to the May 1958 Revolt in Algeria. Under the threat of the quasi-coup being extended to metropolitan France, de Gaulle was thrust into power, ushering in the Fifth Republic. France's constitution, and with it the fundamentals of her political system, were radically changed overnight by the backlash of a failing counterinsurgency campaign across the Mediterranean.

In the early stages of the Algerian rebellion, successive French governments sought to placate the insurgency by enacting political and economic reforms. Although Galula would come to advocate the need to eliminate the root cause of an insurgency in his works, he thought that these particular reforms had been ill-timed and ill-dosed. New concessions emboldened the insurgency, and led the people to believe that (1) the FLN was to be credited; and (2) more concessions could be obtained by extrapolation.

Having failed to appease the rebellion during the first two years, the French opted to quash it. Galula's deployment to Algeria in the summer of 1956 coincided with a hardening of policy and a surge in the deployment of troops. The FLN's uncouth declaration to the effect that Europeans in Algeria would have to choose between "the coffin or the suitcase" had instantaneously reduced the "optionality" of the conflict for France, leading her to a call to arms.

The total strength of the French contingent reached its peak of 400,000 men at the time of Galula's arrival in Algeria. (This figure, however, included a large number of Indigenous units, a fact not taken into consideration by contemporary pundits who automatically dismiss comparisons with the Algerian War on account that the French contingent had had the luxury of being so large.) Opposed to this was an FLN strength estimated at 29,000, of which approximately one third were regular *fellaghas* ("outlaw fighters") and the rest were auxiliary *mousseblines*.[23]

The end of hostilities in Indochina proved to be a mixed blessing for the FLN. Although France's appetite for colonial warfare expeditions had been reduced, the bulk of her fighting troops, many of whom were battle-hardened *à l'outrance* as depicted in Jean Larteguy's bestselling novels of the era, could now be redirected toward the Algerian theater of operations.

A key impediment to the French war effort in Algeria lay in the lack of a unifying counterinsurgency doctrine, according to Galula. "The sad truth," he wrote in *Pacification*, "was that in spite of all our past experience, we had no single, official doctrine for counterinsurgency."[24] The conventional warfare imposed by World War II had pushed the reset button on the pacification experience for a majority of officers, including those who belonged to the Colonial Army. The Indochina War too, where so many of them served, had taken an essentially conventional form in its final years (though true to Maoist doctrine, the Viet Minh never abandoned terrorism and guerrilla warfare as auxiliaries to maneuver warfare). French officers recognized that immaterial forces had been at play in the build up of the Viet Minh's power, but as Galula related in *Pacification*, common wisdom in the army was that the mistakes that had been made in Indochina should not be repeated—without knowing what should be done instead.[25]

France sought to diagnose the problem in Algeria through what remained of its traditional military administration apparatus in North Africa, embodied by the *"Sections d'Affaires Indigènes."*[26] These "native affair" officers were well versed in the historical causes and remedies to insurrection in Algeria. Fluent in local dialects, in tune with local customs and power structures, these men were part of the colonial elite. They maintained that Algeria had been insufficiently administered for too long, and that pacification efforts would have to be sustained through the bias of reforms. But the lack of immediate progress that such reforms seemed to yield, combined with the arrival of General Salan and his staff from Indochina, resulted in a new orientation being given to the French war effort. Lessons learned from Indochina were systematically transposed to Algeria, sometimes blindly, or without cultural adaptation, much to the dismay of the North Africa specialists.

The *Bureau d'Action Psychologique* was also sprung from doctrinal notions imported from Indochina. With incredibly wide-ranging mandates that extended from propaganda to politico-civil affairs, the Bureau appropriated itself a doctrinarian role. Psychological Action staff officers were embedded at nearly all levels of headquarters. Operational- and tactical-level guidance on what and how interactions should be carried out with the population was sporadically issued by these officers through orders, instructions, journals, and indoctrination sessions. Still, the French Army would have to wait until 1959 before it could lay claim to having a pacification doctrine. Four years of counterinsurgency in Algeria had gone by.

In fairness to the French Army, its counterinsurgency effort had been neither hopeless nor wholly unsuccessful prior to the dissemination of a formal doctrine. In terms of military deployment, the army adopted a scheme that was simple and sound. It first proceeded to convert the majority of its supporting ground units (armor, artillery, air defense, etc.) into light infantry battalions that were needed most for this type of warfare. (It is difficult to imagine the amount of resistance that such a pragmatic move would meet in a Western army today, as it probably did then!) These battalions were then assigned to either "mobile" or "static" roles. Mobile units acted as reserves, maneuvering and striking where needed, particularly along the borders. Static units, on the other hand, were tasked with occupying and "pacifying" inhabited areas through *quadrillage*.

The French Army succeeded in starving the rebellion of foreign aid. This had been Salan's number one priority as he took over from General Lorillot in 1956. Algeria's vast coastal area to the north was blockaded by the French Navy, and the vast deserts to the south were interdicted through surveillance combining technical and human means. As for the permeable borders with Morocco and Tunisia, the French Corps of Engineers resorted to building a formidable complex of barriers. So effective was the seal that, according to Galula, the rebellion was all but starved of ammunition and food by 1958.

Salan's second priority lay with the eradication of urban terrorism. The torture-reliant interrogation of suspects in the Kasbahs of Algiers by General Massu's 10th Paratrooper Division gained notoriety, even as it yielded a spectacular stop to the bombings in early 1957. Paratroopers had been tacitly authorized to use any means required to gather intelligence that would lead to the arrest of bomb makers and their support networks. However, Massu's claim that he had subjected himself to every interrogation technique his men had employed did little to alleviate the moral burden of this operation on the overall campaign.

Salan's third priority was to proceed with the said *quadrillage* of rebel-prone areas. But *quadrillage* was not a stand-alone solution to pacification; it was a useful tool by which the conditions for success—stability, proximity to the population, etc.—could be set. Without a standing doctrine, however, battalion and company commanders such a Galula were generally left to their own devices within their grid assignments. This led to a challenge sourced in the complexity of irregular warfare, which remains true to this day. Galula wrote:

> The army officer has learned in military academies that combat is divided into distinct phases. . . . For each phase, he has been taught, there is an appropriate standard deployment and maneuver . . . in accordance with the current doctrine. [. . .] Such a process unfortunately does not exist in counterinsurgency warfare. How much time and means to devote to tracking guerrillas or, instead, to working on the population, by what specific actions and in what order the population could be controlled and led to co-operate, these were questions that the *sous-quartier*[27] commander had to answer by himself. One can imagine the variety of answers arrived at and the effects on the pacification effort as a whole.[28]

Galula felt that it was an imperative to indoctrinate counterinsurgent troops, just as the communist revolutionaries had done for their own. He also felt that it was the duty of leaders to identify among their subordinates which ones were predisposed for such work, and which ones weren't.[29] Indeed, it remains far from certain that counterinsurgency warfare *can* be taught as effectively as other military fields of practice. It remains a cognitive art, that calls for a desire to understand human behavior and the circumstances by which it is molded in a given theater of operations. It further requires from its practitioners an ability to critically observe, learn, and adapt, as well as the willpower to think and act courageously.

Proof of this can be found in Galula's success and influence in Algeria, to which we cast our attention next.

13

Le Capitaine de Kabylie

In today's Revolutionary Warfare, victory will go to those revolutionary leaders.

—*Instruction for the Pacification of Algeria*[1]

... I started pacifying here in October, and arrived to these results within six months. Now, armed with my present experience, I am ready to start from scratch, and achieve the same results anywhere within four months. That is a statement which I can safely make considering how Kabylia, and my douar in particular, were wholly rotten when my battalion arrived here.

—*David Galula*[2]

"IN KEEPING WITH THE PERENNIAL amnesia that has long surrounded the study of insurgency and counterinsurgency," Dr. Bruce Hoffman wrote in his foreword to the declassified release of Galula's *Pacification*, "[the report] too was generally forgotten until a chance conversation at a social event between Fred C. Iklé, a head of RAND's Social Sciences Department during the 1960s, and *Washington Post* reporter Tom Ricks set in motion the chain of events that led Michael Rich, RAND's executive vice president, to decide to reissue it now."[3]

Galula drafted *Pacification* for the RAND Corporation under the umbrella of a one-year, part-time consultant's contract beginning in the fall of 1962. Galula welcomed the contract to supplement his modest Harvard pay during his sabbatical leave from active duty. RAND offered 65.00 USD per day spent on researching and drafting,explaining perhaps why Galula would write such an uncharacteristically lengthy text.[4]

Pacification and *Counterinsurgency* were drafted quasi-simultaneously. Only, the latter would be published commercially by Praeger in 1964, and the former would be kept in classified form by RAND until 2006. This had been done on Galula's request, for he was reticent to release sensitive content about the Algerian War whose aftershocks were still being felt in France. This, of course, would narrow the report's dissemination until its rediscovery some forty-five years later.

Pacification is a rich and insightful text. It is the story of the testing and honing of a doctrine Galula had premeditated for nearly a decade from the sidelines of Greece and southeastern Asia. The evolution of the stepwise framework he formalized in *Counterinsurgency* is clearly apparent in *Pacification*. The latter is replete with practical examples of success and failure as its author attempted to put his embryonic theories into practice. A great number of lessons applicable to small wars may be drawn from the rawer work. From a biographic point-of-view, *Pacification* offers not only a window on its author's character and personality, but also a very good account of Galula's experience in Algeria. It follows that the goal here is not to summarize the contents of the RAND report, but to draw from it highlights, and complement these with new information from sources unknown to the public.

Galula adhered to the advice he had offered Guillermaz in the aftermath of Dien Bien Phu by choosing a field command over a staff appointment in Algeria. A scientist needs a laboratory to test a hypothesis. Field command would afford Galula direct contact with the population—an indispensable condition for him to trial his theories. Galula was, furthermore, adamant on the necessity to test doctrine incrementally, in both scope and scale, as Chinese revolutionary doctrine prescribed. Command of an infantry company would offer that possibility. Galula commented in *Pacification*: "The company commander in his *sous-quartier*, being directly in contact with the population, had the key job in the war. Echelons above him could always issue orders; he was the man to translate them into concrete action. And in the absence of sensible orders from above, he had to make his own if he wanted to achieve anything."[5]

Galula commanded the 3rd Company of the 45th Colonial Infantry Battalion (45th BIC). The latter was assigned "static" duties, meaning that its responsibility was to enforce security and pacify the local population in the *quartier* it occupied. Static assignment favored the pacification endeavor, as it afforded stable and continuous interaction with the *quartier*'s inhabitants. Galula's battalion commander was Lieutenant-Colonel Denoyes, whom the former referred to as Major Renard (Major "Fox") in *Pacification*. Denoyes

Galula in an outpost of his sous-quartier.

had been a classmate of Galula's at Saint-Cyr.[6] Familiarity procured an advantage; Denoyes would be more trusting and amenable to the unorthodox suggestions offered by his classmate.

The 45th BIC operated in Greater Kabila, in northeastern Algeria, where the insurgency had been particularly rife since the beginning of hostilities. The region was inhabited by Kabyl Berbers, a hardy breed of men from whom the French had recruited elite mercenaries like the original Zouaves, and against whom, simultaneously, the French had had the most trouble in earlier pacification campaigns. Galula's *sous-quartier* was devoid of European settlers, making it difficult to find natural sources of information, let alone an obvious "active minority favourable to the counterinsurgent party." Galula reasoned that success in light of these challenges would surely prove the ruggedness of his technique.

Journalist Joe Alsop visited Galula's *sous-quartier* of 10,000 people in June of 1958, as American public curiosity (and criticism) about the Algerian War was on the rise. Of the four articles Alsop dispatched for the *Herald Tribune* and other papers, "In David's District,"[7] was entirely devoted to his friend's achievements. The journalist related how Galula described the situation he had inherited in 1956:

> "The worst part of the job was over," David said, "when the battalion left and I moved in with a company of troops. But the rebels still had a field force of 20 men on the djebel. The villagers paid tribute to them, and fed them, and clothed them, and kept them constantly informed about our movements. They were the real rulers. To us the villagers were closed, absolutely closed people. The people did not speak to us. They would do no work for us. We could not even go amongst them, except in armed groups."[8]

Galula's predecessor in Algeria had been killed, and two of his successors would suffer the same fate in the same *sous-quartier*. It follows that Galula displayed commendable physical courage by constantly exposing himself to dangers through his interactions with the population. Moral courage, however, is what distinguished him most; his efforts to push the military to adapt to an evolving style of warfare proved to be his most arduous task. "I am not writing this to show what a genius I was," he wrote in conclusion to *Pacification*, "but to point out how difficult it is to convince people, especially the military, to change traditional ways and adapt to new conditions."[9] David Petraeus, John Nagl and Bruce Hoffman would all recuperate this statement in their forewords to Galula's works, resonating how true and relevant similar challenges remained fifty years later.

Galula understood that it would not only be his peers and subordinates who would need to be educated on counterrevolutionary warfare, but also "a few of [his] superiors, which was no easy task."[10] His experience in Hong Kong as a quasi-independent attaché had added confidence to his impressions. He was now accustomed to voicing his bold and often unorthodox views to receptive commanders at the uppermost echelons of the French Army. He continued, therefore, to be outspoken in Algeria as he had been in Hong Kong; his modest position as a commander of 100 men or so, in a 400,000 man-strong contingent, did little to curtail his habit. Still, he required self-assuredness to tell his men, who had participated in the horrors of a savage war upfront, and his superiors, who had witnessed military defeat on the battlefields of Indochina, that traditional military operations would have to be shelved in favor of working to win the *sous-quartier*'s active support, once the conditions were ripe for such a transition.

By the same token, Galula issued a stern warning to his men, as generals Petraeus, Mattis, McChrystal, and other notables would decades later in Iraq and Afghanistan against any action that would further alienate the population. "I explained the nature of this war," Galula related in *Pacification*. "Our forces were vastly superior to the rebels. Then why couldn't we finish them quickly? Because they managed to mobilize the population through terror and persuasion."[11]

Galula surmised the timeless imbroglio of irregular warfare: "We were caught in the classic vicious cycle of an insurgency. [Because] of the repeated and costly operations, the Kabyle population was solidly against us; because of the attitude of the population, our soldiers tended to treat every civilian as an enemy."[12] The company he had inherited had yet to truly engage with the population on a continual basis. His predecessor had organized frequent patrols within the *sous-quartier* to be sure, but according to Galula, ". . . Not to visit the population but to hunt rebels."[13] He further lamented how the company had commuted to work[14] from its isolated base. Alsop summarized Galula's description of his early pacification process:

Oddly enough, the fellaghas owe their defeat on Djebel Aissa Mimoun to the theory of Mao Tse-tung that an army must live among the people "like a fish in water." The whole process started when David moved his company from an isolated, fortified farmhouse into the very midst of one of the hostile villages. From there, the process went by steps. Getting the people to work for the company was the first step. The next was strengthening their confidence that the company would protect them from the fellagha's vengeance.[15]

"It can be done anywhere," Galula told his journalist friend. But Alsop was skeptical, not of the process, but of the "availability of men of David's character"[16] to repeat such a process elsewhere. Galula took the issue into consideration. He did not wish for his legacy to be limited to the pacification of a *sous-quartier*, a feat that other capable officers were also able to achieve in Algeria. He wished instead to formulate an accessible counterinsurgency process, founded on sound principles and laws that a majority of leaders would be capable of applying to practice. As for the minority that would prove incapable of doings to, for lack of adaptability, resourcefulness or initiative, Galula would later suggest that they be left to the exercise of more traditional military functions.

Galula had witnessed this inability to adapt in a senior commander he described as being "blind to the peculiar nature of this war":

[The first sector commander had] wasted the critical years of 1956 and early 1957 when the rebels, although large in number, were actually weak in both their military and political organization.... He concerned himself with purely military operations, ignored the population, thus allowing the rebels to build a tight OPA.[17] As a result, the rebels he killed—and he killed many—were instantly replaced.... Moreover, since he did not control the population, he did not control the terrain either, in spite of having companies stationed in so-called strategic positions on the ridge.[18]

For some officers serving in Algeria, interestingly, the obstacle to success in counterinsurgency operations was neither a question of adaptability, nor one of enlightenment, but one of morality. Such was the case for Jacques Guillermaz who felt that it was wrong for the army to get involved in the political affairs of France—for Algeria was French. And moreover, that it was immoral to lure Muslim Algerians to commit to the French side knowing full well that this was contrary to the tide of history, and because France would not be able to protect those who had sided with her from the vengeance of the FLN and its supporters, in the eventuality of a French withdrawal. Veterans of Indochina felt particularly strongly about this point, as loyalists had been massacred in droves by the Viet Minh following the French pull-out. History would indeed repeat itself in Algeria. Thousands of French-paid militiamen (known as *harkis*) were slaughtered in cold blood (sometimes with their families) on the morrow of the French departure.

I discovered through archived correspondence—and was later told by Ruth—that the officer, whom Galula would refer to as "Colonel Bertrand" in *Pacification,* the "man for whom [Galula had] the greatest admiration and respect and with whom [he] had been closely associated for most of [his] career . . ." was none other than Jacques Guillermaz. Guillermaz became Galula's sector and regimental commander in Algeria when the 45th BIC was disbanded, resulting in Galula's transfer to the 2nd Battalion of the 9th RIC. "I took advantage of our long friendship to plead for a change in our tactics,"[19] Galula wrote. But Guillermaz refused. And yet, the older *marsouin* was not a stranger to revolutionary warfare, or to its dependence on political activity. Not a question of know-how then, it was one of principle. ". . . I am a soldier," he had rebuked his protégé, "and I refuse to be anything else."[20] It is for this very reason that Guillermaz would delegate Galula to represent him at the *Comité de Salut Public* (Public Safety Committee),[21] following the May 1958 *Révolte d'Algiers.* It was a quasi-political appointment with which Guillermaz would have been ill at ease, but for which Galula was perfectly suited.

The four "essential laws of counterinsurgency warfare" Galula included in his conclusion to *Pacification* became the pillars of his capstone treatise, as well as the basis from which he derived "principles of counterinsurgency" and a stepwise operational design framework. His first two laws—the population is the objective, and support is gained through the active minority in favor— and the fourth—scale and intensity of efforts—were most heavily influenced by Maoist doctrines. His third law—support from the population is conditional—was most heavily inspired by his experiences in Algeria.

Galula's third law stipulates that effectively protecting the population while demonstrating one's resolve to prevail in the long term are imperatives to success. These are the preconditions to obtaining the population's active support. It is only afterwards that the counterinsurgent can hope to enact effective political, social, and economic reforms that will render his gains sustainable in the long run. From a military perspective, it is only once these preconditions have been met that reliable intelligence about the enemy can be obtained from the population by troops on the ground. In terms that behavioral scientists would probably agree with, Galula wrote under the heading of his third law: "when a man's life is at stake, it takes more than propaganda to budge him."[22]

As Mao had opted for a stepwise approach to revolution, Galula opted for a stepwise approach to counterrevolution. The eight-step operational design framework he crafted would favor control, unity of effort and accessibility at all levels of the chain of command. Algeria allowed Galula to test and prove the validity of his first steps in the field, leaving the final few, for which he neither had the time, nor the power to achieve on his own, as well-considered hypotheses. (Resultantly, his elaboration of these final steps was sparser in *Counterinsurgency*.) Local elections (step 5), testing local leaders (step 6), organizing a [new] political party (step 7), and winning over or suppressing the last guerrillas (step 8) were something of a dialectic tie-back to the first steps of Maoist revolutionary doctrine.

The first semblance of a pacification process to appear in Galula's papers is not his own. Instead, it is the "thirteen-point program" that had been devised by the general in command of his zone in August of 1956, and which Galula would later transcribe in *Pacification*. Although the program did not prove to be entirely successful, it confirmed Galula's impression that a highly structured (i.e., stepwise) approach to a counterinsurgency doctrine was critical to its application in the field.

In terms of contents, the thirteen-point program offered a partial answer to the ubiquitous question of how to involve the population on the side of the counterinsurgent. Galula commented, "[The Zone Commander's program] was based on the idea that pacification would be achieved if we could gradually compromise the population in the eyes of the rebels."[23] The theory was just. The program also spoke of a crucial theme integral to Galula's doctrine: "All the population needed to side with us, provided protection was assured by our forces—was a certain amount of mild pressure on our part so as to have an excuse vis-a-vis the rebels [to cooperate with us]."[24] Here too, the logic was sound. Galula's commentary spoke to his formidable ability for analytical dissection:

> The solution is first to request, and next to order, the population to perform a certain number of collective and individual tasks that will be paid for. By giving orders, the counterinsurgent provides an alibi that the population needs vis-a-vis the insurgent. . . . Just as the counterinsurgent, by forcibly imposing his will on the population, gives it an excuse for not cooperating with the insurgent, the opposite is true. By threatening the population, the insurgent gives the population an excuse, if not a reason, to refuse or refrain from cooperating with the counterinsurgent. The counterinsurgent cannot achieve much if the population is not, and does not feel, protected against the insurgent.[25]

Finally, Galula saw merit in how the thirteen-point program "conditioned" the population into obedience; an unwritten precept of Chinese revolutionary doctrine. The following passage drawn from *Counterinsurgency* reveals the influence this experimentation in Algeria had had on him: "Starting with tasks directly benefiting the population—such as clearing the village or repairing the streets—the counterinsurgent leads the inhabitants gradually, if only in a passive way, to participate in the fight against the insurgent by such work as building roads of military interest. . . ."[26]

(As a military officer with a contemporary perspective, I was most of all impressed by the thirteen-point program's structural simplicity, while recognizing that its contents would be incompatible with present-day constraints on expeditionary forces. The program was issued as a brigade-level operational order to achieve an inherently complex pacification objective. And yet, the entire program was contained on three-quarters of a typed sheet of paper; the direct result of the zone commander's vision and intent, based on the advice received from an undoubtedly restricted staff. In all likelihood, the program was similar in the level of detail to what a rebel commander responsible for a similar-sized zone would have issued verbally or in writing to his fighters. The program was devoid of fanciful language, concepts, or ridiculously grandiose PowerPoint graphics and figures much more suited for maneuver warfare than for pacification work; and all of which leads to a superb control of one's own troops, but rarely of the population, let alone of the insurgency that resides within it. There was no requirement for dozens upon dozens of staff officers to undertake unnecessarily complex and "templated" processes to draw up such a program, sapping along the way the commander's *coup d'oeil*! What's more, is that the program, being phased in accordance with progress and not with operational timings, was much better suited to the problem at hand.)

Impressed as he was by the program upon his arrival in Algeria, Galula produced a four-page set of instructions of his own the following month. He addressed these to the first platoon he would soon send out to occupy a village. Following Mao's teachings on the matter, Galula opted to test the embryonic pacification process his instructions contained in a first village, prior to spreading it to the rest of his *sous-quartier*. The first lines of the instruction read as follows: "In the present Phase, our detachments will establish themselves within the villages to rally the population to our Cause, and to eliminate all hostile elements in order to restore peace. To this end, the detachments' necessary tasks can be divided into four categories: Control of the Population, Action on the Population, Operations [against rebels], and Routine [sustainment]."[27]

Under "Control of the Population," Galula included instructions on how to survey the villagers and their households, how to control their movements and visits, and how to pay particular attention to all aspects of village life. Under "Action on the Population," he instructed his men on the use of propaganda, the appointment of local leaders, and the creation of a medical dispensary and of a school (both of which were to be staffed by handpicked soldiers). Galula stressed the important dual role that every soldier would have to play: gathering intelligence on the enemy and disseminating propaganda messages to the population. In an effort to promote familiarity with villagers and their patterns of life, he ordered, finally, that squads be assigned to patrol certain areas and that this not be changed.

Six months later, Galula recuperated the thirteen-point program's goal of establishing a sustainable self-defense force. In February of 1957, he issued a second secret-labeled set of instructions, titling these, *Creation of a Self-Defence Force in Bou Souar*.[28] He gave orders for the recruitment and arming of a dozen able-bodied men from the village. He placed the administration of this small militia in the care of the elected mayor of Bou Souar, and tellingly defined three categories of tasks for the militia to undertake: military, police and political. The instruction bore the mark of the Chinese revolutionaries he had studied. In the elaboration of political tasks, for instance, he wrote: "Screening of good and bad elements within the population, putting up posters and distributing leaflets, verbal communication of messages to the illiterate, writing slogans on walls, recruitment of other militiamen, etc."[29]

Neither of the above two sets of instructions I found in Galula's papers are mentioned in his published works. The documents are significant, nonetheless, because they contain the embryo for the framework of operations he would elaborate years later in *Counterinsurgency*. The first of these documents, drafted in September 1956, is particularly significant to the biographic study of Galula because it provides additional proof that he had been incubating a response to revolutionary warfare well prior to his arrival in Algeria; the first month spent in a new theater of operations is hardly enough time to understand such a problem and foment such a theory.

In early 2010, I was put in contact with *Commandant* P. L. Bléhaut by a helpful Saint-Cyr alumnus. As luck would have it, Bléhaut had been a classmate of Galula's at Saint-Cyr, and had served with him in the same battalion in Algeria. "In 1956–1957, we were situated, you could say, in the third phase of Galula's [process]—control of the population," the elderly veteran wrote me after describing in great detail the *quartier* they had shared. "Galula knew how to perfectly impose his authority on that population by protecting it through his actions. This allowed him to gather valuable intelligence."

"Galula summed up his methods to us as follows: 'the carrot and the stick',", Bléhaut continued. "In order to have the ability to reward the population [for its collaboration], he was first compelled to take away some of its liberties. He imposed, for instance, a very strict curfew, and would then slacken it gradually. He imposed stringent cleanliness and sanitary rules in the villages, while gradually improving their living conditions by dispensing education and medical services. His method came to be used by the entire battalion. We built a road going up to the peak of the djebel, as well as a large school in this fashion. The method earned us the trust of the majority of the population."

The micro-pacification of Igonane Ameur, the first village where Galula had embedded a platoon (and indeed his own headquarters to be close at hand to his first experimentation), had been a success. Confident in what practical results his theory could obtain, he drafted two unsolicited memoranda destined for his superiors that described his process and what lessons he had learned, but recommending above all, that a unifying doctrine be adopted in Algeria. Galula appended both memoranda in integral form to *Pacification*.[30] These memoranda represented yet another important step in the evolution of his doctrine, as many essential themes in *Counterinsurgency* can be traced back to these.

The first memorandum was titled *Notes on Pacification in Greater Kabylia*. Written in November 1956, barely three months after his arrival, the memo made its way up to the very top of the chain of command, where General Salan, the theater commander, undoubtedly recognized Galula's name. Salan forwarded the memorandum up to National Defense Headquarters, resulting in Galula being invited to make an oral transcription of it during his New Year's leave in Paris, for the benefit of General Ely, the Chairman of the Joint Chiefs of Staff. The latter would have the Minister of Defense listen to it too according to Galula. Colonel Goussault, the commander of the powerful Psychological Action Bureau in Algeria, was also made aware of the report, undoubtedly by Colonel Lacheroy, his superior in Paris, and the godfather of the important Psychological Action branch in the French military. Goussault congratulated the much more junior Galula on the recording, and published a sanitized version of it in his Bureau's classified journal.[31] Galula's luck was such that *Le Monde*, France's widely disseminated center-left newspaper, would publish a nasty editorial in reaction to a leaked copy of the journal. Referring to Galula anonymously as "*Le Capitaine de Kabylie*," the editorialist attacked Galula's proposal to address the "lack of firmness" he perceived in dealing with the population, which placed the counterinsurgent at a disadvantage.

Of the second Algeria memorandum drafted in March of 1957, and titled *The Technique of Pacification in Kabylia*, Galula wrote: "I decided to synthesize a step-by-step process for the pacification of Kabylia. This document was approved by every officer to whom it was shown. General Lacomme[32] agreed with my formula, General Guerin, the new zone commander, concurred ... I was asked to take it myself to General Dulac, General Salan's Chief of Staff in Algiers."[33] But despite the exposure, Galula was disappointed: "Once more, it had no effect." He was frustrated that the progress in his *sous-quartier* did not seem to suffice to prove to upper echelons that he was not swimming in theory. "Indeed," Galula continued, "whenever the zone commander, the préfet, or even Algiers wanted to show visitors that pacification was no dream, they sent them to my area. Thus I received General Salan (twice), General Ely, the then-Minister of Defense M. Morice, plus any number of lower officials and foreign journalists."[34]

Galula sold his influence short. He preceded his second Algeria memorandum with the following note to which we return in the following chapter: "The

VIPs visit Galula's sous-quartier. Galula, on the right, plays host to Defense Minister André Morice (in civilian attire in the center), General Paul Ely (left of Galula), and General Raoul Salan (second officer wearing a trench coat from the left).

ideas contained in this report were embodied in the Challe Plan and became the basis of our counterinsurgency doctrine in 1959–1961." The Challe Plan's significance to the Algerian War surpassed that of the Strategic Hamlet Program to Vietnam, and matched that of the U.S. military's counterinsurgency manual—FM 3-24—to Iraq and Afghanistan.

As another example demonstrating his influence, Galula participated in a series of briefings given to U.S. Army officers on the Algerian War during his summer leave in 1957. He omitted to mention this in his otherwise exhaustive *Pacification*. He and two other handpicked officers delivered presentations at three U.S. bases in France. The outline of his presentation notes include the core doctrinal themes he would later elaborate. The English-speaking Galula was highly appreciated by his American audiences. France's top soldier, General Ely, addressed a personal letter to General Salan to highlight Galula's performance. The latter was praised for simplifying matters into succinct but strong arguments, and as always, for adding a personal touch of humor. Ely wrote to Salan: ". . . thanks to his excellent grasp of the [English] language, American mentality, and of the true conditions related to guerrilla warfare, this officer was able to captivate an audience which was, in general, rather ill-disposed to fully comprehend the overall situation [in Algeria]." Although Ely felt that the United States had turned its back on France at Dien Bien Phu, and then again during the Suez Crisis, he was still hopeful that U.S. foreign policy would change in favor of France's interests.[35] He concluded his letter to Salan, "It is for these reasons that these conferences may be considered successful; and there is ample reason to hope that they will have been profitable and beneficial [to us]."[36] Salan forwarded Ely's letter to Galula, adding a note of his own to congratulate his old acquaintance.[37]

Was Galula rewarded for these achievements in Algeria? Yes. Not through pomp, but in the manner he appreciated most: acknowledgment of his opinions and intellect at the highest levels. His performance in Algeria contributed to earning him a prestigious assignment under de Gaulle, as of August of 1958, on which he kept mum in *Pacification*.

Although there may appear to have been a discrepancy between Galula's achievements and his progression in rank, it is well to note that promotions were notoriously slow in the French military of the 1950s. Joe Alsop was correct in writing that the French officer of Galula's era was ". . . Rather lower in rank than an officer of comparable age in the American Army. . . . In experience, on the other hand, he is far older than most members of post-war generation in any other army. He has in fact been almost continuously at war his entire adult life."[38]

I gleaned from Galula's military file at Vincennes that he had been recommended for promotion by his battalion commander immediately following his arrival in Algeria. One year later, *Commandant* Denoyes would give him a resounding performance evaluation, acknowledging his subordinate's exceptional intelligence, personable character, and desire for increased responsibilities. He also recognized that Galula had "perfectly succeeded" in the pacification of his *sous-quartier*, while noting that he was "more interested in operational or pacification questions, than in material questions."[39] (Unsurprisingly, the cerebral Galula would recommend that a deputy position be created at the company level to alleviate the commander's administrative burden, so that he could devote himself to pacification work.)

Denoyes kept pushing for Galula's promotion. On August 5, 1957, he wrote his subordinate up for a divisional citation. General Guerin, the zone commander who had come to notice Galula's achievements, approved, as would General Allard, his Corps commander. Galula was attributed the Silver Star for his *Croix de la Valeur Militaire*. What Galula referred to as his "drummed-up"[40] citation read as follows:

A knowledgeable and courageous officer in command of a company responsible for a *sous-quartier* in the Djebel Mimoun (Greater Kabylia), [Galula] perfectly succeeded in the pacification of his area by destroying the political cells of Bou Souar, Ikhelouiyene, Ait Braham, and Timizar Laghbar.

He Participated on September 21st and 22nd, 1956, in the clearing of the north flank of Djebel Aissa Mimoun, which translated in the arrest of ten suspects. He particularly distinguished himself as an infantry company commander during operations conducted on the 27th and 29th October 1956 in the Beni Smenzer during which the outlaws suffered 7 killed, 1 wounded, 1 prisoner, and where 12 weapons were captured. He distinguished himself once more from the 10th of April 1957 to the 10th of May during an operation to control Greater Tizi Ouzou, which concluded with the arrest of 27 rebels belonging to adversary organizations.[41]

Galula criticized the very system that required a combat citation to justify a promotion in a pacification campaign. (Lyautey had railed against the same phenomenon some sixty years earlier in *Du rôle colonial de l'armée*.) His contention lay with the fact that the capture or destruction of a handful of replaceable insurgents and weapons could trump the more comprehensive pacification of his area. And why, for that matter, was the fact that schools and medical dispensaries were up and running in his *sous-quartier*, and manned by his own soldiers, not commended as well?[42] He deliberated in *Pacificaiton*:

> Medals were given on the basis of valor in combat. If there was no combat because the local commander had succeeded in pacifying his area, too bad for him—no medal. It was no doubt much easier to assess the efficiency of an officer by glancing at the "score" (how many rebels killed or captured? How many weapons seized?) than by making an estimate of the support he received from the population; what criteria was one to use in this case?[43]

However, as mentioned earlier, Galula's true frustration resided in the reluctance of some of his superiors to endorse his pacification process despite its demonstrated success. His battalion commander in 1958, *Commandant* Ginabat, whom Galula would serve as deputy, although of equal rank, would laud Galula for being "dynamic, robust, with a keen sense of tactics, capable of making clear and prompt decisions, and issuing neat orders"; but would also remark, as others had in previous years, that "amongst his very original ideas, some were difficult to translate to reality."[44] A more poignant case of incredulity occurred when the Inspector General of the Infantry visited Galula's *sous-quartier*. The general expressed his horror at the dispersion of Galula's company among six villages: "With your forces spread out as they are, you have lost all military value. Your posts are utterly useless, their strength too small to allow any serious sortie against the guerrillas!"[45] To this, Galula answered what would still be valid today: "Wasn't the risk in not controlling and protecting the population much greater than the risk of dispersion?"[46] (Fifty years later, the U.S. Army's and Marine Corps' FM 3-24 would address this issue head-on as one of the "paradoxes"[47] of counterinsurgency warfare.)

I stumbled upon a confidential post-mortem report in Galula's papers regarding the deaths of Asli Ahmed,[48] the elderly World War I veteran turned mayor in Galula's *sous-quartier*, and of his son, twenty-year-old Asli Mohamed. The report speaks to Galula's consideration for those Algerians who had actively supported the French cause. The young Asli had been killed "walking point," along with Captain Mauduit, Galula's successor, during a night ambush described in *Pacification*. The young man's father would be killed in the following year by French forces who mistook him for a *fellagha* during a clearing operation. Galula had learned about this in May of 1959, during his one and only trip back to Algeria.[49] Eight years later, Galula concluded his testimony to the French Veterans' Affairs administrator investigating the accident with the following:

> The mayor's family is thus reduced to his widow, his son Asli Ali, and a still younger son. I do not know what has happened to Asli Ali. If he is still alive, I wish that he be brought to France so that I may take personal care of him. As for his younger brother, it seems to me that he should be entitled to become a *pupile de la nation*. I have included here a cheque of 100 francs. I ask . . . that it be remitted in cash to the mayor's widow in the interim; as I hope that official aid will become available to her soon.[50]

Regular Algerians had called for Galula in return. He had become popular not only through charisma and devotion to their cause, which he saw as a match to the French cause, but also through the real protection he had afforded them in his *sous-quartier*. I have no reason to doubt that Galula was genuine when he wrote: "Villagers from Tikobain and nearby hamlets petitioned the préfet for permission to be included in my sous-quartier, 'Where one knew where one stood.'"[51]

Ruth remembered attending a popular rally held in Bordj Menaiel, in 1958, while visiting her husband. "David was treated as a guest of honour." The *préfet* of Tizi Ouzou had wished to make her husband mayor of the city because of his talent in organizing the population, and because of the respect he commanded. Ruth also remembered attending a *meshoui* (spit-roast) feast in Aissa Mimoun held in their honor. "We were treated with a lot of deference by these Kabyles," she told me. Rainy weather had caused the *meshoui* to be postponed by one day, but the lambs had already been slaughtered. "The meat was rancid by the next day," Ruth recalled. "David wouldn't let me eat it. But he did, to my surprise . . . him of all people! I suppose he did not wish to offend his hosts."

Troop morale and attitude were also important considerations for Galula. He complained in a confidential report to his hierarchy:

> With the exception of one post, accommodations consist of Kabyle shacks, where the troops live together in little "rooms" that are impossible to heat. This has lasted for too long. . . . It would have been easy to build during the good season; work undertaken this late is often interrupted by bad weather, which leads one to believe that this will be yet another winter in poor shelter.
>
> The country offers no distraction. There are no women, [only] three movie showings per year, and silly movies at that; no light in the evenings to play cards, not a single room that could be used for recreation. Even hunting is not made possible.[52]

Galula's leadership had been put to the test from the moment of his arrival. He had elaborated a pacification plan that steered away from conventionalism. "You do not catch flies with vinegar"[53] was a favorite line of his. Counterproductive use of force and attitudes had been his primary concern, particularly among his junior leaders. To this end, he had held multiple indoctrination sessions for his troops, the notes of which have survived in his archives. The results of his approach soon convinced the majority of his men of its merits. He gradually evicted from his company those men who couldn't be swayed. He would state the following to higher headquarters:

> The Company's moral has generally improved in comparison to the previous year. The improvement was due to the departure of worthless leaders and to better overall leadership; in addition to improvements in pacification work, which have transformed the *sous-quartier* into a "peaceful corner," and to the semblance of "family life" and camaraderie present in the little outposts that offsets the difficult living conditions. . . . The reduction in the number of disciplinary measures imposed does well to reflect the state of moral.[54]

The 3rd Company indeed grew fond of its leader, and vice versa. Galula related candidly in *Pacification*:

> Having been away from troop duty for so long and not knowing the true state of the Army, I expected to find reflected among the draftees

the fact that 25% of the French people vote communist. I expected to
have to deal with soldiers who loathed Army life, who would question
the reason of this "colonial war." I was completely wrong. I never commanded soldiers of such quality, not even in 1944–45 when we were
fighting for the liberation of France.[55]

Galula had shared these same fears with his wife, who recalled, "He complained, before his departure, that his troops would all be from the Marseilles
area. He expected to command a bunch of 'leftists.' But his men had witnessed the atrocities committed by a Muslim mob on a European neighborhood prior to his arrival in Algeria. He found himself having to rein them in
instead." Adding to this challenge was the fact that Galula's company would
be reinforced with Moslem draftees and a locally raised *harka*. Of these soldiers he wrote: "we treated them exactly as we did the French soldiers, except
for food (they did not eat pork). They behaved in a normal way, mixed easily
with their French comrades, and took part in every operation, firing at *fellaghas* with as much gusto when the occasion arose."[56]

Galula exerted a style of leadership that brought him close to his men and
that, at times, had been reproached by his superiors. Chinese revolutionaries
had practiced a quasi-egalitarian system in their ranks, raising the question
of whether Galula had been influenced in this aspect too. Mao had preached
for this not only from an ideological standpoint of communist equality,
but also from a practical one of allowing for ample initiative at lower levels for guerrilla operations to succeed. Marshal Lyautey, who devoted this
later career to colonial wars and administration, had also famously pleaded
for narrowing the gap between the French officer corps and *les hommes de
troupes*, while vaunting the merits that pacification work had on "decorpo-
ralizing" soldiers.[57] This was quite contrary to General de Gaulle's point of
view, for instance, which insisted that a military leader should be reserved,
and sparse of words, in his classic work *Le Fil de l'Épée*. De Gaulle had
been right within the context of a looming German threat, when firm discipline and unquestioning obedience would be the more useful attributes
of soldiers. But the dichotomy was (and remains) a faded one. Small wars
require more intellectual initiative from soldiers, and a more cognitive
form of devotion, not instead of, but in addition to warrior ethos, discipline
and obedience.

Galula's cavalier consideration of death lent itself well to his leadership
style. He preferred to spend the majority of his time on the ground, meddling
with his troops and the population under his protection. He rode a horse
between hamlets not because he was an avid equestrian, which he was, but to
show that he was in control, and that *fear* wasn't in his *sous-quartier*, keeping
with the old colonial tradition of displaying confidence and interest in the
local population.

Léon Junalik was a sergeant in the 2nd Battalion of the 9th RIC orderly room. I was able to reach him in 2010 through a French veterans' association dedicated to the Algerian War. Junalik had known Galula when the latter had been promoted and transferred to the position of deputy battalion commander in Bordj Menaiel. In our correspondence, Junalik recalled how the *quartier* had been particularly difficult. "We were in an operational area where the FLN was very aggressive. They exacted a heavy toll on prisoners, and even on our deceased," he wrote me. "But Galula nonetheless took the task of pacification quite seriously."

Another veteran I corresponded with, Guy Boyer, had soldiered in Galula's 3rd Company when the latter was still a captain in the 45th BIC. Boyer was stationed with his platoon in the village of Igonane Ameur, and was therefore part of Galula's first pacification trial. Boyer was saddened to learn that Galula had passed away at a relatively young age. "When I had known him," the veteran wrote me, "he was a young man, *très sympatique*, and full of humour." Boyer recalled how Galula had assigned him to teach French in the town's makeshift school. "One day, as I was teaching, Captain Galula was patrolling with another platoon on horseback. He stopped to come and see me. He said hello, and then jokingly: 'Boyer, the girls here are in love with you, I bet you will end up getting married with one of them and staying here!' He then congratulated me for the work I was accomplishing and left."

Boyer's description of his former commander's leadership style was in line with what could be extrapolated from the latter's character. "He was not an authoritarian man," he informed me. "He was, on the contrary, very close to the men he led. He commanded in a very participative style, infusing a bit of humour wherever he could." The next recollection that Boyer offered made me laugh more than just a little. When Galula had assembled his men for the first time to announce that they would soon be sent in small detachments to garrison the *sous-quartier's* hamlets, he concluded with: "Oh, and please do not worry, you will have opportunities to go down to the city ... Tizi Ouzou ... *pour vous dégorger les olives!*" (I'll the leave the translation of this particular French expression to the reader!)

14

Interlude: French Pacification Tradition, Revolutionary Warfare, and the Challe Instruction

The best means by which to achieve pacification in our new colony is to combine force and politics.

—*Marshal H. Lyautey*[1]

"No politics" is an ingrained reaction for the conventional soldier, whose job is solely to defeat the enemy, yet in counterinsurgency warfare, the soldier's job is to help win the support of the population, and in so doing, he has to engage in practical politics.

—*David Galula*[2]

DAVID GALULA HAD NOT BEEN TAUGHT, as discussed earlier, French colonial history at Saint-Cyr. His cadet class did not have the luxury of studying the exploits and methods of Bugeaud, Faidherbe, Gallieni, Lyautey, and others. Rushed by a declaration of war, training was condensed to cover the bare essentials of junior field command. After fighting a conventional campaign in Europe, Galula would follow Guillermaz to the heart of China where he remained isolated from France and her traditional colonial areas. Assigned to Peking, then briefly to Greece, and finally to Hong Kong in the shadow of the Indochina War, Galula worked quasi-autonomously for nearly a decade until returning to troop duty in Algeria. Until then, Galula's exposure to "*l'école coloniale*," which informally instituted a century of lessons drawn from French pacification tradition (from Bugeaud's conquest of Algeria in the 1830s, to the final pacification of the Moroccan Rif a century later), had been very limited. Moreover, a new school of thought on counterinsurgency, known as *Guerre Révolutionnaire*, or revolutionary warfare, was set to supersede it. Spurred by the belief that France and her colonies had become the target of concerted communist subversion, revolutionary warfare evolved from the theoretical conception of a globalized insurrectionary threat, into a counterrevolutionary pseudo-doctrine, which would bear an important influence on Galula's generation of officers.

The questions to which this interlude is owed are: (1) Were Galula's writings influenced at all by *l'école coloniale*?, and (2) Were they influenced by revolutionary warfare theory and its apostles? An affirmative response to one, does not exclude an affirmative response to the other.

There is little risk in assuming that Galula held some knowledge of *l'école coloniale* despite his lack of formal education in the matter. Galula, we recall, was an avid reader of military literature. His military file evaluations referred to his having an excellent "*culture générale*," historically, a mark of pride for Colonial Army officers. He may very well have been familiar with some of Lyautey's works such as *Du rôle colonial de l'armée* and *Paroles d'action*. These were replete with reflections on pacification, all of which were underpinned by the belief—proven by decades of experience—that the population, more so than the enemy, should lay at the center of all pacification efforts.

But to what extent were Galula's writings *directly* inspired by *l'école coloniale*? Two simple factors complicate the answer. The first is that what may appear to be inspired similarities may very well be based on independent observations. The mechanics and counter-mechanics of insurgencies and small wars, whatever their historical context, seldom present parameters that differ so fundamentally that similar conclusions about the art cannot be drawn. The second complicating factor is that the superseding school of thought, revolutionary warfare, would itself borrow a number of lessons from *l'école coloniale*. It is therefore difficult to precisely determine from where certain theories originated.

We note, nonetheless, that references to colonial pacification are very nearly absent from Galula's writings. The latter made a single telling association when he wrote in *Pacification*: "It soon became obvious that military operations alone could not defeat the rebels. The population had to be protected, controlled, won over, and thus isolated from the rebels. Work in depth was necessary. This is how we had pacified Morocco in the 1920s and early 1930s."[3] But otherwise, Galula's stated belief, for instance, that *quadrillage*, or gridding, was a "new method"[4] may indicate how little conscious acknowledgment he lent to *l'école coloniale*. Gridding had been used well before and after the turn of the twentieth century in Tonkin, Madagascar and Morocco.[5] Furthermore, we note that though references to Mao, Chu Teh and other Chinese revolutionaries abound in *Counterinsurgency*, the same cannot be said of references to Gallieni, Lyautey or other illuminati of *l'école coloniale*. Gallieni, who had written of *tâche d'huile* a century before the Algerian War, does not earn a single mention in Galula's works, nor does Lyautey, who is credited for committing to paper the wisdom acquired from decades of French pacification campaigns.

Alas, this is somewhat disappointing. Seventy years before Galula wrote on the subject, Lyautey had already shared lessons that have not lost an ounce of relevance to this day. During the pacification of the Tonkin, for instance, Lyautey had responded to the French Governor General's plea for a greater focus on hunting Chinese raiders along the northern borders with the following:

Firstly, past experience has proven that we are rarely if ever capable of destroying a pirate band uniquely by fire. In the fox hunt that characterizes the pursuit, the pirates hold all of the advantages for obvious reasons that need not be reminded here. The fox hunt offers only incomplete results at a cost of fatigue, losses, and expenses which are seldom justified by success. . . . Secondly, we must not lose sight of the fact that "the pirate" is, by figure of speech, "a plant that grows only in certain types of land," and the surest method [to counter it], is to make the land inhospitable to it. . . . If we push the analogy further, I would add that when we consider cultivating a parcel of land that has been overtaken by weeds, cutting these down does not suffice—as the work will have to be repeated the next day—and so one must, after having ploughed the earth, isolate the land, and plant good seed which will deny the weeds from growing back. . . . Finally, we plant good seed by organizing and rebuilding the population, providing it with arms for its defence, establishing markets, enabling agriculture, and building roads, all of which renders the conquered land uninhabitable to the pirate, which sees himself transformed by this evolution to a point of cooperating with it.[6]

Nonetheless, themes such as these resonate in Galula works. Long before Mao or even Lenin, Lyautey had written, "It is through a combined action of force and politics that we must achieve pacification of the country, and the organization that we wish to bestow on it later," to which he added, "Political action is by far the most important."[7]

Lyautey stated that a colonial officer was required to adopt a "triple role" once open resistance to his forces had been swept away: ". . . diplomatic, . . . political, . . . and administrative."[8] The marshal rebuked the critics in Paris who accused him of demilitarizing expeditionary forces (a concern echoed by some today) by employing them in civil duties he believed were required to achieve a state of pacification. Lyautey skillfully countered that the Colonial Army only "decorporalized" its men, by asking each of them to make every use of his initiative and ingenuity.

That every soldier had a responsibility to "work on the population" by administrating surveys, dispensing education, organizing village committees, acting as a vector of propaganda, etc., was certainly not lost on Galula. Lyautey also believed in the importance of continuity in the civil and military administration entrusted with pacification. Consciously or not, this too would be recuperated by Galula who even felt that the same squads should be assigned to the same neighborhoods, as mentioned earlier.

Lyautey argued, as would Galula later, that not all leaders were cut out for pacification work. While campaigning in Madagascar, Lyautey wrote: ". . . this brings me to discuss a second issue that presents a serious obstacle to my command function. This issue relates to personnel. It is clear that to put the above [pacification] instructions into practice, our provincial leaders and their subordinates, both military and civilian, must be selected with the greatest care. These must be perfectly capable of exercising multiple functions: military, administrative, judicial, economic, etc."[9]

The marshal also cautioned against the employment of "laurel-seekers" in pacification campaigns, a topic that Galula and others of his generation tackled head-on. Lyautey wrote bluntly that participation in colonial operations should be denied to those ". . . mandarins who, possessing all of the academic qualifications, only require a quick campaign to be propelled upwards to the next rank." He continued his scathing reflection in *Du rôle colonial de l'armée* with, "We must be very weary of all of those who wish for another Austerlitz. Firstly, there are no Austerlitzs in the colonies. And secondly, these men are ill-prepared for the protracted, thankless and lacklustre work that characterizes the everyday tasks of the colonial officer. . . ."[10] Lyautey criticized the misalignment between the military's recognition process with that of the objectives sought in pacification operations. Galula would do the same in *Counterinsurgency*: "A system of military awards and promotion, such as that in conventional warfare, which would encourage soldiers to kill or capture the largest number of enemies, and thus induce him to increase the scope and frequency of his military operations, may well be disastrous in counterinsurgency warfare."[11]

Lyautey thus militated against the excessive use of force that was susceptible of alienating a population. He wrote, "When one must seize an objective, but keeps in mind that he will have to establish a market there on the morrow, one does not seize the objective in the same fashion."[12] (Lyautey and other contributors to *l'école coloniale*, we note, could simultaneously embrace a population-centric approach to counterinsurgency while ordering *razziahs*—punitive raids—against recalcitrant villages. Similarly, the Chinese communists and the Viet Minh had set the population as their objective, but had nonetheless enacted very brutal repressions. Population-centricity, morality, and "hearts and minds" are not synonymous issues; regrettably they are often confused as such, leading some to propagate misconceptions.)

Other themes in Galula's works, such as the importance of dispensing education and medical care, also appear, at first glance, to find their roots in *l'école colonial*, where the expert wielding of "the carrot and the stick" had always been instrumental to a successful campaign. We may note, for instance, how Lyautey was alleged to have sent a telegram to Gallieni colorfully asking him, "send me four doctors, and I will send you in return four battalions."[13] Galula wrote, "At some point in the counterinsurgency process, the static units that took part initially in large-scale military operations in their area will find themselves confronted with a huge variety of non-military tasks which have to be performed only by military personnel, because of the shortage of reliable civilian political and administrative personnel. . . . Thus a mimeograph may turn out more useful than a machine gun, a soldier trained as a pediatrician more important than a mortar expert, ..."[14]

Beyond the tangible pacification benefits that humanitarian and economic development safeguarded, subscribers to *l'école coloniale* believed that France's *mission civilizatrice* was intrinsically good. Indeed, Lyautey's theme of adding a "parcel of love" to pacification work would be recuperated later by the French high command in Algeria.[15] "In the human form that the present type of conflict undertakes," read the Challe Instruction for the Pacification of Algeria in late 1959, "only those who know to place a parcel of love in all of their actions will win."[16] Needless to say that not all were swayed.

And yet, despite all of these similarities, it would be unfair and imprudent to conclude that Galula had been deeply influenced by colonial pacification tradition beyond an elemental degree. In contrast with the Chinese Revolutionary school of thought, it is far from certain that the influence of *l'école coloniale* on Galula had been direct.

The second, more certain French influence exerted on Galula's writings belonged to his own era. The revolutionary warfare school of thought emerged in the tumultuous aftermath of World War II in France.[17] It grew out of the contradiction that a modern, well-equipped, and well-trained army—the French Army—could be defeated by revolutionaries in Indochina that had seemingly grown out of nothing. The fear that such a scenario could be repeated elsewhere, such as in Algeria, or even in Metropolitan France, lent the movement impetus.

Mounting communist agitation in France and across her empire led to the creeping belief in military circles that the Nation found itself engaged once more in an existentialist struggle *after* 1945. "World War III has begun,"[18] was an often repeated statement. Café bombs and violent labor-union demonstrations alike were blamed on external communist subversion. It was thought that such subversion was aided by a homegrown "Fifth Column," affiliated to the increasingly powerful *Parti Communiste.* The adherents to this theory believed that the Communist Bloc had chosen to target France because of the strategic location of her territories. Only France remained as a bulwark to communist expansion in Asia, Europe and the Mediterranean. Air Force General Lionel Chassin believed, quite alarmingly in hindsight, that if France and the West ". . . loses this ideological war, and Mao's designs for encircle-ment come to fruition, then all will be lost!"[19] Revolutionary warfare pun-dits considered that the adversary was already fighting on the psychological plane, taking advantage of the West's obliviousness to the notion that war, even if undeclared, could be waged just as effectively through subversion. The Colonial Army, which stood to lose everything in the conflict, was particu-larly taken to these views.

"The communists have revealed to us in recent years the secrets of this new form of war that we call revolutionary warfare," lectured Colonel Goussault, the man in charge of psychological operations in Algeria, at a high-profile conference. "These are the secrets that are being used by the rebels in Alge-ria."[20] Thus, Algeria too was seen through the prism of East vs. West, and *not* (as it should have been) through the prism of localized nationalism. "Con-sciously or not," read the French campaign plan in Algeria as late as 1959, "the FLN serves [the Marxists] as a vector in the present universal struggle in which mankind is at stake."[21]

Revolutionary warfare was set to take over doctrinal thinking in the French military, particularly among the younger generations of officers. (An effect similar to the one the "COIN" phenomenon has had on Western armies in the past decade.) "Revolutionary warfare" came to describe a counterinsurgency theory as much as it did a military subculture. The term received approval from Bernard Fall who preferred it to "counter-insurgency," or to "counter-guerrilla warfare," or even to "political warfare." "Revolutionary warfare," Fall wrote, "is the only expression which . . . combines both method and pur-pose in one comprehensive and uncomplicated term."[22] Galula, on the other hand, was more reticent to embrace it, "because it automatically relegates us to the 'counterrevolutionary' camp,"[23] but would nonetheless employ it often himself. More importantly, he would ascribe to many of the principles, which its underlying theory upheld.

It is beyond contention that Galula was exposed to a profusion of writings and conferences on revolutionary warfare, and that moreover, he would him-self contribute to the theory. He remained critical, however, of the cult-like following it inspired, and particularly of the psychological action program through which it was formally instituted.

Among the most ardent supporters and proselytizers of revolutionary warfare theory were those officers recruited into the psychological action bureaus. These specialists were often selected as a consequence to their internment in the Viet Minh's infamous prisoner camps. It was felt that their intimate knowledge of communist indoctrination techniques would come in handy, if properly adapted, to rallying rebellious segments of the Algerian population to the French cause. (Oddly enough, even though the indoctrination techniques used by the Viet Minh were generally proven to be ineffective against French prisoners of war, they would be recuperated energetically in Algeria.) Otherwise, the Psychological Action Bureau sought to recruit the most dynamic, intelligent, and articulate officers the army could provide.

General Raoul Salan's arrival in Algeria in late 1956 marked a decisive shift towards the adoption of revolutionary warfare theory in that theater. *L'école coloniale* and the central role previously granted to the old guard of Indigenous Affairs officers were cast aside in favor of the lessons imported by counter-insurgents who had fought in Indochina. Salan surrounded himself with officers who had served with him there, and who were generally taken to the view that communist subversion was at the root of all contentions against French rule. The Indigenous Affairs officers cried out in protest that a woefully insufficient administration of Algeria had led to the rebellion. Algeria had been under-governed, and in that vacuum, the FLN and its shadow governance cells had prospered. And that was it. The problem in Algeria had little to do with the Soviet Union or China. Moreover, the Old Guard felt that transposing propaganda tools between such culturally different places was senseless.[24] When fundamental differences between the Viet Minh and the FLN were pointed out by those who were skeptical of the universality of revolutionary warfare theory, upholders of the latter simply acknowledged that the FLN were waging a campaign that was technically inferior to the Viet Minh![25]

As has already been discussed, Galula could also be guilty of similar biases and oversimplifications. And yet, he was critical of any overreliance on psychological means of warfare. (Analogously, the Israel Defense Force was compelled to review its doctrine following its campaign against the Hezbollah in 2006. Its doctrine had become too impregnated with lofty concepts such as Systemic Operational Design that rely on complicated assessments of the psychological impact of operations.[26]) Galula related in *Pacification*:

> At the other extreme [of the warriors] were the "psychologists," most of them recruited among officers who had undergone the Viet Minh brainwashing in prisoner camps. To them, psychological action was the answer to everything, not merely the simple propaganda and psychological warfare adjunct to other types of operations, conventional or otherwise.
>
> "You use force against the enemy," one of their leaders told me, "not so much to destroy him but in order to make him change his mind on the necessity of pursuing the fight. In other words, you do a psychological action." They were convinced that the population could be manipulated through certain techniques adapted from communist methods.

There were others in the French Army, however, such as Colonel Jean Nemo, who were still more nuanced in their subscription to the theory of revolutionary warfare. Nemo's keen interest in social and ethnological studies led him to resist the dogmatism that inevitably resulted from the internationalization of an ideological conflict, as revolutionary warfare theory sought to do. In what may be seen as a precursor to "human terrain" or "cultural terrain" often spoken of today, Nemo wrote in the 1950s: "The organization and composition of the military force of a country depends largely on the social organization, the mores and customs of its population. France's mistake was to wage the war without understanding Vietnamese social structure(s), while its enemy mounted its strategy and tactics on a careful study of that 'social terrain.'"[27]

Galula's writings lack, in my view, an adequate treatment of the importance of culture, which, in its broadest sense, extends to the formation of local power structures that must be leveraged if pacification efforts are to succeed in the long term. (Power structures need to be first studied and understood if they are to be leveraged.) Galula's treatment of the issue was scant, perhaps, because he preferred to believe—not without good reason in many cases—that human beings were fundamentally motivated by similar things.

To be sure, Galula was not entirely oblivious to culture. He had written in a memorandum, for example, "Among the customs of the Algerian rural population there is one that we must absolutely take into account: the weekly market, which is a natural focus of agitation and propaganda. It would be futile to expect decisive results in the countryside as long as these souks have not been purged and controlled."[28] Galula had also cautioned the commander of the Psychological Action Bureau in Algeria against the use of simple slogans and thinly veiled propaganda inspired from Indochina.

Galula was wary, above all, of Pavlovian techniques. In his first memorandum to his chain of command, he warned, "those who see propaganda a simple instrument for stuffing the brain underestimate dangerously the people's common sense. We are dealing in Kabila not with naïve virgin minds but with people who have been abroad many times. We will not convince them with mere talk but only with the truth. . . . If we do not inform them properly, others will, and against us."[29]

At the core of revolutionary warfare theory lay the belief that individuals and entire peoples could be sold to any cause or ideology *if* the appropriate "*embrigadement,*" or indoctrination, was employed. The theory thus massively favored technique over ideology. A good indoctrination could always defeat a good cause. If the communists could win over populations by promising nothing more than a cause that "enslaved" them and culminated in totalitarianism, the theorists argued, then surely the East was winning based on technique alone! Professors Villatoux perfectly summarized the issue as follows:

Whether it is the Moslem from the highland, the peasant in the rice paddy or the docker in Marseilles, none has a valid reason to be dissatisfied to the point of clashing with the established power according to the promoters of *l'arme psychologique*. The aspirations of the people, whether they be of social or nationalist nature, are brushed aside at once by this theory, or denied on principle. The population is viewed as a shapeless and malleable dough to be worked on by a communist ideology with global designs. This rhetoric, far from being the product of a paternalistic or racist colonialism, was instead marked by virulent anticommunism, which suffocated any notion that did not fall in-line with a dogmatic framework that had become obsessive.[30]

Galula was not absolved by this, as he too believed that "provided we have a firm and continuous policy in which our action in every field . . . could be integrated, it is possible, by using the technique of revolutionary warfare, to win this war in Algeria."[31] This said, he acknowledged that a cause or contradiction upheld by an insurgency needed to be addressed, or rendered less acute, *if* it was possible for the counterinsurgent to do so. He tampered this with his knowing belief, however, that successful insurgents invariably remained flexible in their choice of cause, preferring those that could not be resolved or adopted by the counterinsurgent.

Colonel Charles Lacheroy became France's principal theorist on revolutionary warfare and psychological action.[32] Lacheroy had coined the term revolutionary warfare himself, describing it as "the alliance between parallel hierarchies and psychological warfare methods."[33] He had given his first conference on revolutionary warfare in late 1952, in Indochina, to an audience of subordinate officers who were mesmerized by the charismatic and brilliant orator that he was.[34] Lacheroy would make his first mention of "parallel hierarchies" then, a concept that would be recuperated ten years later by both Galula and the famed Colonel Roger Trinquier in their writings. Lacheroy described how individuals living under effective communist rule—official or shadow—were indoctrinated throughout their lives. A territorial governance structure, the "vertical hierarchy" was complemented by an overlay of functional and social committees, the "horizontal hierarchy." Both hierarchies, he believed, were nimbly controlled by a politico-military apparatus that culminated in the Communist Party.[35] The tighter the parallel structure, the more likely an individual was to fall prey to its architect's indoctrination. Lacheroy reasoned that the system enabled the communists to "out-control" and therefore supplant, the weak, sometimes notional, French colonial administration.

After the fall of Dien Bien Phu, Lacheroy published a first brochure on revolutionary warfare. General Blanc, introduced earlier, ordered the publication of thousands of these according to Lacheroy's memoires.[36] Lacheroy also penned editorials in *Le Monde* describing revolutionary warfare and the threat it represented to the Western world.[37] His eloquent portrayal of the Algerian War as an extension of Soviet and Chinese subversion earned him the acclaim of many, even in the political classes. If the Algerian War and other decolonization crises such as the Suez Campaign could be painted in the colors of East vs. West, politicians would have a much easier time harnessing support at home and abroad among allies for France's costly interventions.

Lacheroy's crowning achievement lay in the institution of a powerful psychological action program. The program grew into an organization that spread to the very top of the military hierarchy, at the ministerial level, where Lacheroy's own position was held. In Algeria, a central Psychological Action Bureau was created in March 1955.[38] By August 1, 1957, at the halfway point of Galula's tour of duty, Lacheroy had already obtained that Bureau staff be added to all divisionary headquarters.[39]

The scope of Lacheroy's psychological action program far exceeded its equivalents in other Western armies (PsyOps or PsyWar). Although the equivalent U.S. program had a superb array of technical means, Lacheroy considered its mandate to be completely sterile in comparison to his own. His had been designed to play a central role in revolutionary warfare, not a supporting one. In Algeria, for instance, the French program's mandate went well beyond seeking to convince rebels to drop their arms and embrace the French cause. It also sought to indoctrinate friendly troops—Indigenous and French—to embrace the techniques of revolutionary warfare, and to adhere to the notion of *l'Algérie Française*. The program also sought, finally, to win over the Algerian population politically and, to no small extent, bolster the Metropolitan population's support for the war. The program had thus allowed itself (and had been allowed) to creep into the sacrosanct political domain.

The psychological action program became "the cornerstone of a vast doctrinal system."[40] Journals, brochures, and roving psychological action teams were entrusted with "orienting staff in the area of pacification."[41] The program's propagation was facilitated by the doctrinal void Galula had described in *Pacification*. Far from being satisfied with such an outcome, Galula criticized the labeling of everything related to pacification operations as "psychological operations." Another reticence of his was echoed by a general who warned of "the danger of making psychological action a standalone specialty, when instead, it should be integrated and practiced at all echelons."[42] (The same could be said of misuses of Civil Affairs and Civil-Military Cooperation troops in modern times. Commanders sometimes mistakenly seek to rely exclusively on these to interact with the population, just as one would rely on field engineers to address mobility and counter-mobility issues.) Galula expressed his own disapproval with the program in *Pacification*:

[The Psychological Action officers] managed to take hold of the professional French Army magazines in which, month after month, they published their thoughts and gave the impression that theirs was indeed the official doctrine. In fact, so ridiculous was their position when their theories were submitted to the test of reality in the field that the whole idea became the subject of standard jokes in the Army in Algeria. Psychological action was sunk with whatever valid points the theory might have had.[43]

Galula was at odds with himself over this issue, for despite his broad criticism of the program, there were indeed many themes belonging to revolutionary warfare theory, which he would come to embrace.

It is entirely possible that a certain degree of animosity persisted between Galula and a few of the "psychologists" who had vulgarized, after all, Mao's revolutionary teaching he had come to specialize on. Five months prior to the addition of Bureau staff at subordinate echelons, Galula had submitted the following bold recommendation to his chain of command:

In pacification work political action is a command prerogative. . . . It is a great psychological mistake to have labeled it "psychological action," thus confusing it with propaganda, and to have dropped the responsibility into the lap of a Bureau of Psychological Action. In classical warfare, the leader reaches his decision by studying logistical and tactical factors. In revolutionary warfare, the additional political factor enters into the picture, and with great force. It would seem logical, therefore, for the chief of a large unit to rely on a "political" bureau, which should . . . carry the same weight as the other staff bureaus.[44]

Galula's appeal for "political" officers to be embedded in field headquarters was supplanted when the Psychological Action Bureau received the green light to place its own officers there. Galula had been, no doubt, inspired by the Chinese Red Army model; such an idea was potentially dangerous, but not as dangerous as the Psychological Action Bureau alternative. Galula, at least, had called on his political officers to remain independent from any central bureau, and answer only to the field commander to whom they were assigned. On the other hand, Lacheroy was accused by some of creating a state within the army, of creating nothing less than a "parallel hierarchy" of his own through a network of psychological action officers who remained, under his new construct, technically subordinated to the centralized Bureau in Algiers.[45] Others went further in their accusation by likening these officers to political commissars to the dreaded Viet Minh's Can Bo.

Lacheroy and his Program's sponsors retorted to these accusations that if the army's role was to defend the Nation from all aggression, including that which was manifested on the psychological plane, then the army could no longer afford to practice ideological abstinence.[46] Their argument was bolstered by an unlikely source; General Vo Nguyen Giap was alleged to have claimed after Dien Bien Phu, "the French Army lost [to us] because it refused to engage in politics."[47] However, by 1958, and again in 1961, this lack of political abstinence would cause the army to overstep its republican bounds.

(The issue of military abstinence from political affairs has lost none of its relevance today. The reliance on the military to conduct full-spectrum irregular warfare, including counterinsurgency work, in the absence of a Foreign Service with capabilities or a mandate akin to yesterday's colonial administrations will continue to pose a challenge. I do not pretend that the answer *is* to bolster foreign services with such capabilities, as the challenge would only be replaced with a dilemma of institutionalizing neo-colonial capabilities. There is undoubtedly, however, a greater advisory role in developing governance that can be played by the Department of State and the Foreign Services of allied nations.)

The 1960 Barricades Revolt that followed de Gaulle's announcement that Algeria would be granted its independence convinced the French President to disband the psychological action bureaus. "These bureaus," he wrote in his memoires, "whose original purpose was to keep commanders informed of the state-of-mind of local populations, have become cesspools of trouble and agitation under the impulse of a few military theoreticians specialised in activism."[48] Lacheroy, and others like Goussault's successor Colonel Gardes, were cast away. Many would come to play key roles in the splinter faction of the French Army known as the *organization armée secrète* (OAS), and were consequently court-martialed for mutiny and treason. Galula tellingly cautioned in *Counterinsurgency*, albeit almost as an afterthought, "Needless to say, if political reliability is a problem, as it may well be in a revolutionary war, it is the most reliable cadres who should be assigned to work with the population."[49]

Lacheroy's legacy to counterinsurgency theory today has been eclipsed by two factors. The first is circumstantial. Lacheroy had been one of the chief perpetrators of the OAS. He therefore remains stigmatized. The second is practical. Lacheroy was an unparalleled public speaker capable of captivating an audience of thousands of officers—as he did in the summer of 1957 on the topic of revolutionary warfare—with "electrifying" style, but he was neither an intellectual nor a writer. (There is some debate among historians as to whether he had even fully read Mao's seminal works, which he referred to occasionally in his speeches.[50]) He did not leave behind a written legacy. Jacques Hogard, who was perhaps his most faithful subordinate and disciple, would be the one to do so in his stead. Hogard, a classmate of Galula's at Saint-Cyr, and a decorated veteran of Indochina, published multiple works related to revolutionary warfare.[51] But these, in my view, lack the genius, clarity, and humanity one finds in Galula's.

What then, had been Lacheroy's influence over Galula?

Lacheroy's fame was inescapable, and their career paths had often crossed. A Colonial Army officer himself, Lacheroy had served in Morocco as the deputy commander of a Senegalese Tirailleurs regiment under none other than the charismatic Colonel Groussard who would soon command Saint-Cyr.[52] During the Liberation of France, Galula and Lacheroy would serve in the same infantry division.[53] It is very possible that Galula would meet Lacheroy in Indochina too, particularly in Saigon, where Galula often traveled to brief the theater headquarters on the latest happenings in China. The two would very certainly be reunited later at the historic SEATO conference on counter-subversion held in Manila, in September 1955.[54] The French delegation had been headed by Charles Lacheroy,[55] and would be augmented by Galula on Guillermaz's recommendation. (Galula would later speak of this trip to the Philippines on a number of occasions, and would meet Edward Lansdale in all likelihood there, too.)

The transcript of the 1962 RAND Counterinsurgency Symposium Galula participated in relates a curious statement made by him regarding "an unorthodox but extremely successful experiment with the 'one-man ambush,' which had been tried by a friend of his who commanded a sector in Indochina. A single man, it turned out, was almost invulnerable, and the system permitted the setting of a large number of ambushes."[56] This "friend" had undoubtedly been Lacheroy. The latter had spoken of this favored technique of his repeatedly in his conferences, and had indeed brilliantly commanded a sector in Indochina.

Given their common professional affinity for counterrevolutionary warfare, it is just about certain that the two had had exchanges on those occasions when they saw each other. It is likely, therefore, that the senior Lacheroy exerted some degree of influence over Galula. It is puzzling, at first glance, that Galula never mentioned Lacheroy in his writings. But viewed in the appropriate context, Galula had probably been deliberate about his omission.

Firstly, we note that Galula may have fostered some dislike for Lacheroy, just as there appeared to be bad blood between Trinquier and Lacheroy who never mentioned each other's names in their respective writings, despite having worked closely together on those very things they wrote about.[57] Lacheroy had been somewhat ostracized by the Colonial Army for his proximity to the political elites of the Fourth Republic.[58] As Lacheroy's psychological action program gained momentum, Galula's criticism of the personalities behind it mounted. "Although the pure 'psychologists' were few," Galula commented in *Pacification*, "they were very articulate."[59] The sly remark had certainly been inclusive of Lacheroy.

Secondly, we note that Galula had written *Counterinsurgency* and *Pacification* between 1962 and 1963, while Lacheroy was still on France's wanted list of senior OAS perpetrators. As shall be discussed in a latter chapter, Galula had been working against Lacheroy and his collaborators throughout the attempted putsch. This too may have led to some resentment.

Finally, there was a matter of perception. Mentioning the contribution of the stigmatized Lacheroy to the equally stigmatized revolutionary warfare theory in *Counterinsurgency* would have attracted considerable trouble for Galula in France, where the writings of Lacheroy and even those of Trinquier were banned from publication.[60] Galula would have suspected that the association of his theories to those of a coup-plotter would never favor his book or reputation in the United States.

Still, one wonders what convenience Galula drew from this situation that played in his favor; for in the end, he had very certainly borrowed a few ideas from Lacheroy to support his thesis. The most significant of these were those related to the concept of "parallel hierarchies" described previously, and those related to the "Orthodox Pattern" of insurgency. Though Galula only gave the former topic a fleeting treatment in *Counterinsurgency*, he treated the latter in detail. His "Orthodox Pattern" of insurgency was an elaboration of the "*scénario type*" Lacheroy had described at a counterinsurgency conference in 1957—the transcript of which survived in Galula's personal papers.[61] Galula stated in *Counterinsurgency* that the "Orthodox Pattern" was "based essentially on the theory and experience of the Chinese Communists and was offered by Liu Shao-ch'i as a blueprint for revolution in communist countries. . . ."[62] True, but the articulation into five phases was Lacheroy's.

Lacheroy was not the only revolutionary warfare theorist to exert an influence over Galula. Colonel Goussault was another officer of the Psychological Action Bureau whom Galula would acknowledge more readily. "In January 1957," Galula related in *Pacification*, "I had a long discussion with Colonel Goussault, chief of General Salan's 5th Bureau [psychological action] in Algiers. Colonel Goussault is a brilliant officer who had served on General de Lattre de Tassigny's staff (a real distinction, for de Lattre had a genius for spotting fools and kicking them out) and who later headed our PsyWar section during the Suez expedition."[63]

Galula had met Goussault during one of his many trips to Saigon, and possibly as early as World War II. Goussault, like Trinquier, was one of Salan's close associates from Indochina.[64] Goussault held Galula in high esteem. The head of the powerful Psychological Action Bureau in Algeria remained remarkably attentive to this single company commander's opinions after discovering his exceptional understanding of counterinsurgency warfare. (The Colonial Army seemed characterized by a culture amenable to intellectual exchanges unhampered by differences in rank.) A telling letter written by Goussault to Galula opened with, ". . . we have been able to exploit your dispatch very constructively. I am very thankful for it. Do not fail to send me other letters or documents of this type when you will have them."[65] This adds credence to the hypothesis that the exchange of ideas between Galula and the revolutionary warfare theorists had gone both ways.

In such an open climate, Galula did not hesitate to voice his disagreement with some of the Bureau's practices. True to his habit of attaching import- ance to semantics—for they convey purpose and especially scope—Galula remarked to Goussault, for instance, that it had been wrong to name the Psychological Action Bureau as such, as it overextended what should have been a mandate limited strictly to propaganda. Galula also disagreed with Goussault's Salan-approved plan to secretly recruit young Algerians, train them, and then reinsert them to lead clandestine organizations rivalling the shadow rebel political organizations (OPA) as a panacea to end the war. Galula summarized[66] his objection as follows:

> From my experience in China, I can assure you there is not much room for rival movements in clandestine situations. Even professional ban- dits, and they were experienced, disappeared when the Chinese Com- munists came into an area, they were absorbed or eliminated. I don't deny the possibility of promoting rival movements on a small scale occasionally and for short periods, but this cannot represent our main form of counterinsurgency warfare, it will never bring decisive results. I would rather stick to my methods. Let's compare notes in six months. Meanwhile good luck.[67]

Galula's insistence that counterinsurgency work requires a continuous, sys- tematic, meticulous, and above all, patient and determined approach would come to typify his doctrine. He felt that spectacular actions could seldom lead to lasting results. He also felt that leaders and active supporters from the popu- lation had to emerge naturally by proving their loyalty to the counterinsur- gent, and that no amount of training or indoctrination could make up for this.

Goussault replied emphatically to Galula's reproach above that his moti- vation for the daring plan stemmed from how dire the political situation in France had become; in other words, unless a spectacular victory was achieved quickly, Algeria would be lost. Goussault was generous in his rebuttal, for Galula had, after all, roundly criticized his painstakingly put-together plan. Goussault allowed that such discussions were healthy and enriching, and reasserted his desire to have Galula transferred to his staff.[68]

Goussault had submitted a first request for Galula to be transferred to him in April of 1957.[69] But the Corps commander had refused, preferring to see Galula employed on the ground, in direct contact with the population. (Gal- ula did not seem to object to this, and was reticent, if anything, to join the Bureau.) After Galula's promotion to rank of *commandant*, in early April of 1958, Goussault tried once more to convince him:

I do not know what your plans are now that you have promoted. . . . But if you are not slotted to command a battalion immediately, then I believe, and I say this candidly, that you have absolutely no right to remain in a regiment. The [High] Command is in dire need of people who are qualified and capable of working on the population. Your duty is therefore to orient yourself on that activity as you await Staff College. . . . And if the [headquarters] bureaucracy in Algiers scares you, I would be able to offer you the position of 5th Bureau chief in Orléansville. . . ."[70]

Galula would soon be transferred to National Defense Headquarters instead. Goussault wrote him to congratulate him on his appointment, adding that he "would not fail to come and visit. . . ."[71]

Colonel Roger Trinquier represents another potential source of influence worth exploring. An officer of the Colonial Army, Trinquier spent his World War II years commanding a company of garrison troops in Shanghai and Peking, where he may have crossed paths with Galula. Trinquier also learned to speak Chinese, even though his role had little to do with intelligence gathering.[72] Trinquier did not join the Free French during the war, and according to Bernard Fall, he would carry a grudge towards de Gaulle throughout his career.[73] In 1946, Trinquier left for Indochina, where his career-long involvement in irregular warfare began. His talent for planning unconventional operations led him to command a famed partisan force known as the *Groupements de commandos mixtes aéroportés* (GCMA); a group he allegedly expanded to include nearly 20,000 fighters.[74]

Trinquier came into yet greater renown during the Battle of Algiers in 1957. He was entrusted by General Massu, the commander of the 10th Paratrooper Division, with planning and coordinating the pacification of the capital and the Kasbah. "The conduct of military operations in a large city, in the midst of the populace, without the benefit of the powerful weapons it possesses, is certainly one of the most delicate and complex problems ever to face an army,"[75] Trinquier would later write. True as that was, the purge he had orchestrated had been effective. The bottom-up approach to intelligence gathering he adopted allowed for the dismantlement of the rebel organization and its bomb-making cells in a matter of days. But the pacification had been in the image of its planner, technically sound and efficient, but politically catastrophic. The systematic use of physical coercion during the interrogation of suspects had stigmatized the counterinsurgent and the cause he was intended to uphold to a point of no return. A few years later, Trinquier was saved from participating in the OAS only "by circumstances"[76] according to Fall.

Trinquier would come to author nearly a dozen books on military affairs. His first book, *Modern Warfare—A French View on Counterinsurgency*, represents his most significant contribution to the art of warfare. Other works followed, such as *La guerre* and *Guerre, subversion, révolution* circling around the same themes, but these failed to receive the same level of recognition as his undiluted first. *Modern Warfare* most closely competes with Galula's *Counterinsurgency*. The two works essentially deal with the same subject, and are similar in scope and scale. It is on *Modern Warfare*, therefore, that I chose to dwell on.

Trinquier's original version of *Modern Warfare*—published as *La guerre moderne* in 1961—precedes Galula's *Counterinsurgency* by three years. In the United States, however, the two books were published nearly simultaneously by Praeger in view of U.S. involvement in Southeast Asia. One American reviewer deemed that of the two, *Modern Warfare*, prefaced by none other than Fall, dealt with the counterinsurgent's problems "in harsher terms and in much greater detail as to methods"[77]—a reflection of Trinquier's technical leaning as opposed to Galula's more philosophical one. Otherwise, critics seemed to favor Galula's work. Trinquier's career, however, was popularized by French novelist Jean Larteguy in three bestselling novels—*The Centurions*, *The Praetorians*, and *Hounds of Hell*—propelling Trinquier's works to the forefront of military readership interest. Trinquier had become, from a fame and notoriety point of view, France's Edward Lansdale.

Modern Warfare and *Counterinsurgency* are written in similarly clear prose. Both carry undeniable notes of revolutionary warfare theory, and with it, Lacheroyesque influence. Both also carry unaware or unacknowledging notes of *l'école coloniale*. The basis for their authors' respective arguments, however, differs somewhat more. Trinquier draws heavily on his experiences in Algeria and Indochina, whereas Galula draws more heavily from his firsthand witnessing and study of the Chinese Revolution. (With regards to Mao, for instance, Trinquier limits himself to recuperating the "fish out of water" analogy.) Nonetheless, the two works share a good number of themes and deductions. Both adhere to a population-centric approach to counterinsurgency. Both favor "minds" over "hearts," and both favor technique over ideology, although Trinquier comes across as the more extreme.

That Galula may have been influenced by Trinquier's French edition of *Modern Warfare* is not an excludable hypothesis, but in my opinion, it is a rather unlikely one. As shall be seen, Galula had already drafted a direct precursor to *Counterinsurgency* in 1960, and had committed the seeds of his theories to paper still much earlier. Instead, I believe that resemblances can be attributed to the two officers having evolved in common environments, studied the same wars, and having been driven by their anti-communist convictions to ascribe to the broad theory of revolutionary warfare.

The degree of political acumen exhibited by the authors differentiates their works. (I do not simply mean their political correctness, but their understanding of the constraints and limitations that typify modern "small wars" waged by modern democracies.) Trinquier's lack of political acumen constitutes his greatest handicap. He wrote in *Modern Warfare*, for instance, that he foresaw the Communist Party in Metropolitan France waging terrorist and guerrilla operations in order to accede to power.[78] Galula may have occasionally shared such thoughts, but was sensible enough to keep them for himself, or at the very least, not publish them! On the whole, Trinquier leans much more to the right; his anti-communism very likely surpassed Galula's. Although multiple factors may be singled out for this, I would venture that a difference in cultural backgrounds was also at play. Trinquier could go to the extreme of writing in *Modern Warfare*:

> The nation attacked must fall behind the government and its army. . . . [The army's] unquestioned actions should be praised by the nation to maintain the nobility of the just cause it has been charged to make triumphant. The army, whose responsibility is to do battle, must receive the unreserved, affectionate, and devoted support of the nation. Any propaganda tending to undermine its morale, causing it to doubt the necessity of its sacrifices, should be unmercifully repressed.[79]

The reader is entitled to question whether such "propaganda" included domestic political opposition to a given war. Would American university campus opposition to the Vietnam War have qualified under this? And as such, according to Trinquier, should it have warranted "unmerciful repression"?

No other theme discredits Trinquier as much as his treatment of the interrogation of terrorist suspects. As mentioned much earlier in this work, Trinquier was neither immoral nor amoral. Only, his rationale for the justification of torture reveals the war technician in him; confronted with a problem, he unquestioningly seeks a solution that will enable him to achieve his mission in the immediate. The following passage is drawn from *Modern Warfare*:

> But [the terrorist] must be made to realize that, when he is captured, he cannot be treated as an ordinary criminal, nor like a prisoner taken on the battlefield. . . . If the prisoner gives the information requested, the examination is quickly terminated, if not, specialists must force his secret from him. Then, as a soldier, he must face the suffering, and perhaps the death, he had heretofore managed to avoid. . . . Once the interrogation is finished, however, the terrorist can take his place among soldiers. From then on, he is a prisoner of war like any other, kept from resuming hostilities until the end of the conflict. It would be as useless and unjust to charge him with the attacks he was able to carry out, as to hold responsible the infantryman or the airman for the deaths they caused with their weapons.[80]

Trinquier fails the test of realism here. In the absence of judicial prosecution, what consequence is left to impose on insurgents or other "outlaws" for violent acts committed in the name of a political cause? Indefinite detention? Torture? And what moral and political repercussions would the systematic use of torture have at home and abroad? Galula's prescriptions in *Counter-insurgency* stick out in comparison for being ultimately more compatible with Western jus in bello.

But, entirely compatible, they are not either.

Galula was also capable of pushing moral relativism, albeit not as far as Trinquier. I asked Ruth whether her husband had discussed the use of torture with her. "No, not really," was her answer, to which she had added her own opinion: "When I heard some of the atrocities that some of the rebels had done, particularly with this one school bus whose passengers had been forced to exit and then executed, I realized ... me the devout liberal ... that torture, when one knew for sure of a person's guilty knowledge, was a very relative thing."

In *Pacification*, Galula admitted to employing physical deprivation and psychological coercion in the interrogation of suspects. His first technique consisted of placing suspects in shallow trenches closed-off with barbed wire, and then denying them food and water until they provided information. (Galula may have recuperated the idea from the Vichy days, when the French Army had used this as a disciplinary measure in the work camps it maintained in North Africa.[81]) A second technique of his consisted of locking up a suspect in a bread oven, and threatening to turn it on. Galula considered this more "effective" technique to be "psychologically very impressive, but otherwise quite harmless."[82] Addressing himself to a military audience through the medium of a classified memorandum, he ensued with:

> I wish to make myself clear to the reader on this score. Insurgency and counterinsurgency are the most vicious kind of warfare because they personally involve every man, military or civilian, on both sides, who happens to be in the theater. . . . While the insurgent does not hesitate to use terror, the counterinsurgent has to engage in police work. In order to achieve any result, he has to overcome the prisoners' fears, not their fears of the counterinsurgent but their fears of what the insurgents will do to them if they give out information. If anyone seriously believes that mere talk will do it, all I can say is he will learn better when confronted with the problem. This police work was not to my liking, but it was vital and therefore I accepted it. My only concerns were: (1) that it be kept within decent limits, and (2) that it not produce irreparable damage to my more constructive pacification work. This is why, being an amateur in the field, I wanted to stay in complete control of the action and not be led by eager and still more amateurish subordinates.[83]

In the commercially published *Counterinsurgency*, Galula addressed the topic of interrogation more summarily, under the fourth step of his operational framework: "Destruction of the insurgent political organization." There, he strongly advised that professionals be entrusted with the task, and that this not be left for the counterinsurgents who were in daily contact with the population. The local commander would have to remain ultimately accountable and in charge.[84] Otherwise, he remained deliberately vague: "Under the best of circumstances, the police action cannot fail to have unpleasant aspects for both the population and for the counterinsurgent personnel living with it. This is why elimination of agents must be achieved quickly and decisively."[85]

Notwithstanding his own approach to interrogation in Algeria, Galula stated that the "press campaign against tortures" perpetrated by Massu's paratroopers had been "90 percent nonsense and 10 percent truth."[86] Still, his feelings were betrayed when he recalled his relief that the army had decided to take the "interrogation out of the hands of amateurs," by creating specially trained groups for the purpose, which included turned insurgents.

Galula's belief in the timelessness and superiority of the Maoist framework for insurgency led him to draft a counterinsurgency doctrine that focused heavily on political primacy and grassroots interaction with the population. Trinquier's enthrallment with the terrorism-reliant method of revolution ("*modern warfare*")—which more or less coincided with Galula's "bourgeois-nationalist shortcut" pattern—yielded a counterinsurgency doctrine that focused more on the intelligence-led destruction of terrorist cells. (Still, Trinquier's doctrine remained essentially population centric.) The incidence of their differing experiences in Algeria on their respective doctrines should not be discounted. Galula was assigned to pacify a rural cluster of hamlets in Kabila, while Trinquier was assigned to pacify a densely urbanized Algiers.

Marked no doubt by his orchestration of the Battle of Algiers, Trinquier's emphasis on terrorism as a tool of insurgency in revolutionary warfare is much stronger than Galula's. True to his technical orientation, Trinquier painstakingly describes the composition and modus operandi of bomber cells in *Modern Warfare*, while glancing over the enemy's subtler means of political action. This is in contrast to Galula who considers terrorism as a mere catalyst to Mao's protracted warfare.

Of fundamental importance, Trinquier acknowledges the power of a cause or ideology in insurrectionary wars even less so than Galula does. "Even a band of gangsters, lacking any political ideology at all," Trinquier writes dismissively, "but without scruples and determined to employ the same methods [of insurrection] could constitute a grave danger."[87]

On the need to control the population, however, Trinquier and Galula agree in principle. Only, Galula considers the exertion of control as a means by which protection of the population can be achieved. Trinquier infers something of an end; "Control of the masses," he writes, "through a tight organization, often through several parallel organizations, is the master weapon of *modern warfare*."[88]

Trinquier describes in his work techniques that had proven their effectiveness in the Kasbah of Algiers: *quadrillage*, censuses, the establishment of local hierarchies, self-defense units, and the ordering of simple tasks to be carried out by the population. A year before the Battle of Algiers began, Galula had written a set of orders detailing similar control measures. He instructed his soldiers: "The population can only be controlled if it is surveyed and known by every soldier in the detachment. The census is therefore the base of all [pacification] work. Additionally, it will later serve the Administration that will replace us."[89] Galula detailed how censuses should be taken, what information should be gathered, and by what means this information should be consolidated (census cards, family booklets, etc.). He also described the labeling of each house with the number of inhabitants, and the family name. Complementing these control measures, Galula forbade villagers to absent themselves for longer than twenty-four hours, or from hosting visitors without his permission.[90] All of these techniques would resurface later in Algeria, and in Trinquier's *Modern Warfare*, leaving the original ownership of certain theories and methods up to speculation. Galula's exchanges with the Psychological Action Bureau in Algiers could have conceivably provided a medium for crosspollination between him and Trinquier.

The emphasis on "organising" the population—a purposefully loose term with roots in colonial tradition—is central to Trinquier. Like Galula, Trinquier views this as a command prerogative. Trinquier, the Special Forces warrior, harshly attacked conventionalism:

Traditionally attracted by the purely military aspects of warfare—that is, by the pursuit and destruction in combat of guerrilla bands on the ground—operational commanders invariably hope to succeed in manoeuvring them like regular units and to gain a rapid and spectacular success. They have little interest in the less noble task, however essential, of subtle work with the population and destruction of the clandestine organization that enables guerrilla bands to survive despite local defeats the forces of order periodically inflict.[91]

Echoing Lyautey's reflections on the eradication of pirate bands quoted earlier, Trinquier adds: "We are trying, in the course of repeatedly complex operations to seize an adversary that eludes us. The results obtained bear no relation to the resources and efforts expended."[92]

Galula and Trinquier perfectly agree on the issue of troop deployment in pacification operations. Both subscribe to French *quadrillage*, or gridding, while rejecting the idea of establishing military outposts in isolation from the population on tactical pretenses of self-defense, or on pretenses of controlling key terrain and lines of communications. Trinquier writes categorically: "Since the control of the population is the aim of *modern warfare*, any

element not in direct and permanent contact with the population is useless."
To which he adds spectacularly, "Furthermore, if we try to make strongholds
of outposts, we would be surrounding them with walls built to support a siege
the enemy has neither the intention nor the possibility of undertaking."[93]

Trinquier joins Sir Robert Thompson but diverges from Galula on the use
of "strategic hamlets" (*villages de rayonnement*) aimed at concentrating and
controlling populations so as to deny the insurgency material support.[94] Here
again, Trinquier could wander into a style of war *à l'outrance*. In guerrilla
"refuge areas," for instance, he proposes to finish any clearing operation by
"interval troops"[95] with what rings of British methods in Malaya: "Anything
that would facilitate the existence of the guerrillas in any way, or which could
conceivably be used by them—depots, shelters, caches, food, crops, houses,
etc.—must be systematically destroyed or brought in. This will actually per-
mit the methodical recovery of material and food, which can be distributed to
the regrouped civilians. All inhabitants and livestock must be evacuated from
the refuge area. When they leave, the intervention troops must not only have
completely destroyed the bands, but must leave behind an area empty of all
resources and absolutely uninhabitable."[96]

Galula, in contrast, argues against forced resettlement: "... such a radical
measure is complicated and dangerous. Complicated because the population
has to be moved ... and given ... new, independent means of living. Dangerous because nobody likes to be uprooted and the operation is bound to
antagonize the population seriously at a critical time...."[97]

The *Instruction pour la Pacification d'Algérie*, better known as the Challe
Instruction, was disseminated on December 10, 1959. It was named after
Air Force General Maurice Challe who had been appointed by de Gaulle to
replace Salan in 1958 as the commander-in-chief in Algeria.[98] Galula, who
claimed in *Pacifcation* that the ideas presented in his Second Algerian Memorandum were "embodied"[99] in the instruction, also claimed that much of
the latter had been drawn up by Salan and his staff.[100] In fairness to Challe,
however, he too understood population-centric counterinsurgency, and was
taken to revolutionary warfare theory. He had sat in the front row of Lacheroy's famous conference on the subject delivered in 1957.[101] Challe prefaced his
instruction with statements such as, "feats in pacification will be rewarded
on the same level as purely military ones, as I attribute as much valor to one
as to the other," and "The destruction of the OPA must go hand-in-hand
with the destruction of the armed rebel bands. One exists because of the
other."[102] Moreover, Challe considered self-defense and self-administration
(*l'auto-encadrement*) as decisive steps towards the Algerian population's
self-determination.

One discovers the hybrid of a doctrine and a campaign plan when reading
through the 100-page-long Challe Instruction. The document, which remains

classified to this day, embodies the essence of revolutionary warfare theory, which had matured significantly after a decade of French counterinsurgency campaigning in Indochina and Algeria. Its significance to the Algerian War, as mentioned previously, sizes up to that of FM 3-24 to Iraq and Afghanistan. The French instruction and U.S. field manual share analogous beginnings. Both were drafted with a sense of urgency in the middle of failing wars. Both incorporated new knowledge that had been acquired and tested in battle, while relying on history as their foundation. The principal difference lay in the fact that the Challe Instruction had been notionally drafted for a particular theater of war in mind, but in practice, its authors had broadened its applicability to the global insurgency they perceived.

"Our world is at war," reads the opening line of the instruction. "This war of our times opposes two irreconcilable conceptions of man. One rests on the respect and dignity of man, the other, essentially materialist, leads to the enslavement of the individual and proselytizes to the entire world." And then, as if to leave no possibility of misinterpreting who the global contenders were:

> Cautious to avoid the risks of a nuclear war, the Marxists are operating insidiously. They are using to their advantage every factor of disequilibrium, every gap in political and social evolution between nations, and every difficulty encountered by man to surpass himself and to stay on top of technological progress. They insist on transforming these contradictions into ferments of hatred and discord, and to turn against the West those young nationalists belonging to underdeveloped regions, as they propagate a myth of a fatalistic historical current to destroy in the Free World the will to resist.[103]

The Instruction was drafted, therefore, with an un-admitted versatility in mind. *Officially* directed at Algeria, it was equally applicable to the rest of the French dominion threatened by a perceived global insurgency.

The Challe Instruction appears to be built around three core counterinsurgency objectives: (1) the protection of the population, (2) the destruction of the enemy's political framework, and (3) the engagement of the population through self-defense, self-administration and political action. Unity of command is stressed as an overarching requirement to achieve these.

Challe assigned four distinct roles to his forces, which exceeded in their sum the traditional bounds of employment of a Western military force:

1. The *military* domain, which ensures the security of the population and the destruction of the rebel military apparatus.
2. The *police* domain, which aims to free the population of the O.P.A.
3. The *administrative* domain, which aims to hasten a return to normal life.

4. The domain of *information*, education, and organization of the population, which encompasses every action against those ferments of hatred
and the techniques of enslavement used by our enemy.[104]

This fourth point was a catch-all fitting the revolutionary warfare view
of what "political work" entailed. The door was opened dangerously wide to
interpretation, but nevertheless imparted the theater commander in Algeria
with a freedom of action reminiscent of France's nineteenth-century colonial
era; a carte blanche that extended to civil affairs, and translated into unques-
tionable unity of command. Most of all, the Instruction sought to impose
a standardized framework for the conduct of counterinsurgency operations
in Algeria, addressing the doctrinal void Galula had described, but stopping
short of proposing a stepwise framework as he later would.

Galula's claim to the effect that the Challe Instruction embodied some of
his ideas could be interpreted in different ways. The wording he chose could
either signify that the Instruction's authors drew deliberately from his memoranda, or that they simply arrived at similar conclusions by themselves. It is far
from impossible that certain parts of the Instruction were inspired by Galula's
memoranda submissions in Algeria given the strong thematic resemblances.
Nor is it impossible, in fairness, that Galula had in turn been influenced by
other parts of the Instruction following its dissemination. The complication
stems again from the fact that revolutionary warfare theory had multiple contributors. Still, given the very evident contribution made by the Psychological
Action Bureau to the Instruction, and therefore by Goussault, who was open
and eager to receive Galula's views, there is no lack of credence that some of
Galula's ideas had indeed found their way under Challe's signature.

Important sections of the Instruction resonate Galula. "We may conclude
that overall," reads a middle one, "the Muslim population remains closed
to the ideology of the FLN, redoubts its armed and terrorist activities, but
continues to pay it and materially support it because it is uncertain about
the future and therefore requires insurance. The deliberate refusal to pay the
till[105] constitutes the truest indicator of the population's siding with us."[106]
Equally as *Galulesque* is the following excerpt drawn from an early section:
". . . The final goal of our entire effort in Algeria warrants that every leader,
regardless of the echelon he finds himself in, and whatever his particular mission, plans, prepares and executes his manoeuvre exclusively in accordance
with the effect that is sought on the state of mind of the population."[107]

Commonality can also be found in the deployment of forces. The Instruction breaks away from earlier enemy-centric practices in Algeria by calling
for the ". . . dilution of our military concentration on the ground, every time
that the enemy's dispersion allows it, in order to provide optimal and direct protection to the population."[108] The Instruction devotes its entire second

chapter (there are only four chapters in total) to the imperative of protecting the population, and how to go about this. "The population is the objective of the struggle," a summarizing excerpt reads. "The adversary relies most of all on terror to chain it to its cause. Protecting the population is the precondition for its commitment to our side"—indeed, Galula's third law of counterinsurgency.[109] The instruction mirrors other themes found in Galula's works such as the fostering of grassroots political engagement, and the enabling of leaders to emerge naturally.[110]

Finally, eerie similarities can be found in the finer telltale details. In an annex devoted to the importance of understanding the local population, the Instruction calls for the use of a *cahier de contacte* (contact log) by junior leaders. These were to inscribe, on a daily basis, their impressions of their interactions with the population, and the latter's general mood. We note that Galula had proposed this exact procedure in his First Algerian Memorandum, which received wide distribution.[111]

The Challe Instruction concludes with three case studies of successful pacification efforts in Algeria. The last one of these draws on the pacification of the Bordj-Menaiel sector, where Galula had served as a deputy battalion commander with the 9th RIC. In *Pacification*, Galula deemed the early counterinsurgency effort there to have been a "fiasco." French troops had killed large numbers of rebels in open clashes, but the counterinsurgents remained physically isolated from the population, and incapable, therefore, of affording it any semblance of protection.[112]

The case study detailed by the Challe Instruction spanned the 12 months that *followed* Galula's departure from Algeria. Had he had anything to do with the success described in the case study then? He related in *Pacification* how he had proposed to Guillermaz, his Sector commander, measures ". . . to start doing more constructive work with the population, spreading the static companies in villages and, if necessary, regrouping the population that we could not easily control."[113] He continued:

> I submitted a plan for the reorganization of the sector along these lines, but it was turned down. The zone, it was objected, had a permanent option on a battalion from the sector . . . and it would not relinquish it. I was vindicated in 1959, when a new colonel took over the sector and adopted my suggestions. His achievement made the headlines in French newspapers, which spoke of 'a new look on pacification.'[114]

There is little doubt that Galula was being genuine. The appended case study very obviously betrays Galula's mark. "The ideas which led to the modification of our military deployment were essentially as follows," the incumbent colonel was quoted as saying:

- Draw our troops out of their military posts to redistribute them among the population. . . . Wherever one company position existed, four, five or even six positions were derived.
- Draw our troops out of the city centers. The command, support and service companies have been reduced to 185 men, from 360, in order to make up for the regiment's shortage in personnel, a burden previously shouldered by the combat companies.
- The battalions' headquarters have been moved up to the mountains, leaving behind, at the Sector headquarters, only a reduced presence.
- The number of harkis has been augmented. . . .[115]

Villages of one thousand inhabitants had been garrisoned by detachments of twenty men or so. Of these, a dozen were assigned to tasks such as dispensing basic education and medical care. Later stages of Galula's counterinsurgency framework were also reflected therein. "The Sector Commander strives to detect and foster [leaders within the population] to enable them to replace us politically and administratively," reads the case study. "The first of these leaders were selected based on their local relative importance, eventually these will be replaced by genuine elites whom we will seek from within the *harkis*, the rallied members of the rebel OPA."[116]

It cannot be denied that as in Hong Kong previously, Galula had an influence in Algeria that was well out of proportion with his rank.

15

Under de Gaulle

We had reached the point where some believed that an armistice had marked the end of our effort, while instead, it had only marked our success, and the beginning of the most delicate mission that could be assigned to an army: winning the Peace, which we had lost in 1918 and 1945.

—Instruction for the Pacification of Algeria, 1959[1]

The revolutionary creates and exploits disorder, uses ruthlessness, appeals to passion, fights a cheap war, whereas the counter-revolutionary camp has to maintain order, stay within the bounds of law, appeal to reason, fight an expensive war, and must prevent the war from lasting.

—David Galula[2]

THE ORDER TO RETURN TO PARIS came on July 22, 1958, or six months ahead of what should have been for Galula. He had thus far served twenty-four months in Algeria, but the norm for his rank called for thirty. A brief message from Vice-Admiral Cabanier's office—the de facto highest military authority in France at the time—instructed the *commandant* to report to Paris the following week, affording him no rest, but a stiff transition from the field to national headquarters instead. Galula would henceforth fall under the newly instituted *état-major de la défense nationale*, or National Defense Headquarters (EMDN). The order was signed by the fateful air force Brigadier Fourquet, himself assigned to the *état-major particulier* of the

Présidence du Conseil; a subset of the EMDN serving as Charles de Gaulle's privy military staff.[3]

These scant details were all that were known to me at the onset of my research of an episode of Galula's life that seemed shrouded in secrecy. I had found the above message in a yellowed shadow file Galula had maintained for his personal records, as all soldiers tend to do. His correspondence, which had proven to be a rich source of information when researching other periods of his life, was dry. And yet, even during his busiest assignments, Galula had regularly maintained his contacts, exchanging views on the significant geopolitical happenings of his era.

Still, I had found my first clues in Fourquet's order.

The opacity persisted through my interviews with Galula's widow, in spite of her best efforts to the contrary. It seemed that once again, but especially here, she had been kept in the dark regarding the contents of her husband's work. Galula had been conditioned to adhere to the *secret d'état* ever since his selection for counter-espionage training at Saint-Cyr, a conditioning that his involvement with the intelligence branch (G2) afterwards would reinforce. This particular assignment had undoubtedly warranted additional discretion. In a time of political turmoil and violence in France, Galula's proximity to the president's office—especially in the roles I would discover him to have held—compounded by the overhanging risk of his identity being revealed in connection to the *Le Monde* affair, were all genuine security concerns. Yet thankfully for our purposes, his widow had known enough about her husband's final few years of active service to offer another clue. "He belonged to what was essentially a 'crisis group.' His team's primary function was to alert de Gaulle and his cabinet to any troubles that occurred around the world. The government went as far as installing a telephone line in our home, which was a rare luxury in France back then." France was confronted with a myriad of national security issues ranging from FLN and OAS perpetrated terrorism in the metropole and in Algeria, to the massive "symmetric" threat posed by the Soviet Union. The existence, therefore, of a standing "crisis-group" capable of combing through high-level intelligence, and formulating strategic courses of action for the president to decide on, was unarguably warranted.

I would find the next set of clues some time later in the cases of personal archives Ruth had granted me access to. I discovered there three bullet-pointed résumés drafted by Galula at the end of his term at Harvard's Centre for International Affairs, which coincided with his retirement from the military. The résumés were addressed to a handful of well-connected American, French, and Japanese businessmen he had befriended in Hong Kong. "While posted at our National Security Council in Paris in 1959," read the first résumé, "I worked on the preparation of laws concerning our national defence and took part in many committees at cabinet level. One of my tasks was to conceive and direct a program for the expansion of the French shortwave broadcasting network; the project, which was successfully completed, involved some 20 million dollars."[4]

I discovered later through the course of further interviews that this description of Galula's assignment had been unrepresentative of the full scope of his responsibilities at the EMDN. He had chosen to emphasize the civilian aspects of his work with the intent of demonstrating the transferability of his skills to the business world. His likening of the EMDN—later renamed EMGDN[5] and finally *Secrétariat général pour la défense nationale* (SGDN)—with the U.S. "National Security Council" betrayed the American audience he had in mind for this particular résumé. (The French EMDN and American NSC organizations were similar in the un-intermediated advisory role they played to the presidents of their republics. However, the French organization was endowed with a much broader mandate during those years.)

De Gaulle's creation of the EMDN in July of 1958 was consequent to his perception of the First Algerian Revolt that had returned him to power two months earlier. In circumstances that were not devoid of irony—a recurring characteristic, it seems, of French politics during that era—de Gaulle wished to exert a firmer grasp over the same military establishment whose unlawful ultimatum to the shaky Fourth Republic had led to his return. To this end, he installed a politico-military command relation that was similar to what he had devised in World War II, and with which he was most at ease. Under this reincarnated construct, the power to employ military forces would be withdrawn from the *ministre des Armées* (minister of defense), Pierre Guillaumat and his subordinated Chairman of the Joint Chiefs of Staff, General Paul Ely, and given to the EMDN headed by Vice-Admiral Cabanier—a well-known de Gaulle supporter. Guillaumat and Ely were thus relegated to playing force generation roles. Furthermore, under this construct, the EMDN would henceforth report directly to the president, and not to the minister of defense, nor even to the chairman. The odd but temporary result of this was to de facto subordinate the commandership of Ely to that of the EMDN under Cabanier, despite a difference in rank that called for the opposite.

A few months elapsed before the EMDN (by then renamed "EMGDN") would see France's top soldier, General Ely, transferred to its head. Ely replaced the outranked Cabanier as if some period of probation imposed by de Gaulle had come to an end. As for the EMGDN, it would be placed under Michel Debré, de Gaulle's prime minister responsible for inter-ministry and inter-agency coordination. The subordination of the EMGDN to Debré existed more in theory than in practice, however; for in the latter, Galula's streamlined headquarters would remain directly subordinated to de Gaulle. The president maintained his direct and absolute control over the EMGDN through various defense committees he created and chaired.[6] Galula's participation in "many committees at cabinet level," as he had written in his résumé, undoubtedly brought him in close proximity to de Gaulle on numerous occasions. De

Gaulle made the Algerian War, and that of NATO and nuclear deterrence, his exclusive domains. He recognized these areas as his military centers of gravity, and entrusted their daily management and planning primarily to his EMGDN. (Galula unsurprisingly became passionate about issues of nuclear deterrence and missiles during this time, dropping hints to this effect in his writings. Jere Rowland related how Galula often spoke of nuclear "*meessiles*," and the challenges they presented to traditional military and geopolitical thinking.)

In a second résumé, written in French this time, Galula stated that he had been transferred to Paris, on special request from General Ely.[7] Was it plausible for the Chairman of the Joint Chiefs of Staff to pay such close attention to a field-ranked officer serving in Algeria? Ely had known Galula by name and repute as early as Hong Kong. In Algeria, the general had visited Galula's *sous-quartier* to witness his success in pacifying a difficult area. Ely had also summoned him to elaborate on his First Algeria Memorandum, and had personally congratulated him on his presentations about the Algerian War to American officers stationed in France.

Next, we note that Galula's hurried appointment to the EMDN occurred within three weeks of the latter's creation, and that Ely would have had good reasons to place a trusted horse in de Gaulle's new stable. Galula, after all, owed a certain loyalty to Ely for the recognition the latter had bestowed upon him. Galula's inclinations on Algeria could also be trusted by Ely, who was a loyal but decidedly pro-*Algérie Française* officer. Galula could be trusted because he belonged to the Colonial Army and had spent much of his life abroad—strong indications that he was attached to the vision of *La France d'outre-mer* (the French Dominion). Moreover, Galula's file very clearly revealed his North African origins, and the inescapable fact that he owed his citizenship to the French colonization of Algeria. Finally, in contrast with many of the officers that had been assigned the EMDN, Galula was not a Free French alumnus with a cult-like loyalty to de Gaulle.

We note, finally, that only the most exceptional recommendation could have landed Galula within de Gaulle's inner circle at a time when anybody associated with General Salan, or especially with Lacheroy's Psychological Action Bureau and the broader revolutionary warfare movement, was treated with suspicion by the president, or outright sacked to minor roles.[8] (General Salan was recalled from Algeria to act as the "military governor of Paris"—a ceremonial role, while Colonel Lacheroy was assigned to instruct at a reserve officer academy in France.) Compounding all of this was the fact that Galula had actively preached that winning in Algeria was a matter of political determination at the top. All things considered, it is nothing short of remarkable that even Ely's recommendation had sufficed to get Galula so close to de Gaulle.

A third and final résumé added precision to Ruth's recollection of a "crisis group." Galula wrote that he had served in an operations center geared for "unconventional warfare."[9] The interviews I conducted in 2010 combined with the information I retrieved from his military file at Vincennes corrobo-rated this particular role. My impression that there had been two stages to his four-year assignment under de Gaulle was also confirmed. (The stages were separated by a six-month attendance of U.S. Staff College to which the next chapter is devoted.) Both stages of his assignment were concerned with irregular warfare. He thus remained professionally involved in his subject matter of expertise beyond his tour of duty in Algeria. In all likelihood, it was for reasons of operational security that he failed to mention this additional experience in his writings.

Combing through Galula's correspondence once more, I came across two pieces of information that would speak to the prestige of his new position. The first was a letter written by Galula's second successor in Kabila, Cap-tain Zwilling,[10] shortly before he was killed in an ambush. Knowing well his addressee and his sense of humor, Zwilling asked his friend "if de Gaulle had appointed [him] as a Minister in his cabinet yet?!"[11] The second letter, written by Guillermaz, expressed happiness to see his long-time friend and disciple "finally employed to the full extent of his aptitudes."[12] This prestigious appointment had been, in my view, Galula's reward for his success in Algeria.

At the EMGDN, Galula was no longer "first in Rome"[13] as he had written of his time in Kabila, but a *commandant* among hundreds of others; he was not either. The EMGDN was a lean machine meant to regroup the smartest (and most loyal) staff officers under de Gaulle. Once more in his career, Galula would have the opportunity to exert a level of influence that was well above his rank on issues he was passionate about.

"There were two other officers in the group, a colonel and a young lieuten-ant," Ruth volunteered, to help me find potential sources of information who had worked with her husband under de Gaulle. "We would meet socially from time-to-time, and have them over for dinner too."

The colonel, whose name she could not recall, would later head Paris's storied firefighter brigade—the *Sappeurs Pompiers de Paris*.[14] His name sur-faced months later, once I had been granted access to Galula's military file at Vincennes. Colonel Casso (later General Casso) had been an illustrious figure of the French Army Corps of Engineers. He had fought with the *Résistance* during World War II, and had served with distinction in Indochina. Halfway through Galula's assignment at the EMGDN, he would be sent off to com-mand the Corps of Engineers in Algiers. Casso's benevolence and leadership earned him enormous popularity in Paris. Upon retiring from the military, he would continue his public service career as the mayor of the city's 17th *Arrondissement*.[15]

An end-of-year evaluation of Galula by Casso reveals that the two had belonged to the EMGDN's *division de l'information*. The handwritten entry offered some definition about Galula's role from 1958 to 1959. Casso's praise

Picnicking in the Forest of
Compiègne.

for his subordinate was unequivocal: "Brilliant. Distinguished linguist. He is
an excellent officer capable of immediately adapting to any given situation.
In charge of electronic warfare at the Information Division. Carries out his
duties with a very uncommon dynamic tenacity. Perfect morality and appearance. Superior officer to be pushed upwards."[16]

It is under Casso then, that Galula worked on a project to upgrade France's
shortwave radio network in the colonies and protectorates. His wife recalled
his travels across Africa. "He brought me back a gold watch from Djibouti
during one of his trips," she told me smiling youthfully at the memory. It
was during this time too that Galula returned to visit his old *sous-quartier* in
Algeria.

A project intended to bolster France's ability to conduct strategic information operations across her dominion undoubtedly received considerable
attention from de Gaulle. His becoming a known politico-military entity
capable of inciting rebellion against Vichy and the Nazi occupier was in great
part due to his use of radio broadcasting. (It was said that some of France's
protectorates had failed to rally to him because they had been out of range
of his BBC broadcasts!) Twenty years later, it was de Gaulle's turn to stave
off subversive propaganda throughout the French dominion. Beyond broadcasting French government content, Galula's radio project had included other
electronic warfare capabilities, the sensitivity of which undoubtedly warranted "the preparation of laws," as he had written with intended vagueness
in his résumé. This assumption is strengthened by Lacheroy, who wrote in his
memoires of the " . . . the struggle against Arab radio stations, which we tried
to counter in two ways: defensively, through scrambling and neutralization,
and offensively, through very high powered broadcasts covering the Mediterranean in its entirety."[17]

Casso's evaluation of Galula the following year shed light on the second stage of the latter's assignment, from 1960 to 1961. Galula would henceforth be detached to the *groupe opérationnel*—the "crisis group" to which Ruth had alluded—at the EMGDN. There, his role would shift to one of collating and interpreting intelligence in support of France's counterinsurgency efforts.

"Who had been the young lieutenant on David's team?" I asked Ruth.

"Why, none other than the *Comte* Henri de Clermont, the Prince of Orleans, the Pretender to the throne of France!"

I couldn't believe it. Her husband's life and career never failed to surprise. The Prince of Orleans was, and remains, an important member of France's elite—a symbolic link to Europe's royal community. It is sometimes forgotten that the French monarchy returned to power long after the French Revolution. The House of Orleans's regency during the mid-nineteenth century would leave behind a strong royalist adherence in French society, as would the return of a Bonaparte emperor (Napoleon III) later in the century. Marshal Lyautey, for one, had been a devoted monarchist, as were many other senior officers of his generation who had witnessed the defeat of 1870 early in their careers. The forced exile of the House of Orleans by the republican government in 1886 further demonstrated the "realness" of the royalist adherence. Count Henri was the first of the royals to be granted permission to return to France. President Vincent Auriol had personally intervened to allow the young prince to be schooled in Bordeaux after the Second World War. Henri studied political science at the university, an interest he would share with Galula. Favoring Franco-German rapprochement, the Count would marry the duchess of Württemberg, shortly after which he sought a commission in the army and volunteered for Algeria.

Before I could reach him, Count Henri's short online biography had left me with the impression that his assignment in the shadow of de Gaulle had been a high mark of pride. "Summoned to Paris by General de Gaulle in 1959," the biography reads, "Prince Henri became a *chargé de mission* at the *Secrétariat Général de la Défense Nationale*. He met the Head of State regularly in the conduct of his duties, or during hunting parties at Rambouillet and Marly. He also acted as the intermediary between General de Gaulle, and [Henri's father] the Count of Paris."[18]

Having missed each other during my research trip to Paris in the summer of 2010, Henri kindly agreed to correspond in writing. "I spent three years, from 1959 to 1962, in the company of *Commandant* Galula at the [EMDN]," he prefaced his recollections. Galula had been 14 years his senior, but nonetheless, "A true friendship developed between us and our immediate superior [Lieutenant-Colonel] Brillaut."

"We worked in an immense office whose access was tightly controlled because of the national defence secrets it contained," Henri continued. "When a rare visitor was allowed in, we would shroud the map-covered walls on which our latest troop dispositions were indicated along with what significant events had occured in our hotspots around the world: Algeria, the Tunisian and Moroccan borders, Laos, Cambodia, Berlin, etc. . . . We were the 'Algeria Team,' which slowly became known as the *groupe opérationnel*. We were assigned multiple tasks, amongst which was the production of intelligence reports. We submitted these to the Prime Minister and to General de Gaulle. Every morning, Galula and I marked a map with the significant events of the previous 24 hours. General de Gaulle received a reduced a copy of that map, along with our daily intelligence briefing—a *bulletin de renseignements quotidien*—at 9 am."

"Occasionally, there were long waiting periods during our shifts," the Count offered. "Galula would tell me great stories about his experiences in China, and about Mao Tse-Tung . . . showing off his ability to speak fluent Chinese. He made me discover the teachings of the great strategist Sun Tzu, for [Galula] too was a clever strategist, and an excellent chess professor."

"During the Putsch in Algiers organized by generals Salan, Jouhaud and Zeller, the activity on our team was so intense that we would sleep and eat in our office cooped-up like monks in their cell. . . . We were also responsible for coordinating the efforts of the various military intelligence branches. We were in constant liaison with the *SDECE*[19] and the *DST*."[20]

I considered this last piece of information to be significant to Galula's legacy in France, where the uncertainty surrounding his stance on the Third Algerian Revolt of April of 1961 may have disfavored his recognition.

Fifty years after its end, the Algerian War remains a politically sensitive issue in France. Mixed national feelings of guilt and loss continue to persist strongly. Even today, tensions between those who had been pro-*Algérie Française* and those who had been against remain high. Any involvement or even sympathies Galula may have expressed for the Salan and Challe-led revolt against de Gaulle's authority, or the radical anti-independence movement (OAS) it sprung, would suffice to stand in the way of an "official" recognition. Trinquier and Lacheroy are cases in point.

I asked Ruth what had been her husband's impression of de Gaulle, after she had told me that he had read the general's memoires on his deathbed.

"David admired de Gaulle," she cautioned me immediately, "and continued to do so even after *La paix des braves* affair. He realized that de Gaulle had had little choice in granting Algeria its independence in the end."

And that was it.

"My husband was on particularly familiar terms with de Gaulle's son," she added, to provide some personal context to the affair. "He would meet Philippe quite regularly in professional and social contexts." Philippe had been roughly the same age as Galula. He would reach the rank of admiral prior to retiring to become a senator.

A quick inspection of Galula's published writings and military file at Vincennes—the only two printed sources of information that have so far been available to French authorities—eliminates the possibility of his *direct* involvement with Salan's mutiny. But in defense of French authorities, this inspection does not disprove Galula's hypothetical sympathies for the attempted putsch. Quite on the contrary, the inspection imposes a strong bias against him. Many of the reasons for this have already been discussed: North African origins and a naturalization that inevitably made him pro-*Algérie Française*, a career in *La Coloniale*, a proximity to Salan since World War II, a lack of recorded ties to de Gaulle's Free French, a professional passion for counterrevolutionary warfare, a stated belief that winning in Algeria was a matter of technique, etc. The cherry on the cake surfacing from his file was a request to be *mis en disponibilité* (placed on sabbatical leave) for three years, in the near immediate aftermath of the Third Algerian Revolt.

Galula remained relatively neutral on the outcome of Algeria in his writings. He shared, however, the common belief that France had won the war on the ground—ipso facto raising the question regarding the need to withdraw. (Galula thus highlighted a well-known paradox of counterinsurgency warfare; a war could appear to be won on the ground, and yet still be lost for lack of political sustainability.) Dr. Stephen Hosmer, who chaired the RAND Counterinsurgency Symposium Galula attended in 1962, recalled over the phone how the latter had been guarded about the political issues surrounding Algeria: "David answered my questions about the turmoil during the breaks only very generally at first. It was clear to me that he personally knew many of the high people involved on both sides. During the sessions, he was always adamant on the importance of determination at the top levels of government. He knew that the French Army had won in Algeria, and that the FLN had been on the run, especially after the Challe Plan was implemented. He recognized that a political decision to withdraw had been made." (Galula refrained from relying too heavily on the Algerian War as a case study in *Counterinsurgency* for these very reasons. "Although [my counterinsurgency process] met with great success," he wrote to a potential publisher of his work, "the final outcome of the Algerian war makes it very difficult for me to use Algeria as a convincing example. I would have to prove that the insurgents actually lost the war but were set in power only because the French government so decided."[21])

And yet, despite these indicators, Galula could not have been overly opposed to the decision to grant Algeria its independence. As early as September of 1959, de Gaulle had made his first public announcement to the effect that Algerians would be given the right to choose between independence and "integration" following a referendum. (The British case in Malaya did not differ much from Algeria in this sense.) De Gaulle went as far as downplaying the significance of his *"J'ai compris"*[22] speech in his memoires.[23] It follows that Galula must have been either in agreement, or obediently resigned to de Gaulle's intention to withdraw from early on; failing which, he could not have remained, nor have been *allowed* to remain at the EMGDN until mid-1962. His loyalty to the State in light of all of this is doubtless in my view.

Galula sought a three-year period of leave from the military in 1961, at the apogee of his career. He retired definitively following the completion of this sabbatical. And yet, his performance evaluation in 1961 had positioned him for an eventual promotion to the rank of colonel. What had pushed him to retire from active service at the age of forty-two?

The French withdrawal from Algeria was unlikely to have been the reason. Whatever strong initial objections Galula may have had to the decision of granting Algeria its independence, he had been able to overcome. His employment at the strategic level under de Gaulle had afforded him an appreciation for the politico-economic difficulties of sustaining a counterinsurgency effort in Algeria. It had also made clear the continued burden that such a colony would represent even in the event of a "total" victory, which such a savage, politicized war could never realistically offer. I believe instead that any combination of three reasons would push Galula to a premature retirement.

The first likely reason was one of conscience. Circumstances were such that Galula had found himself at the center of the counterrevolutionary effort waged against the perpetrators of the Third Algerian Revolt by virtue of belonging to the "Algeria Team." Overnight, he had transitioned from countering an Algerian insurgency to countering a French one. What had been the psychological toll of contributing to the foxhunt of Raoul Salan on Galula? Was the latter not intimately familiar with the legendary Colonial Army general and his past service record? Had Salan not shown consideration for Galula, and for his unconventional ideas regarding both Indochina and Algeria? How could Galula not be moved by Salan's rebellion against a government he felt had betrayed him, the army and the nation, when Galula himself had once entertained thoughts on the creation of a first revolutionary "cell" as a result of the trauma and guilt he harbored over Indochina?

I have little doubt that Galula subjected himself to more than one *examen de conscience* during the period leading up to his request for a lengthy sabbatical. But here again, as he had done in 1940, he remained loyal to the established Order. Leaving for the United States as he did, immediately after being *mis en disponibilité,* would allow his conscience a bit of relief by forcing him into neutrality. Once more, he retreated to the fringes of the military, where it seems he had always been most at ease, particularly when his conscience and sense of identity became conflicted.

The second reason likely to have motivated Galula towards seeking a sabbatical was hinged on his ideological convictions and France's rapidly morphing foreign policy. Galula understood that France, despite her acquisition of the nuclear weapon in 1960, would more or less resign herself to focusing on domestic affairs after her withdrawal from Algeria. The Fifth Republic would seek to reacquire a sense of political identity, requiring it to strike a balance between Left and Centre at home. Abroad, she would seek foreign policy independence from the leadership of the United States under the guise of NATO, requiring her to strike a balance in her relations between East and West.[24] For many French officers, and without a doubt for Galula, these shifts in policy signified the end of the Empire. The Colonial Army had lost its prized colonies, and with them, much of its raison d'être. As such, Galula's perception of the world after 1960, as a struggle between Western democracy and Eastern totalitarianism, would outlive his country's ability to influence the outcome. He understood that from then on, the burden of counterrevolution would rest on the United States. His interpretation of world affairs, including that of a growing U.S. involvement in Vietnam, convinced him that his expertise would be of greater use to American institutions.

As a third and final motivator for retiring from active duty, Ruth informed me that her husband was "tired of earning a pittance in the French Army." America, in the early 1960s, promised better opportunities. Moving to the United States would also please his American wife who had not lived there in a permanent fashion since she had joined the Foreign Service fresh out of college. Family reasons were indeed the only ones that Galula would later offer to potential employers for leaving the military. Doing so would quash inferences that he was leaving France on account of sympathies for the *putsch*. In his letter of motivation to Harvard, he had even felt the need to mention that he had never joined a political party![25]

We may conclude, then, that Galula's knowledge of counterrevolutionary warfare would henceforth be of little value to a former colonial power, but of growing value to a superpower that was increasingly willing to act on its policies of containment. Worse than being of little use, Galula's area of expertise would rapidly fall out of fashion in de Gaulle's circle and become taboo. The *troupes coloniales* were compelled to mark the end of an era by reverting to their original name of *troupes de marine*. De Gaulle thus unplugged the French military from its colonial past, and reoriented it, with the help of the likes of General Fourquet,[26] towards a modern, nuclear-capable striking force more relevant to the Cold War. As Bernard Fall would later relate: "General de Gaulle, in his inimitable icy style, allegedly smothered a junior officer who attempted to speak to him about revolutionary warfare with the pithy remark: 'I know of two types of warfare: mobile warfare and positional warfare. I have never heard of revolutionary warfare'[!]"[27]

Galula remained convinced that the principal future of warfare lay in low-intensity conflicts waged against the proxies of symmetrically opposed powers. The U.S. and French militaries would swap orientations in 1960, with one now headed towards symmetric deterrence, and the other headed towards an asymmetric quagmire. The assignment under de Gaulle had exposed Galula to the panoply of constraints a Western democratic government had to face in insurrectionary war. The politico-strategic assignment afforded him the time, the *recul* and the "30,000-foot" view needed to further foment the original doctrinal concepts he had mulled over in Asia, and tested in Algeria.

16

THE FRENCH EXCHANGE STUDENT

A modern army is first of all one that is capable of winning the conflict in which its country is engaged.

—*Roger Trinquier*[1]

Yet, it is important to know how to meet the challenge of revolutionary wars. The Communist bloc imposes on the Western nations a life or death struggle. It is generally admitted that total nuclear war is improbable short of an accident, and that limited wars have also become unlikely because no one knows exactly how to keep them limited. Therefore, revolutionary wars seem to be the only field open.

—*David Galula*[2]

RUTH GALULA WAS OFTEN ILL during the first year of her husband's assignment under de Gaulle. She suffered from recurring abdominal pains, which kept her confined to their apartment in Paris, while her husband worked long hours shrouded in the secrecy of the tiny "Algeria Team" at National Defense General Headquarters. Returning from work one evening, David found his wife in agony, her arms clutching her abdomen as she lay curled up in bed. He associated her state to something he had experienced himself in China. On account of a ruptured appendix in 1948, the surgeon in Beijing had prohibited him from undertaking a much anticipated trip to the southern interior provinces; a repeat of sorts, of his daring exploration of the western hinterlands that had brought him and Guillermaz as far as Lake Koko Nor.

"David rushed me to the hospital," Ruth recalled. "He had convinced himself that I would die if I wasn't treated immediately."

Following a battery of tests, Ruth was informed that an ovarian cyst was causing her pain. She would have to be operated on the next day.

"This added yet another item to my list of health misfortunes," Ruth noted with a sigh. She had suffered from angioedema, which had often led her to being bedridden. She had also suffered from asthma, and would later contract chronic obstructive pulmonary disease despite never having been more than an occasional smoker, like her husband. "We had a live-in Spanish maid named Dolores who would take care of house chores when I was not of much use."

"In any event," Ruth reminisced, "neither angioedema, nor the recovery from the operation was at the forefront of my concerns. David and I had wanted to have a child for quite some time." After ten years of marital life, it had become abundantly clear to Ruth that fertility was an issue. "I started hinting about child adoption."

"David was not favourably inclined to the idea, at least not initially," she continued. "He desperately wanted us to have a child, but for him to adopt one was like admitting that something was wrong with me ... his wife ... and this, he couldn't do. It was yet another manifestation of his traditional attitude towards women. He, as the man of the house, and as an officer, had to bear responsibility for everything."

"My gynaecologist, whose opinion we highly valued, took David aside to tell him that the only alternative was to use fertility drugs. But he cautioned him against it. The science was still very new back then, and the side effects were not yet completely known. The doctor felt that some of my other health complications were at risk of being exacerbated by these drugs. He told David that he wouldn't give the treatment to his own wife under similar circumstances." Galula's desire to protect his wife overruled his desire to spare her from the admittance that she could not bear children. "He finally agreed to it. But that too was not easy. As a couple, we were neither Catholic nor Protestant. We were, therefore, unable to qualify for the majority of adoption agencies."

Their luck would turn for the better in the early summer of 1959, when Ruth, still alone in their apartment, received a phone call from Dr. Lemire. "She was a reputed child psychologist, and a good friend of ours. She worked closely with a few adoption agencies in France, some of which were, thankfully for us, non-denominational. One of these, *Le Rayon Soleil*, had just taken custody over a newborn boy."

Born on the 21st of April 1959, Daniel was only two months old when Ruth and David Galula would cradle him for the first time in the comfort of their home. The infant's biological mother, from the little that Ruth had been told by Dr. Lemire, was a devout Catholic. The archived adoption papers I came across revealed, for their part, that Ida Franci, a Corsican-born,

Daniel's first Christmas.

twenty-seven-year-old housemaid, had originally named her son Christian Henri Franci. "His biological father was an Alsatian who had held a high position in the French judiciary system," Ruth offered. "He was apparently endowed with an exceptionally *difficult* character." I did not press the issue any further. Daniel's biological father's name remains unknown to him. Much to his dismay, he has never met his biological mother.

Daniel's adoption was rendered official by a *Tribunal de Grande Instance* on September 20, 1961.[3] Colonel Casso and Lieutenant Henri de Clermont were present as official witnesses. In later years, Daniel would be affection- ately teased by his parents for having had such prestigious witnesses present at his adoption. His parents would also tease him about the denominational peculiarity of his baptism held at the Morgan family home in Falls Church, near Washington, D.C. Present at the ceremony had been a Congregationalist minister, a Jewish godmother, and a Catholic godfather. Galula's eldest sister, Lolette, had warmly accepted to be Daniel's godmother, and Colonel Forrest, who had befriended Galula as his American counterpart in Hong Kong in the 1950s, had accepted to be Daniel's godfather.

On the Galula side of the family, not everyone supported David's deci- sion to adopt a child. Religion, and the fact that Daniel would be baptized in Christian tradition, had little do to with the disapproval expressed by some.

"Hélène was against it," Ruth shared. "But then again, she had never approved of her brother's marriage to me. She was disdainful. Through her marriage to an affluent man, she felt that she had the right to establish herself as the mainstay of the family. For me, her disapproval revolved around the simple fact that I was American, and therefore supposedly lacked culture, etcetera. Her disapproval of the adoption was based on her opinion that her brother was entitled to have 'legitimate' children of his own. The fact that I was not able to bear children only lowered her consideration of me."

Hélène's disapproval could reach hurtful proportions.

"She asked David one day, in front of Daniel and me in our apartment, whether her brother '*really* thought he could ever love *that* child?'" Her brother's reply had been vicious. "I had never heard David speak rudely to someone, let alone to one of his sisters."

Notwithstanding the disapproving minority, Daniel, by all accounts, grew up a cherished child. "David had to rely on Ruth to do much of the raising," Jere Rowland, David's brother-in-law, told me over the phone. "He travelled a great deal for work, causing him to be often away from a son who grew up idolizing him. But Daniel was his pride and joy, and he spoiled him as best he could."

David Galula had already spent a fate-determining six months in the United States before returning on Harvard's invitation in 1962. From February to July of 1960, he had attended the U.S. Armed Forces Staff College, known today as the Joint Forces Staff College. There, his reputation as an expert on counterrevolutionary warfare was quickly confirmed. His attendance, furthermore, had opened his eyes to the need for his expertise in the United States. He would be lured from then on to return.

U.S. Staff College was a bonus for Galula. While assigned to the EMDN under de Gaulle, he had already earned his *Diplôme militaire supérieur* at the *Collège de l'enseignement militaire supérieur de l'armée de terre* in Paris. Guillermaz had strongly recommended that he undertake these studies ever since Galula's return from Hong Kong, as he had felt that it would add "*rigueur*" and "*pondération*" to his protégé's work, in addition to fulfilling a prerequisite for career advancement.

Staff College, to the benefit of the non-military reader, is a nearly universal course. It is intended to render army officers proficient in all aspects of headquarters work, such as planning, operations, intelligence analysis, and logistics. Allied nations have a tendency to exchange students to promote interoperability and foster long-standing relations. These exchanges result in a cross-pollination that favors innovation in doctrine, tactics, and, of course, staff procedures. It is not uncommon, therefore, for an officer having recently completed his or her staff training to be sent abroad to attend another nation's Staff College. Generally speaking, armies have a tendency to send their brightest candidates to represent them.

Ruth emphasized that her husband's opportunity to attend U.S. Staff College had not come out of the blue. Beyond his affinity for America, his proficiency in English, and his enduring desire to share his knowledge and opinions on matters he was passionate about, there had been a simple motivation for him to apply for the exchange: the College was located in Norfolk,

Virginia, some 200 miles away from Falls Church, where his wife's family lived. The relative proximity would allow Galula to commute over the weekends, while his wife raised Daniel surrounded by her family, which she had not seen in nearly a decade.

Galula's formal admittance to the College required him to complete an English proficiency test. As he already held a *brevet de langue anglaise* with the French military, the test was expected to go smoothly. And it did. But Ruth recalled that the episode had not been devoid of humor. "His written English was fine by then, and he spoke with a very rich vocabulary," she said. "But the American professor administering the test was just horrified by his accent! Much to my husband's delight . . . he had a great sense of humor when it came to such things . . . the professor told him that he sounded like the Warner Brothers character Pepé le Pew!" French words did not always translate as Galula intended them to. One sinisterly funny instance saw an American instructor at Norfolk patiently correct an error Galula had made on his thesis. Galula wrote, ". . . specially trained counter-intelligence units . . . will take care, among other things, of every suspicious individual arrested by the army." To which, the instructor commented, "Dave, [the] expression 'to take care of' has, to an American, the connotation of 'to beat up' or 'kill.'"[4]

Galula's reputation for expertise on counterrevolutionary warfare preceded his arrival at the Staff College in Norfolk. During the first week of classes, Colonel (later Brigadier) George M. Jones, commandant of the Special Warfare School in Fort Bragg, wrote to Vice-Admiral Charles Wellborn, his counterpart at the Staff College, asking for Galula to lecture at an upcoming Special Forces officer course. Jones justified his request with the following: "I feel that [Galula's] knowledge of Mao Tse-tung's political warfare doctrine and tactics as well as his methods of 'counter-revolution,' as he calls it, would be of great value not only to the students in the United States Army Special Warfare School but to the staff and faculty as well."[5]

This was no small measure of flattery for the just-arrived candidate. Jones's reputation added weight to his request. He had led the 503rd Parachute Infantry Regiment in New Guinea and the Philippines during the Second World War under MacArthur. Some two decades later, he would pilot Special Forces development through a new era under a president who foresaw their value to the irregular wars the future promised.[6] Jones underscored the seriousness of his request by concluding his letter with, ". . . To assist [Galula], we are prepared to furnish the necessary funds and invitational travel orders, or send in an Army aircraft to pick him up."[7]

Galula was called upon to give another lecture the following month, this time, at the Staff College itself. The deputy-commandant, Colonel E. R. Powell, referred to the presentation as "outstanding"[8] in Galula's course report, attesting to the latter's orating abilities. External guests had been invited for the occasion. One of these was Marcel Vigneras, author of *Rearming the*

Lecturing without notes on counterrevolutionary warfare at the U.S. Armed Forces Staff College, or at the U.S. Army Special Warfare School.

French, who was working then as a consultant at John Hopkins University's Operations Research Office. He was accompanied by the office's director, Ellis Johnson, and other academic peers. Vigneras expressed his appreciation for the "excellent" presentation, and reaffirmed his interest in reading Galula's forthcoming thesis, which, like all other candidates, he would be required to complete. In the same letter, Vigneras asked Galula if he would be amenable to sharing his views on ". . . logistics in 'exotic' theatres of operation, such as extreme terrain, vegetation and climates."[9] Vigneras added that his U.S. Army-contracted research team was particularly interested in ". . . the security of logistical nodes and axes, guerrilla and counter-guerrilla [warfare], sustainment and convoy operations, medical evacuations and treatment, the employment of aviation—the helicopter in particular; [and] the use of local labour." In short, Galula was being asked to provide insights on counter-guerrilla warfare in anticipation of direct U.S. involvement in Southeast Asia; he agreed.

Galula was solicited to give other lectures during those six months. He spoke of irregular warfare theory—counterrevolution in particular—and proselytized the French views on a globalized communist insurgency. A thank-you note addressed to Galula by the Norfolk Rotary Club in May of 1960, stated that: "[Galula's] ideas on the [communist] methods of infiltration showed us a clearer picture of the universal problems."[10]

The remarkable interest Galula generated during his short stay in the United States persuaded him that he would find both a purpose and an audience for his knowledge should he later choose to return. (He would not be the only Frenchman with counterinsurgency experience to do so.)

Galula's demonstrated interest in political warfare earned him the role of Political Advisor for his class's final exercise. Colonel Powell wrote to the French attaché in Washington that the candidate ". . . displayed a thorough grasp of the situation and its politico-military implications. . . ." He continued his praise of Galula with the following well-corroborated observations:

> . . . Galula has a mature, inquisitive mind and the ability to analyze a problem rapidly and arrive at a sound and practical solution. He holds strong, forceful convictions but is tolerant of the views of others and does not hesitate to accept valid counterproposals.
>
> With his cheerful, pleasing personality and ready humor, he has no difficulty in adjusting to any military situation. . . . He is a good extemporaneous speaker who can 'think while on his feet.' . . . He works equally well as an individual or as a member of a team and in group endeavours he is always willing to do more than his share.[11]

The twenty-one-week–long course Galula completed along with seventy-two U.S. Army and Marine Corps candidates had included academic classes, seminars, and tabletop exercises related to general staff work and planning. Each officer had been required to produce a short, individual thesis on a military topic of his choosing. The choice of topic had been obvious for Galula. He titled his thesis "On the Conduct of Counter-Revolutionary War."

The similarities between Galula's Staff College thesis, written in 1960, and *Counterinsurgency*, written between 1962 and 1963, are such that I can confidently state that the former was the closest and most direct precursor to the latter. Only the level of detail would naturally differ between his thirty-three-page thesis and his Praeger publication. The layout, ideas, and arguments are identical in both works, with very few exceptions. All evidence points to the fact that *Counterinsurgency* was written by Galula as an elaboration of his thesis, a fact that may surprise more than a few, and annul the comparative theories of others, based on chronological precedence. Needless to say that I was enthusiastic to have rediscovered Galula's precursory short work in a forgotten file fifty years after it had been submitted.

True to the style of *Counterinsurgency*, Galula's thesis is based nearly entirely on his observations in the field. So little does he rely on research material that only the lucidity of his arguments, one supposes, saved him from being penalized for a lack of academic rigor. The handful of quotes and references he includes are drawn from his recollection of Chinese communist writings and speeches he had analyzed in Hong Kong and earlier in Peking.

He makes almost no mention of Algeria in his thesis. Nor does he refer to any particular French doctrine or doctrinaire, save for a single superficial mention of "tâche d'huile."[12]

To motivate his American readership, which, in 1960, was likely to relate more to the Cold War than to the brush fire wars fought by waning European powers, Galula introduced his thesis with a Lacheroy-*esque* observation that had been used to indoctrinate French forces in Algeria: "unconventional" warfare had become as "conventional" as warfare between sovereign states in their time. Galula impressed that accordingly, "unconventional" warfare deserved a serious treatment even in the context of the Cold War. He wrote: ". . . it is important to know how to meet the challenges of revolutionary wars. The Communist Bloc imposes on the Western nations a life or death struggle. It is generally admitted that a total nuclear war is improbable short of an accident, and that limited wars have also become unlikely because no one knows how to keep them limited. Therefore, revolutionary wars seem to be the only field open."[13]

The logic was clairvoyant. Although it may seem unoriginal today, as history itself has validated it, it must be reminded that these words were written long before Western armies had formally opened themselves to such notions. Galula further motivated his readership with a second observation; a doctrinal void persisted in the realm of counterrevolutionary warfare. "Starting with Lenin," he wrote, "a long line of Communist military thinkers have set forth the laws of revolutionary war, the chief proponent being Mao Tse-Tung. . . . But one would search in vain for a counter-revolutionary doctrine: the bookshelves are empty, the military reviews are silent."[14] Galula inferred that a counterinsurgency doctrine suited for democratic nations was being written for the first time. The authoritative tone he adopted in his prose was meant to reinforce that impression on the reader.

The Staff College thesis recuperates many of the tactical-level notions from Galula's Algeria memorandums. It includes, for instance, the following prescriptions:

1. No unit must be allowed to be set up away from the population, on so-called strategic positions. Even if a village is dominated by a hill, the unit must be installed in the village and not on the hill.
2. No sizable group of inhabitants must be left alone. The risk of establishing a small post of a few soldiers is smaller than the risk of not controlling the inhabitants.
3. At each level from the company up, units must organize a small force ready to act in the unit's area.
4. No matter how small are the posts, how scattered are the units, [or] how busy the soldiers [are] during the day, each commander must see that patrols and ambushes are out every night from every post. In this type of war, a four man patrol is strong enough at night.[15]

To these tactical aspects of counterinsurgency warfare, and others, such as the requirement to purge political cells at the village level, Galula added strategic-level considerations such as the enactment of political reforms in "uncontaminated areas." He also touched upon issues of morality, law, and the compatibility of his method with Western democratic values. All this reveals maturation in his thinking afforded by his participation in national security spheres under de Gaulle. His return to the EMGDN after Staff College would only further this maturation process prior to his writing of *Counterinsurgency* at Harvard.

To illustrate this last point, we note how Galula would later add two prerequisites for a successful insurgency—"requirement for external support" and "suitable geographic conditions"—to the two he originally outlined in his thesis: "the existence of a problem" and the presence of a "deficient administration and police." The first of the prerequisites he added was indeed critical. Galula's exposure to strategic intelligence regarding Soviet involvement in Algeria convinced him of that, as did perhaps, his witnessing of the instrumentality of Chinese support during the Indochina War. The second prerequisite—suitable geographic conditions—was a notion that was gaining popularity at the time. In truth, however, difficult terrain only became a real hindrance when an army adopted a highly enemy-centric approach to counterinsurgency. (Terrain is much less of an issue today given modern developments in mobility, surveillance, and target acquisition capabilities. Moreover, history has seen insurgencies triumph in every type of terrain. In Galula's defense, he would later remark that "once the insurgents had established a strong foothold and organization, terrain ceased to be an overriding factor; population density . . . then becomes decisive."[16])

Galula's stepwise counterinsurgency framework is very nearly identical in his thesis and in his publication. The reaction of his readers at the Staff College to the later stages of his framework would have been worth noting. There, Galula decidedly entered the realm of political action; an exercise that his service with *la Coloniale*, particularly in Algeria, had accustomed him to, but that U.S. military thinking in 1960 would have been ill at ease with.

Finally, Galula's thesis deliberately confounds strategic issues with tactical ones; a consequence of its author's belief that irregular warfare seldom allows for such distinctions to be made. The thesis also includes deliberations about the Sino-Soviet threat to Western democracy. Galula appended the same communist "ideological maps" of the world he would later include in *Counterinsurgency*. He surmised that the world was not doomed to succumb to the Communist Bloc's ambitions or to the Domino Effect, concluding his thesis with the following statement: "There is no reason why a good cause, a democratic cause, the West's cause, has to be defeated by a bad cause, a totalitarian cause, the East's cause. Assuming the same amount of will to win on each side, victory becomes a matter of technique."[17]

17

Writing *Counterinsurgency* in the Company of Lansdale and Kissinger

The race is not to the swift, nor the battle to the strong.
—*Edward Lansdale quoting Ecclesiastes 9:11*[1]

In a revolutionary war where one side attacks the established order and the other one defends it, the initiative belongs to the revolutionary camp.
—*David Galula*[2]

"THE PRIMARY PURPOSES of the Center are to explore and throw light on basic problems in world affairs and at the same time to provide an intellectual meeting place where senior officials from all continents mingle with scholars from diverse disciples,"[3] read the Harvard brochure in Galula's hands. With his son on his lap, he considered how the offer would translate into a new career or, at least, a hiatus from his current one. Harvard could afford a respite from the plots and internal strife of an army undergoing a transformation that would ultimately not favor the colonial officer that he was. It would be well to try something else. And Harvard of all places! He would wish to share the news with his American friends, and with Guillermaz who had already started an academic career of his own. Most of all, he would have to thank his friend Henry Lieberman of the *New York Times* for having suggested that he apply, and for putting in a good word with Dr. Brown.[4]

Galula remained on the living room couch peering over the letter that accompanied the Harvard brochure describing the first two years of the Center for International Affairs. The letter was signed by Professor Benjamin H. Brown, the center's secretary, and dated September 30, 1961. Brown extended a tentative invitation for Galula to join the center either as a fellow, or as a research associate, on condition that he find a suitable research topic. A fellowship, Brown explained, required that the candidate be "lent" to the center by his government, and that the latter continue to pay his salary. Attendance as a research associate, on the other hand, required the candidate to join the center as a civilian on Harvard's payroll.

Galula's formulation of a research proposal was not long in coming. By December 22, Brown had drafted a contract offering him a one-year term as a research associate.[5] Confident in what chances he would have of being renewed, Galula submitted a request to his chain of command for a three-year sabbatical from active duty. Harvard would grant him a nominal salary of $8,000.00 per year, and an additional $1,000.00 to cover his moving expenses. Admittedly, this was not the boost in living conditions he had wished for his family. But as Ruth would recall, salary was no longer at the forefront of her husband's preoccupations. "He was excited about the work that awaited him."

Dr. Brown related the following regarding Galula's research proposal:

> We had some discussion about your outline . . . there was some feeling that it might be a mistake to start with too ambitious a plan. That is to say, it would perhaps be preferable to undertake at the outset to write a careful, analytical article or two concerning aspects of guerrilla warfare with which you have direct experience.
>
> There might grow from discussions and from your future research a concept of a larger work, possibly a book, which would not necessarily correspond to your present outline. . . . In the meantime, be assured that there is great interest in your project and full realization of its importance.[6]

It follows from this and other pieces of correspondence that Galula had originally outlined a broader-scoped project about the rise of the Chinese communists, and the development of the revolutionary process they sought to export. He had proposed a similar outline to the Council on Foreign Relations earlier, but it had been rejected there too. Harvard's desire to narrow the scope of his research to more practical "aspects of guerrilla warfare with which [Galula had] direct experience" would be fateful in aligning *Counterinsurgency* with the Staff College thesis he had already written, and fateful, therefore, in the publishing of the field-oriented doctrinal work that defines Galula today.

Interestingly, Galula's correspondence also reveals that Harvard would have preferred to see him attend as a Fellow, because, as Brown wrote, "Men in [the Research Associate] category are usually from academic life,"[7] which of course, Galula was not. The latter's final performance evaluation from the French Army reads that ". . . he would have preferred to be detached to Harvard while remaining on active duty."[8] This means that his decision to leave the army may have been tentative at first, explaining his preference for a sabbatical over early retirement.

If Galula had wanted to remain on active duty while at Harvard, then why had the French Army refused? I would venture that it was either a simple policy matter of not wishing to lend a paid officer to the *Américains*, or alternatively, of failing to make a sufficient effort to retain him. The army's decision to award him the Legion of Honour two days after he submitted his request for three years of leave was an unlikely coincidence, however. Was the decoration bestowed as a parting gift in recognition of his achievements, or in a hurried attempt to convince him to return in three years? The reader may decide. The final entry in Galula's military file read: "Possessing a sharp and active mind, disorderly at times but always effective, he is not lacking in initiative or originality. It is in the Army's interest not to lose sight of him. Rank potential: COLONEL."[9]

"I have circled April 11th in my book," Professor Howard Boorman of Columbia University wrote back to his friend Galula. "[I] will notify Messrs. Barnett, Durdin, and other refugees from the *Extrème Orient* to lay down a few bottles of brandy to celebrate your arrival." Boorman and Galula had been close friends ever since Hong Kong. The sinologue added with humor:

> Actually, Harvard called me long-distance last November to inquire after your bona fides and all that sort of thing. Despite the very negative report I turned in, I am delighted that they saw fit to go through with the appointment anyhow. It is all very exciting, and I am sure that you will find the environment at Harvard most stimulating provided you can keep out of debates as to whether or not the Western world should or should not build fallout shelters and all that.[10]

In a second letter, Boorman jokingly thanked his friend for his intention to "help the Americans and Harvard fight creeping communism." He also looked forward to inviting the Galulas over in Boston, "Where no communists except the selected works of Mao Tse-Tung have been reported recently."[11] Galula received other such letters of congratulations, including one from the French attaché general in Washington.[12]

Only the obtaining of a visa now stood in the way of Galula's departure for the United States. His marriage to a U.S. citizen played in his favor. Galula had been to China, however, which had the result of throwing U.S. officials into a tizzy. He was informed that a special clearance would have to be obtained following an investigation into what clubs and associations he had belonged to.[13] The irony of investigating a virulently anti-communist, allied-nation officer invited by Harvard to "research" how to counter the spread of communism in the developing world was unlikely to be lost on him. Galula turned to General Edward Lansdale, and Arthur Hummel, the director of Voice of America, whom he had also befriended in Hong Kong, to intervene in his favor. The visa was awarded just in time.

A mere month before departing from France, Galula received an invitation from the RAND Corporation to attend a five-day counterinsurgency symposium serendipitously scheduled to begin on the first day of his term at Harvard. He was granted permission by the latter to attend. His participation would be fateful.

Some forty-five years after he had organized and moderated the April 1962 counterinsurgency symposium at RAND, Dr. Stephen Hosmer wrote: "The purpose of the symposium was to distil lessons and insights from past insurgent conflicts that might help to inform and shape U.S. involvement in Vietnam and to foster the effective prosecution of other future counterinsurgency campaigns."[14]

I was able to reach Dr. Hosmer over the phone in January of 2011, thanks to Rufus Phillips, an alumnus of the symposium, and a close friend of the former. I discovered a terrific sense of humor and humility in Dr. Hosmer, who is still a contributor at the RAND Corporation. A Detroit native, he has a passion for hockey, over which we connected easily. He chuckled over the phone as he recalled how fifty years ago, he had "purposely kept out the academic-types" from his symposium. "And that worked well," he added, "it was as if a dozen long-lost brothers had been reunited in a room. I had kept it informal so that all could speak candidly."[15]

Among the forum participants was the man who had proposed that Galula should attend. Brigadier-General Edward Lansdale, later awarded a second star, was the most senior ranking of the participants. He had also been responsible for proposing Galula as a lecturer to the Special Warfare School during his attendance of Staff College. Galula and Lansdale had been on friendly terms for almost a decade ever since meeting in Hong Kong, when Lansdale was on his way to Indochina with General John W. O'Daniel in 1953. Lansdale and O'Daniel had been tasked with reporting back to Washington on the French war effort. In all likelihood, Galula had been responsible for arranging their travel, as well as for facilitating their introductions with the French High Command. Galula and Lansdale were later reunited at the SEATO conference on counter-subversion held in Manila. Galula very certainly alluded to Lansdale when he wrote in *Pacification*, "Two trips to Manila and long talks with officials involved in the struggle against the communist Huks had acquainted me with the insurgency in the Philippines."[16]

In addition to being passionate about the same subject, Galula and Lansdale were born networkers who knew the value of connecting with the right people. Galula and Lansdale shared common friends in Hong Kong, including star correspondents Tillman Durdin and Hank Lieberman.[17]

"Lansdale was a big supporter of Galula, and that had its weight," Hosmer informed me, referring to the fact that attendance at his symposium was restricted to a dozen handpicked field experts. Hosmer had met Lansdale in Vietnam during a research trip in 1955, and would contact him first, six years later, with the idea of bringing together a small group of English-speaking, irregular warfare experts. Lansdale had also ensured the participation of his long-time associates Charles "Bo" Bohannan, Rufus Phillips, and Napoleon Valeriano, each of whom was considered a counterinsurgency expert in his own right, and would come to write on the subject. To these five were added seven other participants of various ranks. Notable among them was Lieutenant-Colonel Frank Kitson of the British Army who rose to become the U.K.'s Chief of Defence Staff. "Although we had no difficulty in making our views understood to each other," he would reminisce many years later in his book *Bunch of Five*, "We had mostly been unable to get our respective armies to hoist in the message."[18]

I spoke with Rufus Phillips on a number of occasions in early 2011. A kind and bright gentleman, he had recently authored *Why Vietnam Matters*. We spoke about the past and about Galula, but also about the present given that he had traveled to Afghanistan as an advisor. He had related his impression of Galula in the popular online *Small Wars Journal*:

> I did not participate in the first few symposium sessions, but heard from Lansdale that there was a very unusual French officer named David Galula present, who had a lot of good ideas that sounded very much like our own. As I got involved in discussions with Lt Col Galula, I discovered he wasn't anything like the vast majority of French officers I had tried to work with as part of a joint American-French military advisory mission (called TRIM) in the 1954–55 days in Vietnam. Most had a colonial attitude toward the Vietnamese and saw them as lesser beings. Lt Col Galula, however, was different. He didn't maintain an attitude of superiority. Rather, his mission involved trying to help the local Algerian population as their friend, and he imbued his troops with that attitude.[19]

Phillips elaborated the kinship between Lansdale and Galula over the phone: "It was rather unique. Here were these two men who had evolved independently from each other, but who were like soul mates intellectually." The resemblance was made more striking by the cultural divide. "Lansdale and I had generally not been impressed with the French," Rufus candidly admitted, "although of course there had always been exceptions. Still, it was surreal to find a Frenchman holding such enlightened views about counterinsurgency. He had broken out of the Algeria mould." The perception was representative of American criticism vis-à-vis French counterinsurgency methods of that era. A lack of awareness, in my view, of what legacy stood behind Galula's had been perhaps partly to blame. Naturally, the colonial taboo tainted the perception from the outset; not to speak of the punitive atrocities that had been undertaken at times. Cecil Currey, in his biography of Lansdale, relates how the latter had reacted to being sent back to Vietnam by John Foster Dulles in 1954: "Not to help the French! Hell, the goddamn French *colons* with their colony."[20]

I asked Phillips if Galula's nationality affected his credibility at the symposium. "It is feasible that it did at the beginning," he answered earnestly. "There was some stigmatism associated to the French, who after all, had lost Indochina, and were about to withdraw from Algeria. But that would have been short-lived." Professor Hosmer agreed: "There was no contempt towards Galula, despite the disproportionate amount of space he took up at the symposium. The other members were genuinely interested in what this French officer had to say. He was quite unlike what they were accustomed to."

The animosity between French and U.S. officers in Indochina had indeed been strong at times. Many French officers, including Galula, believed that they had been sold out at Dien Bien Phu by Eisenhower's refusal to commit U.S. airpower to support their defense. The French also felt that the Americans had willingly antagonized their relations with the non-communist Vietnamese. Jealousy too was part of the equation. A French officer had told Phillips amicably during the handover of South Vietnam to U.S. advisors that it was like "seeing your beautiful mistress, whom you could no longer afford, throwing herself at the next man who arrived in a Cadillac."

I asked Dr. Hosmer why he had chosen Galula alone to submit a comprehensive report detailing his counterinsurgency experience following the symposium.

"I felt it was important to get Galula's experience on paper. We had had case studies done on Malaya, and even on Indochina through George Tanham's work on the Viet Minh, but we wanted to know more about the Algerian experience.[21] It was obvious that Galula was extremely analytical, and that he would be able to write a very insightful piece. *Pacification* is proof of that. He was unquestionably the star of the symposium. He was also unique in that he was extremely knowledgeable of both sides of the issue: insurgency and counterinsurgency."

Neither Rufus Phillips nor Stephen Hosmer could recall the topic of Vietnam being addressed head-on at the symposium. But according to Phillips, "the possibility of a more direct form of U.S. involvement was certainly known to all of the participants." RAND sent a copy of the symposium's transcript to Bobby Kennedy. "He was setting up a COIN effort at the time," Hosmer told me. "But in many ways of course, Washington and the Pentagon were like bottomless pits. One didn't really know if or how the symposium's findings or Galula's memorandum were ever used. Officers like Fertig and Kitson returned to their respective armies to partake in counterinsurgency operations, undoubtedly influenced by the discussions we had had together. It was only six years later, in 1968, that we had a senior officer from the Joint Chiefs of Staff come in to ask us questions about the symposium, and request a copy of the transcript." Forty years later, Dr. Hosmer would receive many more inquiries and even congratulatory notes from U.S. officers. "I received testimonials from young men going into Iraq and Afghanistan to the effect that the transcript had been part of the most useful readings they had found. When they asked me if I had any other texts to recommend, I drew heavily on Galula to educate them."

Ed Lansdale was a walking legend by 1962. He had acted as a top advisor to Philippine Defense Minister and later President Ramon Magsaysay in his successful campaign against the communist Huks. Lansdale had also advised the top spheres of the nascent Republic of South Vietnam in its struggle against the Viet Minh in the years 1954 to 1956, and later, at the side of the doomed President Diem. Whereas General O'Daniel had reported some degree of confidence in the French war effort prior to Dien Bien Phu, Lansdale had not. He had felt that the French had failed to understand the war they were fighting.[22] It would not be long before he would reach the same conclusion about his own countrymen. For his objections to U.S. policy in Vietnam, Lansdale was ostracized by Defense Secretary McNamara—for whom he had served as an advisor on irregular warfare—and by the likes of General Curtis LeMay, who believed in achieving "victory through air power," and by "bombing insurgents back to the stone age."[23]

In October of 1961, just a few months prior to the RAND symposium, Lansdale was invited by President Kennedy's top military advisor, General Maxwell Taylor, to return with him to Vietnam. Taylor was tasked with evaluating the requirement for direct U.S. military intervention on the side of South Vietnam. (U.S. ground troops would still be referred to as "advisors" for the sake of appearances under the MAACV construct.[24]) Skeptical of Taylor's real understanding of the situation, Lansdale's impression was that "Very few of the military minds understood the problem we were facing or who the enemy was or how he was trying to fight, the political basis behind their military activities. . . . We went out to kill the enemy—a very different thing—and wouldn't try to understand him."[25] Lansdale advised President Diem against the direct involvement of U.S. troops. "I was against U.S. troops going [into] combat [there]," he told his biographer decades later, "I'd seen the French and figured we'd do much what they did—even with good intentions."[26]

Upon his return from Southeast Asia, Lansdale was oriented towards the Cuban issue by President Kennedy, who sought to redeem his administration following the Bay of Pigs fiasco. Lansdale took on the position of chief of operations for what soon became Operation MONGOOSE—the subversion of the Castro regime, and the assassination of its leader.[27] The planning for MONGOOSE was underway as Lansdale sat through the RAND symposium. This operation too amounted to a catastrophic brouhaha for the Kennedy Administration, culminating, it can be argued, in the Cuban Missile Crisis. Lansdale's name had been splashed in the press, sealing his fate as a CIA-affiliated black sheep in Department of Defense circles. His position under McNamara was abolished. The advisory role he had played regarding irregular warfare was taken over by the Marine Corps' General Krulak who became the Special Assistant for Counterinsurgency and Special Activities (SACSA). Krulak started off knowing "very little" about counterinsurgency according to Phillips. Cecil Currey wrote that Krulak would "savage and undercut"[28] Lansdale, barring him from any future participation in Vietnam affairs.

Despite his official belonging to the Air Force, Lansdale had been heavily involved with the C.I.A. throughout much of his career. His uniqueness inspired three authors—American, British, and French—to base characters of their satirical novels on him. His portrayal depended on the novelist's nationality. The first of these novels, *The Ugly American*—written by an American—was laudatory. It solidified Lansdale's reputation as America's counterinsurgency expert. So poignant and à propos was the satirical novel that it would trigger a formal review of U.S. foreign aid policy in Southeast Asia (it even led to a Marlon Brando movie).[29] The other two novels were much less flattering. The one written by a Brit, titled *The Quiet American,* would be produced into a movie, albeit much later, featuring Michael Cain and Brendan Fraser (as an underhanded and conniving Lansdale). The second, *Le Mal Jaune* (Yellow Fever), written by Jean Lartéguy, was representative of the general French sentiment towards Lansdale: a brutish, unrefined, and vehemently anti-French *agent provocateur.*

(French suspicion of Lansdale may explain the absence of correspondence between him and Galula in the latter's personal papers. The only correspondence that survived there dates back to the beginning of Galula's sabbatical leave from the army, despite the fact that the two had very certainly corresponded prior to this time and that Galula was meticulous about preserving correspondence. As an intelligence officer with access to Cabinet-level secrets in France under de Gaulle, Galula may have legitimately worried about how his friendship with a high-profile American C.I.A. agent would be perceived.)

Lansdale and Galula shared similarities beyond their affinity for intelligence work and a common revulsion of communism. Both were proper "misfits" within their respective militaries, and both had been happiest while employed on the fringes of these. "The military institutions just didn't understand Lansdale, nor could they understand Galula," Phillips agreed. Both officers were endowed with humanistic qualities that led them to crusade against what they interpreted to be thinly veiled totalitarianism underpinning the revolutionary movements of their era. (History has proven that they were generally not wrong.) In charisma and character too, they were similar. Both had been charming and engaging in their interactions, necessary assets for the intelligence gathering that was integral to their work. "Galula impressed you with his thoughts," Phillips recalled. "Just like with Lansdale, you were marked by his powerful intellect." They were also excellent public speakers, falling only shy, perhaps, of the electrifying Charles Lacheroy.

But Lansdale and Galula differed on one important point that came to be reflected in their respective counterinsurgency theories. Galula was pragmatic to a point of cynicism when interpreting the motivations of men. Lansdale was not. Lansdale believed most of all in the intrinsic power of a cause and of a worthy ideal. Galula believed in the leveraging power of a cause to polarize a population; a cause was only required to operate the basic tenet of "power-through-segmentation." Drawing on the "hearts and minds" idiom again, Lansdale believed in a counterinsurgency theory built primarily around "hearts." Galula believed in one built primarily around "minds."

The difference of opinion was perhaps best demonstrated in their respective views of colonialism. Lansdale believed that the French had lost Indochina as a result of their never having offered anything beyond the prospect of continued subjugation. Galula believed that the French had lost because of their inability to protect the population from the Viet Minh's control. Galula felt that the average person's overriding concern for security had led—and would always lead—to a de facto loyalty that had little to do with nationalist or other aspirations.

Understanding this difference of opinions remains exceedingly relevant to irregular warfare. If the first split in counterinsurgency theory lays at the juncture of enemy-centric and population-centric approaches, the latter splits again on the issue of "hearts" and "minds." The "minds" approach—belonging to the Galula school of thought—calls for controlling the population to enable its protection against the insurgency's harassment and intimidation. The "hearts" approach, belonging to the Lansdale school of thought, requires the counterinsurgent to invest heavily in the marketing of a worthy cause (democratic freedom, prosperity, etc.) that can sway the population to its side. Naturally, neither approach is entirely exclusive of the other. Common sense would dictate that the "minds" approach be favored initially, progressively yielding to a "hearts" approach as the population's basic needs are successively met.

Was the difference of opinion between Galula and Lansdale due to a difference in national cultures; the American idealized view of freedom through

national self-determination, versus the French view of freedom, more focused
on the individual and less on a collective aspiration? The difference of opinion between Galula and Lansdale may also have stemmed from their different practical experiences. Although Lansdale had been in contact with local
populations, he had not had to command troops in a counterinsurgency campaign. Nor had he been faced with the daily obstacles and frustrations associated with pacifying a *sous-quartier* as Galula had been. Lansdale had worked
in much higher spheres, without the constant exposure to the nitty-gritty
motivations of a population stuck in the middle of a war. Lansdale could
therefore remain somewhat aloof, as many contemporaries do, when singling
out lofty contradictions to explain the persistence of insurgencies.

The transcript of the 1962 RAND counterinsurgency symposium is telling
of Galula's voluble participation. Surrounded by experts drawn from U.S.
and Commonwealth armies, it is undeniable that the French officer came
across as the most articulate, knowledgeable and opinionated of them all.
His interventions not only appear to be the most numerous, but are also the
most thorough and structured. Basing himself on his previous deliberations
on the subject, he would outline in detail his interpretation of the dialectically
opposed frameworks for insurgency and counterinsurgency.

The very first intervention of the symposium belonged to Galula. (He was
also more often than not the first to intervene whenever the moderator, Dr.
Hosmer, introduced a new topic.) Galula expressed his view that both insurgent and counterinsurgent shared the same intermediate aim—"control of the
population."[30] In the same breath, he audaciously warned the participants of
a pitfall to avoid: "Although the Symposium's main interest would appear to
be centered on the military aspects of guerrilla warfare, it is well to realize (a)
that we must concern ourselves at least equally with what precedes military
activities (that is, what creates the guerrilla movement) and what will follow
them; and (b) that the political aspects of guerrilla movements are highly
important if not decisive."[31] He complemented this viewpoint with a reproach
he had made ten years ago to his friend Pierre Bourgeois in Saigon, when
France had been losing the war in Indochina: "Those accustomed to planning in terms of conventional war do not realize, for example, that it is difficult and sometimes futile to try to 'identify prior targets for counter guerrilla
operations,' because one of the principles of the insurgent is his willingness to
abandon a base rather than fight for it. . . ."[32] The assertion attacked the future
relevance of Operations Research to guerrilla warfare, which McNamara and
others would come to rely on heavily in Vietnam.

Similarly, when the symposium members spoke of special equipment and
tactics, Galula weighed in with great lucidity, "Guerrilla warfare does not, in
general, call for elaborate equipment beyond that at hand. Though climate,
terrain, and other special factors may create certain special requirements, the

unique demands of this kind of warfare are not so much for a new technology as for a novel philosophical approach to its overall conduct."

Like Galula, Bernard Fall had also been clairvoyant in his distinction between the French and American schools of thought regarding this kind of warfare. The French had learned what the Americans were about to learn in Vietnam. Having quoted the theories of Lacheroy and Trinquier on revolutionary warfare, Fall wrote, "All this differs radically from the American emphasis on *guerrilla techniques* alone and almost total discounting of the primacy of the political factor in revolutionary warfare operations."[33] Incidentally, this perhaps explains the American fascination, going back to the Kennedy era, with Special Forces for counterinsurgency operations. Capable of mimicking and even surpassing guerrillas in terms of stealth, agility, and autonomy, they indeed present a lethal and effective counter-guerrilla alternative to regular forces if the desire is to disrupt the enemy. But in the broader picture of a counterinsurgency campaign warranting a population-centric approach (not all campaigns do), they serve as a complement, and not a substitute, to regular forces who are entrusted with the static protection of the population, which will be needed to set the conditions for governance to be reformed or bolstered. Special Forces are otherwise also invaluable in the "constructive" aspect of counterinsurgency when properly employed towards training specialized host nation forces.

Galula also emphasized the need for methodical *quadrillage* at the discussion table. A phased approach was best, he advised the symposium's members, as there would seldom be sufficient troops to adequately cover an entire theater of operations. He steered clear from the competing method of population concentration. The latter was not only logistically difficult to achieve, but it could also be politically unpalatable and morally questionable. Concentrating and cloistering locals into guarded villages had met success under unique demographic circumstances in Malaya, but the failure of the "Strategic Hamlet Program" in Vietnam would prove Galula right. (The sheer difference in population sizes between the two cases had been to blame according to Fall.[34])

There were, to be sure, a few points of discord between the symposium participants. The importance of ideology in insurgency was among these. Galula gave the example of how French-African students made apt recruits for the Communist Party in France because the latter promised to "raise them from obscurity." He wished to demonstrate that men were seldom motivated by the merits of an ideology itself, but more from what they could gain from it. Bohannan and Lansdale disagreed. Bohannan pointed out that the "generalization failed to take account of the significant minority of genuine believers [in the ideology itself]."[35] To Galula, however, true believers of communism seldom, if ever, could exist. Nor could there be many Algerians who would genuinely prefer to live under the FLN than under the French. "Persuasion," Galula would soon write in *Counterinsurgency*, perhaps influenced *en finale*

by the symposium, "brings a minority of supporters—they are indispensable—but force rallies the rest."[36] Still, it was his experience that the veracity
of any particular cause could be fleeting. This had been the case in China,
for instance, where the Communists had invented the "land-tenure" cause
despite the existence of a relatively "fair spread" in ownership according to
Galula; and that afterwards, instead of redistributing the land, the Communists collectivized it, robbing everyone of ownership in a single swoop.

While Galula believed in the imperative of controlling a population,
Lansdale believed in leaning on the American Revolution and Constitution
to inspire people in the contested developing world. Lansdale noted that,
"Against those communist beliefs, rooted in nineteenth-century philosophy,
we should at least pit our own ideals, rooted in eighteenth-century philosophical concepts, to show that we are *for* something and not just fighting a
negative, defensive battle."[37] This reasoning, in truth, sat well with Galula too.
In Hong Kong, as discussed earlier, he had written at length about the need to
propagate a positive alternative to communism, instead of stubbornly propa-
gating *anti*-communism.

Galula placated his objectors by conceding that there were four possible motivations that could fuel a guerrilla fighter: "belief in the ideals of
the movement, personal ambition, fear (for oneself or one's family), and the
desire to join the bandwagon after initial successes." Galula had thus diluted
the importance of ideology through the grouping. (I would add that even
simpler sources of human motivation such as the prospect of risk and excitement, a sense of belonging, camaraderie and a desire for recognition, honor
or revenge, will motivate young men to take up arms well before any given
ideology does.)

Nevertheless, Galula believed that propaganda mattered, and that it should
be anchored on two themes: the first being that the counterinsurgent's cause
is a good one, and the second being that the counterinsurgent's position is as
strong as it is resolute. With Algeria in hindsight, Galula felt that the "determination of the top leaders" was the biggest asset in a counterinsurgency
campaign. He would revisit this theme in *Pacification,* in reference to de
Gaulle's return to power: ". . . And what a lesson, for what ultimately counted
most was not the tenacious, dedicated effort of officers in the field but a sudden political change at the top. This battle for the minds of the people, which
I believe I had won in my Aissa Mimoun area when the situation was black or
grey everywhere else in Kabylia, a revolution in Algiers had won in a single
stroke."[38]

Bohannan, however, felt that there were two other equally important
counterinsurgent assets to add to political resolve, namely: "an understanding of revolutionary warfare" and a "wise political goal."[39] This triad of sorts
was certainly clever. Galula disagreed, however, on another point expressed
by Bohannan, who felt that "people will revert to their normal political

indifference once the leaders of the guerrilla have been eliminated."[40] Galula considered that the elimination of leaders was rarely decisive. The French had spectacularly captured the top leadership of the FLN, but to little avail to the overall campaign. Galula would also come to write that if an insurgent leader could be killed by the counterinsurgent, he could just as easily be arrested, and that a public trial would serve the overall cause better than a dead rebel leader who would quickly be replaced. Further yet, he cheekily argued that eliminating rebel leaders only hastened the natural selection process among them! And that this rendered promotions of rebel cadres that were much more effective than the slow and bureaucratic process required to promote able counterinsurgents within a professional army!

Bohannan and Galula disagreed finally on a matter that continues to haunt counterinsurgency campaigns today. Still according to the transcript, Galula "thought that, where the guerrilla already has the support of the people, you cannot hope for support until you have purged the area of rebels and created new political organizations."[41] This was a central stance he had previously elaborated in his Staff College thesis: "Political and social reforms alone have no advantageous effect on the population once it has been organized by the revolutionary camp. No matter how good or well they are, the population is in no position to appreciate them and to manifest its support for them. Reforms serve only to encourage the rebels and increase their claims."[42] However, Bohannan felt that reforms and improvements to living conditions should not be delayed on such pretenses.

Galula believed that the elimination of the root cause of the insurgency was actually secondary in both priority and sequence to the reestablishment of order. Galula concluded that "firm and unequivocal rules, a scale of punishments to fit the crimes, and the will to enforce these penalties were essential if [the counterinsurgency] hoped to achieve perfect control."[43] But, to some extent, this reasoning was the product of his era, where the aim of the counterinsurgent generally revolved around the *re-establishment* of order and not the establishment of a new one; a matter that is discussed in the conclusion to this work. Galula's argument has merit, albeit not to the extent of discounting Bohannan's. Reforms and attempts at economic development fall flat when the insurgency remains in firm control of the population. Improperly timed endeavors can even be counterproductive, as unfulfilled promises result in loss of face for the counterinsurgent.

Harvard's Center for International Affairs offered a golden opportunity for Galula to expand his network of intellectual acquaintances. The permanent faculty included titans the likes of Robert Bowie, Alex Inkeles, Henry Kissinger, Edward Mason, and Thomas Schelling. These were joined by a dozen handpicked Fellows and twenty research associates of the calibre of Zbigniew Brzezinski, Fred C. Iklé (who I reached over the phone in the summer of

2011),[44] and Rupert Emerson. All of these were, or would soon become, men of great influence in U.S. foreign policy circles. For over a year, Galula mingled and interacted with them on a daily basis.

The notes and exchanges Galula kept of that era led me to believe that he had quickly become a well-integrated and esteemed member of the Center. According to Ruth, however, an important exception to this harmony lay with the Center's co-founder and director, Dr. Robert Bowie. "Bowie was much more of a liberal than David," she told me. "He was much more of a liberal than Kissinger for that matter too. On many issues, unfortunately, my husband could not see eye-to-eye with Bowie. He was frustrated that Bowie considered him to be a reactionary in his views of international relations." Ruth conceded with a sigh, "David must have spoken his mind a bit too often." His hawkish position on China may very well have been at play.

Galula's contract was not renewed for a second year. It would only be extended to eighteen months to allow him to finish the manuscript for *Counterinsurgency*. "This caught him by surprise. He hadn't been looking for another job," Ruth recalled. But his correspondence spoke otherwise. Galula had started looking for a job as early as March 1963, five months prior to the end of his contract. He had perhaps withheld from telling his wife so as not to worry her, which would have been in line with his character. His future intentions were made clear in a letter to a Hong Kong acquaintance: "Although I may be offered another academic position by a different institution, I prefer to enter the business field; such in fact was my main intention [upon] retiring from the Service. I am looking for a position in an organization . . . active in international trade, where my experience and aptitude could be rapidly put to use."[45]

Dr. Bowie's parting letter to Galula was as short as it was dry: "As I said when you left I wish you every success in the next stage of your career. I very much enjoyed having you here at the Center, and hope you will return to pay us a visit sometime in the future."[46]

I was able to reach Dr. Thomas Schelling, the renowned Nobel laureate of economics, in January of 2011, and Dr. Henry Kissinger's office a few months later, in July. As regrettable as it was understandable, both had difficulty remembering the research associate who had sojourned with them at Harvard fifty years earlier. Over the phone, Schelling recalled some of the differences of opinions that persisted between Kissinger and Bowie at the time. These would get worse as Kissinger ascended Washington circles until he was ostracized completely from the center's faculty members. "We went to see him at the White House in 1970. We warned him that if he pushed for the invasion of Cambodia, we would break off ties with him."[47] Kissinger and Schelling never spoke again.

At Harvard, Galula and Kissinger had grown close to the point of friendship. "The Kissingers were also living off a single academic salary at that time," Ruth sympathized. "I remember when Ann, Henry's first wife, would pick us up with her car . . . you could see the ground through the rusted bottom! We hosted each other on a number of occasions. David, of course, much to my embarrassment and to Ann's, never ate anything." Over dinner, the men invariably talked about politics and foreign affairs. "They were kindred spirits in how they thought American foreign policy should be exercised," Ruth said. "My husband felt that the U.S. should throw more of its weight around on the international scene, but that this should be done intelligently, especially when placating the communists. Kissinger, of course, was bitter that the Kennedy administration had discarded him so-to-speak. He and my husband were critical of JFK's foreign policy, but approving of his domestic one." Kennedy's criticism of the French war effort in Algeria, and of France's foreign policy in general, had done little to endear him to Galula. It is unlikely too that Kennedy's track record in dealing with the Soviets, or the Cubans for that matter, had impressed him.

I discovered that Dr. Schelling had been instrumental in the publication of *Counterinsurgency*. He had been the first to review Galula's draft in the summer of 1963. "I read your manuscript with extraordinary interest about ten days ago," he wrote Galula in a piece of correspondence I found in the latter's papers. "I have not read many books on your subject but yours is the only one from which I think I really learned something."

Schelling was critical, however, of the undertone in Galula's opening chapter. "First, most of us have found the first chapter somewhat pedantic. It is well written; nevertheless, some of the terminology, and some of the style make the reader get ready for a sermon. No great harm is done since most readers will discover soon that the book is extremely creative. But if you can somewhat relax the discussion of laws and principles, I think it would help."[48] (The critique was just, because even after Galula's editing, the Maoist tone can still be detected there and in other parts of the publication.) "The style of the book," Schelling continued, "is not that of the usual book published under the sponsorship of the center. That does not bother me. The style is effective, self-confident, and authoritative . . . I find it quite persuasive. . . ." Galula would be indebted to Schelling for his open-mindedness. It was true that the center seldom if ever published a book with such little academic rigor, or that was prescriptive to the point of resembling a field manual in some sections. Schelling would take it upon himself to forward Galula's manuscript to publisher Frederick Praeger, "ahead of any decision from my colleagues and me about Center publication, just to speed up the process."

Otherwise, both Kissinger and Schelling believed that the manuscript could have benefited from more illustrative examples drawn from his experiences in Algeria.[49] Galula resisted. He was worried about what confidentiality issues such inclusions would raise. He was also mindful about not stigmatizing his work. Finally, he replied to his reviewers: "Because I deal with the essence of the problem, I deliberately kept the manuscript's length short, avoiding overuse of details. Also you may note that examples are visibly lacking in the constructive parts[50] of my work. The reason is simply that my theory has only been applied in part in Algeria."[51] (Such integrity, consistent throughout Galula's works and correspondence, contradicts what some have recently tried to establish.)

Kissinger perceptively asked Galula, "Is the experience of the Chinese Civil War the same kind of problem as where a foreign country is engaged in guerrilla warfare?"[52] The question was of fundamental importance then, and remains so today, as Galula had written with a domestic or *defensive* view of counterinsurgency.[53] (We return to this question in the conclusion.) Kissinger was impressed: "My general comment is that your book is very good. I think it is a first-rate effort."[54]

Galula devoted the duration of his contract period at Harvard to drafting *Counterinsurgency* from Room 305 at the center's borrowed facilities at 6 Divinity Avenue. He drafted *Pacification* during his off hours. The titles he chose for those two works is worth noting. *Pacification* borrowed a term that was more reflective of his view of the subject; however, it echoed colonialism. Lending a stigmatized term to a confidential report was one thing, but lending it to a commercial publication was quite another. Galula did not choose the term "counter-revolutionary warfare" either, because of its negative connotation. "Counterinsurgency," on the other hand, had been popularized by Edward Lansdale, according to Rufus Phillips, and validated in Galula's mind, perhaps, by the RAND symposium. For to *New York Times* columnist Hanson Baldwin, however, the term was little more than "the highfalutin new name for a type of warfare as old as man's inhumanity to man."[55]

Sponsored by Harvard, Galula had written *Counterinsugency* in English for an American audience. This had nothing to do with allegiance, as some French critics have inferred. It was a matter of addressing demand where it stood, and, yet more practically, of abiding by a contract he had signed. Nor did Galula try to hide his book from the French military establishment. The first letter he would write in view of publishing *Counterinsurgency* was addressed to the French attaché general in Washington. Galula submitted two copies of his manuscript to General Jean Compagnon. He asked the latter whether he, or the *Ministre des Armées*, would object to an eventual publication. Galula wished to act transparently at a time when the works of Trinquier, Lacheroy and others were censored in France. Cognizant as to what sensitivities persisted regarding the Algerian War, Galula chose his words carefully in describing his book to the attaché:

> As you will see, my study does not base itself on any official regulations or doctrines. The study is first and foremost a product of my own experiences and reflections, most of which I have acquired a long time

ago principally in China and Greece. You may also note that in the constructive part, I have deliberately withheld from including many examples from Indochina and Algeria, despite the risk of appearing dogmatic by doing so. And of the few examples that are included, they are very broad, publicly known and often drawn directly from Michael Clark's *Algeria in Turmoil*.[56]

Compagnon, a scholarly general whose ascension in France's armored corps had been stellar, wrote back to Galula two weeks later. He had read his manuscript and found the texts to be "interesting and inclusive of the various aspects of the 'counterinsurgency' problem." Otherwise, the general felt confident that the book would not become the target of "criticism from official sources."

"However," Compagnon warned, "seeking ministerial permission to publish would cause delays that are entirely incompatible with your publication schedule." He recommended that Galula withhold any reference to the effect that he was an officer, so as not to be bound by the obligation to obtain any official permission. Nevertheless, the political climate prevailing in France led Compagnon to add: "On a strictly personal level, I think I should give you the following piece of advice: Refrain from promoting your book in French circles in France or in the United States if you wish to avoid any interference with its publication."[57]

Galula heeded this advice.

Fifty years later, it would be ironic yes, but wholly explainable in light of this discovery, that his writings remained unknown within French circles.

To potential publishers of *Counterinsurgency*, Galula wrote:

My manuscript may be summed up as follows: Each type of war has its own set of laws, principles and rules. In conventional wars, they apply equally to both sides. In revolutionary wars, what holds true for the insurgent does not hold true for the counter-insurgent. It is the same war in terms of time and place, yet there are two distinct warfares (*sic*). . . . My theory revolves around the fact that in any circumstances the people are divided pro and con (both a minority) and neutral (a majority). Principle: identify the "pro" group, test it, train it, organize it and set it to work to rally the neutrals and eliminate the "cons."[58]

Rejected by John Wiley & Sons for addressing a topic that was "too narrow" in scope, Galula found better luck with Frederick Praeger; the "most prolific" of publishers in the field of counterinsurgency according to Hanson Baldwin. A mere two weeks after receiving Galula's manuscript, Praeger wrote Thomas Schelling an opinionated, but thoughtful response:

As to the book itself, it is an extraordinarily intelligent book, not brilliant, but very methodical and exceptionally orderly. I like books of this kind because I had the impression that the really gifted people in the military field do too much thinking at the frontiers of knowledge, become too fascinated with solutions, and do not do enough "inventory" thinking, cataloguing, defining, and discussing problems comprehensively and exhaustively, including the very basic, almost primitive ingredients. This Mr. Galula's book does.[59]

Praeger stated that the French author's language and grammar errors could easily be fixed. He was more critical, however, of the subjectivity found in some of the information presented. Specifically, Praeger felt that Galula employed a "simplistic approach when talking about the international communist apparatus."[60] Consequently, some shallowly sourced statements would have to be removed. Otherwise, Praeger proposed that Schelling, Bowie, or Kissinger write the foreword. The least enthused of these was unfortunately chosen. Bowie's foreword fell expectedly flat. Galula reacted politely to his editor that the foreword was "... rather cautious and uncommitted, but I don't blame him, it's a tricky subject on which he has no direct practical experience."[61]

I found other editions of *Counterinsurgency* on Ruth Galula's bookshelves. The translation rights for the work had visibly been sold to Turkish and Portuguese publishers. Turkey had faced insurgency in its Kurdish provinces, and Portugal in Angola. The book would also be translated to Spanish, in light of the Basque rebellion, communist subversion in Latin America, or both. It appears, therefore, that *Counterinsurgency* had not remained untapped in the last half century. To what degree the book was leveraged in those and other conflicts would be worth looking into.

Counterinsurgency received a strong share of media attention in the United States. Hanson Baldwin penned a review in the *New York Times*. Baldwin, who Galula felt was generally biased against the French, nonetheless deemed the author to have been "somewhat more successful" than others at defining the "terms and laws and principles" of counterinsurgency.[62] A review in the *Journal of Politics* read that Galula's book "contrasted" with the recent "dreary parade" of political science works on insurgencies; "it is, therefore, a considerable pleasure to be able to report that Galula ... [has] something of value to contribute. It is almost as great a pleasure to note that the contributions are made with style and, even, with verve."[63] The *Journal of International Affairs* commented for its part, "Well written and well reasoned, this book illuminates the complexities of counter-insurgency in such a manner as to be useful to the policy-maker and to inform others. The author's most significant contribution is his formulation of a framework of laws and principles for counter-insurgency, the basis of which is the building or rebuilding of a political machine from the population upward."[64] Dr. Robert Waelder, famous for applying psychoanalysis to the study of political science, would congratulate Galula by writing, "It is the best I have so far read on the subject."[65]

Perhaps most significant of these was the U.S. Marine Corps *Gazette's* review. In the opinion of the *Gazette's* editors, *Counterinsurgency* contained "some of the best thoughts on the development of tactics from a positive strategy and the actual operations that we've read . . . this book will make you think."[66] In 1964, as the United States prepared to intervene more directly in Vietnam, Galula would write to a friend, "I have met . . . for the first time a perfect stranger . . . who heard about my book. Apparently, he [attended] a lecture by a Marine Colonel . . . on counterinsurgency and the lecturer mentioned my book as the one to read."[67]

As could be expected, not all reviews were positive. Some were politically flavored. Galula had written to his editor, Phyllis Freeman, "This book, I strongly suspect, will make me the Clausewitz of the counter-revolutionaries and as such the target of a lot of ill-minded people, on both sides of the iron and bamboo curtains. Please be kind enough to send me any clippings you may see on the book once it comes out of your presses, I need to be amused."[68] Galula's sense of humor and self-confidence were left unshaken. He would later comment sardonically to his editor, "Thank you also for the reviews. So far, they are exactly as I expected. 'Retired French officer, experience in Algeria, O.A.S. guy, bad guy, lousy book, no need to read it in order to comment on it' . . . Be sure to let me know what comes next!"[69]

To Joe Alsop's congratulations, Galula replied with as much confidence and humor:

> I was very touched to receive your letter. Now that you have read it all, I hope you found my book as interesting as I did myself. But of course, being the father, I am prejudiced. I put into it the quintessence of my experience and observations in the business. I may go down in History as the "Clausewitz of the counter-revolutionaries," and as such the target of the Communists (Soviet and Chinese) as well as their friends. Unless they choose to ignore it. If they do not label me a first class "vipère lubrique," or a "tool of Wall Street," or an "arch-imperialist," I will be really mad.[70]

Freeman forwarded a letter Frederick Praeger had received from the White House. "You really made a hit in high quarters," she wrote Galula excitedly. The letter had been sent by Lansdale, who was serving as a consultant for the U.S. Food for Peace Program after retiring from the Air Force. Lansdale agreed with Praeger on the "astuteness of [Galula's] writing." In the same letter, he supplied Praeger with the names of people who were in charge of counterinsurgency at the White House, presumably so that the latter could circulate Galula's work on the subject: "The man really in charge of counter-insurgency is Secretary McNamara. The other two who are supposed to be are: Maj. Gen. Rollen H. 'Buck' Anthis, SACSA, JCS (who took Krulak's place) and Maj. Gen. James D. Alger, Special Warfare, U.S. Army, Pentagon (who took Bill Rosson's place)."[71]

Did McNamara receive a copy of Galula's work? And even if so, would he have read it? Fast-forwarding fifty years, history had come full circle. U.S. Army General Jack Keane was pulled out of retirement in 2006 by the Pentagon to become the top advisor to rectify a spiraling situation in Iraq. Keane took it upon himself to impress upon Defense Secretary Donald Rumsfeld that funda-mental principles of counterinsurgency were being systematically violated on the ground; a drastic change of strategy was required. The population would have to be controlled and protected. Counterinsurgent forces would have to leave their massive fortified bases and live among the population to achieve this. Their commanders would have to be held accountable for progress. Finally, Keane recommended that the secretary take a deeper look at the ratio-nale behind all of this; of all of the existing works on counterinsurgency, Keane would choose to recommend Galula's for the secretary of defense to read.[72]

Lansdale's acclaim of *Counterinsurgency* was accompanied by criticism that highlighted his disagreement with Galula regarding how population-centric counterinsurgency should be waged. Lansdale wrote to Praeger:

[Galula's] analysis of insurgency was superbly well done. I sort of wish he had stopped there, because his analysis of the strategy and tactics of counterinsurgency, while interesting (and probably a much more pain-ful task for David), simply isn't as good as his wonderful depth of under-standing of insurgency. He comes mighty close on counterinsurgency, but the policeman in his nature seems to keep gaining the ascendancy over the politically sensitive side of his nature.[73]

Lansdale's recollection of Galula from the Hong Kong and Manila years clashed, to some extent, with the post-Algeria Galula who believed that rev-olutionary warfare technique mattered as much, if not more, as ideological contentions. Lansdale did not appreciate Galula's dismissive treatment of the counterinsurgency victory in the Philippines, which he attributed to the insur-gency's adoption of a cause that could be usurped by the counterinsurgent.[74] Galula had written to this effect that it was easier to win when, "The insurgent has a cause that the counterinsurgent can espouse without unduly endanger-ing his power. This was, as we have seen, the situation in the Philippines dur-ing the Huk's insurgency. All the counterinsurgent has to do is promise the necessary reforms and prove he means it."[75] To this, Lansdale retorted:

I wish he had had more perception about the Huk campaign in the Philippines, which only looked simple because so many hard-to-do things went right. Beyond the blood, sweat, and tears which there were, as elsewhere, there were some strong political lessons which I have yet to discover a Frenchman understanding. I had hoped that Galula would be an exception. It's the winning ingredient he almost touches. Maybe the difference between the French and American Revolutions is the gap still.[76]

It can be inferred from this that even if the idealistic Lansdale had not been ostracized from Pentagon circles, it is unlikely that he would have pushed for the adoption of Galula's doctrine among Vietnam War planners. Despite all of this, Lansdale felt that his friend Galula should be the one to tackle a pivotal issue for U.S. foreign policy in Southeast Asia. He continued his note to Praeger with:

. . . all signs point to there being an even better second book in Galula. I believe you should encourage and develop his writing this second book. He has most of the adrenalin of his Algerian counterinsurgency experience out of his system in this first book, so now he should be ready to do the task which I have long believed he is rather uniquely capable of doing (and which both Hank Lieberman of the *New York Times* and I urged him to tackle some ten years ago in Hongkong.)

The second book should be a description of Chinese Communist insurgency and its exportable qualities. I believe that the Chinese having discovered the farmer-intellectual combination, in contrast to the Soviets' proletariat-intellectual, makes the Chicom doctrine the one which we will up against in country after country for years to come. We need a Free World portrayal of this great danger to us, done in firm honesty and understanding, and I believe Galula is the one to provide it. He owes us all this one![77]

Praeger was enthusiastic. Phyllis Freeman asked her author with flattering humor, "Could we then induce you to take time out from the golf course to write along the lines that Lansdale suggests? We quite agree that this book would be very valuable (in the non-monetary sense) and that you are certainly the one to write it. And among 'the exportable qualities' that [Lansdale] mentions, I am sure there would be some good cuisine."[78]

Galula declined, stating that he was ill-at-ease with "working from research material" and otherwise busy with his new post-Harvard career. He reminded Freeman that the Council on Foreign Relations had rejected his proposal to write a book on the rise of the Chinese Communist Party and the "exportability" of its doctrine when he had had the time and inclination to do so.[79] Undeterred, Lansdale wrote a second letter, this time directly to Galula, in a final effort to convince him.

> I urged [Praeger] to get you to write a second book solely on the subject of subversive insurgency or revolutionary warfare as practiced by the other side. I felt that this first book of yours merely skimmed a tiny surface part of your deep feelings and knowledge of this subject and how the enemies of free men go about gaining control of populations. What you have to say on this subject would be invaluable to many of us, and certainly far more pertinent than the academic treatment which other scholars give it.[80]

Regrettably, Galula could not be swayed.

Offers to write and lecture continued to come Galula's way from some of the most reputable universities, think tanks, and journals. He declined a majority of these for lack of time to devote to writing.

He thus refused an offer from the Civilian Defense Study Conference to lecture along with Alastair Buchan and Liddell Hart.[81] He declined an offer by Leopold Labetz of the London-based *Survey—A Journal of Soviet and East European Studies*, to contribute an article on "polycentric communism."[82] He declined another opportunity with the Ford Foundation, interested in China, which had found out about him through his friends Howard Boorman from Columbia University and Stanley Hoffman from Harvard.[83] He also declined an invitation to contribute articles to an encyclopaedia prepared by the Soviet System and Democratic Society, whose contributors included the likes of Brzezinski.[84] To these, Galula typically responded, "My present activity has left me no leisure even during the week-ends for last eighteen months. There is no sign of relaxation of my work."[85] He was also approached by Oxford with an offer for him to lecture on guerrilla warfare and the legal ramifications of counterinsurgency operations, in the context of a special course being put together for senior civilian and military officials of the British Ministry of Defense.[86] This too he rejected, but on account of his health in 1967.

Among the few solicitations he did accept was a request from the journal *Current Thought on Peace and War* to publish extracts from *Counterinsurgency*.[87] In 1964, he also accepted an invitation from Alastair Buchan to lecture at the Institute for Strategic Studies's annual conference in Oxford. Titled "Conflict and Co-existence in Asia," the conference included his friend Samuel Griffith and nine other presenters. Buchan wrote Galula in the summer of 1964, "I know the valuable work that you have been doing in the study of subversive warfare and of counter-insurgency, and I am writing to ask whether you would be willing to write a paper on this question, dealing in particular with the means by which Asian countries, with or without American assistance, can defeat subversive warfare."[88] Galula agreed. However, after the conference, he confided to Freeman that he "would not be invited again, as [he had] deflated a few theories that seem fashionable these days."[89] During the same period, Galula was solicited by *U.S. News & World Report* for a televised interview regarding the looming Vietnam crisis. The reporter, Joseph Fromm, wrote Galula, "With a New Viet Nam crisis coming to a head, I thought a good deal about the points you had made in our talks."[90] Galula accepted the invitation, but disappointingly, the interview would be canceled at the last minute to allow for additional coverage of the presidential election. What impact such an interview would have had is unknown. I would venture, however, that Galula's renown in the United States would have benefited from it, and that the United States may have benefited from it too.

18

Five Short Years

In this form of war that has been imposed on us, every action we undertake to engage the population must respect the fundamental principles of our civilization, that is to say, to concretize through action our ideal of justice, freedom and brotherly love in the service of man.

—Challe Instruction, 1959[1]

I do not try to pretend that my work is the final one of the subject, but I feel certain that it is the first and only one that tries to go beyond lame formulas such as, "We must win the support of the population."

—David Galula[2]

BASKING IN THE SUN of a beautiful Cape Cod day, David Galula spoke of his future career plans with his brother-in-law who sat in the beach chair next to him. The two had been watching their kids play in the sand, when Galula lowered his Wayfarers and announced that he intended to go into business once his contract at Harvard expired. He was at peace with not returning to active duty in France and had failed to fall in love with academic life, which, after all, his extroverted character was rather ill-suited for.

"He was thinking of opening up a consulting firm that would cater to large corporations wishing to operate in unfamiliar or risky countries," Jere Rowland reminisced about a conversation he had fifty years earlier. "His analytical mind, and his accumulated experience would have lent themselves well for that." His large network of influential acquaintances would have also played in his favor.

Prior to going into business on his own, however, Galula wished to gain a better feel for what such work in the private sector would entail. Mao had preached, above all, the merits of testing a concept prior to fielding it in full scale. Galula would seek employment in a similar field first to test the market and to gain a better financial footing. To his friend and editor at Praeger, Phyllis Freeman, he wrote jokingly but clairvoyantly that there were "commercial applications to be drawn from guerrilla warfare!"[3]

The publication of *Counterinsurgency* provided Galula with the closure to the longest chapter of his existence. "The book finally written and out," he confided to his journalist friend Joe Alsop, "I am now trying to become a businessman. I did not like the idea of spending the rest of my life idling in futile tasks in the French Army of today. I hope to find in business the same moral and intellectual challenges that made my previous career so interesting."[4] Galula asked to be definitively retired from active service at the end of his three-year sabbatical on October 1, 1964, at the age of forty-five. Transferred to the Reserves, he would be promoted to the rank of lieutenant-colonel the following year, but would fall short of becoming a full colonel despite what his file foretold.

Galula applied to a number of companies in the United States, France, and Hong Kong where he had maintained numerous contacts. His first serious job offer came from a large U.S. oil and gas company that wished to hire him as a political-risk analyst. He wrote self-mockingly to Freeman, "The job was with Sonoco-Mobil . . . 4 billion dollars a year in revenue, of which 17,000 for me!" But the offer was tied to a condition that led him to reject it; "I had every qualification but one, I was not—and did not plan to become—an American citizen." Nevertheless, Galula confided that he deemed the company's position to be "understandable."[5] Sonoco-Mobil wished for him to acquire U.S. citizenship in order to become eligible for a security clearance. "He replied that he had enough acumen of his own to provide good analysis and advice without having to consult U.S. Government documents," his widow recalled, adding after a pause: "He was very proud of his French citizenship you know." It certainly had been hard earned.

With no further employment prospects in sight, Galula returned to France with his family in October of 1963. They stayed temporarily at an apartment located at 43bis, *rue* Madeleine Michelis, in Paris's 16th *Arrondissement*, before settling into the pretty suburb of Neuilly, on the Seine River. In France too, the retired officer had difficulty finding suitable employment. "As the months went by," Ruth told me, "we ran out of what little money we had been able to save." The royalties from *Counterinsurgency* alone were not sufficient to support the family. "This led him to undertake the writing of *Les*

Moustaches du Tigre, for no other reason but to pay the bills. He drafted the novel between job applications and interviews."

Frederick Praeger would have preferred to see Galula devote himself to writing on issues of growing importance to the United States: irregular warfare and Vietnam. Nonetheless, Praeger offered to put Galula in touch with the *Economist's Intelligence Unit* in London where he could help him find a job. But Galula politely declined, stating that he had already received offers from think-tanks and universities, but that he was now seeking to acquire a hands-on commercial experience.[6]

Galula's luck changed for the better by mid-1964. Unrelenting in his humor, and displaying the resilient morale Guillermaz had highlighted before, he wrote to a friend:

> I have been hunting for a job for the last five months, receiving only negative answers. Then suddenly everyone wants to hire me and my problem is to choose between various exciting offers, in France, Africa, and the Far East. From the way things look, I may end up in Hong Kong as the Far Eastern representative for a large French firm manufacturing earth moving equipment; something the Chinese Communists aren't interested in, so it won't bother my employers if I am persona non-grata in Peking![7]

Galula soon received a more appealing offer from a French defense firm. And although that may have seemed to be the obvious option for a military retiree, the technology-intensive milieu was unfamiliar to the Colonial Army officer that he was. He was recruited into the company's business development arm, where his people skills would make up for his lack of technical knowledge. Presumably, his experience in managing a shortwave radio project under de Gaulle had proved to be an asset in his résumé.

Galula started his new job at *La Compagnie Française Thomson Houston* (CFTH) in April of 1964. "I am selling radars, all kinds," he announced smartly to Phyllis Freeman. "We start with a cheap model for foot soldiers at $4,000, and we have a giant model for $3,000,000. We can give a discount for customers with large families.[8]" The editor replied to her often-flirtatious French author, "I think I'll take the three million dollar one if they make it in a color that matches my office." In a letter to Frederick Praeger, Galula offered greater detail, but without foregoing his characteristic humor:

> My job is to find out what are the long term prospects in order that the bosses make the right business decisions. I must say that the prospects are not so hot, I can smell a strong danger of peace. That would be my

luck! Anyway, it's intellectually interesting, particularly since I have to disguise myself in a hurry into an electronics expert, and God knows that my electronic background is very close to zero. I am trying to absorb as fast as I can the proper technical terms and I can already discourse about the radarmonopulse with compressed impulsions, side beams, using coherent technique . . . My son Daniel (5) is really impressed.[9]

CFTH owed its name to the two American founders of General Electric who had created a French subsidiary at the turn of the century. CFTH was merged with Hotchkiss-Brandt, and then again with *La Compagnie générale de la télégraphie sans-fil,* acquiring the name of Thomson-CSF shortly after Galula's death. In 2000, the company was renamed Thales. It was, and remains, one of France's, and indeed of the world's, largest defense companies. (Coincidently, it is also one for which I have had the pleasure of working briefly for.) In 1964, the company was in the midst of forming a consortium dedicated to the NATO Air Defense Ground Environment (NADGE) project to which Galula would be assigned. CFTH partnered with America's Hughes and other Western European aerospace companies such as Marconi to provide a "modernised, semi-automated air defence system, comprising new radars, new ground-to-air communications and computer-based control sites."[10]

CFTH identity card.

Ruth discussed her late husband's work at CFTH over her favorite Chinese tea. She showed me some of the company's 1960s catalogues in the makeshift office space we had set up in her bedroom, using an ironing board in lieu of a desk. As fate would have it, Ruth would work for an entire decade at Thomson-CSF as an administrative assistant to a senior executive to support herself and Daniel after her husband passed away. It had been her husband's dying wish that she remain in France to raise Daniel. And so she had.

Despite the frenetic tempo and the constant traveling that his new occupation required of him, Galula was content. By all accounts, he did well under the *sytèmes éléctroniques radar* (SER) subdivision to which he belonged. Two years had not gone by before the English-speaking Galula was moved to London to assume greater responsibilities within the NADGE consortium.

In late 2010, I was able to reach Gérald Cauvin, Galula's supervisor at CFTH, with the help of the resourceful Colonel René Lantelme. Cauvin had served as an officer in the French Navy prior to starting a successful civilian career at CFTH. Ruth remembered him as a man with an exceptionally kind heart.

Galula had been referred to Cauvin by a common military acquaintance. "I was immediately impressed by David," Cauvin described their first encounter. "His temperament, vivacious mind, sense for human relations, and naturally, his experiences convinced me that he would be a great asset for our team." The division's president, Mr. Bouysonnie, would later corroborate this, "We saw a future executive in him. He very quickly adapted to civilian life, and proved himself to be a worker and a friend whose drive, intelligence and competence were appreciated by all."[11]

"Indeed, he excelled," Cauvin remarked. "I was very grateful for his efficiency, and we soon became close friends. He had in him this character and attitude that are so particular to North African Jews ... this brought back pleasant memories of my youth. Finally, we were also bound by a common passion for Asia. We had both spent considerable time serving there in our previous careers, me at sea, and him, on the ground."

In the first few days of May of 1967, the Rowlands received a distressed phone call from France. David had been declared terminally ill. Ruth's sister, Freddy, told her husband Jere that she would be leaving him alone with the children for some time. Freddy left on the next available flight to Paris.

In November of 1966, David had moved to an apartment in Earl's Court, in Greater London. "He went alone," Ruth explained, "because we wanted Daniel to finish his school year in France before we joined him." She visited her husband twice, once in February, and once in late March of 1967, by which time he had started to feel ill. "He resisted seeing a doctor for lack of time. It was only when boils started appearing on his body that I was able to convince him to get a check-up in London. That yielded a faulty diagnosis.

"The doctors told him that he was sick because he had a tiny gallbladder!" Ruth scoffed, recalling how silly that had sounded even then. When it became apparent that Galula's condition was not improving, an executive at NADGE referred him to a reputed specialist at the American Hospital in Paris. An appointment was set for April 1.

David flew in the day before in high spirits, as his wife recalled: "He kept saying how good it was that he would finally get this issue solved once and for all. I think he knew that it was something serious, but he had a lot of faith in American medicine. I do not think he was overly worried. He had been such a strong, healthy, and dynamic man throughout his life." Ruth regretted being upset with him for taking a taxi from the airport, instead of calling her to pick him up. "I reminded him that we couldn't afford such luxuries, and that it was not like him to spend for the sake of convenience. That's how clueless I was about his condition. I was still thinking on such silly terms!"

The specialist, Dr. Hughes, telephoned Ruth at home the following week with the results. David had cancer. It had aggressively spread from his lungs to his liver. Hughes estimated that David had no more than six weeks left to live.

By mid-April, Galula, still in Paris, became bedridden by the pains. "It must have been unbearable," Ruth recollected, on the verge of tears. "He suffered from incredible nausea and abdominal pains. I also knew he had chest pains from the way he coughed. He decided to sleep in another room so that Daniel and I could get some rest at night. In the mornings, I could hear his muffled groaning in his room. He never complained to me, and refused to show pain in anybody's presence. He was a military man. An officer who had belonged to *La Coloniale*."

David's correspondence spiked during this period. In addition to the invitations he continued to receive to write or lecture, he received a profusion of notes from friends wishing him a speedy recovery. Professor Doak Barnett, the White House advisor on Chinese affairs who had recalled Galula's sound analysis, was the first one to write.[12] Tom Straker, a reputed scientist, who had known Galula at NADGE followed next: "As you know, Bill [Quill] and I have been out of NADGE affairs for some time now but we both look back to the good old days when Cauvin, Galula, Todd, Quill and Straker really got the consortium off the ground and made things go. It was a pleasure and a privilege to work (and sometimes relax) with you David, and I look forward to the time when you are fully recovered and we shall do so again."[13]

Dr. Hughes urged Ruth not to tell her husband the truth about his prognosis. He felt that it would be better for her husband to not lose hope of recovering. To David, Dr. Hughes would only say that he had cancer, but that it had reached an intermediate stage, and was therefore curable. "We had received a lot of poor advice over the years," Ruth reflected painfully. "But on this particular occasion, the consequences would haunt me for the rest of my life." She felt that this advice, which she diligently followed, had robbed her and her husband from saying their proper good-byes. The lack of closure extended to their entourage, exacerbating the shock of his death. Ruth had nonetheless tried to warn close members of her husband's family of the gravity of his state in late April. But few believed that the intrepid David could be dying at forty-eight. His sister, Madeleine, who Ruth had always found to be aloof, categorically refused to believe any of it. "She thought she had seen him in high spirits, when in fact he had been hiding his pain. She thought I was over-reacting. *'Penses-tu!?'* she had told me."

Nonetheless, a man of Galula's perceptiveness could not have been so easily duped. While he still could, Galula took his wife and son to sign a will in the last days of April. On the way back from the notary's office, he turned to his wife in the car and said: *"Tu vois, je pense à ces choses aussi."*[14]

David lost consciousness on May 10, 1967.

"He and I had been talking about the most trivial things the evening before on the balcony," his widow told me, unsuccessfully fighting back tears. "I remember him sitting there on his rocking chair, looking out, as I left him to his thoughts." He had reminded Ruth in a conversation earlier that day that whatever became of him, he would want Daniel to be raised in France. Before going to bed that evening, an eight-year-old Daniel told his father that he loved him, just as he had on every other night, to which his father could only reply: *"Je t'aime aussi."*

David passed away at eight o'clock on the morning of May 11.

"I lay there next to him, I do not know for how long," Ruth muttered, with tears slowly streaming down her face. "His lips turned cold. His sister Hélène kept insisting that I leave the room, but I refused. I was no longer rational. I locked myself in to be left alone with him. I felt as if I had been hit by a train. I refused to accept how quickly the man I had loved and admired so much had been taken away from me."

Hélène was infuriated by Ruth's insistence on staying in the room. Although David's sister had been very much secularly assimilated, she had been raised by a mother who was mindful of religious traditions and superstitions; one of which was that a corpse should be left alone and buried as soon as possible. Hélène forced the door open. "Her physician injected me with a sedative," Ruth said. "I must have been in hysterics. The drug only made things blurrier, worsening I suppose, my state of emotions. I could not even recall where I had stored David's uniforms, as people around me started discussing funeral arrangements."

Gérald Cauvin helped Ruth and her sister plan the funeral, along with Aunt Mathilde, who hosted David in his preparatory year for Saint-Cyr. She would become like a mother to Ruth and a grandmother to Daniel while they remained in France. Ruth had wanted a military funeral for her husband. Cauvin did his best to give the funeral as much of a military semblance as he could. To his deep regret, he would not be able to remain for the funeral due to a scheduled business trip to Israel. Mr. Colombé, whom Ruth referred to as a top-executive at CFTH attended in his stead. "He and his wife were very kind to me. Mrs. Colombé offered to drive Daniel to school that week, and even had the thoughtfulness to purchase me the black clothing that I would have to wear. She was an elegant and charitable lady belonging to a class of people that has unfortunately ceased to exist."

Freddy Rowland arranged for the funeral to take place at the American Cathedral in Paris, in the 8th *Arrondissement*. I asked Ruth whether any thought had been given to burying David in the Jewish rite. "Yes, some was," she answered, "but we wouldn't have known how to go about it. David had never spoken of such things. Some of his sisters, I think, were upset by this, but I don't think they would have known how to go about it anymore than I did."

The funeral was held on Saturday, May 13. Sadly, David's own mother was not in attendance. "Hélène had insisted that her mother not be told that David had passed away," Ruth told me. "Some of the sisters thought that Julie would succumb to sorrow if she found out." This was indeed extreme, beyond the typical idiosyncrasies of Sephardic family dynamics I thought. "Hélène told me to keep writing to her mother, and to find some excuse or other for David's absence. I tried. I wrote her a single letter stating that David had been captured, once again, by communists in Asia, but that he would surely be released . . . it was ridiculous, and emotionally unbearable. I never wrote another one."

Cauvin was deeply saddened by the loss of his friend. He had visited him often in his final days, with the accord of Ruth, who was glad to see her husband's spirits lifted by him. Cauvin shared with me a secret he had kept dear for five decades. I interpreted it as a kind man's confession of an act that had marked his life. "At the very end, on the day before he passed away, I was left alone in David's room. I felt taken over by a formidable emotion for this dying friend. I laid a kiss on his forehead, and traced a cross on his emaciated face, saying, 'I baptize you, in the name of the Father, the Son, and the Holy Spirit.'"

"Let this not shock you," he would add with benevolent intent. "As a Catholic wishing to contribute to the salvation of a man who had become a true brother to me, I wished to leave it up to God to decide. I cannot tell you anything more; if not that his writings on counterinsurgency are a legacy to his intelligence. But I can testify that behind his fine sense of humor, there was an exceptional sensibility and the kindest of hearts."

The short delay between Galula's death and burial did not allow Ruth to contact all who had known her husband. "Sadly, we were so hurried, that many of David's friends and acquaintances would learn about the funeral only after it had taken place. I've already told you about Pimienta," Ruth said. Still, I counted more than eighty signatures of friends and colleagues who attended the service. (The presence of spouses very likely doubled this figure.) Present at the funeral were many of the people Galula had known at NADGE, but also from much earlier times: Colonel Lantelme from Saint-Cyr, Pierre Bourgeois from China, Lieutenant-Colonel Desnoyes from Algeria, General Casso from the EMGDN, and of course, General Jacques Guillermaz, his lifelong mentor and friend. It was the latter who Ruth would entrust to deliver the eulogy. Ruth's esteem of Guillermaz had always been boundless. "I felt that for as long as Guillermaz was alive, there was a still a part of David in this world. He kept me going."

Fifty years later, I would find a copy of Guillermaz's moving eulogy in a case of archives at the Galula home. Ruth, who had not read it since, cried as she did now. The eulogy read with brotherly affection and respect for a disciple who had truly demonstrated his worthiness in all facets of life. Guillermaz described David's remarkable passage and career, but also his remarkable character. "David's formidable intelligence never eclipsed his big heart," Guillermaz had said. "He was a man of character, always moving forward and heeding to his conscience and judgement, but always adhering, in the end, to an exact discipline."

Portrait taken in the final year of his life.

Galula was buried in La Norville, on the outskirts of Arpajon, to the south of Paris. His stone is engraved with both his name and his widow's.

David Galula's untimely death meant everything in the world for the woman in whose life he had played such a central role, and for the eight-year-old boy who had lost his second chance of having a father. Mother and son were never able to fully come to terms with the monumental loss. To them, David had been a titan, a center of gravity, and a hope.

I believe that by remaining in France for so long after her husband's death Ruth not only kept her promise to her husband, but also took comfort in what little continuity this could provide. She would wait an entire decade before returning to the United States. To my astonishment, Ruth had never reread any of her husband's letters to her since his death; so deep was the pain. When I met her for the first time in late 2008, we would peer over documents and letters together that had not been looked at in fifty, and in some cases, sixty or seventy, years. I digitized microfilms for her to see; pictures of her and her husband that had not been viewed in as long. The emotion was heart wrenching. And then, there was relief. She told me that she was experiencing closure at last. I was honored and humbled to be told that this book would bring her peace.

For the mother and her son, materially, life was not simple either. Ruth had had to struggle through multiple levels of bureaucracy to receive her husband's modest military pension, despite his notarized will. The royalties from David's books, paid by Praeger and Flammarion, had dwindled by the time of his passing away to just a few hundred dollars per year. "What saved us," Ruth told me, "was that David's colleagues at CFTH had had the gallantry to help me, perhaps at the risk of their own careers. They gave all of the credit of securing a large business deal to him, which resulted in a substantial bonus being paid posthumously."

When Ruth finally left France with a teenaged Daniel, she would settle in the rented basement of a house in Stamford, Connecticut, next to where the Rowlands and her mother had moved to. Naturally, it had not been easy for her to leave France after so many years. "David's aunt Mathilde was the closest thing to a mother for me there. She had somehow fallen out with her daughters during those years, and yet, she accepted me as her own child. I had lots of friends in France too, and so did Daniel. We had been attached to the house in Arpajon and its lovely garden. For Daniel, the change of schools, language, and even culture proved to be difficult.

I allowed myself to ask Ruth if there had been another man in her life after David's death. She replied that there hadn't. But after a pause, she added, ". . . it would have been perhaps better for Daniel if there had been . . . but I would have never been able to replace him."

Ruth continues to receive her husband's army pension, paid through the French consulate. She also receives royalties from her husband's books, which have been resuscitated in recent years. She lived with Daniel, his wife, and their two young children in California until late 2010. She now lives in a retirement home. Her greatest joy is to be visited by her grandson named David, after his grandfather.

EPILOGUE:
THE CLAUSEWITZ OF
COUNTERINSURGENCY

OVER THE SUMMER OF 2011, as I drafted the conclusion to this work, I interviewed a number of American counterinsurgency experts who had come to mention Galula's influence over contemporary thinking and operations. Retired Lieutenant-Colonel John Nagl was among the first I would call. His doctoral thesis, *Learning to Eat Soup with a Knife*, a comparative study of the Malayan Emergency and the Vietnam War, had earned him much acclaim, as would his contribution to the drafting of FM 3-24. Pleasant and down-to-earth, he was eager to contribute to the story of the man he and David Petraeus had knighted as the "Clausewitz of counterinsurgency."[1]

"I discovered Galula through the *Warlord Loop*," Nagl answered my first question over the phone, in his quick and upbeat tone. "It was an email community driven by retired Colonel John Collins, but Terry Daly was the sponsor of Galula."

To Nagl, *Counterinsurgency* was a forgotten treasure.

"It was very exciting to read through Galula for the first time. It felt new. No one had previously achieved that level of clarity. Perhaps this was so because Galula was both a practitioner and a theorist. . . . His was a real 'how-to-guide.'"

Nagl's involvement with FM 3-24 dated back to his return from Al-Anbar province in late 2004 to work under Deputy Secretary of Defense Paul Wolfowitz. In October of that year, he would read the just released interim version of *Counterinsurgency Operations*, FMI 3-07.22 (an offshoot of FM 3-07

Stability Operations and Support Operations drafted in 2003). "It was a first stab at a counterinsurgency doctrine. The updated draft came out the following year. I felt that it was worse than the first." FM 3-24's predecessor had been written by a staff officer at Fort Leavenworth who had little to no practical experience in counterinsurgency. "The officer wasn't to blame. Counterinsurgency was viewed as an arcane field of study, and it had simply been this officer's fate to be assigned to that desk."

Nagl believed that an entirely new doctrine was warranted. He would mention this to David Petraeus who had just returned from a second tour in Iraq. Nagl offered the visiting general a list of recommendations he thought would help reverse the spiraling insurgency. "The first point on that list expressed the need for a new doctrine," Nagl recalled. It boded well for change, for Petraeus was set to take over the Combined Arms Center and Fort Leavenworth, where he would overlook doctrine development and professional education for the officer corps.

In November of 2005, Nagl would meet Petraeus again at a conference on counterinsurgency organized by Sarah Sewall, a young and dynamic professor from Harvard's John F. Kennedy School of Government with White House and Pentagon experience. She would later author the introduction to the Chicago University Press edition of FM 3-24, while Nagl authored the forward. The latter told me that a few notables in the field of counterinsurgency had found Sewall's thirty some-odd page introduction to be as good as, if not better than, the doctrine itself.

"In his keynote address," Nagl recalled, "General Petraeus announced that a new doctrine would be written, and that I would be the one to produce it! I spent the evening drawing up an outline at the Front Page bar on a cocktail napkin." But Nagl's boss at the Pentagon did not wish to part with him completely. "There were twelve of us involved, and Con Crane led the drafting effort instead. He acted as the editor-in-chief, so to speak, while I acted as his managing editor." Dr. Conrad Crane, a seasoned professor of military history, had graduated from West Point with Petraeus.

"We kicked off in December 2005, and submitted in February 2006," Nagl asserted. I was astounded by how quickly the draft had been put together. "We were losing a war," was Nagl's reply.

In his foreword to the Chicago University Press's edition of the field manual, Nagl wrote with characteristic verve, "Chapter authors were selected, given their marching orders, and threatened with grievous physical injury if they did not produce a draft in short order."[2]

The final draft of FM 3-24 was released in December of 2006. It was downloaded 1.5 million times in the first month alone.[3] It had in fact become a bestseller, with an audience that extended well beyond American military circles.

I was intrigued by the inclusion of a bibliography in a field manual.

"I plead responsibility for that," Nagl said. "It was something I insisted on. We wanted to send a clear message about us being a *Learning Organization*. The troops had to keep learning if they wanted to be good at counterinsurgency." This was laudable.

What of the manual's subsequent publication by a commercial press?

"This was a first to my knowledge," Nagl replied, "with the exception of the 1940 *Small Wars Manual*, which has been reprinted in recent times."

Nagl had contributed to FM 3-24's first chapter, *Insurgency and Counterinsurgency*, and had drafted major sections of Chapter Five, *Executing Counterinsurgency Operations*. These two are among the most important chapters in my view, the doctrine's heart and brain, respectively. I asked him what his degree of awareness of Galula's writings had been at that time.

"I was deeply immersed during the drafting," he replied. "I had already been invited to write the foreword to Praeger's new edition of *Counterinsurgency*. Galula's book simply never left my desk." He conveyed the image by sharing that he was holding the book as we spoke over the phone. "Galula's influence was huge. If you look at the field manual's *Executing Counterinsurgency Operations* chapter, for instance, and compare it to Galula's on counterinsurgency operations, you could switch them up, and nobody would bat an eye."

And on the imperative of protecting the population?

"General Petraeus made that, and the importance of learning and adapting, his two central themes."

In his foreword to the commercial edition of FM 3-24, Nagl concluded just as categorically: "Of the many books that were influential in the writing of Field Manual 3-24, perhaps none was as important as David Galula's *Counterinsurgency Warfare: Theory and Practice*."[4]

In his bestselling book, *Fiasco*, about the invasion of Iraq and its aftermath, *Washington Post* journalist Thomas Ricks related retired Lieutenant-Colonel Terry Daly saying, "*Counterinsurgency Warfare* is the primer, and at the same time, the bible."[5] Daly informed me over the phone that some attempts of applying Galula had been made by Special Forces and others in Vietnam, where he had served as an intelligence officer with provincial reconnaissance units. Daly had been frustrated to no end that many valuable lessons from that war had been discarded. "The army wanted nothing to do with counterinsurgency after Vietnam." This had motivated him to shed light on an old problem American forces were facing in new theaters of war.

Daly put me in touch with Thomas X. Hammes at the Institute for National Strategic Studies in the fall of 2011. "T.X. Hammes published a resounding review of Galula's *Counterinsurgency* in the *Washington Post* on July 17, 2005," Daly had told me. Indeed, Hammes, the author of *The Sling and the Stone*, wrote that Galula's treatise ". . . remained one of the most useful books on counterinsurgency ever written."[6] Hammes, a retired USMC colonel holding a PhD from Oxford, had been one of the three retired officers to call for the resignation of Defense Secretary Donald Rumsfeld in their testimony to the U.S. Democratic Policy Committee in late 2006.[7] Hammes understood small wars and counterinsurgency. He wrote me that he had discovered Galula in the mid-1980s, to which he added simply: "I had been studying insurgencies since joining the Corps in 1975."

I shared my belief with Hammes that Galula had written with "defensive counterinsurgency" (to preserve existing regimes) in mind; but that human motivations being what they were—relatively consistent in their hierarchy—Galula had been translated for "offensive counterinsurgency" (to install a new regime) with relative ease. Still, there were differences between seeking to defend a pre-existing friendly regime, and seeking to impose a new one after having toppled its predecessor. His insightful response to employing the Galula Doctrine by proxy was as follows:

> You hit the fundamental problem with an expeditionary power using Galula. His book is written for the domestic power. It is based on creating legitimate government. If you are the domestic power, you can simply fire those who are incompetent or corrupt. As we have found in Vietnam, Iraq and Afghanistan, you can't fire the host nation people; you have to try to persuade them. When you have committed major forces, you lose leverage to force change. Your threats to cut resources to the government or depart are not believable. In contrast, in the Philippines (1950's and present), Columbia, Thailand, and El Salvador, we could make real threats to leave if they didn't make the necessary political adjustments to defuse the insurgency. Galula can apply when working by a proxy but, the historical record indicates it can only work if the outside power keeps its commitment small and thus can withdraw if the host nation refuses to change.

(Admittedly, however, the proposition of a lighter form of intervention may be difficult to apply to scenarios where the foreign party intervenes directly to topple a regime. The onus of the ensuing chaos and disruption to governance belongs to the foreign intervener. This may inevitably require a substantial footprint on the intervener's part to bring back a state of normalcy. The exception to the rule occurs when the intervention itself is carried out in a minimalist fashion, as had been the case in Libya in 2011. But how "light" or "heavy" an intervention must be to topple a regime is not entirely the intervener's prerogative; it is very much a function of the targeted regime's strength and resilience [to invasion, subversion, or even domestic political opposition], as well as a function of environmental circumstances [revolutionary momentum, demographics, etc.].)

I followed the above question with another one regarding Galula's position within the enemy vs. population-centric dichotomy. Had Galula's works been misinterpreted in some circles? "The problem is defining population-centric counterinsurgency," Hammes offered. "Recent U.S. writings have neglected the hard side of counterinsurgency while Galula certainly didn't."

I next corresponded with Tom Ricks, the veteran journalist who brandished *Counterinsurgency* at the Command and General Staff College at Fort Leavenworth as the "must read," and who likened Galula to the "Chuck Berry" of counterinsurgency in his popular foreign policy blog. (As I am Canadian, and younger than thirty when this work went to press, I had to Google "Chuck Berry" to discover that he had been one of the most celebrated pioneers of Rock 'n Roll. The comparison was favorable.) I got my questions through to the Pulitzer-winning[8] Ricks after heeding his request that I read *Fiasco*, and its sequel, *The Gamble*, as both of these contained passages on Galula's influence over U.S. military thinking. Ricks offered the following interesting point of view regarding Galula's applicability to "offensive counterinsurgency":

I think you put your finger on a fundamental problem in the American military using Galula that has never really been addressed: The French in Algeria, like the British in India, were fighting to stay. The Americans say they are fighting to leave Iraq and Afghanistan, but leave them relatively stable. I believe that is true. But it means that the Franco-Anglo COIN approach may not be right for the Americans. How do you establish a credible government that can stand after you leave? In some form, it has to go into opposition against you. I think we are seeing this paradox play out in both Baghdad and Kabul right now.

I asked Ricks about his promotion of the book in 2005. "I began my talk at Leavenworth by writing 'GALULA' in big, white letters on a green chalkboard," he wrote back. "I asked who knew what that word meant or indicated. One or two hands went up, of about 900 officers in the lecture hall. I said, 'If there is one thing you take away from my talk today, it is that you need to read this guy's book. You can do it in one evening.'" Ricks was met by skepticism at first. "I heard from a friend a couple of years later that after my talk, one officer turned to another and said, 'Who does that reporter think he is, coming in here and telling us what to read?' Of course, a couple of years later, I was back at Leavenworth and went down to their great bookstore, and there were stacks of Galula's books for sale." This was in contrast with the year before, when according to Ricks, "used copies were going for more than one hundred dollars." *Counterinsurgency* had been added to the mandatory reading list for all Staff College attendants. It remains, to this day, one of the three recommended "first reads" on the college's counterinsurgency "short list," which includes seven titles in total.[9]

Knowing how attuned he was to Pentagon circles, I asked Ricks whether there had been much discord about Galula. He considered that what push-back there was had come later. "[There is] a sense that Galula has [the military] doing stuff that is not really their job. I think that people who think that don't understand Galula. He could be very tough." His inference agreed with my view that the debate between enemy and population-centric approaches had careened away from the essence of what was required to get the mission accomplished. Dr. Sarah Sewall, the author of the introduction to the Chicago University Press edition of FM 3-24, observed in an email that, "misreading [Galula], or oversimplifying him, remains a challenge for practitioners." I agreed. That was an inherent challenge for any doctrine and certainly for one that was so succinct.

Dr. Conrad Crane, the leader of the FM 3-24 drafting group, offered additional lucid insights in our email exchange in the fall of 2011. "During the review process for the [field manual] in 2006, we got over 4,000 comments from Soldiers and Marines in the field. The field very much agreed with [Galula's ideas]. . . . The main shots at Galula came from those outside commentators who wanted to criticize the manual, and who used him as a strawman." Crane felt that these critics perceived FM 3-24 as trying to impose Algeria on Iraq. "In reality we did not look at Algeria very much, except to condemn torture as a tool. And we were smart enough to ignore those aspects of Galula that were outdated." Crane impressed that in any event, the large share of the intellectual input for the field manual had come from generals David Petraeus, James Mattis, and Peter Chiarelli. With regards to Galula, Crane was ". . . struck by [his] concise yet complete vision for [counterinsurgency], and how most of his ideas still made sense 40 years later. I was particularly impressed by his realization of the importance of propaganda, as he called it, and how there were different audiences for it, and also his acknowledgement that soldiers had to do a wide variety of non-military acts in [counterinsurgency], as well as how the rules of the game favored the insurgent."

Dr. Bruce Hoffman was another titan in the field I was able to reach over the summer of 2011. A professor at Georgetown's School of Foreign Service, he had penned the foreword to the public release of *Pacification* in 2006, while chairing the Terrorism and Counterinsurgency Department at RAND. He and Michael Rich, the think-tank's executive vice-president, had agreed to reissue the memorandum in declassified form. Hoffman laughed over the phone as he recalled how he and John Nagl had found themselves writing forewords to *Counterinsurgency* and *Pacification* at the same time without knowing it. "The reissue of *Pacification* was a big hit," Hoffman told me. "Word spread quickly within the COIN community. *Pacification* complemented, by way of practical examples, the theories found in *Counterinsurgency*."

I discovered Hoffman to be one of the rare experts who had known about *Counterinsurgency* through his own research before the book's reappearance in 2005. But despite working at RAND, he would discover *Pacification* later. "*Pacification*'s classification had kept it under the radar," he explained. "It was very unusual for a work of that type to be classified; so it hadn't come up in our inventorying of our counterinsurgency literature."

Hoffman's view of Galula was unequivocal.

"Galula is very clearly one of the best out there," he told me. "He's the superstar in the field. It's his holistic view of counterinsurgency that differentiates him. There are very few contradictions in his works, in comparison with Trinquier, for instance. Galula was able to boil it down to the fundamental essentials. He was very much like Mao or Clausewitz because of it. His analytical ability allowed him to extract the essence of the Algerian War, for example, and relate it to the Chinese Revolution."

"He understood human needs and behaviour?" I ventured.

"Absolutely. In my view, he was as much of an anthropologist as he was a soldier."

I reached Colonel Peter Mansoor next at Ohio State University, where he teaches military history. Another well-known figure in counterinsurgency circles, he commanded the 1st Brigade, 1st Armored Division in Iraq, participated in the famed Joint Chiefs of Staff's Council of Colonels, directed the foundation of the Counterinsurgency Training Center at Fort Leavenworth, and acted as General Petraeus's executive officer in Iraq prior to retiring to his present academic career. He had also contributed, I was told over the phone, to the editing of the second draft of FM 3-24 on Crane's invitation. "I insisted that we include a troop ratio prescription," Mansoor told me casually. "This would serve as a benchmark that would be useful in the planning of future COIN operations. We didn't want a Secretary of Defense coming in and saying, you could do the job with twenty guys."

"Had the ratio affected the surge in Iraq?" I asked out of curiosity.

"Oh no," he said. "At that point, we just figured out how much the entire U.S. Army could supply, and went with that! We had taken a 'let's end it here' approach to the whole thing."

The theme of protecting the population, and of having to control it in order to be able to do so, came up a few times in our conversation about Iraq. I asked Mansoor whether Galula had had an influence in that.

"Huge, massive," he answered instinctively. "Galula had an enormous influence on all of us. He wrote the most fundamental texts on the matter. His writings completed whatever each of us knew individually from our past experiences, or from having studied history."

Mansoor's position at the Council of Colonels very much echoed Galula's theory. "The debate at the Council at that point was pretty straightforward," Mansoor confided. "It was a question of whether we stayed in Iraq, or pulled out and cut our losses. The position I held was that we could win with the right approach, and the right amount of forces. I also cautioned that it would be a long run affair."

We discussed Galula's applicability to scenarios where a foreign party intervened against an insurgency, such as in Iraq and Afghanistan.

"It had been extremely difficult for my brigade to engage the local population in Iraq" he reflected. "The insurgent has an incredible psychological advantage, you know. All he has to do is point towards the flag-patches on our soldiers and say 'USA,' that's not 'Iraq' or whatever. . . . You therefore need, desperately need, that local brush to paint your efforts."

How did a surge of additional U.S. troops factor in then?

"Timing," he answered. "It coincided with the end of a phase of training for a large number of host nation forces. Lots of these became available to partner up with us everywhere we went. They modeled our behavior. It had taken time and lots of effort to get there, but as you may recall, someone had taken the boneheaded decision to disband the Iraqi army completely."

I recalled the error, and recalled thinking that it was an error.

"What of the Awakening Movement?" I asked, again out of curiosity. "It seemed to have come out of the blue?"

"Not at all, different units had been trying to leverage the sheikhs for quite some time. But those who cooperated were often murdered or otherwise terrorized. It took some commanders longer than others to understand the tribal conditions and power structures, but we finally got it. Then, two things happened. Firstly, the tribes had had enough of Al Qaeda's brutality; and secondly, the Sunnis suddenly realized that they would never be able to reclaim total power, and moreover, that the tribal heads would lose everything if they did not unite and cooperate."

Mansoor believed that Galula "was the first Western thinker to clearly state that it was not about us, nor about the enemy, but *really* about the population," to which he added, "This will be his lasting influence."

Before parting, Mansoor wished to share a recollection of what he considered to be an incredible occurrence at a 2009 conference on irregular warfare at the Naval War College.

"There we were with many of the big shots in the COIN world, all of whom had studied Galula by then. A French presenter got up, and announced that Galula had just been translated into French, which meant that the French Army could *start* studying him! None of us in the audience could believe it! How could it have taken them so long?"

I informed the colonel that I was not surprised to hear that at all. The translation had been undertaken in 2007–2008 as a personal initiative by French Army Lieutenant-Colonel Philippe de Montenon, who had ironically been introduced to Galula's writings while on exchange at the U.S. Army Command and General Staff College (GCSC).

I reached de Montenon at the French Minister of Defense's cabinet in Paris where he was assigned. A clever young officer sprung from an elite reconnaissance unit, de Montenon attended the GCSC in 2005–2006. His attendance coincided with the transfer of command of the Combined Arms Center (which oversees the GCSC) from General William S. Wallace to Petraeus. According to de Montenon, General Petraeus ordered that a mandatory course on counterinsurgency history be added to the GCSC curriculum and that four specific case studies be included: U.S. forces in Vietnam, the Soviets in Afghanistan, the British in Malaya, and the French in Algeria.

"My colleagues instinctively turned to me when Galula's book surfaced at the top," de Montenon recalled. "They asked me what I knew about him. I had to tell them the truth; I had never even heard the name!" De Montenon was far from the exception in this regard. He inquired about Galula upon his return to France. "Nobody had heard about him. He was unknown to defence historians and to the instructors at our doctrine school. This convinced me to translate the book myself the following year." Beyond the translation, de Montenon would also include an insightful *note du traducteur* of his own. He has, in my view, significantly contributed to the recognition of Galula in France. This was opportune, as I came to notice how a handful of vociferous critics there, possessing very limited knowledge of Galula, let alone any practical counterinsurgency experience of their own, were attempting to play down his legacy and originality for reasons that eluded me.

I asked de Montenon what had motivated him to take on the task of translation in addition to his military duties. His explanation was genuine. "I had attended the Staff College at a time when some of my colleagues were driving around Kansas with bumper stickers that read 'Boycott France'! I felt that Galula and the value of his writings represented an opportunity to rebuild a bridge between the French and American armies." After a pause, he added, "I also felt that an injustice had been done. Here was this officer who had been expelled on racial grounds from the French Army during the War, and for whom, it seemed, no effort had been made to retain, or to recognize his achievements."

This second part of de Montenon's motivation echoed the one I had discovered in Nagl, who co-authored with Petraeus the preface to the French edition of *Counterinsurgency*. "Your motivation to write the preface?" I asked Nagl at the end of our conversation. "General Petraeus told me to do so!" had been his immediate reply. "That's too easy an answer!" I retorted, causing us both to laugh. "I also felt that he was a prophet without honor in his own country," Nagl reflected.

De Montenon's efforts to reintroduce Galula in France were complemented by General Vincent Desportes, who was then serving as the commander of the Force Employment Doctrine Center, the French equivalent to Fort Leavenworth. Desportes would solicit his U.S. counterpart, General Petraeus, to pen the foreword to the French edition, thus credibly championing Galula's reintroduction in France. Still, the uptake in a cautious French military culture was mitigated. "There was no immediate reaction in France, no sudden boom," de Montenon candidly recalled. "But slowly, by late 2008, mentions of Galula were starting to be heard at Saint-Cyr and at *L'École de Guerre*. Our new counterinsurgency doctrine, published in 2009, also refers to him."

Galula's endorsement by senior U.S. generals such as Stanley McChrystal and David Petraeus, both of whom have confided to French media that Galula had been the author they read before going to sleep, has had a tremendous impact.[10] Many have petitioned the French Defense establishment (and even the Presidency) to name a Saint-Cyr promotion after him, or to bestow an equivalent honor. The future will tell if Galula's abnegation for his adoptive country and his masterful contribution to military thought will receive its just recognition. Unofficially, it would seem that it already has.

CONCLUSION:
THE GALULA DOCTRINE

Our enemy has made similar mistakes. He did not recognize that fighting against the Red Army required a different strategy and different tactics from those used in fighting other forces. Relying on his superiority in various respects, he took us lightly and stuck to his old methods of warfare.

—*Mao Tse-Tung*[1]

There is clearly a need for a compass, and this work has as its only purpose to construct such an instrument, however imperfect and rudimentary it may be.

—*David Galula*[2]

WHAT WILL BE DAVID GALULA'S LEGACY to the art of irregular warfare? Will it match, in significance, Clausewitz's legacy to the art of war between sovereign states?

Galula synthesized an immutable core of wisdom around which others will surely come to add, sometimes subtract, and forever interpret and reinterpret. I write this because I believe that the *fundamental* parameters of counterinsurgency warfare, the basic ingredients that make up the art, can be defined, and that Galula was able to do just that. There is an ineluctable degree of science to war, which makes Galula applicable beyond his era, just as it does Clausewitz beyond his. Had these soldier-intellectuals' writings been devoid of timeless truths, they would surely be of academic interest today, but would come short of resonating with practitioners this long after they were penned.

And yet, they do resonate.

Naturally, I also believe that *circumstantial* parameters found in insur-rections, revolutions, and civil wars[3] will forever vary between eras, regions, and contenders. The motives that fuel insurgencies and counterinsurgencies will surely keep evolving, though perhaps not as radically as we are made—or would like ourselves—to believe. Societies engaged in such conflicts will also evolve, morphing what limitations they may set themselves, and what doctrinal amalgams they may adopt when rebelling against oppressive authorities or when countering those that do. Information technology and social communications in particular will progress by leaps and bounds, and this too will play on circumstantial parameters dictating how quickly revo-lutionary ideas are spread, and how efficiently populations are first "polar-ized" and then "organized." Galula had written cynically but wisely, "the problem may even be artificial so long as it is accepted as fact. . . . The first task of the insurgent is to make it acute by 'raising the political[4] conscious-ness of the people.'"[5]

Despite these evolutions, the finite core ingredients—people and what motivates them to take up arms, or just as importantly, *side* with those who do—will remain essentially the same. For the majority of people, the motiva-tion will seldom *truly* stem from galvanizing ideologies—religious, racial, political, or other. No more than a minority of people driven by desperation, righteousness, or fanaticism will *actively* subscribe to such ideologies to the point of risking their lives before a movement has gathered seemingly unstop-pable momentum. Instead, the majority's motivation to commit to one side or the other will continue to be driven by universal needs. The need for security will forever come first, followed by the desire for prosperity in every sense of the word: fair and adequate access to water, food, housing, utilities, med-ical care, education, employment, justice, and political freedoms. The desire to preserve a sense of honor and dignity, personal and collective, will also remain paramount.

Insurgency and terrorism—the two are clinically (but not morally) identi-cal in my view for their appendage of violence to what is ultimately political activism—are not about to disappear. These two phenomena will continue to crop up when alternate forms of expression are barred, or more often yet, when non-violent forms of expression are deemed inefficient by those who seek to force change: the expulsion of an occupier, the toppling of a dicta-tor, the secession of a territory, or their own self-interested bid to reign over others. And to these ends, the reader will surmise from history and cur-rent events that societal thresholds for the recourse to violence—that single ingredient that differentiates an insurgency from what would otherwise be viewed as a democratic desire for change—are not long in crossing. Reasons to cross these thresholds, Galula's "causes" and Mao's "contradictions," will always abound in regions where stability is artificially maintained.

Galula's counterinsurgency theory, indeed his intellectual legacy, boils down to the following: To win, the counterinsurgent must outdo the insurgent in addressing the needs of the population *effectively* and *sequentially*.

Protect first, please second.

THE PRIMACY OF PROTECTION

Security is the first need that must be addressed, as it generally overrides all others without regard for local culture or other circumstantial parameters. Galula believed that security primes over ideology for the majority of people. "Hearts" are overridden by "minds." It is not unreasonable to claim that throughout history, security has always been the first item populations have come to expect from their governing authorities in return for allegiance and civil obedience. Galula cautioned the counterinsurgent to remember that "when a man's life is at stake, it takes more than propaganda to budge him."[6]

And yet, a terrorized population's fear of collaborating with the counterinsurgent must be swung or at the very least alleviated. A totalitarian counterinsurgent can swing fear to the other side by imposing consequences and punishment for collaborating with the insurgent that surpass what the latter imposes for collaborating with the state. Collective punishment, torture, and summary executions carried out by the state are far from unheard of in insurrectionary wars. A Western democracy operating abroad, however, is generally bound by the spirit of the international laws of armed conflict to which it ascribes, and by the host nation's justice system, which will often resemble (or be made to resemble) its own. Limited, therefore, in what consequences it can impose, a Western democracy is left with the nobler but more difficult task of *protecting* the population against the insurgent's always-harsher consequences and punishment.

This is the premise of the Galula Doctrine. Once fear has been sufficiently alleviated, the population becomes free to choose the side it wishes to embrace and the cause it wishes to uphold. Here, contemporary history seems to prove that the Western democratic construct generally has the upper hand when it is intelligently presented. It follows that it is always to the West's advantage to protect, so that free men and women may choose in its favor.

An extrapolation of the Galula Doctrine is in order; the above argumentation holds equally true for Western intervention to protect a population against a fear-instilling insurgent—as in Afghanistan—as it does for Western intervention to protect a population against a fear-instilling counterinsurgent state—as in Libya.

PROTECTION IS ACHIEVED THROUGH CONTROL

Control brings about the very order that the insurgent seeks to destroy.

The Galula Doctrine achieves protection through control. Control of the population eliminates the insurgent's freedom of action on the physical plane by restricting his movements, resupply, and communications, and on the moral plane by restricting his ability to force the population's collaboration. This is why Galula calls for the counterinsurgent to occupy villages and live among the people. It is also why his doctrine requires a heavy investment of troops on the ground to conduct censuses, man checkpoints, and impose travel restrictions and curfews.

THE GALULA DOCTRINE BRIDGES POPULATION AND ENEMY CENTRICITY

Properly interpreted, the Galula Doctrine erodes the dichotomy between "population-centric" and "enemy-centric" theories. Enemy-centric counter-insurgency does well at neutralizing the visible growth of the proverbial plant that is an insurgency; population-centric counterinsurgency does well at neutralizing the invisible root. The Galula Doctrine does both.

Galula's "population-centric" interpretation of irregular warfare does not categorically imply benevolence.[7] Far from it. Fundamentally, the act of protecting a population leads to a grim contest. The more the counter-insurgent protects, the more the insurgent is compelled to toughen the consequences it imposes on the population to achieve the required degree of coercion. For this, in the absence of sufficient counterinsurgent misdeeds, is necessary to keep the insurgency alive. Pushed beyond a certain point, this dark cycle plays in the counterinsurgent's favor; the population is slowly turned off by the insurgent's brutality, leading it to rebel against the rebels. The insurgent's key task consists of compromising his enemy in the eyes of the population, and the reverse holds true for the counterinsurgent. Benevolence for the sake of benevolence has little to do with this sinisterly pragmatic equation.

Finally, protecting the population requires the neutralization of armed insurgents and of the shadow governance structure that seek to cow the population to their side. This is inherent to the Galula Doctrine. Doing so additionally creates a strong deterrent to participation in the insurgency, which the Judiciary alone may be unable to provide.

A strong caution is in order, however. Here stands a conceptual fulcrum balancing the two competing theories. The trade-off of imposing a lethal consequence to participation in the insurgency must be carefully weighed. Situations where the population witnesses the counterinsurgent squandering vast means and resources to endlessly pursue and kill opponents emanating from the host population while leaving the majority in the same state of insecurity and misery must be avoided at all costs. It is much better to target key, irreconcilable insurgents and publicize the act in spades, than it is to target their subordinates in spades; as this will create human collateral damage and animosity along the way that will recruit scores of others. The first alternative gives the impression of exemplary justice and order, the second that of unbounded war and disorder.

Clausewitz and Jomini do not translate well to the struggle. The expectation that the insurgent will agree to partake in a duel against the counterinsurgent, and then lose his will and abandon his cause once defeated, is senseless. Similarly, the defeat of the insurgent through attrition, or at a decisive point in time, can also be deemed impossible because of how instantaneously any civilian may take up arms (as Mao had claimed and Fall endorsed) and because a mature insurgency is a popular movement with infinite shades of grey.[8]

PROTECTION IS A MEANS TO AN END

Effective protection of the population is not an end in itself. Security as anything but an enabling objective is a mistakenly diminutive view of Galula. Once protection is sustainably achieved, and therefore increasingly assumed by the population itself, the counterinsurgent must quickly move on to address the next set of basic needs. (The same holds true for the Western-backed insurgent on the morrow of having toppled the oppressive domestic regime.) Electricity must be restored. Roads and railways are built. Schools, markets, and banks are reopened. Political, economic, judicial, and electoral reforms are enacted. All of this, of course, must be undertaken against the background of a cause designed to appeal to the majority from the outset. And all of this, the Galula Doctrine stipulates, must be undertaken with a strong political determination to prevail that must be made clear to the population at stake, for the latter will side with whomever it perceives as the long-term victor. Siding with the long-term loser, regardless of the merit of the cause he proposes, would dissatisfy the first universal need.

The importance of vigorously addressing post-security needs cannot be overstated; nor can the importance of rendering a counterinsurgent force capable of doing so.[9] Insurgencies, after all, are not only bred in power vacuums. Insurgencies can spring where governance is absolute, and where the state security apparatus is strong. The recent "Arab Spring" has demonstrated this well. It is not, therefore, only a contest in the degree of governance insurgents and counterinsurgents seek to impose, but also in the style. An artificially maintained stability that discounts higher needs is bound (and merits) to collapse rapidly once fear has swung.

The term "pacification" to these ends, it must be admitted, was semantically more far-reaching than its contemporary equivalents.[10] Military forces partaking in counterinsurgency campaigns in recent years have been attributed mission statements such as to "secure," or to "provide for a safe and secure environment." There is nothing wrong with these tasks per se since they must be achieved, but the scope of work they convey unfortunately deludes some commanders to believe that their role is solely limited to the performance of military and security duties. And yet, wide is the gap between that and the end-state of leaving behind a sovereign, democratically governed nation aligned with Western interests. A force, Indigenous or foreign, that has been assigned a pacification task cannot refuse to partake in what Galula refers to as the "constructive" part of counterinsurgency, or alternatively, the "build" function in today's commonly known "clear, hold, build" strategy. Counterinsurgency, as defined by Galula, *is* nation building, or rebuilding, in many ways. It is delusional to shy away from this notion, just as it is delusional to believe that nation-building interventions can be consistently avoided by Western armies in the future. We return to this topic shortly.

Steeped in Maoism, the Galula Doctrine does not allow for the tidy separation of politico-civil and military affairs. For a host of reasons, practical politics, in the Galulan sense of the term (which includes reinforcing local governance and conducting "information operations"), cannot be left entirely to civilian administrators, as would be ideal. This is especially true at the local level, where military commanders exercising their authority over segments of the "battlespace" are more often than not left with little choice but to engage in localized forms of statecraft.

As such, a military engaged in a counterinsurgency campaign cannot content itself with conducting purely military tasks, and then raise its hands in the air when other areas of governance have been neglected. Bernard Fall had said that a war could be militarily unlosable but politically unwinnable.[11] This is true at first glance, but non sequitur upon further reflection. An army claiming to have never lost a battle in an insurrectionary war from which it was withdrawn prior to a favorable conclusion, only indicates that it never found its way to the battlefield.

Hence, the Galula Doctrine stresses the requirement for close collaboration between civilian and military authorities. It also implies that officers partaking in counterinsurgency warfare must be trained, at least rudimentarily, in civil affairs as Marine Corps and Colonial troops once were, naturally, with varying degrees of specialization. Without understanding the basics of governance, officers are at loss in how to engage in localized statecraft. Armed with basic knowledge, much-needed accountability can follow.

THE COMPLEXITY PARADOX

One of the many paradoxes of irregular warfare is that its principles must be understood and adhered to by every soldier, civil servant, and elected official involved, and yet, it is unarguably the most difficult form of warfare to grasp, because in the end, as Samuel Griffith had written, "its basic element is man, and man is more complex than any of its machines."[12] And so, lucid and intuitive as the Galula Doctrine may be, counterinsurgency indeed remains a "thinking man's warfare."[13]

The blend of political and military acumen required to succeed in small wars can be as relatively important to the statesperson who must forge alliances to deny the insurgency external support, as it is to the expeditionary force commander who must leverage existing power-structures, and as it is, finally, to the infantry sergeant who must seek the collaboration of his neighborhood's shopkeepers, while denying that collaboration to the insurgent. The possibilities for interaction between the sergeant and the shopkeepers are infinite. Ironically, therefore, the interaction is more complex than if the shopkeepers were firing at his squad, for this would trigger a finely honed response.

Faced with such complexity and the circumstantial variance alluded to before, a counterinsurgency doctrine is limited in the extent to which it can outline a standard operating procedure. What it does instead is guide behavior and develops a common operating culture. Technical proficiency does not suffice in irregular warfare. Soldiers and civil administrators must be capable of applying their own creative solutions to the realities they face, inspired by the core of wisdom the doctrine provides. General Petraeus had aptly stated prior to the drafting of FM 3-24 that the new doctrine would have to teach officers *how* to think, not *what* to think.[14]

This has proven to be both an opportunity and a challenge, since engaging in "practical politics," for instance, is obviously not part of traditional troop-leading procedures. Tactical-level commanders are trained to think doctrinally in Jominian terms of finite operations that yield specific, immediate effects on the battlefield. Irregular warfare requires that longer-view "strategic thinking" be instilled in these officers as well, without eroding their ability to think, decide, and act faster and more effectively than their enemies in combat. Irregular warfare requires both cognitive skill sets.

Still, the "complexity paradox" sets a trap for doctrinaires. The more enlightened and open ended a counterinsurgency doctrine becomes—naturally driven towards complexity by the problem it is trying to solve—the more difficult it becomes for practitioners to translate into practice. The risk resides in an over-systemization and *technocratization* of this form of war. Manifestations of this pitfall are common through the use of fanciful buzzwords, and the laborious staff processes they designate such as "non-kinetic targeting"! This can detract from core, common sense laws, principles, and operational frameworks of the likes Galula devised, while leaving the rest to acumen and experience. Most of all, mission accountability and the *desire to win* must be invoked in counterinsurgency doctrines, because the opposite tendency to command through risk management is unproductive in the short term and yet worst in the long term. Force protection in war is a consideration, not an objective. This is why officers should be held accountable for their achievements, and not only for their losses.

We may wish to acquiesce that broad-based knowledge and patient Determination are as important to counterinsurgency as technical know-how and aggressive shock action are to maneuver warfare.[15] Whereas technical training is imperative to the latter, culture, in its broadest sense of general education and openness of mind, is imperative to the former. But one does not preclude the other. Training and culture matter to both forms of war. It behooves any military to instill a versatility that renders its soldiers and especially its officers and senior NCOs capable of adapting to either form of war without having to undergo reactive institutional overhauls midway through campaigns. To this end, cultural, anthropological, and language studies should not be neglected. Nor should history studies. An officer not knowing, for instance, when the Soviet Union occupied Afghanistan may seem absolutely trivial, but it is a good indicator that he or she does not know either what pacification efforts had succeeded there or failed. Nor why. Soldiers must be made to value knowledge, in all its forms, as much as they do advanced tactical shooting, field craft, or physical fitness, which are all important to fighting small wars.

A RETURN TO THE BASICS: TECHNOLOGY DOES NOT REPLACE COGNITION

The inherently static nature of counterinsurgency warfare has teamed up with the complexity of modern technologies to create disproportionately large headquarters. What should have resulted in a bottom-heavy style of warfare, due to the importance of being in contact with the population, has resulted in quite the opposite. The larger the amount of personnel involved in staff or specialist support functions retrenched in bases, and often behind computer screens, it irrefutably follows that fewer are in contact with the population, and the day-to-day reality by which it lives. Soldiers on the ground are thinned out on the basis that technology can be leveraged as a "force-multiplier." Agreed. But the extent to which this is true is also dictated by context. In conventional warfare, a single hi-tech sensor platform can arguably replace a squadron of scouts in a screening role. In insurrectionary wars, where the problem is subtler, and much more linked to—precisely—what cannot be seen from the air, the multiplier does not carry the same weight. Relying too heavily on technological solutions to problems that have human dimensions is known to disappoint.

The ever-so-important function of command does not profit from head-quarters that grow beyond a certain point. This leads to managerial issues, classic information overload, and situations where work is often created for the sake of creating work. Moreover, this represents a cognitive burden by which commanders are tied to cumbersome planning and decisional mecha-nisms, often driven by parallel realities rooted in fanciful metrics. A better middle ground must be found.

THE GALULA DOCTRINE ENABLES COMMAND

The Galula Doctrine requires commanders to establish operational frame-works that offer tangible, no-nonsense direction for their troops fighting a protracted, irregular war. This requirement goes deeper than the mount-ing of punctual operations with cleverly worded intent-paragraphs and spe-cific timelines that are often incompatible with the continuous context of population-centric struggles as commented by Trinquier.[16] Galula, however, was unique in proposing to overlay the non-linearity inherent to counter-insurgency warfare with a linear, stepwise framework within which military operations could be planned and executed. He thus opted for simplicity and *sequentiality*.[17] "To control is to command [in counterinsurgency]," he wrote. A senior commander's elaboration of such a framework to his troops, tailored for the area and people he has been tasked to pacify, is more important than any set of disassociated finite operations.

"With the step-by-step approach," Galula wrote, "the counterinsurgent provides himself with a way of assessing at any time the situation and the progress made."[18] He was right in my view, despite the inherent risk of pro-ducing an overly rigid formula. What lacked perhaps in his proposal was a series of simple and sound measures that a commander could use to evaluate when a step up or down the pacification process was warranted. Galula left this to the commander's discretion and *coup d'oeil*—maybe as it should be in the end. Failure to adopt a unifying process, he cautioned, would lead to "an accidental mosaic, a patchwork of pieces with one well pacified, next to another one not so pacified . . . an ideal situation for the insurgent, who will be able to manoeuvre at will among the pieces. . . ."[19]

No-nonsense campaign plans are mandatory, therefore, in complement-ing doctrine. It seems unpardonable that recent campaigns persisted for years without them. Elementally, campaign plans assess the present, stip-ulate the end state, and chart the path in between. They have the added benefit of forcing commanders to think strategically, and on longer terms, without precluding future adjustments as the situation unfolds. By virtue of this, and to account for regional variances, the drafting of campaign plans should be encouraged at subordinate levels. Every province, city, town, and village warrants its own simple and appropriately scaled campaign plan. This would favor synchronicity and unity of effort throughout the "mosaic" Galula describes. A campaign plan should be one of the first deliverables required of a commander entrusted with the pacification of a segment of population, just as a range card is the first deliverable required of a commander entrusted with the conventional defense of a frontage of ground.

THE DECISION TO ENGAGE IN COUNTERINSURGENCY

The difficulty of consistently translating theory into practice presents the major risk in aligning a military with adaptations of the Galula Doctrine, which is—if we accept our previous discussions—more complex than purely enemy-centric alternatives. I do not at all share in the belief that the risk lies instead with corroding a military's fighting prowess, if fundamental war-fighting ethos, capabilities, and conventional doctrines are properly maintained.[20]

The "counterinsurgency-turns-an-army-soft" argument must be debunked. Well-led armies have turned their counterinsurgency experiences to their advantage. They have transformed themselves into learning organizations that foster a culture of innovation, and that demand of their soldiers unprecedented levels of initiative, adaptability, and courage. These skills and attributes, along with the battle hardening that such conflicts have provided (earned at a great cost of suffering for soldiers and their families), will not be lost on future high-intensity battlefields.

Turning back to the snapshots of French history we have described in this book, we recall how Lyautey had famously claimed that pacification work only "decorporalized" his expeditionary forces, as each man was asked to interact intelligently with the population without losing an ounce of combativeness when it was required of him. Or, we may think of the French paratroopers that had had no trouble in reorienting themselves from pacification work in Algeria to conventional operations against Egyptian forces in the Sinai within the span of a few weeks.

Questioning whether an army should maintain a capacity to wage counterinsurgency operations is tantamount to questioning whether an army should maintain a capacity to operate abroad. The risk of having to face an insurgency has always, and will always accompany an army in its foreign expeditions. Entirely symmetric scenarios such as the first Gulf War are few and far between. I can think of no country in the world today, or over the next two decades, that would repeat the mistake of taking on the U.S. military conventionally with anything else but a political objective that factors in military defeat.

The argument that a modern army's role should *not* include "nation building" is equally narrow minded and myopic to the evidence that other, less-benevolent actors will always be willing to step in to fill geopolitical voids. There is little sense in self-limiting what foreign policy tools a nation maintains in its arsenal, and what purposefulness it bestows to its standing army, as long as the latter's capability of defending the sovereignty and security of the nation is never compromised. We note, furthermore, that nation-building enterprises such as the one that had been occurring in Afghanistan at the time of this writing, will often originate from this defensive mandate.

Similarly, in light of recent successes, it is doubtful that the West will renounce employing military resources in a direct or advisory role to lend support to insurgencies against regimes it wishes to pressure or topple. Here too, the extrapolation of the Galula Doctrine applies. Protecting a foreign population against its regime's heavy-handed repression, while demonstrating international resolve to see the regime fall, are central precepts to favoring a genuine revolution from within.

Nevertheless, the decision to intervene militarily must be weighed carefully, as this comes with the risk of drawing the intervener into protracted, irregular wars that may include a requirement to partake in costly counterinsurgency. A government must be intelligently certain that the politico-economic capacity and national determination to see the endeavor through will be at hand. Most of all, as has been highlighted often in this work, the politically chosen end state must reflect the "optionality" of the intervention; because national *will* to sustain a war, and the latter's optionality are reciprocal. This equation matters a great deal. Heeding it is first and foremost a moral responsibility towards those who will lay down their lives in pursuit of the set objective.

MAO SITS AT THE CORE OF THE GALULA DOCTRINE

"Counterinsurgency," Galula wrote, "is only an effect of insurgency."[21] It would be well, therefore, to shed a new light on what sits dialectically at the core of his doctrine.

Galula relied on the five-stage Maoist framework for insurgency (MAO-FIN)[22] as a baseline to describe all revolutionary insurgencies. This framework, which he labeled as the "Orthodox" pattern, begins with the creation of a political entity (stage 1), and the achievement of a "united front" (stage 2).

It then escalates to "guerilla warfare" (stage 3), "maneuver warfare" (stage 4), and culminates, finally, in a "battle of annihilation" (stage 5).

Over the last thirty or forty years, we may ask, how many insurgencies have truly fit the MAOFIN? Not many it would seem. The Tamil Tiger insurrection, which was well into the maneuver warfare stage before being destroyed in conventional battle by the Sri Lankan Army in 2009, comes to mind as a recent, but incomplete example. The Hezbollah provides somewhat of a second one. The movement teetered between the third and fourth stages of the MAOFIN against the I.D.F. over the summer of 2006, thus demonstrating its "progression" after over two decades of terrorism, and the establishment of a "united front" among Lebanon's Shiites. But even such loose examples have depended on rarely lined up circumstances.

The authors of FM 3-24 brought an update to the framework:

Effectively applying the Maoist strategy does not require a sequential or complete application of all . . . stages. The aim is seizing political power, if the government's will and capability collapse early in the process, so much the better. If unsuccessful in a later phase, the insurgency might revert to an earlier one. Later insurgents added a new twist to this strategy, to include rejecting the need to eventually switch to large-scale conventional operations. For example, the Algerian insurgents did not achieve much military success of any kind, instead, they garnered decisive popular support through superior organizational skills and astute propaganda that exploited French mistakes. These and other factors, including the loss of will in France, compelled the French to withdraw.[23]

The above warrants further precision. Today, the later stages of the MAOFIN are more susceptible to be manifested in the context of civil war and revolution, such as the one that had occurred in Libya in 2011, than in the context of a counterinsurgency campaign undertaken by a developed world power. In Libya, the insurgency's build-up of a military force past the guerrilla warfare stage in such short order was only made possible by important defections in the armed forces that were catalyzed, to no small extent, by foreign support and intervention.

Much has changed since Galula observed the modern-equipped French expeditionary corps's defeat by a MAOFIN-ascribing insurgency in Indochina some 60 years ago. By the Second Indochina War, seasoned Viet Minh commanders that had defeated the French conventionally at Dien Bien Phu would come to regret their every attempt to wage large-scale maneuver warfare against American forces. Yet despite the absence of a battle of annihilation, U.S. forces ultimately withdrew, allowing South Vietnam to collapse. Two decades or so later, in Afghanistan, the Mujahedeen would content themselves with waging aggressive guerrilla warfare against the communist invader without ever attempting to progress to the maneuver warfare stage. Nevertheless, the Soviet Union also withdrew. In none of these cases did the insurgencies evolve to the point of waging a true battle of annihilation against their enemies as prescribed by the Maoist framework. And yet, all of these insurgencies ultimately succeeded.

Galula wrote, "guerrilla warfare cannot win the decision against a resolute enemy."[24] Evidently, then, the foreign counterinsurgents had not been resolute. Or alternatively, the "optionality" of those foreign expeditions had translated into insufficient national will to see them through to their initially set objectives.

TECHNOLOGICAL DISPARITY ALTERS THE LATER STAGES OF THE MAOFIN

The incidence of optionality on the above campaigns may have removed the *need* for insurgencies to see the MAOFIN through to the end, but another factor has been at play to remove the very *possibility* of their doing so. The potential for technological disparity between insurgent and counterinsurgent has increased dramatically since Galula's *Counterinsurgency* was penned.[25] This is consequential to the later stages of the MAOFIN where symmetry rises between insurgent and counterinsurgent.

Despite advances in the lethality of IEDs and other weapons available to terrorist groups and insurgents, technological progress generally favors the counterinsurgent who has unlimited access to it.[26] The last few decades have seen marked improvements in precision weaponry, personnel survivability, signals intelligence, UAV-based targeting, etc. The caveat persists, however, that none of this is decisive. Technological disparity only offers the counterinsurgent a "defensive" advantage that prevents his opponent from acceding to higher stages of the MAOFIN.[27]

Already during the last decade, as much as Iraqi and Afghan insurgents ventured into the third stage of the MAOFIN—guerrilla warfare—one never expected them to undertake sustained maneuver or even "positional" warfare against U.S. and NATO forces. On those few occasions when they did on relatively limited scales (such as during the battle for Fallujah in Iraq), they were not long in reverting back to guerrilla warfare and further back yet to terrorism against "softer" targets such as local officials, police forces, and other icons of collaborationism.

The future widening of the technological disparity between insurgent and counterinsurgent, particularly in the areas of intelligence, surveillance, and targeting, may very likely recede the ability of insurgencies adhering to the MAOFIN to sustain even primitive guerrilla operations against developed world powers. (*If* the trend holds, which it should, and as long as competing powers do not intervene to narrow the technological gap, which is less certain.[28]) Resultantly, insurgencies fighting against Western powers may be increasingly confined to the earlier stages of the MAOFIN: creating a solid "united front" through civic action and political agitation centered on a particular cause, complemented by fear-instilling terrorist activity, preferably in urban settings, where clutter and the risk of collateral damage will continue to play in their favor.

Insurgents may also choose to export the first stage of the MAOFIN—blind terrorism—to the foreign counterinsurgent's home front. There is nothing new about this phenomenon. The IRA had done so in Great Brittan, the FLN in metropolitan France, the PLO in Israel, etc. But this strategy remains a double-edged sword for the insurgent and his foreign backers, as it can suddenly decrease the optionality of the conflict for the counterinsurgent, bearing a reciprocal effect on his resolve.[29]

THE INSURGENT PREMISE TO THE GALULA DOCTRINE REMAINS VALID

The *essence* of the MAOFIN remains valid. What differs is the plane on which the later symmetrical stages ("manoeuvre warfare" and the "battle of annihilation") are often waged. Contemporary history indicates that modern insurgencies will seek to enter the fourth and fifth stages not on the battlefield—the "kinetic" or "physical plane" in modern military doctrinism—but on the politico-diplomatic plane. The insurgent's achievement of politico-diplomatic symmetry, or *recognition* in other words, has become tantamount to entering the fourth stage. There, the insurgent's diplomatic dealings, analogous to maneuvers on the battlefield, secures concessions from the counterinsurgent. If the insurgent succeeds in garnering clout on the international stage, and continues to inflict casualties on the counterinsurgent—sapping what remains of the latter's political support for the war, he soon progresses to the fifth stage, where a negotiated withdrawal of counterinsurgent forces is analogous to annihilation. A cataclysmic battle *à la* Dien Bien Phu need not occur. The endgame sees the counterinsurgent withdraw, and the insurgent accede to power in one form or another. Southern Afghanistan, it can be argued, was on the cusp of this at the time of this writing.

Half a century ago, the Algerian War had already provided an example of this phenomenon, which Galula had failed to entirely see. And yet, he had come very close. The "shortcut pattern" he described was flawed in the sense that it was false to believe that it would ever seek to "rejoin the orthodox"[30] one. However, he had added that this would only happen "if necessary," and that "at anytime during the process, the insurgent may make peace offers, provided there is more to gain by negotiating than by firing."[30] In truth, this reasoning would always apply to both insurgent *and* counterinsurgent.

THE GALULA DOCTRINE VIEWS THE POPULATION AS THE METAPHORICAL GROUND OVER WHICH CONTENDERS FIGHT FOR POWER

Galula wrote: "The population represents this new ground. If the insurgent manages to disassociate the population from the counterinsurgent, to control it physically, to get its active support, he will win the war because, in the final analysis, the exercise of political power depends on the tacit or explicit agreement of the population or, at worst, on its submissiveness."[31]

As insurgent and counterinsurgent fight for control over this metaphorical ground, their centers of gravity remain rooted in their respective populations. The insurgent is defeated once the population from which he emanates no longer supports him. The foreign counterinsurgent is defeated once the population from which he emanates no longer supports the war objective. It follows that a modern power's capacity to wage war against an insurgency abroad is only limited by popular will at home. And it follows from all of this that when faced with a foreign counterinsurgent, the insurgent's initial objective consists of gaining control over his population, but that his final one consists of persuading his enemy's home front of the excessive cost and futility of the war. Unquestionably, the importance of this exercise for the insurgent has risen since Mao recognized the role a sympathetic minority in Japan would play in ushering the latter's withdrawal from China.

Protracting the conflict and inflicting casualties on foreign counterinsurgent forces will generally suffice to spread anti-war sentiment from a minority of voters, pundits, and policy makers to the mainstream. Numerous channels combine to provide the medium through which the insurgent can act against the counterinsurgent's will. This is why it is almost invariably in the insurgent's interests to publicize what losses he has inflicted, and what "spectacular" actions he has undertaken. Better yet, the media provides an excellent gauge of the foreign counterinsurgent's will to stay the course, and of what opinion prevails in the rest of the world, where the insurgent hopes to find circumstantial if not ideological allies.

IRREGULAR WARFARE REQUIRES DETERMINATION AND UNDERSTANDING AT THE TOP

The determination at the top level of government to defeat an insurgency represents a central pillar of the Galula Doctrine. The perception of this resolve is just as vital to sustaining troop morale as it is to undermining the opponent's. Most importantly, it is vital to convincing the population being pacified of which side will win in the long run. Galula offered the following lucid analysis:

> As the war lasts, the war itself becomes the central issue and the ideological advantage of the insurgent decreases considerably. The population's attitude is dictated not by the intrinsic merits of the contending causes, but by the answer to these two simple questions: 1) which side is going to win? And 2) which side threatens the most, and which offers the most protection? This is the reason why a counterinsurgency is never lost a priori because of a supposedly unpopular regime.[32]

In Algeria, Galula and others believed that the war had been won, and that a withdrawal had been ordered on account of a calculated political decision. The tragedy resides in the amount of suffering the French campaign had inflicted on all sides only to achieve an end-state that could well have been achieved without bloodshed. Such a human sacrifice always seems—and very much *is*—unpardonable in hindsight. It therefore behooves the top level of leadership—military and civilian—to intelligently judge the nation's desire and long-term determination to see a campaign through to the end prior to engaging in it. It follows from this too that a clear understanding of the requirements of irregular warfare is needed in the upper echelons of government before such campaigns are undertaken.

I do not share in the common opinion that democracies engaged in counterinsurgency campaigns are handicapped from the outset. History has seen totalitarian states exhibit just as much vulnerability to waning domestic support for protracted wars abroad. (The present NATO-led counterinsurgency effort in Afghanistan has outlasted the Soviet Union's, albeit without having incurred as many losses.) Western democracies have proven their resilience to wars and human sacrifice before. They remain sensitive to victory, and sensitive to not losing soldiers in vain.

Support for a given campaign may be slower to wane if the intervening nation is honestly informed of what commitment is required to achieve the foreign policy aim its government has subscribed to. If support does begin to wane, it is still better to announce a strategy that will lead to an achievable state of affairs that allows for a withdrawal than it is to announce a withdrawal based solely on a time schedule. The latter approach is wholly incompatible with winning counterinsurgencies, and therefore irresponsible if that is the intention. Moreover, a timeline implies a withdrawal come what may, which raises a moral issue once more.

Granted, recognizing the appropriate decision point that will trigger a withdrawal is no easy matter. As Galula writes, "A counterinsurgency seldom ends with a ceasefire and a triumphal parade."[33] The well-known requirement for an exit-strategy to be designed at the outset must be heeded.

THE "GLOBAL INSURGENCY" PERSPECTIVE VERSUS THE GALULA DOCTRINE

It would be a mistake to dismiss Galula on the pretense that we are faced today with a global jihadist insurgency; and that in light of this, his doctrine lacks sufficient scope to confront this modern, globalized paradigm.

It is not without irony that one discovers that Galula, and indeed all of those who ascribed to Revolutionary Warfare theory during his era, had once also believed that they were faced with a global, ideologically fueled insurgency. If there is *some* truth to the global phenomenon that I would not discount, I would argue that the phenomenon was probably truer in Galula's era than it is today. Firstly, multi-state sponsorship of the international Communist movement was stronger in the latter's heyday than it is today for radical Islam. Moderate Muslim states generally fear the risk of domestic backfire brought on by sponsoring revolutionary movements abroad. Secondly, Communism had the greater galvanizing potential on a global scale. As much as radical Islam can make inroads in the West today, the ideology is limited by the simple fact that demographically, the Christian majority cannot be made to ascribe to it. And even in the Muslim regions of the world, we note, the Sunni-Shiite contest precludes a unified bloc.

I do not agree either with the parallel view that the level of fanaticism has radically increased in recent times with the advent of confessional insurgencies, thereby diminishing the relevance of classical counterinsurgency theory. Mao's atheist Red Army had no qualms in using suicide bombers during the Chinese Civil War, and today's Mexican narco-traffickers have demonstrated their resolve to outdo any confessional insurgency in their brutality. Nor do I agree, finally, with the view that contemporary insurgencies are unique from those of the past on account that non-ideological actors (i.e. criminal gangs) are mixed into the fray. Lyautey, we recall, had to contend with "Chinese pirates" in the Tonkin, in addition to nationalist resistance so to speak. Mao too was confronted with criminal gangs, which his forces systematically wiped out or absorbed. Criminal activity thrives expectedly when governance is weak or corrupt.

Of the few truly transnational terrorist movements that exist in the world today, most have acted more as global banners than as global organizations per se. Transnational cross-pollination in doctrine and tactics has unarguably occurred between insurgent movements, and some transnational coordination under given banners has enabled spectacularly grim acts of terrorism. It is nonetheless imprudent to paint a picture of hidden Kremlin-like headquarters issuing orders to a worldwide network of trained sleeper cells, allocating arms and funds, dispatching men and recruiting others in a truly global fashion. The killing of Osama Bin Laden—a figurehead more than a commander-in-chief—in the cloistered home of a residential suburb dispels that myth rather handily.

Even so, this argumentation matters little, for insurgencies and counter-insurgencies are truly fought at the regional level, fueled by unmet needs and political power struggles. Even Al Qaeda, we note, has always had to adapt to the host locality by leveraging local grievances, and rendering these "acute" in order to attract supporters. When it hasn't, it has failed. Attempting to wage a global counterinsurgency can very well have the undesired effect of serving relatively isolated insurgencies by unifying them, when common sense would dictate that the exact opposite is required. Galula had written to Alistair Buchan prior to submitting an essay about China's ambitions: "If insurgency can be practiced on a global scale by a single country like China, counterinsurgency is too piecemeal an affair, too subject to local conditions, to be treated other than verbally, . . . , or at a length impossible in this paper."[34] On this particular issue, he turned out to be wrong about China and insurgency, but right about counterinsurgency.

The validity in perceiving insurgencies, revolutions, and civil wars as globalized phenomena resides more than anywhere in their initiation, which is inevitably sensitive to regional and temporal contagion when a particular ideology gains ascendancy. Circumstantial momentum, as evidenced by the Arab Spring and by similarly sweeping political episodes in previous eras, has a remarkable incidence on swinging fear from one side to the other, thereby allowing for revolutions to take place.

THE GALULA DOCTRINE MEETS
"OFFENSIVE" COUNTERINSURGENCY

What remains to be done now is to answer the question Henry Kissinger had asked Galula regarding the applicability of his writings to counterinsurgency expeditions in the *post*-colonial era.

In all likelihood, Galula's answer to Kissinger would have been "yes," the doctrine he had formulated within the context of domestic and colonial counterrevolution would find applicability to expeditionary counterinsurgency such as the looming U.S. intervention in Vietnam.

Only, Kissinger's question had been ahead of its time. The First and Second Indochina Wars would not differ substantially from one another. France had fought to preserve an existing regime, and so would the United States. (Bernard Fall cleverly noted how the distinction between a French and U.S. soldier was lost on the Viet Minh guerrilla being shot at.) Kissinger's question would find all of its relevance some thirty-five years later in the aftermaths of the invasions of Iraq and Afghanistan. Galula's answer then may have been more nuanced.

Expeditionary counterinsurgency can be split into two categories. The first may be labeled "defensive." It seeks to *preserve* an existing regime, which predates the foreign intervention, as was the case in Vietnam. The second may be labeled "offensive." It seeks to *establish* a new regime after having toppled the previous one through direct intervention, subversion, or a combination of both, as was the case in Iraq and Afghanistan. Although the Galula Doctrine finds applicability to these two forms of intervention, fundamental adaptations are required.

It is an undeniable fact that Galula wrote with *defensive* counterinsurgency in mind; he defined insurgency as, ". . . a *protracted struggle* conducted methodically, step by step, in order to attain specific intermediate objectives leading finally to the overthrow of the existing order."[35] He foresaw the West partaking in counterinsurgency expeditions to prop up friendly regimes that were at risk of succumbing to communist subversion. But his motivation lay not with colonial preservation. "Colonialism is now dead," he wrote in *Counterinsurgency.* "There are no colonies in Latin America apart from the Guianas, British Honduras, and other insignificant places. Yet the whole continent is seething with unrest."[36] The very last lines of his treatise are telling in this regard: "It is safe to assume that the West, almost automatically, will be involved directly or indirectly in the coming revolutionary wars. With the Communists pulling one way, chances are that the West will probably be involved on the side of order, i.e., on the side of the counterinsurgent. That is why this book has been written."[37]

What of *offensive* counterinsurgency; did Galula (or Kissinger) foresee his doctrine being applied to scenarios where the foreign power did not intervene to prop up a regime, but to topple it instead, and then ipso facto take on the role of counterinsurgent against rejectionists and irregular forces loyal to the fallen regime? In the historical context that Galula and Kissinger found themselves, it would be reasonable to assume that they hadn't envisaged such scenarios. Friendly regimes were already proving difficult to safeguard against communist subversion, resulting in little appetite to topple unfriendly ones. Even so, the Cuban Missile Crisis had set a clear precedent as to the risks that such an enterprise could involve.

Elementally, recent counterinsurgency campaigns of the *offensive* type— Iraq and Afghanistan—have shared more commonalities with those of Lyautey's era than with those of Galula's. "Conquest, occupation, pacification,"[38] Lyautey wrote succinctly of the millennia-old sequence of foreign intervention. Only, the sequence has since evolved to reflect a new geopolitical paradigm; the sequence has become "conquest, occupation, pacification, and handover." When the West undertakes a counterinsurgency campaign today, it does not fight to stay; it fights to leave. The foreign counterinsurgent aims to withdraw once the newly installed regime has demonstrated that it will (1) remain reasonably aligned with friendly interests, and (2) be viable on its own.

The distinction between *defensive* counterinsurgency (akin to counterrevolution) and its *offensive* counterpart (more akin to pacification) is important to interpreting Galula. Can his framework for counterinsurgency be reconciled with the Iraq-Afghanistan model of intervention? Nothing in Galula's short works, we know, addresses the question head on. And yet, Galula's overarching prescription seems eerily well suited to *offensive* counterinsurgency: ". . . The basic mechanism of counterinsurgency warfare . . . its essence can be summed up in a single sentence: Build (or rebuild) a political machine from the population upwards."[39] In comparison to other doctrines of its era, Galula's is rather unique in this constructive aspect; for bottom-up governance ultimately leads to democratic self-determination—a ubiquitous goal of modern Western interventions.

(Self-determination in Galula's view was fine as long as it did not lead to communism, just as it is considered fine by the West today, as long as it does not lead to undemocratic forms of government, namely, radicalized theocracies.)

Notwithstanding the apparent suitability of Galula's bottom-up approach, a fundamental question remains: After having replaced a regime by force, how does a foreign intervener employ the Galula Doctrine to lead a population to embrace its new government, and reject the old cause, when we know that the doctrine was originally devised to achieve the exact opposite?

On first impression, the answer can be found in the same Maoist dialectics Galula upheld; the foreign intervener must find the minority that has a stake in embracing the incumbent government, and leverage this minority to sway the neutral majority, and to suppress the rejectionist minority.

All is not so simple, however.

Firstly, prior to imposing a revolution on a sovereign nation, the foreign intervener must be entirely confident in what chances the revolution has of sustaining itself in his absence, because the end-state is no longer one of acquiring a colonial possession, let alone a vassal state, but of leaving behind a stand-alone democratic government aligned with friendly interests. A sound political estimate is crucial. The challenge resides too in the preliminary legitimization of the endeavor in the eyes of the intervener's home electorate, as well as in the eyes of the nation that will be invaded. The most extenuating circumstances and interests must be at hand to justify this right to go to war.

Secondly, the Galula Doctrine forces us to make a set of important assumptions. The first is that a Western power will not invade a nation whose people are *a priori* hostile to it, or whose majority is satisfied with its present government. (The West would be ill advised to invade Iran, for example, according to this reasoning.) The second assumption is that the cause offered by the West will be more appealing to the majority of the population than that which the insurgent—loyalists of the previous regime and rejectionists—will seek to defend or counter-offer. Failing either assumption, the Galula Doctrine becomes ill suited for the endeavor of imposing a revolution; for what would be required instead would be to obtain a people's submission. And if such were the case, it would no longer make sense to protect a population, so as to allow it to rationally choose the side that offered the more appealing prospects. The aim, on the contrary, would be to impose a choice through limitless force. This is where purely enemy-centric theories come in, and indeed, where they have historically been applied. The Soviets had been left with this alternative in Afghanistan where their atheist ideology had proven to be irreconcilable with the theocratic society they sought to assimilate. This is also where purely enemy-centric theories fail to mirror Western values, and negate the "natural" advantage a Western democratic cause would otherwise have over others.[40]

Thirdly, "offensive" counterinsurgency brings about two serious complications for the Galula Doctrine. The first is what Clausewitz referred to as the People in Arms. The second is the upsetting of equilibrium—however artificial—that unleashes a civil war along sectarian fault lines. The Galula Doctrine was not written to counter either of these. And yet, these are the very things it came to be used for over the past decade.

THE GALULA DOCTRINE VERSUS THE PEOPLE IN ARMS

Galula did not write to counter insurrection in the Clausewitzian sense of the "people in arms," who, after seeing their national army defeated by a foreign invader, carry on the "strategic defence." Few, if any of the classic counterinsurgency theories tackle this fundamental grievance that may overshadow any other foreign occupation.

Bernard Fall perceptively commented that populations had sometimes risen to defend dictatorial regimes when confronted with a foreign invader.[41] Indeed, an immediate advantage goes to the insurgent when, regardless of the ideology he upholds, joining his side results in fighting against the invader.

Savvy insurgents do not enlist support on the basis that they wish to accede to power. They enlist support on the basis that they are fighting for national or sectarian liberation. If the counterinsurgent happens to be of a foreign nationality and religion, then so much the better for the insurgent.

A quick example follows. Distracting exceptions aside, the insurgency waged against U.S. and coalition forces in Afghanistan has been led by a Pashtun political base in the South that wishes above all to return to power. This, of course, is not the cause the insurgency has propagandized (because too many still recall the Taliban governance record). Instead, the Taliban leadership has adopted the simpler cause of ousting the foreign occupier.

(The cause is also cast in a religious light, but the Karzai government has been able to reduce the potency of that claim by equally upholding the Islamic standard. The Karzais of the Soviet era, so to speak, did not have the luxury of doing so.)

It can be argued that the presence of U.S. forces in a liberated Kuwait in 1991, or in a liberated France in 1945, did not yield insurgencies seeking to expel them. True, but the United States had not come to impose regime changes there; it had come to liberate those nations from less desirable foreign occupiers. It would be well, therefore, never to confuse again the invasion of a country to liberate it from a foreign occupier with the invasion of a country to forcibly remove a homegrown despot. The latter's mere existence proves that he had benefited, at the very least, from the support of a loyal minority capable of ruling over the rest.

Against "the people in arms," much of what Galula established becomes a doubled-edged sword for the foreign counterinsurgent. The imperative of exerting a tight control over the population demonstrates this well. Doing so is necessary to protect the population, but does it not exacerbate the latter's impression of living under foreign occupation? Galula's prescription for counterinsurgent troops to live among the people poses the same dilemma. The appearance of military occupation is reinforced if foreign troops strive to be in constant contact with the population. Another contradiction lies with Galula's prescription for the counterinsurgent to demonstrate his resolve to see the endeavor through to the very end. Although this goes towards persuading the population as to which side will prevail, it may also give the impression of an indefinite occupation; for the "very end," in the eyes of the population, will rely on the invader's own subjective assessment. Finally, how does Galula's argument in favor of withholding development and restricting civil liberties (so as to progressively restore these as a reward for collaboration) translate against the "people in arms"? This too does not seem to do for the foreign intervener who wishes to avoid the stigma of occupation.

The counterinsurgent's campaign plan, operations, and posture must therefore be made to reflect whether an insurgency is being waged against the incumbent regime, or against its foreign backer. Since insurgencies are seldom homogenous blocs, this determination should be devolved to subordinate echelons. Violence in one part of the country will be directed at the foreign counterinsurgent, while in another part, it will be directed at the incumbent regime. Often, it will be directed at both. Violence may also be wholly sectarian, and therefore, in theory, directed at neither. (In practice, however, attacking the foreign counterinsurgent serves to remove the obstacle standing in the way of a given faction's objectives, as well as a means of self-legitimization.)

Still, it has been my experience that a population's perception of a foreign force as an occupier is secondary in importance to the perception of that force's ability to provide security and to improve daily life. Retrenching foreign troops into isolated bases to limit their interaction with the population can seldom present a solution. No matter how discreet their convoys and operations are made to be, the insurgent would have little trouble, and paradoxically every interest, to render these more aggressive and frequent.

The population caught in the middle asks the following question: "Has the foreign intervention bettered our lives or worsened them?" The answer to this is of critical importance to the foreign intervener that has come to impose a revolution. Firstly, rhetoric and promises of future progress can only go so far to inspire patience in the population, and a willingness to accept sacrifice. Secondly, until the intervention has yielded a state of betterment for the population, the foreign counterinsurgent's withdrawal will be made difficult by the evidence of his failure to achieve a key outcome of the intervention. Such failure raises yet another issue of morality, and sets a spoiling precedent for future legitimate causes for armed intervention.

It follows that after having toppled a regime, the foreign intervener must quickly bring about a state of betterment in the daily life of the population. Exercising a tight control over the population remains a necessity to re-establish order and security. Existing or emerging power structures are leveraged to achieve this. The foreign counterinsurgent acts alone only in the absence of a viable alternative; the perception he may generate as an occupier through the imposition of control is a lesser evil than the violent chaos he would otherwise be held accountable for. The same rationale must apply to the degree of presence the foreign counterinsurgent will need to demonstrate, as well as to the consequences for non-collaboration with the incumbent regime he wishes to impose.

The foreign counterinsurgent's withdrawal is announced early not according to a hard timeline, but in accordance with progress for which his own forces and the incumbent administration will be held accountable for. This has the advantage of sending a clear message that the occupation is transient, but that the incumbent government will emerge the victor. Behind closed doors, the message to the incumbent government differs, and may indeed rely on a timeline so as to impress a sense of urgency.

Against the People in Arms, the Galula Doctrine still applies, but its prescriptions must be conducted by proxy, or at the very least, appear to be so. Galula's entire framework sees itself overlaid with the well-acknowledged need to create host nation capacity in security and governance.

Galula paid relatively little attention to the development of host nation security forces because Indigenous troops had traditionally been integral to colonial formations. This differed from U.S. interventions in the postcolonial era where Indigenous forces had to be closely trained and advised, but notionally kept at arm's length. Galula did, however, pay significant attention to the need of raising self-defense militias, as he had done so himself in Algeria to render hamlets in his *sous-quartier* responsible for their own security.

Properly raised and employed, host nation security forces can provide the backbone to the "active minority in favor" of the incumbent regime. These forces must be sold to the cause they will uphold. They must be rendered proficient in small-scale combat and security operations, as well as capable to "work on the population" and gather intelligence. However, care must be given on developing ethos, so as not to create an overly politicized force susceptible of future undemocratic ambitions.

The foreign counterinsurgent's image must be kept positive at all costs, for otherwise, it will irreversibly taint the incumbent government as the lackey of an unwanted occupier. When an incumbent government finds itself having to publicly denounce the presence of its foreign backer, it is a good indicator of how dire the situation has become since the latter was greeted as a liberator. It follows from this that it is much more preferable for a domestic government to appear harsh (in the prosecution of insurgents, in the imposition of control, etc.) than it is for the foreign occupier to be so. The latter will be held accountable to an entirely different set of standards. Resistance, solidarity, and hypersensitivity towards external authority are engrained in human nature. (Children accept discipline from their parents, but much less from strangers.)

THE GALULA DOCTRINE VERSUS SECTARIAN CIVIL WAR

Galula's definition of civil war fell short of describing what sectarian-based violence the futures of Lebanon, the Balkans, Rwanda, Somalia, and Iraq promised. "A civil war suddenly splits a nation into two or more groups," he wrote in *Counterinsurgency*, "which, after a brief period of initial confusion, find themselves in control of part of both the territory and the existing armed forces that they proceed immediately to develop. The war between these groups soon resembles an ordinary international war except that the opponents are fellow citizens, such as in the American Civil War and the Spanish Civil War."[42]

The politico-economically fueled American and Spanish civil wars were characterized by symmetry between rivals that led Galula to dismiss his own treatise for that category of warfare. But what of the sectarian civil wars that followed his era; particularly those that failed the test of symmetry, and that evolved in tandem with insurgencies against a ruling government or its foreign backer?

I asked Dr. Sarah Sewall to comment on Galula's tendency to downplay the importance of ideology in insurrectionary wars. "I personally buy population centric and security prioritization approaches," she wrote me. "But for tribal, ethnic and confessional conflicts, ideology may be more important than Galula acknowledges." Her point is very valid.

In 1999, professors Barbara Walter and Jack Snyder edited a study describing how sectarian groups engaged in civil war can be driven either by environmental ("structural") security concerns, or by "predation, ideology, and unresolvable conflicts of interest."[43] The distinction is critically important to the Galula Doctrine, for the latter stands on the premise that protecting a population—addressing its primal concern for security—frees it to act rationally (i.e., opt for the side that best addresses higher needs). It follows, at first glance, that the Galula Doctrine applies more to those sectarian civil wars (indeed those insurgencies) that are fueled by structural security deficiencies (where fear and a sense of vulnerability paradoxically lie at the center of the violence) than it does to those civil wars where a faction has predatory motives that include territorial ambitions, the desire to exclude other factions from power, or simpler yet, the fanatical desire to kill and terrorize rival sectarian groups.

Walter lists five fear-producing environmental disturbances that can encourage sectarian groups to go to war against each other despite not having prior aggressive aims: "(1) the government breaks down or collapses, (2) a minority group becomes geographically isolated within a larger ethnic community, (3) the political balance of power shifts from one group to the other, (4) economic resources rapidly change hands, [and] (5) groups are asked to demobilize partisan armies."[44]

The invasion of Iraq in 2003, and the decisions that were subsequently taken would cause not one, but all of the above disturbances. A sectarian civil war erupted in tandem to an insurgency that sought to oust the foreign occupier. Presumably, a large proportion of those Shiites and Sunnis who picked up arms against each other did so out of fear, or more precisely, on account that they perceived belligerent motives in each other. Presumably too, factional subgroups on each side fought with predatory motives or fanatical convictions unrelated to this sense of vulnerability. Such would have been the case for Al Qaeda in Iraq, for instance.

Security-driven factions are more amenable to cooperate in the rebuilding of their nation once their sense of vulnerability has been addressed. Predatory-driven factions, on the other hand, are less likely to cooperate until they are made to have more to lose than to gain from fighting.

There is, in my view, a parallel to be drawn between this latter category of behavior and Galula's depiction of the "active minority in opposition." In a sectarian civil war, the predatory or ideologically fueled faction seeks to rally the rest of its group into armed confrontation against a rival one. In an insurgency, the active minority in opposition to the Authority seeks to rally the majority of the population against the latter. In both cases, the instigating minority is deemed irreconcilable, and warrants neutralization; failing which, this minority will come to represent the entire sectarian group—in the case of sectarian civil war—or population—in the case of an insurgency.

Paradoxically, this representation is often achieved with the help of the pressured counterinsurgent who finds it difficult to resist the appeal of negotiating with such a ready-made interlocutor. (The FLN, the PLO, the IRA, ..., all came to represent their populations at the negotiating table. Muqtada al-Sadr's inclusion in the power brokerage process in Iraq, as a representative of an important segment of the Shiite population, provides another example.)

The above reasoning leads us to believe that the more a conflict is predatory in nature, the more appropriate an enemy-centric response becomes. The more the conflict is structural in nature (i.e., security driven), the more appropriate a population-centric response becomes.[45] "Outsiders might have great difficulty changing the goals and principles of competing groups," Walter aptly writes, "but security dilemmas are one problem they can solve."[46] Indeed, the reestablishment of order remains a key task for the foreign intervener who seeks to convince—through the protection he will afford—that there is no requirement for one sectarian group to take up arms against another. This sets the stage for collaboration—the ultimate guarantor of a lasting peace.

THE GALULA DOCTRINE DOES NOT SUBSTITUTE FOR STATECRAFT

A well-executed counterinsurgency doctrine enables statecraft to run its course, but cannot substitute for it. Successful counterinsurgency operations buy time and afford political freedom of action. However, they seldom if ever achieve victory on their own. Shrewdness and *savoir faire* in the upper spheres of the counterinsurgent party are invaluable to bring about favorable turning points that will lead to the desired political outcome.

Galula skirted this issue in his essay titled *Subversion and Insurgency in Asia* by adding circumstantial "luck" as a sin qua non ingredient to victory in insurrectionary wars. Japan invaded China when Mao's revolution against the Kuomintang was on the brink of collapse; the Greek communists were doomed once Tito broke off relations with Stalin, etc. Galula considered such turning points to be lucky because neither insurgent nor counterinsurgent had deliberately brought them about, and yet, their consequences had been decisive.

Can watersheds be deliberately brought about through statecraft in irregular warfare? The Awakening Movement in Iraq provides a positive example. The deliberate spurring of the Sunni counterinsurgency movement that favorably altered the course of the war did not only prove the importance of money; it proved the importance of employing statecraft to leverage existing power structures towards the attainment of common objectives between the intervener and the population at stake. Galula does not provide how to go about creating such watersheds, but their necessity is implied.

The host nation's political landscape must be considered carefully by the foreign counterinsurgent prior to applying Galula's prescription to rebuild the "political machine from the population upwards." Galula sought to counter insurgencies that succeeded in out-governing authorities at the grassroots. A bottom-up approach to bolstering governance, therefore, made good sense for the counterinsurgent to adopt. In *offensive* counterinsurgency scenarios, however, building or rebuilding governance[47] from the bottom up is only warranted if the structure that is already in place (1) is insufficiently robust to start with, or (2) refuses, for ideological reasons, etc., to bend to the intervener's interests despite concerted attempts, thereby warranting its dismantlement or destruction. Furthermore, in *offensive* counterinsurgency scenarios, the intervener must decide whether to employ a bottom-up, top-down, or combination approach to rebuilding governance; a decision that must take into account local realities. In Iraq, for example, an effective system of top-down central government *had* existed prior to the U.S. invasion. Completely rebuilding a politico-administrative machine from the bottom up would have squandered the opportunity to leverage this existing bureaucracy.[48] But in places like Afghanistan, where central government has mattered little since time eternal,[49] foreign forces would have been ill advised to rely too heavily on top-down governance at the detriment of bottom-up alternatives.

Galula was not blind to these nuances, although he refrained from commenting on them in his works. Rufus Phillips recalled the following:

> My closing memory of Lt Col Galula is tied to a later informal discussion during which he acknowledged the importance of a political cause in motivating the national government from the top down to meet popular aspirations, that insurgencies cannot be won on the local level alone. He understood that only a country's people and government could ultimately win such a contest and he recognized the difficulties inherent in an advisory role of promoting the emergence of national as well as local leadership.[50]

This returns us to the fundamental question of whether a Western military force that is neither accustomed nor mandated to conduct politico-administrative work can simply be complemented by a "whole-of-government" approach (whereby advisors from every realm of government are added to the contingent), when partaking in counterinsurgency operations abroad. Does such a complement suffice for the purposes of rebuilding a political machine from the population upwards if that is deemed to be the optimal approach? How does such an enterprise become viable for a Western military force?

A final question worth raising here is whether expeditionary counter-insurgency can truly be practiced without some form of meddling in the cultural affairs of the host nation. The potential role of education should not be overlooked. Beyond its intrinsic merits, education—not ephemeral propaganda or psychological operations—provides the best means of articulating a cause. The natural predilection for democratic freedoms, human rights, and prosperity is negatively affected when a population remains naive and cut off from the world, and malleable, therefore, to regressive rhetoric and agendas. Education takes time—true. But the present Afghan War, for instance, had just marked its ten-year anniversary at the time of this writing.

Governments and regimes of every kind have been built and undone as a result of insurrections, revolutions, and civil wars. Ongoing events across the Middle East prove that the political landscape around the world continues to be jostled and shaped by these conflicts.

The significance of violent political struggles to U.S. and Western interests should not be underestimated; nor should the significance of these struggles to bettering or worsening the condition of nations and the lives of people be underestimated for that matter. Galula is owed a debt of gratitude for having shed his bright light to further our understanding in this field. It is hoped that all who come to employ his works will do so guided not only by the veracity of his arguments, but also by the moral compass that is intrinsic to us all.

The stable West today may be threatened by spectacular terrorism on its soil, but not by revolutionary insurgency for the foreseeable future. The West's future participation in irregular wars will therefore remain an option of foreign policy. The costs of recent campaigns in Afghanistan and Iraq have been high enough to force decision-makers to think twice before committing their nations again to such wars.

Jihadism, as a politicized ideology, will wither through its present resurgence, or, at the very least, the ideology will be eclipsed by new contests brought on by the ongoing shift in the global balance of power. As a new era of multi-polar competition begins, subversion and foreign sponsorship of small wars are unlikely to disappear as tools of foreign policy once "soft power" fails to satisfy as a lever. Past periods of "peaceful coexistence" were far from devoid of geopolitical jockeying by proxy. The democratic West will therefore have to increasingly invest in proactive diplomacy to ensure global stability, while working to develop economic and scientific agendas that will favor a convergence of international interests through trade and education. And still, the West will have to keep improving on its understanding of irregular warfare to ensure its military relevance to deter future threats to its strategic interests abroad, as well as to address future foreign policy objectives that will be driven by humanitarian concerns.

Ideally, present counterinsurgency doctrine will be expanded to explicitly cover the broader spectrum of irregular warfare, which it already does well to imply. One benefit among others of such an expanded coverage would be to offer a common understanding of what is required for insurgencies and revolutions to succeed, to be of use in those situations where the international community supports regime changes from within. To these ends, what Mao had said of his own doctrine can be equally said of Galula's, which will continue to be adapted to evolving times and challenges: "Under suitable conditions, it has great possibilities."[51]

Appendix A

COMPANY INSTRUCTIONS, OCTOBER 1957

Galula addressed the following unpublished set of instructions to his company in Algeria, in October of 1957. Inspired by Maoist doctrine and practices, he stresses the importance of devolving propaganda (information and psychological operations) and intelligence collection down to the individual soldier. He concludes with "two broad goals" and "nine rules" for his soldiers to memorize; these are similar in form to Mao's "Three Rules and Eight Remarks" that can be found in 'On Guerrilla Warfare.'

PACIFICATION. INTERACTION WITH THE POPULATION. DEPORTMENT

There was a time, when during war, we were satisfied with the Prussian habit of asking soldiers to obey orders without ever seeking to understand these. Obeying orders remains a necessity.

Later, we realized that soldiers carried out orders more effectively when the reasons behind these were understood. So we began to explain orders. Understanding orders remains a necessity.

Today, we realize that in revolutionary warfare, and especially in the revolutionary war that is being waged in Algeria, the soldier must continuously act on his own initiative in addition to obeying and understanding orders from above. In this revolutionary war, thinking and acting is not the sole purvey of leaders; soldiers must think and act individually too. This is why . . .

I. IMPORTANCE OF THE POPULATION
IN REVOLUTIONARY WARFARE

The armed rebels constitute a force of 20,000 to 30,000 men. We are 400,000. The war should have been won long ago. So why have the rebels not yet been defeated? Because they have succeeded through terror and persuasion to organize the population to their advantage in the villages thanks to their shadow political organization.

II. WHAT IS PACIFICATION?

Once the large rebel bands have been destroyed or cleared from a region, pacification consists of cutting these off definitively from the population in the following fashion:

1) By destroying rebel cells in villages.
2) By identifying friendly elements among the population, and by using these to prevent the return of rebel cells on the one hand, and to rally the rest of the population to our cause on the other.
3) By convincing the population that our cause is just and ultimately victorious, and that the rebel cause is bad and ultimately doomed to failure.

III. THE ARMY'S ROLE IN PACIFICATION

The fulfillment of point no. 1 above is the responsibility of your leaders. LEAVE IT TO YOUR LEADERS TO ARREST AND PUNISH THOSE THAT ARE FOUND GUILTY.

The fulfillment of point no. 2 above starts requiring the participation of every soldier. These must help their leaders in identifying the friendly elements.

The fulfillment of point no. 3 can only happen with the total participation of every soldier. EVERY SOLDIER IS A PROPAGANDIST, WHETHER HE LIKES IT OR NOT. His misconduct creates enemies for us, and his passivity does not further our cause. But his tactfulness wins us friends, and his personal involvement advances us closer to the objective of pacification.

IV. SOLDIER'S ATTITUE VIS-A-VIS THE POPULATION

Two overarching principles dictate the soldier's attitude:

1. EXTERIORLY. EVERY VILLAGER IS A FRIEND, as we cannot "catch flies with vinegar."

2. INWARDLY. EVERY VILLAGER IS A SUSPECT. There exists only one formal proof of loyalty: the spontaneous denunciation of rebels.

There are two broad goals that we must continuously be striving to achieve:

1. REDUCE THE NUMBER OF FOES.
2. INCREASE THE NUMBER OF FRIENDS.

Consequently, you must respect the following rules:

1. I will be courteous with everyone. Never insult, never hit, never yell.

2. I will be honest. I will not even take a grape. I will never ask for anything (one does not ask when one is holding a rifle). I will not accept any gift, cup of coffee, fruits, eggs, etc. I will politely refuse and invite those who offer these in turn to come to our outpost and offer them something in return.

3. I will respect local customs. Unless I am ordered to do so (for searches), I will not unveil women; nor will I joke with them. I will instead be courteous and humble; a behavior to which they are very sensitive.

4. I will be firm in carrying out orders. I will not tolerate that the population discuss these. I will never show indecisiveness or weakness.

5. I will never discuss military matters within earshot of the population. I will elude any questions on the matter.

6. I will help the population. I will seek every opportunity to lend a hand (by writing their letters, by offering them rides, etc.).

7. I WILL EXPLAIN OUR CAUSE TO THE POPULATION. I WILL COMMUNICATE OUR ORDERS. I WILL OBSERVE THEIR REACTIONS TO THESE, REGISTER AND MONITOR THESE. I WILL DO SO AT EVERY OCCASION, IN THE VILLAGE, OUT OF THE VILLAGE, AT THE STATION, IN THE HOMES, IN THE STREET, IN THE SCHOOLS, IN THE MEDICAL DISPENSARY, EVERYWHERE AND ALL THE TIME.

8. I WILL FIGHT AGAINST REBEL PROPAGANDA IN THE SAME FASHION.

9. I WILL BE CLEAN, WELL-GROOMED, IN PROPER UNIFORM, AND DISCIPLINED.

To conclude, if every soldier befriends a villager, we shall have 20 or 30 friends in every village, and the game will be quickly won. If every soldier becomes an enemy to a villager, we shall have 20 or 30 enemies in every village, and the game will be quickly lost.

Appendix B

Preface to *Contre-Insurrection: Théorie et Pratique*

David H. Petraeus and John A. Nagl

> I am not writing all this to show what a genius I was, but to point out how difficult it is to convince people, especially the military, to change traditional ways and adapt themselves to new conditions.
> —*David Galula, Pacification in Algeria, 1956–1958*

It is an honor to help the French military celebrate one of their own, David Galula, a brilliant student of counterinsurgency and the author of this classic book. Indeed, many—if not most—of those who helped write the new United States Army/United States Marine Corps field manual on counterinsurgency regard this book as *the* classic in the field.

Bernard Brodie has written that Carl von Clausewitz's *On War* "is not only the greatest, but the only great" book on warfare. In the same sense, David Galula's *Counterinsurgency Warfare* could arguably be called not just the greatest, but the only great book on irregular warfare. And as this sort of warfare is likely to dominate the twenty-first century, an examination

---

"David Galula: The Clausewitz of Counterinsurgency," by General David H. Petraeus and Lieutenant Colonel John A. Nagl. Foreword from *Contre-Insurrection*, used by permission of Economica.

of Galula's career and teachings could hardly be more important or more timely.

Like Clausewitz, Galula grew up a soldier and cut his teeth on war. Born in Tunisia and raised in Morocco, he graduated from Saint-Cyr on the eve of the Second World War in time to fight in North Africa, France, and Germany. Enjoying the life of a soldier, he accepted a postwar assignment to the French Embassy in Beijing and had a front-row seat as the greatest insurgent in history, Mao Tse-Tung, overthrew the government of the most populous country in the world. Posted to the United Nations Special Commission on the Balkans, Galula observed the unsuccessful insurgency in Greece before being assigned back to the Far East as Military Attache to Hong Kong. From there, he kept close watch on the ongoing counterinsurgency campaigns in Indochina, Malaya, and the Philippines. This education in counterinsurgency prepared Galula well for the most important campaign of his colorful career, Algeria. Galula served there as a company commander in the 45th Colonial Infantry Battalion for nearly two years before being promoted to deputy commander of the battalion just before his departure in 1958.

It is these two years of personal experience in counterinsurgency, interpreted through the prism of some fifteen previous years of intense study of the subject, that gave Galula's work its balance of, as he put it, "Theory and Practice." Personal experience of warfare unrefined by intellectual reflection is merely a litany of slaughter; military theory uninformed by personal experience of blood and iron tends toward irrelevance. Galula, like Clausewitz, had both extensive personal experience of war and the intellectual and philosophical bent to reflect for future generations upon the enduring truths of the sort of warfare he had seen.

That reflection took place at the national defense headquarters in Paris for the next four years before a fortuitous assignment as a research associate at Harvard University. During that posting, Galula attended and intellectually dominated a counterinsurgency conference convened by the RAND Corporation in November 1962. Because of his keen insights into the subject, RAND's Stephen Hosmer invited Galula to capture his counterinsurgency experiences in what became *Pacification in Algeria, 1956–1958*, published by RAND in 1963 (and republished, with an excellent new Foreword by Bruce Hoffman, in 2006). This narrative of Galula's combat experiences in the Algerian province of Kabylia was the ore from which Galula mined his 1964 gem, *Counterinsurgency Warfare: Theory and Practice.*

And what a gem it is! *Counterinsurgency Warfare* is, like Clausewitz' *On War*, both a philosophical reflection on the nature of warfare and an instructional manual full of guidance on how to succeed in it. Counterinsurgency is, of course, different from conventional war because an insurgent enemy does not array himself in plain sight on a field of battle, protected by armor and sheer mass, but instead finds protection among the population. An insurgent, in Mao's immortal words, "swims like a fish in the sea of the people." Identifying and defeating such an enemy is impossible unless the counterinsurgent has gained the support of the population. As Galula observed, the "counterinsurgent cannot achieve much if the population is not, and does not feel, protected against the insurgent."

Galula's primary insight is that while in conventional war the focus of combat is the enemy force in the field, in counterinsurgency warfare the focus of all action must be this protection of the native population. All else logically follows in a book notable for its logic, its precision, and its brevity. Securing the people hinges upon identifying those who threaten it; however, as any police officer understands, getting information on bad apples is difficult. "Intelligence has to come from the population," Galula explained, "but the population will not talk unless it feels safe, and it does not feel safe until the insurgent's power has been broken." Because insurgents seldom follow the laws of warfare, they are able to coerce and intimidate the population through violence and terror; defeating this strategy requires the patient, persistent presence of counterinsurgent forces. The best of these forces are local troops, whose professional presence is a constant reminder of the authority and dedication of the national government.

Conventional military forces often struggle with the need to adapt to these demands of counterinsurgency, a kind of war for which they generally have not been designed, organized, trained, or equipped. It is for this reason that the *US Army/Marine Corps Counterinsurgency Field Manual* identifies the need to "Learn and Adapt" as an imperative for success in twenty-first century counterinsurgency campaigns. Conventional forces engaged in a counterinsurgency campaign must be true learning organizations that rapidly adjust their organizations, tactics, and procedures in order to defeat their hidden enemies—putting far more resources into intelligence collection and analysis, dispersing rather than massing their forces in order to provide security to the population, acquiring armored reconnaissance vehicles to protect against hidden roadside bombs, above all else exerting themselves to train the local forces on whom victory depends.

Galula is also clear on the paradoxical nature of this kind of war, in which, at a certain point, "a mimeograph machine may turn out to be more useful than a machine gun, a soldier trained as a pediatrician more important than a mortar expert, cement more wanted than barbed wire, clerks more in demand than riflemen." The scale of the adaptation required is immense, and "it is just as important that the minds of the leaders and the men—and this includes the civilian as well as the military—be adapted also to the special demands of counterinsurgency warfare."

Reading Galula's work is an important first step in that mental adaptation to the demands of modern warfare among the people, but it is only the first step. Timeless as are most of the insights of *Counterinsurgency Warfare*, the field has evolved in the forty-five years since its publication. Indeed, some modern Galula acolytes describe today's conflict environment as a "Global Insurgency" led by radical adherents of misinterpreted religious beliefs. Religious ideology can be an even more virulent motivation for modern insurgents than was the nationalism that spurred the conflicts of Galula's day, while nationalist insurgents could often be coerced through political negotiations, those inspired by religion may have to be imprisoned or killed. The tactic of suicide bombing combined with more powerful explosives dramatically increases the precision and damage that can be inflicted by insurgent forces today. But the most important modern imperative of counterinsurgency operations is the need to manage information and expectations.

In this internet age, easily created and instantly distributed videos serve as insurgent recruiting advertisements, requests for campaign contributions, and propaganda blows at the national will of the counterinsurgent force. Galula spends far more time in *Counterinsurgency Warfare* discussing how to coordinate an information operations campaign than he does teaching us how to kill or capture insurgents; perhaps he knew that the former was a more difficult, as well as a more important, adjustment for conventional armies fighting an insurgency. Today's counterinsurgent must publicize his objectives and his measures of success, and report frequently and honestly upon them—and upon the atrocities committed by his enemy—in a coordinated information operations campaign that is often the key determinant of success in modern counterinsurgency campaigns.

These thoughts lead to one of Galula's most important insights—that counterinsurgency warfare is just twenty percent military and eighty percent political. Defeating an insurgent enemy requires coordinated action along multiple logical lines of operation, designed not just to kill or capture insurgents and train local forces—although those tasks are essential—but also to improve the ability of the national government to govern, to provide economic opportunity to the population, and to ensure that all have access to essential services such as water and electricity. All of these actions should be conducted by, with, and through host nation officials whenever possible, as the final objective is the empowerment of a government that can meet the needs of all of its people, earning their trust, support, and commitment.

Galula's importance to the American military's understanding of counterinsurgency in the Afghan and Iraq campaigns can hardly be overstated; his thinking was the single greatest influence on the *U.S. Army/Marine Corps Counterinsurgency Field Manual* of 2006. Through his book's impact on that doctrinal publication, and through its assignment as required reading at the U.S. Army Command and General Staff College and at the U.S. Army center that prepares advisors for Iraqi and Afghan security forces, *Counterinsurgency Warfare* may ultimately be seen as the most important French military writing of the past century. It certainly is regarded as such in the United States.

Unfortunately, Galula has, until now, been more recognized abroad than in his own homeland. The publication of this book in French is thus an overdue tribute to his importance—just as the renewed recognition of Galula's wisdom has helped change US military doctrine and practice. Ultimately, Galula's work may have implications for modern French doctrine, education, and even defense policy, as well. Indeed, a question he asked forty years ago has great relevance for a world that is today challenged by a global insurgency: "If the individual members of the organizations were of the same mind, if every organization worked according to a standard pattern, the problem would be solved. Is this not precisely what a coherent, well-understood, and accepted doctrine would tend to achieve?"

It is, precisely. And as we work to understand and to defeat what is, in certain respects, a global insurgency, the scale and scope of whose threat Galula would have understood all too well, we would be well served when writing a doctrinal manual, a lesson plan, or a campaign plan to begin with the work of a French Lieutenant-Colonel who died in 1967, leaving behind what is perhaps the only truly *great* book on irregular war.

CHRONOLOGY

1919	January 10. Galula born in Sfax, Tunisia.
1924	October 28. Family granted French citizenship on account of Crémieux Decree.
1926	Family moves to Morocco.
1930	Galula attends Lycée Lyautey in Casablanca.
1938	Prepares for Saint-Cyr admittance exam in Paris.
1939	September 3. France declares war on Germany.
	October. Galula attends Saint-Cyr. Curriculum compressed to six months.
1940	March 20. Galula commissioned in the Colonial Army. Assigned to Morocco.
	May–June. Battle of France.
	October 3. First Statute of Jews decree enacted by Vichy. Galula remains in the military despite ban on Jewish officers.
	October 7. Crémieux Decree abolished. Naturalized Jews are stripped of their citizenship.
1941	April. Galula attends four-month complementary course at Saint-Cyr (Aix-en-Provence).
	June 2. Second Statute of Jews decree enacted by Vichy.
	September 2. Galula discharged from the military on racial grounds.
1942	Undertakes special mission in Tangiers.

	November 8. Operation TORCH. Allies land in French North Africa.
1943	July. Galula reintegrated into French Army.
	October. Crémieux Decree reinstated.
1944	June 17. Operation BRASSARD. Galula lands at Elba with 9th Colonial Infantry Division. Receives Army Corps citation for actions under enemy fire.
	July 19. Promoted to lieutenant, retroactive to March 20, 1942.
	August. Operation DRAGOON. Galula lands on French Riviera. Participates in Battle for Toulon as a platoon commander. Serves as the battalion signals and intelligence officer for the remainder of the Liberation of France Campaign.
1945	October. Arrives in China as assistant-attaché under Jacques Guillermaz. Begins study of Maoist revolutionary warfare.
1948	April. Undertakes first hinterland expedition. Detained by communist forces twice. Witnesses communist methods of controlling and indoctrinating population.
	July. Promoted to Captain.
1949	May. Starts sixteen-month assignment with U.N.S.C.O.B. in Greece. Witnesses insurgency flounder for lack of a proper polarizing cause.
	August 14. Marries Ruth Beed Morgan.
1951–1956	Military attaché assignment to Hong Kong. Continues study of Chinese Communist revolution and neighboring insurgencies. Submits memoranda on counter-subversion.
1954	May 7. Last French positions at Dien Bien Phu fall.
	November 1. FLN launches first attacks across Algeria.
1955	September. Galula attends Manila conference on counter-subversion.
1956	March. Tunisia and Morocco granted independence.
	August. Galula begins twenty-four-month tour of duty in Algeria as a company commander and then as a deputy battalion commander. Receives an Army Corps citation for his actions against rebels. Submits two memoranda relating his pacification techniques, and calls for theater-wide doctrine to be implemented.
1958	April 2. Promoted to Commandant.

May 13. First Algerian Revolt. Putsch leads to return of de Gaulle and instatement of the Fifth Republic.

August 1. Galula begins assignment at National Defense General Headquarters under de Gaulle. Continues to work on irregular warfare at Information Division (information operations and electronic warfare).

1959   April 21. Daniel is born. He will be adopted that summer.

1960   January. Second Algerian Revolt (Barricades Revolt) follows de Gaulle's announcement of Algerian self-determination. Psychological Action Bureaus are disbanded.

February 8. Galula attends six-month U.S. Armed Forces Staff College course in Norfolk. Submits thesis "On the Conduct of "Counter-Revolutionary War," the direct precursor to *Counterinsurgency: Theory and Practice*.

1961   April 22. Third Algerian Revolt erupts under generals Salan, Jouhaud, Zeller, and Challe.

September 30. Harvard Center for International Affairs expresses interest in Galula.

December 27. Galula requests three-year sabbatical from active duty to attend Harvard as a Research Associate as of April 1962.

December 29. Galula receives Légion d'Honneur.

1962   April. Attends five-day RAND counterinsurgency symposium.

Begins writing *Counterinsurgency* at Harvard.

October 1. Begins writing *Pacification* for RAND.

1963   July 2. Completes *Counterinsurgency*. Submits manuscript to French Attaché in Washington.

August 31. Harvard contract ends.

September 30. RAND contract ends. Galula submits *Pacification* as a classified memorandum.

October. Galula returns to France.

1964   January. *Counterinsurgency* goes to print with Praeger.

April. Galula starts work with La Compagnie Francaise Thomson Houston.

September 18–21. Lectures at Institute of Strategic Studies Conference, "Conflict and Co-existence in Asia." His paper will be published the following year.

	October 1. Officially retires from active duty. Transferred to the Reserves where he will be promoted to lieutenant-colonel the following year.
1967	May 11. Galula passes away from cancer.
2001	October. U.S./coalition intervention in Afghanistan begins.
2003	March. U.S./coalition intervention in Iraq begins.
2005	Praeger releases new edition of *Counterinsurgency*.
	RAND releases *Pacification* to the general public.
	December. Drafting of FM 3-24 begins.
2006	December. Final draft of FM 3-24 issued. Downloaded 1.5 million times in the first month.
2008	*Counterinsurgency* published in French by Economica with preface by General David Petraeus and Lieutenant-Colonel John Nagl lauding Galula as "Clausewitz of counterinsurgency."

NOTES

PROLOGUE

1. Galula, *Counterinsurgency*, 54–55.

INTRODUCTION

1. Clausewitz, *On War*, 189.
2. Galula to Freeman, June 30, 1964, DGP.
3. Galula, *Counterinsurgency*, xiii–xiv.
4. Galula to Freeman, June 30, 1964, DGP.
5. Galula, *Counterinsurgency*, xiii.
6. University of Chicago Edition, *Counterinsurgency Field Manual*, xvi.
7. Conrad Crane in discussion with the author, September 2011. Dr. Crane noted that even Pakistan had come up with a counterinsurgency doctrine inspired by FM 3-24.
8. John Nagl in discussion with the author, June 2011.
9. Galula, *Contre-insurrection*, v.
10. Ibid, xii.
11. Philippe de Montenon in discussion with the author, January 2011.
12. Galula, *Counterinsurgency*, xiii–xiv.
13. Clausewitz, *On War*, 184–190.
14. Galula, *Counterinsurgency*, 36.
15. Fall, *Street Without Joy*, 400, and Freeman to Galula, March 11, 1964, DGP.
16. Galula, *Counterinsurgency*, 54.
17. Ibid, 53.
18. Galula, "Counter-Revolutionary War," 2.

19. Kissinger to Galula, August 1, 1963, DGP.

CHAPTER 1

1. Camus, *The Rebel*, 234.
2. Galula, "Counter-Revolutionary War," 33.
3. Literally meaning black feet. The term refers to French settlers who had often been sun–darkened farmers.
4. France, Commune de Sfax, Extrait des registres de l'état civil—Registre des naissances, No. 003277, 1919, DGP.
5. The Semitic word for "Spanish," it denotes members of the Jewish community who were exiled from the Iberian Peninsula as a result of the Inquisition. A majority of these crossed the Strait of Gibraltar to settle in Muslim lands. North African Jews are hence referred to as "Sephardic," regardless of whether their ancestors once lived in Spain or not.
6. Alliance Israélite Universelle website; aiu.org.
7. France, Éxtrait du journal officiel de la République Française du 11 novembre 1924. Page 10002, no. V47587, January 6, 1939, DGP.
8. Galula details the following four counterinsurgency laws: (1) The support of the population is as necessary for the counterinsurgent as for the insurgent; (2) Support is gained through an active minority; (3) Support from the population is conditional; and (4) Intensity of effort and vastness of means are essential (Galula, *Counterinsurgency*, 54–55).
9. A term Galula borrowed from Mao, who had borrowed it in turn from Marxist–Leninist literature.
10. Isaac Crémieux served as Minister of Justice under Napoleon III. He played an instrumental role in the founding of the Alliance Israélite Universelle.
11. Allouche–Benayoun and Bensimon, *Juifs d'Algérie*, 36.
12. Galula, *Pacification*, 161.
13. Fellous, ed., *Juifs et Musulmans*, 472.
14. Galula to Buchan, June 25, 1964, DGP.
15. Galula to Buchan, August 29, 1964, DGP.
16. Hosmer and Crane, eds., *Counterinsurgency*, 63.
17. Fellous, ed., *Juifs et Musulmans*, 472.
18. Yolande Bismuth and Ruth Galula in discussions with author, 2009–2010.
19. Eisenbeth, *Juifs d'Afrique du Nord*, 129, and Toledano, *Histoire de familles*, 447.
20. Tolédano, *Histoire de familles*, 447.
21. Sebag, *Les Noms des Juifs de Tunisie*, 76.
22. Fellous, ed., *Juifs et Musulmans*, 250.
23. Galula to Freeman, June 20, 1964, DGP.

24. Jacques Guillermaz eulogy for David Galula, May 13, 1967, DGP.

CHAPTER 2

1. De Boisboissel, *Dans l'ombre de Lyautey*, 108.
2. Galula, *Counterinsurgency*, 4.
3. Lyautey, *Paroles d'action*.
4. Primault, Christophe. "Le Maréchal Lyautey." Lycée Lyautey website; edulyautey.org.
5. Bensoussan, *Il était une fois*, 213.
6. My grandmother insists that the AIU school in Casablanca surpassed the Lycée in the quality of education it dispensed. She attended the Lycée de Casablanca until Vichy laws saw her expelled on racial grounds. The AIU stood as a welcoming alternative.
7. "Fatima" was a common name for Muslim women in Morocco at the time.
8. David Galula, personal résumé drafted in 1963, DGP.
9. Lycée Lyautey website; "Le système éducatif français sous le protectorat," entry by P. J. Bravo.
10. Jointly administered Muslim schools, which offered a mix of French, Arabic, and Islamic curriculums.
11. France, Ministère des Affaires Étrangères, La France à la Loupe—The Education System in France, June 2007.
12. Lycée de Casablanca honor roll. Tableau d'honneur, Classe de première II, 1937, and Classe de mathématiques élémentaires, 1938. Courtesy of Marcel Kadosch.
13. Marrus and Paxton, *Vichy and the Jews*, 196.
14. Paxton, *L'Armée de Vichy*, 210.
15. Guynemer and Mermoz were two of France's most romanticized figures in aviation.
16. The condemnation of an assimilated Jewish officer for treason in the aftermath of the Franco–Prussian war of 1870 would have a tremendously polarizing effect on French society, as well as a significant impact on the French military psyche (see Bach, *L'Armée de Dreyfus*.)
17. De Gaulle, *Le fil de l'épée*, 46–49.
18. Regrettably, I was unable to find any service records related to that name at the Service Historique de la Défense in Vincennes, France.

CHAPTER 3

1. Lacheroy, "Guerre Révolutionnaire," 24.
2. Galula, *Counterinsurgency*, 59.
3. Bach, *L'Armée de Dreyfus*, 34–37.

4. Latelrne, "La promotion," 119–122.
5. France, SHD, État signalétique et des services, David Galula.
6. Ibid.
7. Lantelme, "La promotion," 119–122.
8. "Historique." École de Saint-Cyr Coëtquidan website; st–cyr.terre.defense .gouv.fr
9. France, École Spéciale Militaire, Livret Matricule d'Homme de Troupe, David Galula, 1939, SHD.
10. France, SHD, État signalétique et des services, David Galula.
11. "Historique." École de Saint-Cyr Coëtquidan website; st–cyr.terre.defense .gouv.fr
12. France, SHD, État signalétique et des services, David Galula.
13. Lantelme, "La promotion," 119–122.
14. Ibid.
15. "Les promotions par époque." La Saint-Cyrienne website; saint–cyr.org, and René Lantelme in correspondence with author, April 2010.
16. Lantelme, "La promotion," 119–120.
17. René Lantelme in correspondence with author, April 2010.
18. "L'École spéciale militaire et l'École Militaire de l'Infanterie à Aix–en–Provence," Revue de l'armée française, No. 4 (January 1942): 9.
19. Considerable attempts were made, nonetheless, by the French Army's Psychological Action program to indoctrinate officers for "Revolutionary Warfare" in Algeria.

CHAPTER 4

1. Clausewitz, On War, 189.
2. Galula, Pacification, 246–247.
3. France and Germany suffered staggering losses: 90,000 and 30,000 men killed, respectively, within six weeks. The swiftness of the German offensive resulted in a total breakdown of French command, control, and communications.
4. Paxton, L'armée de Vichy, 150 (citing Le Figaro, October 15, 1941.)
5. Marrus and Paxton, Vichy and the Jews, 138.
6. Ibid, xii.
7. Ibid, xi.
8. Ibid, xiii.
9. Oliel, Les Camps de Vichy, 38.
10. Marrus and Paxton, Vichy and the Jews, 87.
11. Ibid.
12. Ibid, 98.
13. Ibid, 127.
14. Paxton, L'armée de Vichy, 199–200.

15. France, Journal officiel, Loi du 3 octobre 1940 portant sur le statut des juifs, 1940.
16. Marrus and Paxton, *Vichy and the Jews*, 146.
17. France, SHD, État signalétique et des services, David Galula.
18. France, 1ère Région Militaire, Résumé de notes, David Galula, SHD.
19. Marrus and Paxton, *Vichy and the Jews*, 98.
20. France, Journal officiel, Loi du 2 juin 1941 portant sur le statut des juifs, No. 2332, 1941.
21. Paxton, *L'armée de Vichy*, 151.
22. Willemin, *Images d'archives d'Algérie*, 131.
23. Michel, *Vichy Année 40*, 144.
24. Marrus and Paxton, *Vichy and the Jews*, 195.
25. Ibid., 196.
26. Darlan was caught in Algiers during the Allied landings. He offered his services to the Allies, who accepted him, to de Gaulle's dismay. He was assassinated the following month by a member of the French underground.
27. A veteran of the Moroccan counterinsurgency campaign against Abd-el-Krim, Giraud commanded the 7th Army during the Battle of France. Captured in battle by the Germans, he would later succeed a spectacular escape from Königstein Castle. The United States felt that placing Giraud at the head of French forces in North Africa, instead of de Gaulle, would secure the loyalty of the French military establishment there. De Gaulle, the savvier politician of the two, eventually prevailed. De Gaulle was famously reported to have said of Giraud that he was thick-headed (*bête*) like a general!
28. Oliel, *Les Camps de Vichy*, 39.
29. Allouche–Benayoun and Bensimon, *Juifs D'Algérie*, 280.
30. Clausewitz, *On War*, 189.
31. De Gaulle was court-martialed and sentenced to death in absentia by the Vichy army. Historian E.J. Duval aptly points out that twenty years later, it would be de Gaulle's turn to court martial dissident generals for treason in Algeria.
32. Paxton, *L'armée de Vichy*, 240.
33. Duval, *L'Épopée des tirailleurs sénégalais*, 221.
34. Paxton, *L'armée de Vichy*, 176.
35. Marrus and Paxton, *Vichy and the Jews*, 208.
36. Galula's forced expulsion from the Vichy army shielded him from the stigma that would haunt the careers of those officers who had stayed on.

CHAPTER 5

1. Galula, "Counter–Revolutionary War," 3.
2. Les Troupes de la Marine. Centre Militaire d'Information et de Documentation sur l'Outre-Mer, Versailles, 1978, 44.

3. Singer and Langdon, *Cultured Force,* 46.

4. Galula, *Pacification,* 50.

5. Centre Militaire d'Information, Les Troupes de la Marine, 44.

6. Ibid.

7. David Galula, personal résumé drafted in 1963, DGP.

8. Interview conducted May 12, 2010.

9. Descoubes, *1er Régiment de Zouaves,* 9 and 53–54.

10. Gelez, "Les Zouaves," 7.

11. France, École Spéciale Militaire, Livret Matricule d'Homme de Troupe, David Galula, 1939, SHD.

12. Villatoux and Villatoux, *La République et son Armée,* 299.

13. Mangin, "Un ralliement."

14. Before the war, Groussard led a program to weed out officers with communist sympathies from the French Army. It is very likely that his anticommunism influenced Galula, and others at Saint–Cyr such as Jacques Hogard and Maurice Prestat.

15. Breuer, *Undercover Tales,* 127.

16. Ibid., 126.

17. "History: The Battle for Gibraltar," MI5 Security Service website; mi5.gov. uk/output/the-battle-for-gibraltar.html.

18. Crémieux-Brilhac, "Consignes Provisoires."

19. The tirailleurs were officered by white Frenchmen. In 1927, a decree was passed authorizing that a single Indigenous officer be commissioned per battalion. (Duval, *Les tirailleurs,* 201.)

20. Duval, *L'Épopée des tirailleurs,* 72.

21. In 1940, rumors ran in the Italian camp that the Senegalese sought to fill their pouches with the ears of their enemy. (Interview with the editor of Le Blog officiel du secteur fortifié des Alpes Maritimes).

22. Duval, *L'Épopée des tirailleurs,* 197

23. Duval, *L'Épopée des tirailleurs,* 77.

24. It was said of General Borgnis–Desbordes that he had "inaugurated the method that Gallieni would come to perfect: training and employing troops in all of the endeavours required for pacification: engineering, masonry, carpentry, etc." (Zimmerman, "Le Général Borgnis–Desbordes," 467.)

25. Gaujac, "Débarquement de Provence," 26.

26. Ibid., 26–27.

27. France, SHD, Carnet des notes du feuillet du personnel, David Galula. Entry by Borgnis–Desbordes, 1943.

28. Saint-Hillier, "L'armée française."

29. Bertin, *La Seconde Guerre Mondiale* (vol. de Sicile en Provence, 188).

30. De Lattre, *Histoire de la Première Armée,* 29.

31. Guillermaz, *Une vie pour la Chine,* 126.

32. Citation, "Citation à l'ordre du corps d'armée," Extrait de l'ordre général no. 31 du 1.10.1944 du général commandant le 1er corps d'armée. David Galula. January 10, 1944, DGP.

33. Boré, "La 9e Division d'Infanterie Coloniale."

34. Swanston et al., *The Historical Atlas of World War II*, 283.

35. Bertin, *La Seconde Guerre Mondiale* (vol. de Sicile en Provence, 158).

36. Willemin, *Images d'archives d'Algérie*, 142.

37. De Lattre, *Histoire de la Première Armée*, 42.

38. Bertin, *La Seconde Guerre Mondiale* (vol. de Sicile en Provence, 189).

39. Saint-Hillier, "L'armée française."

40. Bourgund was later killed in action.

41. Gaujac, *Libération de Toulon*, 228–229.

42. Ibid., 281.

43. Ibid., 282.

44. Ibid., 284–286.

45. Ibid., 304.

46. Ibid., 306.

47. Bertin, *La Seconde Guerre Mondiale* (vol. de Sicile en Provence, 191).

48. Ibid., 203.

49. Swanston et al., *The Historical Atlas of World War II*, 283.

50. Gaujac, *Libération de Toulon*, 30.

51. Duval, *L'Épopée des tirailleurs*, 248–249.

52. Les Coloniaux dans les batailles de la libération. Unofficial Troupes de Marine website; troupesdemarine.org/traditions/histoire/hist013

53. France, SHD, État signalétique et des services, David Galula.

54. Les Coloniaux dans les batailles de la libération. Unofficial Troupes de Marine website; troupesdemarine.org/traditions/histoire/hist013.htm.

55. France, SHD, Carnet des notes du feuillet du personnel, David Galula. Entry by Delteil, 1945.

CHAPTER 6

1. Tse-Tung, *On Guerrilla Warfare*, 89–90.

2. Galula to Hanrahan, June 29, 1953, DGP.

3. Guillermaz, *Une vie pour la Chine*, 125–126.

4. Ibid., 32.

5. Ibid., 57.

6. France, SHD, Carnet des notes du feuillet du personnel, David Galula. Entry by Guillermaz, 1946.

7. Guillermaz to Galula, March 21, 1954, DGP.

8. Guillermaz, *Une vie pour la Chine*, 191.

9. Barnett to Galula, April 20, 1967, DGP.

10. Patrick Tyler, "Doak Barnett Dies: China Scholar, 77," *New York Times*, March 19, 1999.

11. Guillermaz to Galula, December 30, 1955, DGP.

12. Galula to Freeman, February 7, 1964, DGP.

13. Lansdale to Praeger, May 21, 1964, DGP.

14. Galula to Freeman, June 30, 1964, DGP.

15. "Collections remarkables–Général Jacques Guillermaz." Bibliothèque municpale de Lyon website; bm–lyon.fr/decouvrir/collections/Guillermaz .htm.

16. Guillermaz, *Une vie pour la Chine*, 68.

17. Ibid., 99.

18. Ibid., 124–125.

19. Ibid., 123.

20. Léouzon passed away in February 2010, just before I could reach him.

21. Guillermaz, *Une vie pour la Chine*, 50 and 66.

22. Ibid., 15

23. Ibid., 57

24. Ibid., 16

25. Ibid., 129.

26. Topping, *On the Front Lines*, 48.

27. Guillermaz, *Une vie pour la Chine*, 158.

28. Peking, or Pékin, as the French had dubbed Beijing 400 years ago. Renamed to its present day Beijing by Mao.

29. Guillermaz, *Une vie pour la Chine*, 18–19 and 157.

30. "La Chine." Alain Peyrefitte 1925–1999 un intellectuel en politique website; alainpeyrefitte.fr.

31. "Seymour Topping." The Journalism School Columbia University website; journalism–columbia.edu

32. Topping, *On the Front Lines*, 3–5.

33. Ibid., 6.

34. Ibid., 9.

35. Ibid., 10.

36. Ibid., 9–10.

37. Guillermaz, *Une vie pour la Chine*, 158.

38. Ibid., 150.

39. Ibid., 160–161.

40. Galula to Hanrahan, June 29, 1953, DGP.

41. Mao Tse-Tung to Anna-Louise Strong in an interview, August 1946.

42. Guillermaz, *Une vie pour la Chine*, 185.

43. Ibid., 179.

44. Ibid., 178, and interview with Ruth Galula.

45. Guillermaz, *Une vie pour la Chine*, 180.

46. Fall, *Street Without Joy*, 32.

47. Chassin, *La conquête*, 106–107. The credit of this discovery belongs to G. Mathias.

48. Guillermaz, *Une vie pour la Chine*, 164–165.

49. Marcel Kadosch in discussion with the author, 2010.

50. Guillermaz, *Une vie pour la Chine*, 164.

51. Ibid.

52. Galula, *Counterinsurgency*, 35.

53. Ibid., 38.

54. Guillermaz, *Une vie pour la Chine*, 165.

55. Ibid., 167.

56. Ibid., 170.

57. Ibid., 172.

CHAPTER 7

1. Tse-Tung, *Guerrilla War Against Japan*, chap 1, sect 4.

2. Galula to Goussault, April 5, 1957, DGP.

3. Ts'ai Ch'ien, "Japanese Combat Methods Against Guerrilla Forces," in *Chinese Communist Guerilla Tactics*, Hanrahan, ed., 134.

4. Galula to Goussault, April 5, 1957, DGP.

5. Galula, *Counterinsurgency*, xi, and Galula to Hanrahan, June 29, 1953, DGP.

6. Galula, *Pacification*, 266.

7. Galula, *Counterinsurgency*, 10.

8. Tse-Tung, *Guerrilla War Against Japan*, chap 1, sect 1.

9. Camus, *The Rebel*, 283.

10. Galula referred to Chu Teh's "commercial operations," where the "basic aim in reference to arms and equipment is to capture from the enemy as many new weapons as possible and to learn how to use them against the enemy himself." Chu Te, "On Guerrilla Warfare," in *Chinese Communist Guerilla Tactics*, Hanrahan, ed., 68–69.

11. Paul and Marie-Catherine Villatoux in discussion with author. The next commercial French translations of Maoist works appeared in 1954–1955.

12. Tse-Tung, *On Guerrilla Warfare*, 38.

13. *Problems of Strategy in Guerrilla Warfare against Japan* was published in English by the People's Publishing House in Peking in 1952 according to Griffith, and reprinted in Bombay, according to Hanrahan. (See Tse-Tung, "On Guerrilla Warfare," p. 39 and Hanrahan, ed., *Chinese Communist Guerrilla Tactics*.)

14. Hanrahan states in his translator's notes, "To this writer's knowledge, none of this material, aside from that of Mao Tse-tung, has been published in this country [U.S.]. An excellent translation of part of Mao's work completed by Colonel S.B. Griffith appeared in the Marine Corps Gazette in

the late 1930s, but this is now largely unobtainable." (Hanrahan, *Chinese Communist Guerrilla Tactics*, I)

15. Boorman to Galula, September 28, 1955, DGP.
16. Galula to Hanrahan, June 29, 1953, DGP.
17. Chassin published a first article in February of 1951 on Mao's conquest of China in *La revue militaire d'information*, before publishing *La conquête de la Chine par Mao Tse-Tung* the following year and L'Ascencion de Mao Tse-Tung in 1953. (Villatoux, La République et son armée, 294 and http://www.salan.asso.fr/Biographies/chassin.htm.)
18. (1) Creation of a party; (2) United front; (3) Guerrilla warfare; (4) Movement warfare; and (5) Annihilation campaign. (Galula, *Counterinsurgency*, 31–39.)
19. Galula, *Counterinsurgency*, 29–30.
20. Tse-Tung, *On Protracted War*, 34.
21. Steps one through three can be directly transposed to Galula's five-phased orthodox pattern of insurgency, while steps four and five can be combined to represent the latter's "movement warfare," and steps six and seven combined to represent "the battle of annihilation."
22. A loose equivalent to conducting guerrilla warfare in Maoist vernacular.
23. Tse-Tung, *On Guerrilla Warfare*, 43.
24. Guillermaz to Galula, undated, DGP.
25. Derogatory term used by communists to denote their foes. Galula often used this term to describe himself and others in jest.
26. Galula, *Counterinsurgency*, 39.
27. Ibid., 6.
28. Ibid., xiii.
29. Tse-Tung, *On Guerrilla Warfare*, 34.
30. Source's italics. The use of this term belies Maoist influence.
31. Galula, *Counterinsurgency*, 2.
32. Tse-Tung, *On Protracted War*, 46.
33. P'eng Te-huai, "Our Strategy and Tactics," in *Chinese Communist Guerilla Tactics*, Hanrahan, ed., 113.
34. Galula, *Counterinsurgency*, 6.
35. Tse-Tung, *On Guerrilla Warfare*, 25.
36. Tse-Tung, *China's Revolutionary War*, chap 3, sect 3.
37. Galula, *Counterinsurgency*, 4.
38. Tse-Tung, *China's Revolutionary War*, chap 1, sect 1.
39. Tse-Tung, *On Guerrilla Warfare*, 33.
40. Galula, *Counterinsurgency*, 51.
41. Ibid., 7.
42. Ibid., 58.
43. Ibid.
44. Ibid., 15–16.

45. Ibid., 46.
46. Ibid., 15.
47. Ibid., 53.
48. Shaoqi, *Onslaught of the Diehards,* para 5.
49. Galula, *Counterinsurgency,* 4.
50. Ibid.
51. Ibid., 55.
52. Ibid., 5.
53. Tse-Tung, *On Guerrilla Warfare,* 7.
54. Ibid., 89.
55. Galula, *Counterinsurgency,* 54.
56. Or Xiao Ke. Hsiao co-commanded the Second Front Army (Snow, Red Star, 434.)
57. "Plains" refer to inhabited areas. Hsiao K'e, "On Plain Guerrilla Warfare," in *Chinese Communist Guerrilla Tactics,* Hanrahan, ed., 73.
58. Galula offers the example of the FLN's ban on smoking in *Counterinsurgency* and *Pacification,* despite the secular-nationalist nature of the rebel movement.
59. Galula, *Counterinsurgency,* 34.
60. Ibid., 53–54.
61. Chu Te, "Problems in Guerrilla Warfare," in *Chinese Communist Guerilla Tactics,* Hanrahan, ed., 67.
62. Tse-Tung, *On Guerrilla Warfare,* 90.
63. See Chapter 7, *Counterinsurgency.*
64. Tse-Tung, *On Guerrilla Warfare,* 92.
65. Galula, *Counterinsurgency,* 55.
66. Ibid., 73.

CHAPTER 8

1. Chu Te, "On Guerrilla Warfare," in *Chinese Communist Guerilla Tactics,* Hanrahan, ed., 66.
2. Galula, *Counterinsurgency,* 55.
3. Topping, *Journey Between Two Chinas,* 276.
4. France, Ambassade de France en Chine, Ordre de Mission–David Galula, November 17, 1948, DGP.
5. Ibid.
6. France, SHD, Copie des notes du feuillet du personnel, David Galula. Entry by Vernier, 1949–1950.

CHAPTER 9

1. Tse-Tung, "Problems in Guerrilla Warfare," in *Chinese Communist Guerilla Tactics*, Hanrahan, ed., 19.

2. Galula, *Pacification*, 69.

3. France, Ambassade de France en Chine, Certificat de cessation de paiement–David Galula, November 19, 1948, DGP.

4. Galula, *Counterinsurgency*, 31.

5. Nachmani, *International Intervention*, 1.

6. Ibid., 2–3.

7. Ibid., 20.

8. Ibid., 36.

9. Ibid., 77.

10. France, SHD, Copie des notes du feuillet du personnel, David Galula. Entry by Vernier, 1949–1950.

11. Nachmani, *International Intervention*, 48.

12. Ibid., 40.

13. France, SHD, Copie des notes du feuillet du personnel, David Galula. Entry by Vernier, 1949–1950.

14. Nachmani, *International Intervention*, 67.

15. Ibid., 71–72.

16. Ibid., 50.

17. Ibid., 11.

18. Ibid., 17.

19. Galula, *Counterinsurgency*, 7–8.

20. Ibid., 31.

CHAPTER 10

1. Fall, *Street Without Joy*, 375.

2. Galula to Goussault, April 5, 1957, DGP.

3. France, Ministère de la Guerre, Permission de fin de campagne, David Galula, September 18, 1950, DGP.

4. France, Secrétariat d'état aux forces armées, Avis de mutation, David Galula, November 18, 1950, DGP.

5. David Galula, Copie des notes du feuillet du personnel, SHD.

6. Guillermaz, *Une vie pour la Chine*, 198–199.

7. Ibid., 199.

8. Ibid., 214.

9. Caran, *Tiger's Whiskers*, 61.

10. Stevenson to Galula, June 25, 1954, DGP.

11. Galula to Rubel, April 6, 1963, DGP.

12. Caran, *Tiger's Whiskers*, 49.

13. Guillermaz to Galula, May 31, 1951, DGP.

14. Ibid.

15. Caran, *Tiger's Whiskers*, 49–50.

16. France, SHD, Carnet des notes du feuillet du personnel, David Galula. Entry by Simoneau, 1952.

17. Guillermaz, *Une vie pour la Chine*, 214.

18. Galula to Guillermaz, January 11, 1956, DGP.

19. Joseph Alsop, "In David's District," Matter of Fact, *Herald Tribune,* June 11, 1958.

20. Guillermaz to Galula, December 30, 1955, DGP.

21. Galula, "Counter-Revolutionary War," 4.

22. France, SHD, Carnet des notes du feuillet du personnel, David Galula. Entry by Simoneau, 1952.

23. Jacques Guillermaz eulogy for David Galula, May 13, 1967, DGP.

24. Bourgund to Galula, April 2, 1955, DGP.

25. Guillaume was an early champion of "Psychological Action" operations.

26. Guillaume to Galula, July 28, 1955, DGP.

27. Laroche to Guillermaz, February 17, 1953, DGP.

28. David Galula, "Sens du Congrès de Pékin" (intelligence note drafted for G2, September 15, 1952), DGP.

29. Guillermaz to Galula, July 8, 1953, DGP.

30. Unknown to Galula, June 2, 1953, DGP.

31. Galula to unknown Commandant of the G2 in Indochina, May 28, 1954, DGP.

32. Guillermaz is alluding to French officers with communist sympathies.

33. Guillermaz to Galula, July 8, 1953, DGP.

34. Galula to unknown Commandant of the G2 in Indochina, May 28, 1954, DGP.

35. Guillermaz to Galula, September 30, 1952, DGP.

36. Galula to Blanc, January 20, 1954, DGP.

37. Guillermaz to Galula, March, 21, 1954, DGP.

38. Navarre replaced Salan as the theater commander in Indochina.

39. Cogny commanded French forces in Northern Vietnam.

40. Morgan, *Valley of Death,* 241.

41. Ibid., 242.

42. Galula to Guillermaz, July 21, 1954, DGP.

43. Guillermaz to Galula, March 21, 1954, DGP.

44. Galula to Guillermaz, January 11, 1956, DGP.

45. Bourgeois to Galula, August 29, 1952, DGP.

46. Galula to unknown Commandant of the G2 in Indochina, May 28, 1954, DGP.

47. Galula is referring to founders of the Chinese Communist Party.

48. Common people.

49. Galula to Guillermaz, July 21, 1954, DGP.

50. Galula to Guillermaz, January, 11, 1956, DGP.

51. The staff function that is in charge of orchestrating operations.
52. Galula to Guillermaz, July 21, 1954, DGP.
53. Guillermaz to Galula, March 5, 1955, DGP.
54. Buchan, ed., *China and the Peace*, 182.

CHAPTER 11

1. Gaddis, *Strategies of Containment*, 16.
2. Galula, *Counterinsurgency*, 34.
3. Jacques Guillermaz eulogy for David Galula, May 13, 1967, DGP.
4. Gérald Cauvin in discussion with the author, 2011.
5. Caran, *Tiger's Whiskers*, 45.
6. Bachollet, *L'Affaire Dreyfus,* 50.
7. Freeman to Galula, May 5, 1964, DGP.
8. Magruder to Galula, May 13, 1964, DGP.
9. Galula to Magruder, June 22, 1964, DGP.
10. Galula to Durand, September 23, 1966, DGP.
11. Durand to Walker, November 2, 1966, DGP.
12. Galula to unknown Commandant of the G2 in Indochina, May 28, 1954, DGP.
13. Galula to Freeman, May 8, 1964, DGP.
14. I only found a partial manuscript of *Germ Warfare* in Galula's personal papers. Ruth was unaware that her husband had undertaken the project.
15. Freeman to Galula, June 17, 1964, DGP.
16. David Galula, "Guerre Bactériologique," 8.
17. Ibid., 16.
18. Ibid., 26.
19. Ibid., 42.

CHAPTER 12

1. Lacheroy, *Guerre Révolutionnaire*, 5.
2. Galula, *Pacification*, 10.
3. Ibid., 1.
4. Guillermaz to Galula, July 25, 1955, DGP.
5. Galula to Goussault, April 5, 1957, DGP.
6. Galula, *Pacification*, 40.
7. Payreffite, *C'était de Gaulle.*
8. Alain de Serigny. "Un moment de l'histoire de l'Algérie." L'Assemblée Algérienne. Revue du Cercle Algérianiste, no. 5, March 5, 1979.
9. Galula, *Pacification*, 270.
10. Galula, *Counterinsurgency*, 11.

11. Israel's counterinsurgency effort in the Gaza strip has been based on a more or less similar approach in the absence of viable alternatives.

12. Galula, *Counterinsurgency*, 72.

13. Ibid., 25–27.

14. Khrushchev, *Memoirs,* 880.

15. The French Army's surge in Algeria required it to divert high–readiness divisions from Europe. De Gaulle's effort to include Algeria within NATO's mutual defense pact was unsuccessful, lending credence to his decision to pull out of NATO.

16. Miloud Barkaoui. "Kennedy and the Cold War Imbroglio: The Case of Algeria's Independence." Arab Studies Quarterly, Spring, 1999.

17. David Galula, "Rapport annuel sur le moral" (secret-labeled memorandum submitted to his battalion commander, November 21, 1957), DGP.

18. Alsop to Galula, December 26, 1957, DGP.

19. Galula, *Counterinsurgency*, 21.

20. Galula, *Pacification*, 262.

21. Ibid., 18.

22. Ibid., 181.

23. Ibid., 19.

24. Ibid., 64.

25. Ibid., 38.

26. Ibid., 24.

27. French pacification strategy of quadrillage divided territory into: zones, sectors, quartiers, and sous-quartiers (Villatoux, *La défense en surface,* 36.)

28. Galula, *Pacification*, 68.

29. Galula considered that officers demonstrating a poor grasp of counterinsurgency warfare should be employed in more conventional roles (Galula, *Pacification*, 279).

CHAPTER 13

1. France, Instruction pour la pacification en Algérie, 29.

2. Galula to Goussault, April 5, 1957, DGP.

3. Galula, *Pacification*, vii.

4. Contract between David Galula and the RAND Corporation, October 8, 1962, DGP.

5. Galula, *Pacification,* 67–68.

6. I was unable to find Denoyes in Galula's Saint-Cyr yearbook. It is possible that he attended the year before or after.

7. Alsop sought to maintain his friend's anonymity by omitting his last name.

8. Joseph Alsop, "In David's District," Matter of Fact, *Herald Tribune,* June 11, 1958.

9. Galula, *Pacification*, 178–179.
10. Galula to Goussault, April 5, 1957, DGP.
11. Galula, *Pacification*, 70.
12. Ibid., 219.
13. Ibid., 57.
14. A term General David Petraeus would employ some fifty years later.
15. Joseph Alsop, "In David's District," Matter of Fact, *Herald Tribune,* June 11, 1958.
16. Ibid.
17. Organization Politique Armée, or Armed Political Organization. The term denotes the FLN's shadow governance structure.
18. Galula, *Pacification*, 216.
19. Ibid, 218.
20. Ibid.
21. The term dates back to the French Revolution when politico-military structures were instituted from the bottom up to govern in times of national crisis.
22. Galula, *Counterinsurgency*, 55.
23. Galula, *Pacification*, 92.
24. Ibid.
25. Galula, *Counterinsurgency*, 83.
26. Ibid., 81–82.
27. David Galula, "Consignes d'un détachement implanté dans un village" (secret-labeled set of orders given to his company, September 25, 1956), DGP.
28. David Galula, "Création de l'autodéfense de Bou–Souar" (secret-labeled set of orders given to his company, February 26, 1957), DGP.
29. Ibid.
30. The original copies, written in French, survived in his archives.
31. Galula considered that the journal was wrongfully employed in lieu of a formal pacification doctrine until the Challe Instruction was produced.
32. The zone chief of staff.
33. Galula, *Pacification*, 178.
34. Ibid.
35. Faivre, Maurice, "Le Général Paul Ély: Un Chef d'état–major face au pouvoir politique." Institut de Stratégie Comaparée website; stratisc.org/RIHM_81_FAIVRE_ELY.html
36. Ely to Salan, July 22, 1957, DGP.
37. Salan to Galula, August 7, 1957, DGP.
38. Joseph Alsop, "The Para," Matter of Fact, *Herald Tribune,* June 9, 1958.
39. France, SHD, Carnet des notes du feuillet du personnel, David Galula. Entry by Denoyes, 1957.
40. Galula, *Pacification*, 179.

41. France, 10e Région Militaire, "Ordre Général no. 507," signed by General Allard, October 29, 1957, DGP.
42. Galula claimed that up to 1,100 boys and girls were schooled in his sous-quartier (Galula, *Pacification*, 164.)
43. Galula, *Pacification*, 65.
44. France, SHD, Carnet des notes du feuillet du personnel, David Galula. Entry by Ginabat, 1958.
45. Galula, *Pacification*, 179.
46. Ibid., 131.
47. U.S. Department of the Army, *Counterinsurgency* Field Manual, 47–51.
48. Asli Ahmed was admitted to the Légion d'honneur in 1958.
49. Ruth Galula in discussion with the author.
50. Galula to Chef de Service Français de l'administration des anciens combattants à Tizi Ouzou, February 25, 1967, DGP.
51. Galula, *Pacification*, 188.
52. David Galula, "Rapport annuel sur le moral" (secret-labeled memorandum submitted to his battalion commander, November 21, 1957), DGP.
53. Galula, *Pacification*, 72.
54. David Galula, "Rapport annuel sur le moral," DGP.
55. Galula, *Pacification*, 49.
56. Ibid., 128.
57. Lyautey, *Du rôle colonial*, 28.

CHAPTER 14

1. Lyautey, *Du rôle colonial*, 16.
2. Galula, *Counterinsurgency*, 66.
3. Galula, *Pacification*, 23.
4. Ibid., 24.
5. Gillet, *Principes de pacification*, 25. Gridding was spread through a process of "triangulation," whereby every new outpost added to the periphery of a pacified area was connected to the nearest other two outposts through protected lines of communication, forming a triangle in which Pacification efforts were undertaken.
6. Lyautey, *Du rôle colonial*, 10–12.
7. Ibid., 17.
8. Lyautey in a letter to General Bichot in Tonkin, 1895 (Gillet, *Principes de pacification*, 11).
9. Lyautey in letter drafted on February 6, 1899 (Gillet, *Principes de pacification*, 10).
10. Lyautey, *Du rôle colonial*, 33.
11. Galula, *Counterinsurgency*, 66.

12. The notion has become increasingly relevant in the age of airpower. Lyautey, *Du rôle colonial,* 14–15.

13. Gillet, *Principes de pacification,* 59.

14. Galula, *Counterinsurgency,* 66.

15. Ironically enough, identical thoughts were held by Edward Lansdale, who roundly criticized the French from a moral standpoint.

16. France, Instruction pour la pacification en Algérie, 29.

17. The history of the Revolutionary War movement has been authoritatively documented by historians Paul and Marie-Catherine Villatoux.

18. Villatoux and Villatoux, *La République et son Armée,* 63.

19. Lionel Chassin, "Vers un encerclement de l'Occident?" *Revue de Défense Nationale* (May 1956) : 551 (Drawn from Villatoux and Villatoux, *La République et son Armée,* 533.)

20. Michel Goussault, "L'Action Psychologique dans la guerre révolutionnaire d'Algérie" (lecture given as part of a broader presentation by General Allard, Ministère de la Défense, November 15, 1957).

21. France, Instruction pour la pacification en Algérie, 5.

22. Fall, *Street Without Joy,* 370.

23. Galula, *Pacification,* 258.

24. Villatoux and Villatoux, *La République et son Armée,* 345–346.

25. Ibid., 348–349.

26. See Milan N. Vego, "A Case Against Systemic Operational Design," *Joint Forces Quarterly,* Issue 53 (2nd Quarter, 2009): 69–75.

27. Jean Némo, "Les facteurs politiques et sociaux dans les opérations militaires (33C5)," lecture, cours de guerre psychologique, 17e promotion, 1955–1956, 30., ESG, FV.675 (drawn from Villatoux and Villatoux, *La République et son Armée,* 322).

28. Galula, *Pacification,* 281.

29. Ibid., 266.

30. Villatoux and Villatoux, *La République et son Armée,* 566–567.

31. Galula, *Pacification,* 262.

32. Villatoux, *Action psychologique en Algérie,* 6.

33. Ibid., 29–30.

34. Ibid., 28–29.

35. Ibid.

36. Lacheroy, *Saint–Cyr à l'Action Psychologique,* 64.

37. Villatoux, *Action psychologique en Algérie,* 39.

38. Ibid., 36.

39. Ibid., 52–53.

40. Ibid., 565.

41. Goussault to Galula, February 25, 1957, DGP.

42. General Bailly to the Chief of Defense Staff, July 13, 1957 (drawn from Villatoux and Villatoux, *La République et son Armée,* 435).

43. Galula, *Pacification*, 65–66.

44. Ibid., 277.

45. According to Pierre Messmer in Villatoux and Villatoux, *La République et son Armée*, 554.

46. Villatoux and Villatoux, *La République et son Armée*, 326–327,

47. Ibid.

48. De Gaulle, *Mémoires d'espoir*, 92–93.

49. Galula, *Counterinsurgency*, 67.

50. Villatoux in discussion with the author.

51. Villatoux and Villatoux, *La République et son Armée*, 315.

52. Lacheroy, *Saint-Cyr à l'Action Psychologique*, 38.

53. Ibid., 35.

54. Guillermaz to Galula, July 25, 1955, DGP.

55. Lacheroy, *Saint-Cyr à l'Action Psychologique*, 70.

56. Hosmer and Crane, eds., *Counterinsurgency*, 32.

57. Villatoux in discussion with the author.

58. Villatoux and Villatoux, *La République et son Armée*, 452–453.

59. Galula, *Pacification*, 65.

60. Villatoux in discussion with the author.

61. Lacheroy, "Guerre Révolutionnaire," 24.

62. Galula, *Counterinsurgency*, 30–39.

63. Galula, *Pacification*, 66.

64. Villatoux, *Action Psychologique en Algérie*, 51.

65. Goussault to Galula, date unknown, 1958, DGP.

66. I found the original letter in Galula's papers. It went into greater detail, but related the same facts and opinions.

67. Galula, *Pacification*, 67.

68. Goussault to Galula, April 9, 1957, DGP.

69. Ibid.

70. Goussault to Galula, date unknown, 1958, DGP.

71. Goussault to Galula, August 1, 1958, DGP.

72. Villatoux and Villatoux, *La République et son Armée*, 285.

73. Fall, introduction to Trinquier, *Modern Warfare*, xiv.

74. Ibid., xv.

75. Trinquier, *Modern Warfare*, 42.

76. Fall, introduction to Trinquier, *Modern Warfare*, xvii.

77. Mark Watson, "Books in Review," review of *Counterinsurgency*, by David Galula, and *Modern Warfare*, by Roger Trinquier, *The Evening Sun*, Baltimore, March 18, 1964.

78. Trinquier, *Modern Warfare*, 20–21.

79. Ibid., 24.

80. Ibid., 19.

81. See Oliel, *Les Camps de Vichy*.

82. Galula, *Pacification*, 119.

83. Ibid., 119.

84. Galula, *Counterinsurgency*, 87.

85. Ibid.

86. Galula, *Pacification*, 183.

87. Trinquier, *Modern Warfare*, 20.

88. Ibid., 28.

89. David Galula, "Consignes d'un détachement implanté dans un village" (secret-labeled set of orders given to his company, September 25, 1956), DGP.

90. Galula, *Pacification*, 268.

91. Trinquier, *Modern Warfare*, 49.

92. Ibid., 4.

93. Ibid., 61.

94. Ibid., 62.

95. Professors Villatoux point out that this notion extends back to colonial times when camel-mounted Méharistes crisscrossed the deserts between French-occupied towns and outposts.

96. Trinquier, *Modern Warfare,* 69.

97. Galula, *Counterinsurgency,* 78.

98. De Gaulle undoubtedly saw a more trustworthy candidate in the Air Force general, than in the Colonial Army officer who lived and breathed *l'Algérie Française.* Nevertheless, both Challe and Salan would end up plotting against him.

99. Galula, *Pacification*, 271.

100. Ibid., 243.

101. Villatoux and Villatoux, *La République et son Armée*, 304.

102. France, Instruction pour la pacification en Algérie, 4.

103. Ibid., 5.

104. France, Instruction pour la pacification en Algérie, 10.

105. Galula, however, felt that a denunciation remained the greatest test of loyalty.

106. France, Instruction pour la pacification en Algérie, 38.

107. Ibid., 18. A precursor to the notion of effects-based operations applied to counterinsurgency; a definitive downside to which is a catastrophic over-complication of things at junior echelons.

108. Ibid., 25.

109. Ibid., 13.

110. Ibid., 77.

111. Ibid., 70.

112. Galula, *Pacification*, 216.

113. Ibid., 220.

114. Ibid., 221.

115. France, Instruction pour la pacification en Algérie, 109.
116. Ibid., 115.

CHAPTER 15

1. France, Instruction pour la pacification en Algérie, 29.
2. Galula, "Counter-Revolutionary War," 15.
3. France, EMDN, Décision d'affectation David Galula, Signed by Fourquet, July 22, 1958, DGP.
4. Galula to Rubel, April 6, 1963, DGP.
5. État-major général de la défense nationale.
6. Philippe Vial, "La genèse du poste de chef d'état-major des armées." *Revue historique des armées,* no. 248 (2007) : 29–41.
7. David Galula, personal résumé drafted in 1961, DGP.
8. This was perhaps offset by Galula's criticism of the Psychological Action Bureau, which may have reassured de Gaulle's inner circle.
9. David Galula, personal résumé drafted in 1964, DGP.
10. Galula refers to him as Captain Hermann in *Pacification.*
11. Zwilling to Galula, August 31, 1958, DGP.
12. Guillermaz to Galula, December 31, 1958, DGP.
13. Galula, *Pacification,* 156.
14. The French Army Corps of Engineers continues to provide Paris with its fire brigade.
15. France, Conseil municipale de Paris, Condoléances, Débat, Discours du Maire, March 17–18, 2002.
16. France, SHD, Carnet des notes du feuillet du personnel, David Galula. Entry by Casso, 1959.
17. Lacheroy, *Saint-Cyr à l'Action Psychologique,* 70.
18. "Le Comte de Paris," maisonroyaledefrance.fr.
19. External Documentation and Counter-Espionage Service, the precursor to the contemporary direction générale de la sécurité extérieure (DGSE): France's spy agency.
20. Direction de Surveillance du Territoire, France's domestic security agency until 2008, after which it was folded into the direction centrale du renseignement intérieur.
21. Galula to Rae, July 10, 1963, DGP.
22. De Gaulle famously stated that he "understood" (j'ai compris) the grievances of French Algerians in his first speech pronounced in Algiers following his return to power.
23. De Gaulle, *Mémoires d'éspoir,* vol. 1, 51–53.
24. De Gaulle did not wish to see France's defense and foreign policy independence disappear under "an American supreme commander headquartered not far from Versailles, exercising on the Old World, the military

authority of the New One" (De Gaulle, *Mémoires d'éspoir*, vol. 1, 15). Moreover, de Gaulle judged it very improbable that the "Soviets would march across Western Europe to try to impose an unappealing totalitarianism on the West's 300 million inhabitants when they had trouble maintaining control over three times as few in their own satellite-states" (Ibid., 212–213).

25. Galula to Brown, March 23, 1962, DGP.
26. Fourquet would energetically oversee the French withdrawal from Algeria and the dismantling of the OAS. He became France's Chairman of the Joint Chiefs of Staff in 1968 after having championed the country's nuclear strategy and doctrine.
27. Fall, *Street Without Joy*, 370.

CHAPTER 16

1. Trinquier, *Modern Warfare*, 6.
2. Galula, "Counter–Revolutionary War," 3–4.
3. France, Préfecture de Paris, Extrait des Minutes des actes de Naissance, no. 64247, 10iéme Arrondissement, September 30, 1975.
4. Galula, "Counter-Revolutionary War," 15.
5. Jones to Wellborn, February 19, 1960, DGP.
6. JFK visited Fort Bragg in 1961, and would soon augment the size and mandate of U.S. Special Forces.
7. Jones to Wellborn, February 19, 1960, DGP.
8. Powell to Office of the Attaché of France in the United States, August 5, 1960, DGP.
9. Vigneras to Galula, March 25, 1960, DGP.
10. Winn to Galula, May 27, 1960, DGP.
11. Powell to Office of the Attaché of France in the United States, August 5, 1960, DGP.
12. Galula, "Counter-Revolutionary War," 17.
13. Ibid., 3–4.
14. Ibid., 3.
15. Ibid., 28.
16. Hosmer and Crane, eds., *Counterinsurgency*, 8.
17. Galula, "Counter-Revolutionary War," 33.

CHAPTER 17

1. In an address to the U.S.A.F. Academy (Currey, *Unquiet American*, 269).
2. Galula, "Counter-Revolutionary War," 13.
3. Harvard Center for International Affairs, "The First Two Years (1958–1960)," pamphlet, DGP.

4. It was not, as I have seen stated elsewhere, General Westmoreland who had introduced Galula to Harvard (Brown to Galula, September 30, 1961, DGP).

5. Brown to Galula, December 22, 1961, DGP.

6. Ibid.

7. Ibid.

8. France, SHD, Carnet des notes du feuillet du personnel, David Galula. Entry by Coussaud de Massignac, 1962.

9. France, 1ère Région Militaire, Résumé de notes, David Galula, SHD.

10. Boorman to Galula, January 30, 1962, DGP.

11. Boorman to Galula, March 14, 1962, DGP.

12. Germain to Galula, February 13, 1962, DGP.

13. Galula to Brown, March 23, 1962, DGP.

14. Hosmer and Crane, eds., *Counterinsurgency*, iii.

15. Stephen Hosmer in discussion with the author.

16. Galula, *Pacification*, 69.

17. Durdin had been one of the few American journalists to have interviewed Ho Chi Minh. He was also a friend of Bernard Fall (Ruth Galula in discussion with author, and Currey, *Unquiet American*, 197).

18. Hosmer and Crane, eds., *Counterinsurgency*, iv.

19. Phillips, "Meeting Lt. Col. David Galula."

20. Currey, *Unquiet American*, 136.

21. The RAND Corporation would also solicit Constantin Melnik's account of the Algerian War at a strategic level.

22. Currey, *Unquiet American*, 135.

23. Ibid., 269.

24. Fall, *Street Without Joy*, 346.

25. Currey, *Unquiet American*, 238.

26. Ibid., 200.

27. Ibid., 239.

28. Ibid., 256.

29. Ibid., 200.

30. That "control of the population" is the objective of revolutionary war, and not merely "the population," is French, *Guerre Révolutionnaire* in its purest form.

31. Hosmer and Crane, eds., *Counterinsurgency*, 2.

32. Ibid.

33. Fall, *Street Without Joy,* 371.

34. Ibid.

35. Hosmer and Crane, eds., *Counterinsurgency*, 5.

36. Galula, *Counterinsurgency*, 37.

37. Hosmer and Crane, eds., *Counterinsurgency*, 60.

38. Galula, *Pacification*, 240.

39. Hosmer and Crane, eds., *Counterinsurgency*, 61.

40. Ibid., 13.

41. Ibid., 21.

42. Galula, "Counter-Revolutionary War," 28.

43. Hosmer and Crane, eds., *Counterinsurgency*, 21.

44. Dr. Iklé was either unwilling to collaborate for this work, or unable to recall Galula. In fairness, I had been warned that he had an aversion to being interviewed.

45. Galula to Rubel, April 6, 1963, DGP.

46. Bowie to Galula, September 26, 1963, DGP.

47. Thomas Schelling in discussion with the author, January 27, 2011.

48. Schelling to Galula, July 29, 1963, DGP.

49. Kissinger to Galula, August 1, 1963, DGP.

50. Galula refers here to the final steps of his counterinsurgency framework.

51. Galula to Rae, July 10, 1963, DGP.

52. Kissinger to Galula, August 1, 1963, DGP.

53. The French were trying to preserve territories they already administered.

54. Kissinger to Galula, August 1, 1963, DGP.

55. Hanson Baldwin, "End Papers," review of *Counterinsurgency*, by David Galula, *The New York Times*, February 24, 1964.

56. Galula to Compagnon, July 2, 1963, DGP.

57. Compagnon to Galula, July 18, 1963, DGP.

58. Galula to Rae, July 10, 1963, DGP.

59. Praeger to Schelling, August 16, 1963, DGP.

60. Ibid.

61. Galula to Freeman, December 15, 1963, DGP.

62. Hanson Baldwin, "End Papers," review of Counterinsurgency, by David Galula, *The New York Times,* February 24, 1964.

63. Walter Jacobs, "Book Reviews," review of Counterinsurgency, by David Galula, the *Journal of Politics,* Vol. 26, 1964.

64. John Youle, review of Counterinsurgency, by David Galula, clipping from the *Journal of International Affairs,* date and title unk, 1964, DGP.

65. Waelder to Galula, December 8, 1964, DGP.

66. Praeger, "Military Affairs," review of Counterinsurgency, by David Galula, clipping from publisher catalogue, date unk, 1964, DGP.

67. Galula to Freeman, December 6, 1964, DGP.

68. Galula to Freeman, June 30, 1964, DGP.

69. Galula to Freeman, October 18, 1963, DGP.

70. Galula to Alsop, February 15, 1964, DGP.

71. Lansdale to Praeger, May 21, 1964, DGP.

72. Ricks, *Gamble,* 89. I was informed by Secretary Donald Rumsfeld's office that he did not wish to comment on that particular encounter.

73. Lansdale to Praeger, May 21, 1964, DGP.

74. Galula was somewhat dismissive of the counterinsurgency effort in Malaya on account that demographic factors had never favored the "Chinese Terrorists," and that the counterinsurgent was able to usurp the insurgent's cause by declaring that the nation would be granted its independence.
75. Galula, *Counterinsurgency*, 71.
76. Lansdale to Praeger, May 21, 1964, DGP.
77. Ibid.
78. Freeman to Galula, May 27, 1964, DGP.
79. Galula to Freeman, June 30, 1964, DGP.
80. Lansdale to Galula, July 29, 1964, DGP.
81. Whitfield to Galula, August 1, 1964, DGP.
82. Labedz to Galula, April 14, 1965, DGP.
83. Jordan to Galula, June 30, 1965, DGP.
84. Gasteyger to Galula, December 15, 1965, DGP.
85. Galula to Gasteyger, December 24, 1964, DGP.
86. McCabe to Galula, May 5, 1967, DGP.
87. Leonard to Galula, May 9, 1964, DGP.
88. Buchan to Galula, June 22, 1964, DGP.
89. Galula to Freeman, December 6, 1964, DGP.
90. Fromm to Galula, August 25, 1964, DGP.

CHAPTER 18

1. France, *Instruction pour la pacification en Algérie,* 19.
2. Galula to Rae, July 10, 1963, DGP.
3. Freeman to Galula, May 18, 1964, DGP.
4. Galula to Alsop, February 15, 1964, DGP.
5. Galula to Freeman, October 18, 1963, DGP.
6. Freeman to Galula, November 6, 1964, DGP.
7. Galula to Alsop, February 15, 1964, DGP.
8. Galula to Freeman, May 8, 1964, DGP.
9. Ibid.
10. "Legacy Products—NADGE", consulted January 6, 2010. http://www.npc.nato.int/htm/legacy.htm
11. Bouysonnie to Galula, May 11, 1967, DGP.
12. Barnett to Galula, April 20, 1964, DGP.
13. Straker to Galula, April 26, 1967, DGP.
14. "You see, I also think of these things."

EPILOGUE

1. Galula, *Contre-Insurrection*, v.

2. Nagl, foreword to U.S. Department of the Army, Counterinsurgency Field Manual, xvi.
3. Ibid., xvii.
4. Ibid., xix.
5. Ricks, *Fiasco*, 265.
6. Thomas X. Hammes, "Expert's Picks," *Washington Post*, July 17, 2005.
7. William Branigin, "Three Retired Officers Demand Rumsfeld's Resignation," *Washington Post*, September 25, 2006.
8. Ricks and his *Washington Post* team had won a Pulitzer Prize in 2002 for their reporting on the beginning of the "US counteroffensive on terrorism."
9. "CAC Commander's Counterinsurgency Reading List." cgsc.edu/carl/resources/biblio/CAC_counterinsurgency.asp
10. Régis Le Sommier in discussion with the author.

CONCLUSION

1. Tse-Tung, *China's Revolutionary War*, chap 3, sect 1.
2. Galula, *Counterinsurgency*, xiii.
3. I consider the distinction between these types of conflicts to be much blurrier than what Galula tried to define (see Galula, *Counterinsurgency*, 1–3).
4. Political consciousness may just as easily be replaced with other ideological levers such as religious consciousness.
5. Galula, *Counterinsurgency*, 14–15.
6. Ibid., 55.
7. One can think of the Maoists and the Viet Minh and how their population centricity did not preclude them from being ruthless with those that would not commit actively to their side.
8. It is for this very reason that traditional intelligence, even that which is human sourced, must be complemented by "political intelligence." The latter is required to provide a commander with an understanding of how to unhinge the rebel from the population, and how to leverage local power structures.
9. Certainly, development programs conducted in the midst of a counterinsurgency campaign must also heed elemental principles such as the requirement to protect first and please second. In Afghanistan, this order was reversed. A tremendous emphasis was placed on imposing ill-suited models of contracting for public works, fueling corruption and nepotism, and squandering incredible sums of money that was often misdirected, thus further putting off the majority of the population, and contributing in no way to the latter's general sense of involvement. Progress was stymied, and information operations were ultimately ineffective in areas where security could not be genuinely ensured. Moreover, insufficient

attention was paid to shadow governance structures, present in every insurgency as both a symptom and a cause of the latter's success.

10. The term "counterinsurgency" is much more misleading than Galula already considered it to be, particularly in the context of a foreign intervention. "Countering" gives the impression that what is solely required is a defensive campaign against the armed insurgency that emerges; when quite on the contrary, what is required beyond that is an offensive campaign to establish a viable political order that is aligned with friendly interests. Comparing enemy-centric to population-centric approaches in this light, the former comes across as the more defensive of the two, since one has to wait for segments of the population to act against the established order in order to strike. Population-centric counterinsurgency, on the other hand, takes the initiative by trying to seize vital ground, the population, ahead of the enemy that seeks to do the same. Whereas the defensive campaign is an easy sell with the intervening military force, as it is traditionally well suited for the job; the offensive campaign is not, for it requires skills and aptitudes that were generally castaway when colonialism went out of fashion, thankfully, or earlier in other nations, when the military function separated itself from the politico-civil function to a point of sterility.

11. Fall, *Bernard Fall*, 229.

12. Griffith, introduction to Tse–Tung, *On Guerrilla Warfare*, 7.

13. U.S. Department of the Army, Counterinsurgency Field Manual, 1.

14. Ricks, *Gamble*, 25.

15. The adoption of technocratic pedagogy was concretized in Western militaries during the Second World War, and reinforced during the Cold War. Officers were trained in the latest technological, doctrinal, and organizational innovations in conjunction with immutable military art. The pedagogy is that much more technocratic because technological innovations more often than not lead innovation in the other two categories. And that is fine, as far as "conventional" or "symmetric" warfare is concerned, where net advantages in mobility and firepower, etc., can "force the decision" when properly employed. But technocratic indoctrination discards, as there is little use for it, the properly human dimension of things, which incidentally is central to irregular warfare. (There is little coincidence in the fact that "psychological operations," regardless of what they are defined to encompass, become so prevalent there.)

16. This had certainly been true of the Zhari and Panjwayi districts of Kandahar Province in Afghanistan prior to the surge of U.S. forces. An insufficient number of combat troops on the ground translated in the proverbial reset button being pressed after every operation.

17. Galula attributed the following principles to his counterinsurgency framework: "economy of forces," "irreversibility," "initiative," "full utilization

of the counterinsurgent's assets," "simplicity," and "to control is to command" (Galula, *Counterinsurgency*, 56–60).

18. Galula, *Counterinsurgency*, 59.
19. Ibid, 60.
20. So as not to fall into traps such as the one the Israel Defense Force fell into in 2006, when critics claimed that it came up short to varying degrees on all of these elements against the Hezbollah after years of low-intensity counterinsurgency work in Gaza and the West Bank.
21. Galula, *Counterinsurgency*, 1.
22. I would ask the reader to pardon my invention of this acronym; I have done so for the sake of brevity.
23. U.S. Department of the Army, Counterinsurgency Field Manual, 13.
24. Galula, *Counterinsurgency*, 36.
25. The disparity is partly responsible [societal evolution has contributed the rest] for accustoming modern powers to engage in war with relatively low human capital investments and losses. And this, as Sarah Sewall and others have commented, has been problematic in terms of setting unrealistic expectations for counterinsurgency campaigns, where human capital requirements are much more intensive.
26. The oft cited lethality of IEDs in Afghanistan, for instance, has much more to do with the insurgency's innovative employment of these than with the use of cutting–edge technology. Moreover, we note that as far back as the First Indochina War, the French had lost nearly two armored division's worth of vehicles to enemy action; of which 84 percent had been lost to "mines and booby traps" (see Fall, *Street Without Joy*). Little there is new.
27. A second caveat persists. Technological advantages may backfire on the counterinsurgent if they are improperly used or abused. The cost-to-benefit ratio of having deployed modern main battle tanks to Afghanistan represents such an instance in my view.
28. The United States had introduced Stinger missiles in Afghanistan (against the Soviets), and more recently, the Iranians had introduced explosively formed projectiles in Iraq.
29. Spain deviated from this rule in the aftermath of the Madrid bombings. This said, Spain had been a reluctant volunteer for Iraq.
30. Galula, *Counterinsurgency*, 40.
31. Galula, *Counterinsurgency*, 4.
32. Galula, *Pacification*, 246–247.
33. Ibid., 244.
34. Galula to Buchan, September 5, 1964, DGP.
35. Galula, *Counterinsurgency*, 2.
36. Ibid., 96.

37. Ibid., 99.
38. Lyautey, *Du rôle colonial*, 17.
39. Galula, *Counterinsurgency*, 95.
40. We can infer from all of this that the eruption of a large-scale insurgency *following* a Western military intervention indicates that either the entire premise for the campaign was flawed or that the initial planning and execution were a failure.
41. Fall, *Street Without Joy*, 71.
42. Galula, *Counterinsurgency*, 3.
43. Walter, *Civil Wars*, 4.
44. Ibid.
45. Accordingly, the dichotomy between both approaches is replaced by a spectrum.
46. Walter, *Civil Wars*, 4.
47. Governance has many forms: elected, confessional, tribal, socioeconomic, etc.
48. Admittedly, there is a fine line as to what extent legacy governance from a toppled regime can be leveraged. Relying on it too heavily alienates the would-have-been favorable minority that was opposed to the regime in the first place, but discarding it completely, as was done in Iraq, simply bolsters the ranks of the minority in opposition.
49. I recommend Michael Barry's *Le Royaume de l'Insolence*, the best and most useful book I have ever read about Afghanistan.
50. Phillips, "Meeting Lt. Col. David Galula."
51. Tse-Tung, *On Guerrilla Warfare*, 58.

BIBLIOGRAPHY

ABBREVIATIONS

DGP: David Galula Papers, held by the Galula family, California, USA
SHD: Service Historique de la Défense, Galula personal military file, Dossier
   d'officier no. 68-07637, Vincennes, France

INTERVIEWS AND CORRESPONDENCE

Barlett, Mimi
Bismuth, Yolande
Bléhaut, P. L.
Boot, Max
Boré, Vivianne
Boyer, Guy
Cauvin, Gérald
Crane, Conrad
Daly, Terrence
De Montenon, Philippe
D'Orléans, Henri
Ericson, Torleif
Ericson-Galula, Magda
Fall, Dorothy
Galula, Daniel
Galula, Ruth Morgan
Greaves, Fielding
Hammes, Thomas

Hoffman, Bruce
Hoffman, Stanley*
Hosmer, Stephen
Iklé, Frederick*
Junalik, Léon
Kadosch, Marcel
Kissinger, Henry*
Lantelme, René
Le Sommier, Régis
Mansoor, Peter
Morot, Richard
Nagl, John
Phillips III, Rufus
Ricks, Thomas
Rosensohn, Anne-Louise
Rowland, Jere
Schelling, Thomas*
Sewall, Sarah
Topping, Seymour
Villatoux, Marie-Catherine
Villatoux, Paul
Walter, Barbara

*Individuals who collaborated with David Galula at Harvard, but who could no longer remember him specifically when I contacted them.

BOOKS, MANUSCRIPTS, REPORTS, ARTICLES, LECTURES

Allouche-Benayoun, Joelle and Doris Bensimon. *Juifs d'Algérie, hier et aujourd'hui*. Toulouse: Privat, 1989.

Amidror, Yaakov. *Winning Counterinsurgency War: The Israeli Experience*. Jerusalem: Jerusalem Center for Public Affairs, 2008.

Bach, André. *L'armée de Dreyfus*. Paris: Tallandier, 2004.

Bacholet, Raymond. *Les 100 Plus Belles Images de L'Affaire Dreyfus*. Paris: Editions Dabecom, 2006.

Barry, Michael. *Le royaume de l'insolence*. Paris: Flammarion, 2002.

Bensoussan, David. *Il était une fois le Maroc, témoignages du passé Judéo-Marocain*. Montreal: Éditions du Lys, 2010.

Bertin, Claude, ed. *La Seconde Guerre Mondiale*. 20 vols. Paris: Éditions de Saint-Clair, 1965.

Beyssade, Pierre. *La guerre d'Algérie*. Paris: Culture, 1968.

Boorman, Howard. *Men and Politics in Modern China: 50 Biographies*. New York: Columbia University Press, 1960.

Boot, Max. *Invisible Armies*. New York: Norton, 2012.

Boot, Max. *Savage Wars of Peace*. New York: Basic Books, 2003.

Boot, Max. *War Made New*. New York: Gotham Books, 2006.

Boré, Pierre. "La 9ᵉ Division d'Infanterie Coloniale." Article Mémoire, Journal de l'Association des anciens combattants et soldats français au Québec website : anciens.combat.qc.voila.net/.

Breuer, William B. *Undercover Tales of World War II*. New York: Wiley, 1999.

Buchan, Alastair, et al. *China and the Peace of Asia*. New York: Praeger, 1965.

Bugnet, Charles. *Le Maréchal Lyautey*. Paris: Mame, 1948.

Camus, Albert. *The Rebel*. New York: Alfred A. Knopf, 1978.

Caran, Jean [David Galula]. *The Tiger's Whiskers*. Translated by Frances Frenaye and Harold Talbott. New York: Walker and Company, 1965.

Centre Militaire d'Information et de Documentation sur l'Outre-Mer. *Les Troupes de Marine*. Versailles : CMIOD, 1978.

Chaliand, Gérard, ed. *Les guerres irrégulières*. Paris: Gallimard, 2008.

Chassin, Lionel. *La conquête de la Chine par Mao Tse-tung*. Paris: Payot, 1952.

Chassin, Lionel. *L'ascencion de Mao Tse-tung*. Paris: Payot, 1953.

Clark, Michael. *Algeria in Turmoil*. New York: Praeger, 1959.

Clausewitz, Carl Von. *On War*. New York: Oxford University Press, 2007.

Coll, Steve. *Ghost Wars*. New York: Penguin, 2004.

Crémieux-Brilhac, Jean-Louis. "Consignes provisoires du comité Français de la libération nationale à donner le jour J." La Fondation Charles de Gaulle website : charles-de-gaulle.org/.

Currey, Cecil. *The Unquiet American, Edward Lansdale*. Boston: Houghton Mifflin, 1988.

De Boisboissel, Yves. *Dans l'ombre de Lyautey*. Paris: André Bonne, 1953.

De Courrèges, Hervé, Emmanuel Germain, and Nicolas Le Nen. *Principes de Contre-Insurrection*. Paris: Économica, 2010.

De Gaulle, Charles. *Discours et Messages*. 4 vols. Paris: Plon, 1970.

De Gaulle, Charles. *Le fil de l'épée*. Paris: Plon, 1971. First published 1932 by Berger-Levrault.

De Gaulle, Charles. *Mémoires d'espoir*. 2 vols. Évreux: Plon 1970–1971.

De Gaulle, Charles. *Mémoires de guerre*. 3 vols. Paris: Plon, 1954–1959.

De Gaulle, Charles. *Vers l'armée de métier*. Paris: Plon, 1971. First published 1934 by Berger-Levrault.

De Lattre de Tassigny, Jean. *L'Histoire de la 1ère Armée*. Paris: Plon, 1949.

Déon, Michel. *L'armée d'Algérie et la pacification*. Paris: Plon, 1959.

Deschamps, Hubert and Paul Chauvert. *Gallieni pacificateur*. Paris: Presses Universitaires de France, 1949.

Descoubes, Ernest. *Historique du 1ᵉʳ Régiment de Zouaves*. Paris: Berger-Levrault, 1882.

Desmazes, Charles. *Saint-Cyr: Son Histoire, Ses Gloires, Ses Leçons*. Paris: Les Ordres de la Chevalerie, 1948.

Dupuy, Trevor N., Curt Johnson, and David L. Bongard. *The Harper Encyclopedia of Military Biography.* Edison: Castle Books, 1995.

Duval, Eugène-Jean. *L'Épopée des tirailleurs sénégalais.* Paris: L'Harmattan, 2005.

Eisenbeth, Maurice. *Les Juifs d'Afrique du Nord.* Paris: La Lettre Sépharade, 2000. First published 1936 by Cercle de Généalogie Juive.

Fall, Bernard. *Hell in a Very Small Place.* Cambridge: Da Capo, 2002. First published 1966 by Harper.

Fall, Bernard. *Street Without Joy.* Mechanicsburg: Stackpole, 1961.

Fall, Bernard. *The Two Viet-Nams.* New York: Praeger, 1963.

Fall, Dorothy. *Bernard Fall, Memories of a Soldier-Scholar.* Washington: Potomac, 2006.

Fellous, Sonia, ed. *Juifs et Musulmans en Tunisie—Fraternité et Déchirements.* Paris: Somogy, 2003.

France, Commandement en chef des forces en Algérie, *Instruction pour la pacification en Algérie,* December 10, 1959.

Gaddis, John Lewis. *Strategies of Containment—A Critical Appraisal of American National Security Policy during the Cold War.* New York: Oxford University Press, 2005.

Gallieni, Joseph S. *Mémoires.* Paris: Payot, 1928.

Galula, David. *Contre-insurrection: théorie et pratique.* Translated by Philippe de Montenon, with a foreword by David H. Petraeus and John A. Nagl. Paris: Economica, 2008.

Galula, David. *Counterinsurgency: Theory and Practice.* New York: Praeger, 2006. First published 1964.

Galula, David. "Guerre bactériologique." Unpublished manuscript, 1964, DGP.

Galula, David. "On the Conduct of Counter-Revolutionary War." Staff college thesis. US Armed Forces Staff College, Norfolk, April 1960.

Galula, David. *Pacification in Algeria, 1956–1958.* Foreword by Bruce Hoffman. Santa Monica: RAND, 2006. Originally submitted in classified form in 1964.

Gaujac, Paul. "Débarquement de Provence—La Guerre en Méditerranée." *Ancre d'Or,* no. 341, July–August 2004.

Gaujac, Paul. *La Bataille et la Libération de Toulon.* Paris: Éditions Latines, 1994.

Gelez. "Les Zouaves: *ceux d'hier, ceux de toujours.*" Documents Algériens— Service d'Information du Cabinet du Gouverneur Général de l'Algérie, Série Militaire, no. 8, October 12, 1950.

Gillet, Maxime. *Principes de pacification du Maréchal Lyautey.* Paris: Economica, 2010.

Gillin, Donald G. *Warlord: Yen Hsi-shan in Shansi Province, 1911–1949.* Princeton: Princeton University Press, 1967.

Gottmann, Jean. *Bugeaud, Gallieni, Lyautey: The Development of French Colonial Warfare.* Princeton: Princeton University Press, 1943.

Gouraud, Henri. *Au Maroc 1911–1914.* Paris: Plon, 1949.

Greene, Graham. *The Quiet American.* New York: Viking Press, 1955.

Guillermaz, Jacques. *Histoire du Parti communiste chinois, 1921–1949.* 2 vols. Paris: Payot, 1968.

Guillermaz, Jacques. *Le Parti communiste chinois au pouvoir, 1949–1979.* 2 vols. Paris: Payot, 1972.

Guillermaz, Jacques. *Une Vie pour la Chine—Mémoires 1937–1989.* Paris: Laffont, 1989.

Hammes, Thomas X. *The Sling and the Stone: On War in the 21st Century.* New York: Zenith Press, 2004.

Hanrahan, Gene, ed. *Chinese Communist Guerilla Tactics.* New York: Columbia University, 1952.

Hogard, Jacques. "Guerre révolutionnaire et pacification." *Revue militaire de l'information,* no. 280 (1957).

Hosmer, Stephen T., and Sibylle O. Crane, ed. *Counterinsurgency, A Symposium, April 16–20, 1962.* Revised ed. Santa Monica: RAND, 2006. Originally published 1963.

Howard, Michael, ed. *The Theory and Practice of War.* New York: Praeger, 1965.

Huré, A. *La pacification du Maroc.* Paris: Berger-Levrault, 1952.

Khrushchev, Nikita et al. *Memoirs of Nikita Khrushchev: Statesman, 1953–1964.* 3 vols. University Park: Pennsylvania State University Press, 2007.

Kilcullen, David. *Counterinsurgency.* New York: Oxford University Press, 2010.

Kitson, Frank. *Bunch of Five.* London: Faber & Faber, 1997.

Lacheroy, Charles. *De Saint-Cyr à l'action psychologique.* Panazol: Lavauzelle, 2003.

Lacheroy, Charles. "Guerre révolutionnaire et arme psychologique." Lecture, Ministère de la Défense—la Sorbonne University, July 2, 1957.

Landau, Philippe E. *Les juifs de France et la Grande Guerre.* Paris: CNRS, 1999.

Lansdale, Edward. *In the Midst of Wars, America's Mission to Southeast Asia.* New York: Fordham University Press, 1991.

Lartéguy, Jean. *Les Centurions.* Paris: Presses de la Cité, 1960.

Lartéguy, Jean. *Le Mal Jaune.* Paris: Presses de la Cité, 1962.

Lasserre, Isabelle. "Afghanistan: Le retour de la contre-insurrection." *Le Figaro.* October 29, 2008.

Latelme, René. "La Promotion Amitié Franco-Britannique—Saint-Cyr 1939–40." Unknown publication, 119–122.

Lawrence, Thomas E., *Seven Pillars of Wisdom.* New York: Penguin, 2000.

Leclerc, Max. *Au Maroc avec Lyautey.* Paris: Armand Colin, 1927.

Lederer, William, and Eugene Burdick. *The Ugly American.* New York: Norton, 1999.

Le Moing, Guy. *Et l'Océan fut leur tombe.* Paris: Marines Éditions, 2005.

Lyautey, Hubert. *Paroles d'action.* Paris: Armand Colin, 1927.

Lyautey, Hubert. *Du rôle colonial de L'armée.* Paris: Armand Colin, 1900.

Lyautey, Pierre. *Gallieni.* Paris: Gallimard, 1959.

Mangin, Stanislas. "Un ralliement." France Libre website : france-libre.net.

Mansoor, Peter. *Baghdad at Sunrise: A Brigade Commander's War in Iraq.* London: Yale, 2008.

Marrus, Michael, and Robert Paxton. *Vichy France and the Jews.* New York: Basic Books, 1981. Originally published 1981 as *Vichy et les juifs* by Calmann-Lévy.

Melnik, Constantin. *De Gaulle, les Services Secrets, et l'Algérie.* Paris: Nouveau Monde, 2010.

Melnik, Constantin. *Insurgency and Counterinsurgency in Algeria.* Santa Monica: RAND, 1964.

Melnik, Constantin. *The French Campaign against the FLN.* Santa Monica: RAND, 1967.

Michel, Henri. *Vichy Année 40.* Paris: Laffont, 1966.

Morgan, Ted. *Valley of Death—The Tragedy at Dien Bien Phu that led America into the Vietnam War.* New York: Random House, 2010.

Nachmani, Amikam. *International Intervention in the Greek Civil War—The United Nations Special Commission on the Balkans, 1947–1952.* New York: Praeger, 1990.

Nagl, John. *Learning to Eat Soup with a Knife.* Chicago: Chicago University Press, 2005. First published 2002 by Praeger.

Netanyahou, Benyamin. *Fighting Terrorism.* New York: Giroux, 2001.

Oliel, Jacob. *Les Camps de Vichy.* Montreal: Les Editions du Lys, 2005.

Onana, Charles. *La France et ses tirailleurs.* Paris: Éditions Duboiris, 2003.

Paxton, Robert. *L'Armée de Vichy—Le Corps des Officiers Français 1940–1944.* Éditions Tallandier, Paris 2004. Originally published 1960 as *Parades and Poltics at Vichy—The French Officer Corps under Marshal Pétain* by Princeton University Press.

Payrefitte, Alain. *C'était de Gaulle.* Paris: Gallimard, 2000.

Phillips, Rufus. "Meeting Lt. Col. David Galula—April 1962." *Small Wars Journal.* Smallwarsjournal.com.

Phillips, Rufus. *Why Vietnam Matters.* Annapolis: Naval Institute Press, 2008.

Prestat. "Stratégie de Mao Tse-Toung. " Lecture, École de guerre supérieure, July 23, 1956.

Ribère, Fabrice. "Faut-il brûler Galula?" *Défense et Sécurité International,* no. 58 (April 2010): 32–39.

Ricks, Thomas. *Fiasco.* New York: Penguin, 2007.

Ricks, Thomas. *The Gamble*. New York: Penguin, 2009.

Saint-Hillier, Benard. "L'armée française dans le débarquement de Provence." France Libre website: www.france-libre.net.

Salan, Raoul. *Mémoires, Fin d'un empire*. 4 vols. Paris: Presses de la Cité, 1970–74.

Sebag, Paul. *Les Noms des Juifs de Tunisie—Origines et significations*. Paris: L'Harmattan, 2002.

Shaoqi, Liu. *Resolutely Smash the Onslaught of the Diehards*. 1940. http://www.marxists.org/reference/archive/liu-shaoqi/.

Singer, Barnett, and John Langdon. *Cultured Force*. Madison: University of Wisconsin Press, 2004.

Slama, Bice. *L'insurrection de 1864 en Tunisie*. Tunis: Maison Tunisienne de l'Édition, 1967.

Snow, Edgar. *Red Star over China*. New York: Grove Press, 1968. First published 1938 by Random House.

Surhone, Lambert, ed. *Roger Trinquier*. Beau Basin: Betascript Publishing, 2010.

Swanston, Albert and Malcolm Swanston. *The Historical Atlas of World War II*. London: Chartwell Books, 2007.

Tanham, George. *Communist Revolutionary Warfare : The Viet-Minh in Indochina*. New York: Praeger, 1961.

Thompson, Robert. *Defeating Communist Insurgency: Experiences from Malaya and Vietnam*. New York: Palgrave Macmillian, 1978.

Tolédano, Joseph. *Une Histoire de Familles—Les noms de famille juifs d'Afrique du Nord*. Jerusalem: Éditions Ramtol, 1998.

Topping, Seymour. *Journey Between Two Chinas*. New York: Harper and Row, 1972.

Topping, Seymour. *On the Front Lines of the Cold War: An American Correspondent's Journal from the Chinese Civil War, to the Cuban Missile Crisis*. Baton Rouge: Louisiana State University Press, 2010.

Topping, Seymour. *The Peking Letter*. New York: Public Affairs, 1999.

Trinquier, Roger. *Guerre, subversion, révolution*. Paris: Laffont, 1968.

Trinquier, Roger. *La guerre*. Paris: Albin Michel, 1980.

Trinquier, Roger. *Modern Warfare—A French View of Counterinsurgency*. Foreword by Bernard Fall. New York: Praeger, 2006. First published 1961 as *La guerre moderne* by Table Ronde.

Tse-Tung, Mao. *La stratégie de la guerre révolutionnaire en Chine*. Paris : Éditions Sociales, 1950.

Tse-Tung, Mao. *On Contradiction*. 1937. http://www.marxists.org/reference/archive/mao/selected-works.

Tse-Tung, Mao. *On Guerrilla Warfare*. Translated with foreword by Samuel Griffith. Mineola: Dover Publications, 2005. Originally written in 1937, and published by Praeger 1961.

Tse-Tung, Mao. *On Protracted War*. Honolulu: University Press of the Pacific, 2001. Drawn from 1938 lecture series.

Tse-Tung, Mao. *Problems of Strategy in China's Revolutionary War*. 1936. http://www.marxists.org/reference/archive/mao/selected-works.

Tse-Tung, Mao. *Problems of Strategy in Guerrilla War Against Japan*. 1938. http://www.marxists.org/reference/archive/mao/selected-works.

Tsu, Sun. *The Art of War*. New York: Barnes & Nobles, 1994.

U.S. Department of the Army. FM 3-07 Stability Operations and Support Operations. Washington: Headquarters Department of the Army, 2003.

U.S. Department of the Army. FMI 3-07.22 Counterinsurgency Operations. Washington: Headquarters Department of the Army, 2004.

U.S. Department of the Army. The U.S. Army/Marine Corps Counterinsurgency Field Manual: U.S. Army field manual no. 3–24: Marine Corps warfighting publication no. 3-33.5 with foreword by David H. Petraeus, James F. Amos, and John A. Nagl, and introduction by Sarah Sewall. Chicago: University of Chicago, 2007.

Vigneras, Marcel. *Rearming the French*. Washington: U.S. Government Printing Office, 1957.

Villatoux, Marie-Catherine. *La défense en surface*. Tulle: Service Historique de la Défense, 2009.

Villatoux, Marie-Catherine. *Guerre et action psychologique en Algérie*. Tulle: Service Historique de la Défense, 2007.

Villatoux, Paul. *La Guerre Psychologique*. Sceaux: L'Esprit du Livre, 2008.

Villatoux, Paul, and Marie-Catherine Villatoux. *La République et son Armée face au 'péril subversif.'* Paris: Les Indes Savantes, 2005.

Walter, Barbara, and Jack Snyder eds., *Civil Wars, Insecurity, and Intervention*. New York: Columbia University Press, 1999.

Willemin, Véronique. *Images d'archives d'Algérie*. Paris: Éditions de Lodi, 2005.

Zack, Lizabeth. "Who Fought the Algerian War? Political Identity and Conflict in French-Ruled Algeria," *International Journal of Politics, Culture, and Society* 16 (1) Fall 2002.

Zimmerman, Maurice. "Le Général Borgnis-Desbordes." *Annales de Géographie*. Volume 9, Issue 48, 1900.

INDEX

About the Author

A. A. COHEN is a senior infantry officer in the Canadian Army. He currently serves in the Reserves and works as a strategic adviser on international trade. Cohen fought in Operation Enduring Freedom in Kandahar, Afghanistan. He was awarded the Chief of Defense Staff Commendation for outstanding initiative and motivation, and for his establishment of vital relationships with the local population.

Galula : the life and writings of the
French officer who defined the art of
counterinsurgency / A. A. Cohen ;
foreword by John A. Nagl.

DATE DUE

PRINTED IN U.S.A.